Discovering Texas History

Discovering Texas History

Edited by
Bruce A. Glasrud
Light Townsend Cummins
and
Cary D. Wintz

University of Oklahoma Press : Norman

Library of Congress Cataloging-in-Publication Data

Discovering Texas history / edited by Bruce A. Glasrud, Light Townsend Cummins, and Cary D. Wintz.
p. cm.
Includes index.
ISBN 978-0-8061-4619-5 (paperback : alkaline paper) 1. Texas—History. I. Glasrud, Bruce A. II. Cummins, Light Townsend. III. Wintz, Cary D.
F386.D57 2015
976.4—dc23

2014010703

The paper in this book meets the guidelines for permanence and durability of the Committee on Production Guidelines for Book Longevity of the Council on Library Resources, Inc. ∞

Contents

Acknowledgments

The essays in this volume represent the work of almost two dozen Texas historians. Each contributor is indebted to people who assisted their research, writing, and editing. The number of people to be thanked by all the authors in this book would constitute a long list of historians, scholars, librarians, associates, and friends. Unfortunately, page-length limitations for this volume preclude the contributors making such acknowledgments.

Several people made signal contributions to the entire volume. This is especially the case for Jay Dew, acquisitions editor of the University of Oklahoma Press. A Texan by background, he graduated with a B.A. in history from Austin College and later earned a Ph.D. in history from Oklahoma. Jay has been a steadfast proponent of Texas history across his entire career. His hard work, constant encouragement, and unflagging desire to see this book in print are reflected in every one of its chapters. Project manager Emily Jerman Schuster's yeoman editing skills helped transform our manuscript into a book. Two distinguished Texas historians, M. Scott Sosebee of Stephen F. Austin State University and Jean Stuntz of West Texas A&M University, kindly read the entire volume while in manuscript, currycombing each chapter with diligence. They improved this book significantly in terms of writing style and bibliographic utility.

The editors also thank the Texas State Historical Association for allowing use of the previously published award-winning article by F. Todd Smith on Spanish and Mexican Texas. Finally, we acknowledge as editors the historians who contributed their essays to this work and effusively thank them for working with us. A faculty grant-in-aid from the Sid Richardson Fund at Austin College underwrote the index for this volume. We three alone accept responsibility for all errors or omissions in the pages that follow.

Bruce A. Glasrud, San Antonio, Texas
Light Cummins, Austin College
Cary D. Wintz, Texas Southern University

Texas History Considered

Light Townsend Cummins, Bruce A. Glasrud, Cary D. Wintz

More than a quarter-century ago Light Townsend Cummins and Alvin R. Bailey, Jr., edited a volume titled *A Guide to the History of Texas*. Published by Greenwood Press, it contained historiographical essays of a topical and chronological nature, each written by experts in their fields.[1] The book also contained a series of chapters that detailed the holdings of archives in Texas that contained records relevant to the history of the state. Archivists at the various repositories wrote the selections for their collection. That 1988 guide had as its primary audience students and beginning researchers who were starting work on their own historical investigations. It also targeted undergraduates in college- and university-level Texas history classes who required an introduction to historical literature about the state, especially those seeking books and articles to read on particular aspects of the history.

Cummins and Bailey conceptualized the 1988 guidebook as an initial point of reference for those commencing their interest in Texas history. The level of coverage in each of the essays therefore existed at what might best be described as the introductory level. It was not anticipated that specialists in a particular part of Texas history would learn anything new from reading the selections that dealt with their area of expertise. The emphasis in each of the essays centered on the presentation of bibliography. For that reason, the contributors did not explicitly attempt to address matters of interpretation, nor did they offer commentary on general historical viewpoints or enter into historiographical debate about the character or nature of Texas history as an intellectual enterprise. As well, each of the essays confined itself to dealing only with academic works of history that existed within the matrix of professional scholarship based on impartial investigation in sources. The authors of each essay avoided genealogical materials, popular or genre writing, narrative nonfiction dealing with Texas history, and other publications from the general area of Texana that failed to manifest an academic frame of reference. Moreover, because there were many guides and historiographical reference books dealing with larger geographic and topical aspects of American history (western, southern, economic, and the like), the *Guide* emphasized books and articles that dealt primarily with Texas only and made no attempt to link this literature to larger conceptualizations of U.S. history of which the state was only a part.

The 1988 *Guide to the History of Texas* met with a level of success unanticipated by those involved in its creation. The American Library Association designated it the best reference book of the year. A nationwide series of similar state-based volumes published by Greenwood Press, with Cummins serving as national editor, brought the concept of the *Guide* to many other states, especially older and larger states which, like Texas, enjoyed long and rich histories. As well, the Texas guide has remained in print for more than a generation and, to the knowledge of its editors, is regularly consulted today by beginning students and researchers. The *Guide to the History of Texas* therefore continues to be a useful reference used by the target audience for whom it was originally published, although its coverage has become dated. This particular deficiency has become compelling inasmuch as, over the decades since publication of the *Guide*, there has been a virtual explosion of writing about the history of the Lone Star State. Each year witnesses the publication of hundreds of professional scholarly books and articles dealing with Texas history.

There are several reasons for the seemingly ever-expanding number of books and articles dealing with Texas history. For example, since the late 1970s there has been marked growth in the number and size of institutions of higher education across the state providing graduate-level training in Texas history. Today, more Texas and southwestern universities offer master's and doctoral degrees in the history of the state than ever before. It may well be that today the total population of graduate students studying Texas history has never been larger. As well, there has been remarkable growth since the late 1970s in the number and size of university presses specializing in Texas history. There are now more than a dozen major presses hosted by universities in the southwestern United States whose catalogs contain Texas history titles; several smaller presses and a half-dozen well-respected commercial publishers are also eager to publish about the state and its past. For example, in August 2013 the University of Texas Press announced a new series titled "The Texas Bookshelf." It will be composed of sixteen topical volumes about Texas including ones dealing with politics, art, music, sports, business, and other aspects of the state and its culture. Each will be written by a University of Texas faculty member who has expertise regarding the respective topic. The first volume, anticipated in 2017, will be a narrative history of Texas written by author Stephen Harrigan.

The Internet has also accelerated research and publication about Texas history, although on first glance one might erroneously assume that this new technology would threaten the existence of books and articles on the topic. Such has not been the case to date because of the increased ability of researchers to consult far-flung sources from their keyboard, to research in digitized databases, and to conduct efficient online searches in ways never before possible. The Internet has indeed revolutionized historical research and made it much easier to accomplish in terms of access. Academic historical research has become more egalitarian in the process, in terms of individual researchers becoming active practitioners. Although the eventual widespread digitization of printed materials may well impact the use of printed books and articles, there is no indication that increased use of online technology will stifle historical research in the future. The opposite will probably be true. It is thus likely that scholarship on Texas history will continue to expand, no matter what combination of digitized or paper-based publication becomes standard.

These developments over the past quarter-century, all of which have made the 1988 Texas *Guide* increasingly dated, eventually became a recurring subject of conversation among the three historians who are the editors of this volume, *Discovering Texas History*. Bruce A. Glasrud first mentioned several years ago while at the annual meeting of the Texas State Historical Association that steps ought to be taken to update and revise the *Guide to the History of Texas*. Light Townsend Cummins and Cary D. Wintz concurred, and the three of them, all old friends in the history profession, set their minds to considering the task. It soon became apparent, however, that something other than a simple update or revision was needed. The 1988 *Guide* remains available for purchase, and large parts of it can be accessed online. Found on the shelves of many libraries and archives, it provides useful bibliographic information up to the date of its publication and will continue to serve as a good bibliographic tool for all time. These realizations resulted in the decision to create an entirely new, different book that would primarily address the bibliography of Texas history published since the mid-1980s. *Discovering Texas History* would thus not be an update or revision of the earlier book but an entirely new, distinct volume to be used as companion to it, the newer book beginning coverage where the older one ended.

Other than this connection (and the editorship of Cummins), there is no relationship between the two volumes. In fact, the very organization of the two books is different. Unlike its predecessor, *Discovering Texas History* does not address any archival repositories or primary sources, coverage that comprises almost half of the 1988 *Guide.* This change resulted from recognition of the relatively easy access to finding aids and detailed holdings of important archives and manuscript repositories, today, via the Internet—access that did not exist twenty-five years ago. Every archival facility listed in the 1988 book now maintains a website that contains as much information, if not more and in greater detail, than was presented in the *Guide to Texas History.* "Texas Archival Resources Online," a website sponsored by the University of Texas Libraries, provides a convenient cross-listing of holdings for approximately three dozen important repositories across the state that can be searched simultaneously. Other websites efficiently put researchers in touch with primary sources that are being assembled into purpose-built hypertext databases, including the Portal to Texas History, the West Texas Digital Archives, the SMU Central University Libraries digital collection of art and photographic archives, and many others too numerous to list.[2]

In that regard, the increasing importance of the Internet and its certain growth presented a special problem to the editors of this new volume—namely, how much attention should be given to denoting online materials and highlighting URLs of interest to readers seeking Texas history bibliography? The decision was made not to emphasize this information at all. This is because online search engines and other vehicles of Internet research, such as WorldCat and JSTOR, along with digitized books, are likely already familiar to users of this volume. In addition, the structure and organization of the Internet is fluid, and, across time, any volume that seeks to comment about or analyze online bibliographic materials will become obsolete and of limited utility. Rather, we concentrate on paper-based publishing, a format that undebatably remains the norm for historical scholarship today.

For students and readers of Texas history, textbooks remain an effective vehicle for historians to have an impact on the public. The best textbooks are those written for university students, and this field has experienced an explosion in the past twenty years. In 1988 there was only one successful college textbook: *Texas: The Lone Star State*, by Rupert N. Richardson, Ernest Wallace, and

Adrian Anderson. Originally published in 1943 by Richardson, who added Wallace and Anderson to his team in the 1960s, this solid work needed a renewed infusion by the turn of the next century. The addition of historian Cary D. Wintz to the writing team for twenty-first-century editions revised the focus and its perspectives. The first serious challenger to this book's dominance emerged in 1990 with the publication of Robert A. Calvert and Arnoldo De León's *History of Texas*. This work incorporated material on common folks in the Lone Star State and offered expanded discussions of such subjects as agriculture, industrialization, urban growth, and demography. Gregg Cantrell joined the writing team for recent editions of *The History of Texas*.[3]

The production of two significant college textbooks on the history of Texas set a high mark for any scholarly competitor. That challenge was met by Randolph B. Campbell with *Gone to Texas: A History of the Lone Star State*, which appeared in 2003. Drawing on the best writings of many of his contemporaries, Campbell produced a text that is both a readable narrative and an insightful analysis. Anglos, blacks, Indians, Hispanics, and other ethnic groups all appear in the narrative, which does not ignore the contributions of women; it became the textbook most commonly used in university classes.[4]

Texas is a big state, and there are a lot of university professors shopping for new perspectives to present to their students. To meet that demand, Jesús F. de la Teja, Paula Marks, and Ron Tyler produced *Texas: Crossroads of North America*. This work employs a thematic approach that emphasizes diversity and opportunity in presenting the history of the initial settlement and then later development of Texas. Rather than present a different perspective, James L. Haley, in *Passionate Nation: The Epic History of Texas*, sought to tell the good stories others left out of their histories. Based largely upon his previous work, Haley's survey of all Texas history proved to be entertaining, but it lacked a compelling analytical focus.[5] Recently, a multiauthored volume developed by Kenneth Howell, *Beyond Myths and Legends: A Narrative History of Texas*, which received contributions from Keith J. Volanto, James M. Smallwood, Charles D. Grear, and Jennifer S. Lawrence, provided an additional venue for the study of Texas history. Some students and professors prefer shorter textbooks. For that purpose, Stephen F. Austin State University scholar Archie P. McDonald gave us *Texas: A Compact History*.[6]

Some Texans, of course, may never read a textbook on the history of their state, much less ponder the implications of the debate between history and myth in telling their story. But they will have questions, and one of the greatest achievements of the past two decades has been the completion of *The New*

Handbook of Texas, a magisterial resource compiled under the direction of a team of editors led by Ron Tyler as the director of the Texas State Historical Association. Containing more than 23,000 articles on a tremendous range of Texas topics, the *New Handbook* became a model for others. Its six volumes with more than ten million words made it somewhat cumbersome to use, if not downright formidable, and a landmark decision was made by former director L. Tuffly Ellis to not only put the text online but to provide access free of charge. Furthermore, the online version of the *New Handbook* would be continuously updated, allowing for a process of inserting new information, or even more articles, as historical research advanced. For those committed to having information literally in their hands, or who perhaps did not have access to an effective computer system, the Association later published *The Portable Handbook of Texas*, edited by Roy R. Barkley and Mark F. Odintz (both of whom worked on the previous six-volume edition). More important, the appearance of *The Handbook of Texas Music*, edited by Barkley and others, reflected the commitment by the Association to continue expanding its services to Texans, amateur enthusiasts and professional scholars alike, in an effort to replace myths, or simply wrong information, with factual material drawn from careful historical inquiry.[7]

Interestingly, some of the most intriguing new work has appeared in collections of essays designed to showcase new perspectives on Texas history. In these volumes, myth has not entirely disappeared, as evidenced by the twelve selections found in *Lone Star Pasts: Memory and History in Texas*, edited by Gregg Cantrell and Elizabeth H. Turner. Embracing the avant-garde notion that constructed histories, which often rely as much on perceptions as facts, are as important as those that emerge from academic research, the edited work bravely asserts that historians must still take into account the value, or at least the influence, of collective memory. Pushing in a similar direction, but trying harder to put aside myth in favor of history, is *Twentieth-Century Texas: A Social and Cultural History*, edited by John W. Storey and Mary L. Kelly. The sixteen authors of the fifteen essays found in this collection discuss Native Americans, Mexican Americans, African Americans, women, religion, the home front in wartime, women in music, literature, film, art, sports, philanthropy, education, the environment, and science and technology. In the same vein, Donald Willett and Stephen Curley edited a volume of eighteen essays titled *Invisible Texans: Women and Minorities in Texas History*. Though not restricted to any particular century, this work owes much to the initiatives in social and cultural history of the past few decades, and thus it provides some indications not only of how much has changed but how much can and will change in the writing of Texas history in the decades to come. And with *Eyewitnesses to Texas History*, Felix D. Almaraz, Patricia Thompson, and Carmen Reyes-Johnson edited a perceptive, broad-ranging study.[8]

A volume honoring the career of Texas historian Randolph B. Campbell, a long-time professor of history at the University of North Texas, contains essays by former students and some of his colleagues that examine the historical nature of Texas identity as well as major chronological periods of Texas history. Patrick L. Cox and Kenneth E. Hendrickson, Jr., edited a volume of fourteen biographical essays dealing with the contributions of historians important to the study of Texas history.[9] Other general studies also have been produced. Coeditor of *Discovering Texas History*, Texas Southern University professor Cary D. Wintz, with Sam W. Haynes, edited *Major Problems in Texas History: Documents and Essays*. Other document books also focus on Texas. George B. Ward updated the source book on Texas history in 2002 that had been produced originally in 1963 by Texas Tech University historians Ernest Wallace and David M. Vigness, *Documents of Texas History*. Worth Publishers printed Randolph B. Campbell's two-volume set *Texas History Documents* in 1997. Six years earlier J'Nell L. Pate published *Document Sets for Texas and the Southwest in U.S. History*.[10]

The list of general texts or studies of the Lone Star state does not stop. Ben Procter and Archie P. McDonald edited *The Texas Heritage*. The third edition, for example, contains seventeen well-written essays and covers topics such as sports, civil rights, and progressivism. Not to be outdone, Ty Cashion and Jesús F. de la Teja, in *The Human Tradition in Texas History*, used biography as a medium to discuss Texas history. They included fifteen biographies by scholars in their respective fields. *Texas Vistas*, edited in its third edition by Ralph A. Wooster, Robert A. Calvert, and Adrian N. Anderson, used selections from the *Southwestern Historical Quarterly* to convey historical insight and meaning to students of Texas history. Charles Swanlund and Kirk Bane, in *A Lone Star Reader*, included thirty-three excerpts from previously published articles and works for their edited volume published by Kendall Hunt in 2010. It should be noted, however, that the Swanlund/Bane work includes no notes or bibliography. The same year, Keith J. Volanto introduced readers to *Texas Voices*.[11]

Two more specialized but nonetheless significant contributions to Texas history should be mentioned. David O'Donald Cullen and Kyle G. Wilkison edited *The Texas Left*, which features eleven original essays by historians of the Texas past. In *Texas Labor History*, Bruce A. Glasrud and James C. Maroney used previously published articles to capture, for the first time, the spirit and essence of the vitally important, albeit misunderstood, Texas labor movement.[12]

In 1991, three years after Cummins and Bailey published their *Guide to the History of Texas*, two Texas A&M University historians, Walter L. Buenger and Robert A. Calvert, produced another historiographical survey of Texas history—*Texas through Time: Evolving Interpretations. Texas through Time* focused on analyzing Texas historical writing and, in the process, challenged historians to move their Texas studies to more relevant and overlooked aspects of Texas history. In 2011, Walter L. Buenger, this time with Angelo State University professor Arnoldo De León, completed a sequel to the original work—*Beyond Texas through Time: Breaking Away from Past Interpretations.* In this work, six articles continued to challenge and ask questions about Texas history and its writing.[13] Other works of a historiographical nature significant to the study of Texas history are Laura L. McLemore, *Inventing Texas: Early Historians of the Lone Star State*, and Richard B. McCaslin, *At the Heart of Texas: One Hundred Years of the Texas State Historical Association, 1897–1997.*[14]

In addition to the topics included in *Discovering Texas History*, it is interesting to note that the most written-about group in Texas history is undoubtedly the infamous Texas Rangers. That process has leapt forward in the past years. Three two-volume sets have been published—one general history by western historian Robert M. Utley and the second by former Ranger spokesman Mike Cox. Bruce A. Glasrud and Harold J. Weiss, Jr., produced *Tracking the Texas Rangers*, a two-volume anthology of Ranger studies. Individual works about the Rangers proliferated also but are too numerous to mention in this short introduction.[15]

As one can notice by the previous paragraphs, not only is the writing of Texas history continuing, it is continuing by studying its historiography. The essays of this volume, *Discovering Texas History*, therefore focus on providing historiographical introductions to the literature about Texas history published in paper form since the mid-1980s, with the knowledge that some of these materials may also be available online but not so noted in this book. The criteria used in the 1988 *Guide to the History of Texas* remain as the overriding standard for coverage in this volume. Both volumes center squarely on introducing beginning users to the historical literature and, in the process, presenting them a place to start. As well, the essays in this volume avoid extensive commentary dealing with schools of historical interpretation, do not seek to analyze Texas history as an intellectual form of social analysis, avoid discussions of historical theory, and do not explicitly relate the state to larger parts of the

American experience and the national-level literature that comments on such. Presentation of, and commentary about, particular items of bibliography is the unifying force in this book. Its authors concentrate on works of professional, academic history that are based on archival research and the accepted standards of scholarship. They overtly avoid localized studies, genre writings, general Texana, and genealogy. It must also be noted that each of the contributors had much more to say than appears in the published version. A great deal of material had to be cut due to the practical vicissitudes of publishing an affordable book within cost-effective page limits. The academic value of this book, in the final analysis, therefore rests on contemplating what was included instead of considering what was omitted.

Discovering Texas History is organized into two sections, one topical and one chronological. All of the essays were specially written for it except the one by F. Todd Smith, which is based on his article that appeared in the January 2010 issue of the *Southwestern Historical Quarterly*. The contributors had a large measure of freedom to address their subject in any manner they wished. For that reason, the editors permitted a level of duplication in which several essays address the same literature, albeit from different perspectives. This was something worthy of encouraging instead of stifling, because such overlap gives readers additional understanding about significant works of Texas history. Each essay can be seen as a free-standing commentary that makes no conscious effort to coordinate or be in tandem with others in the volume. Most anticipated users, anyway, will probably not consult the entire volume in total as part of one integrated process that surveys all of the essays together. This also means that the topical and chronological coverage of this volume is not comprehensive for all time periods and topics. *Discovering Texas History* is not about what happened in the past but instead solely about recent historical scholarship dealing with those parts of the past that relatively recent academic historians have written about.

This volume is also not a textbook. It makes no attempt to reflect the totality of Texas history and its entire literature on all topics. The sole purpose of *Discovering Texas History* is to provide each author with the opportunity to make individual judgments about what has been written of importance concerning mainstream Texas history during the past quarter-century. It is the hope of the editors that the anticipated users of this book as beginning researchers will eventually outgrow its coverage and move toward a deeper, more comprehensive knowledge of the literature of Texas history. In every case where that happens, this volume will have fulfilled its purpose.

NOTES

1. Light Townsend Cummins and Alvin R. Bailey, Jr., *A Guide to the History of Texas* (New York: Greenwood Press, 1988).

2. Texas Archival Resources Online, www.lib.utexas.edu/taro/index.html; The Portal to Texas History, http://texashistory.unt.edu; West Texas Digital Archives, http://wtda.alc.org; SMU Central University Libraries, Digital Collections, http://digitalcollections.smu.edu/all/cul.

3. Rupert N. Richardson, Adrian Anderson, Cary D. Wintz, and Ernest Wallace, *Texas: The Lone Star State*, 9th ed. (New York: Prentice Hall, 2004); Robert A. Calvert, Arnoldo De León, and Gregg Cantrell, *The History of Texas*, 4th ed. (Arlington Heights, Ill.: Harlan Davidson, 2007).

4. Randolph B. Campbell, *Gone to Texas: A History of the Lone Star State* (New York: Oxford University Press, 2003).

5. Jesús F. de al Teja, Paula Marks, and Ron Tyler, *Texas: Crossroads of North America* (Boston: Houghton Mifflin, 2004); James L. Haley, *Passionate Nation: The Epic History of Texas* (New York: Free Press, 2006).

6. Kenneth W. Howell, Keith J. Volanto, James M. Smallwood, Charles D. Grear, and Jennifer S. Lawrence, *Beyond Myths and Legends: A Narrative History of Texas* (Wheaton, Ill.: Abigail Press, 2008); Archie P. McDonald, *Texas: A Compact History* (Abilene, Tex.: State House Press, 2007).

7. Ron Tyler, Douglas E. Barnett, and Roy R. Barkley, eds., *The New Handbook of Texas* (Austin: Texas State Historical Association, 1996); Roy R. Barkley and Mark F. Odintz, eds., *The Portable Handbook of Texas* (Austin: Texas State Historical Association, 2000); Roy R. Barkley et al., eds., *The Handbook of Texas Music* (Austin: Texas State Historical Association in cooperation with the Center for Studies in Texas History at the University of Texas at Austin, 2003).

8. Gregg Cantrell and Elizabeth Hayes Turner, eds. *Lone Star Pasts: Memory and History in Texas* (College Station: Texas A&M University Press, 2007); John W. Storey and Mary L. Kelley, eds., *Twentieth-Century Texas: A Social and Cultural History* (Denton: University of North Texas Press, 2008); Donald Willett and Stephen Curley, eds., *Invisible Texans: Women and Minorities in Texas History* (Boston: McGraw-Hill, 2005); Felix D. Almaraz, Patricia Thompson, and Carmen Reyes-Johnson, *Eyewitnesses to Texas History* (Dubuque, Iowa: Kendall-Hunt, 2007).

9. Richard B. McCaslin, Donald E. Chipman, and Andrew J. Torget, *This Corner of Canaan: Essays on Texas in Honor of Randolph B. Campbell* (Denton: University of North Texas Press, 2013); Patrick L. Cox and Kenneth L. Hendrickson, Jr., *Writing the Story of Texas* (Austin: University of Texas Press, 2013).

10. Sam W. Haynes and Cary D. Wintz, eds., *Major Problems in Texas History: Documents and Essays* (Boston: Houghton Mifflin, 2002); Ernest Wallace, David M. Vigness, and George B. Ward, eds., *Documents of Texas History* (Austin: Texas State Historical Association, 2002); Randolph B. Campbell, ed., *Texas History Documents*, 2 vols. (New York: Worth, 1997); J'Nell L. Pate, ed., *Document Sets for Texas and the Southwest in U.S. History* (Lexington, Mass.: D. C. Heath, 1991).

11. Ben Procter and Archie P. McDonald, eds., *The Texas Heritage*, 3rd ed. (Wheeling, Ill: Harlan Davidson, 1998); Ty Cashion and Jesús F. de la Teja, eds., *The Human Tradition in Texas* (Wilmington, Del.: Scholarly Resources, 2001); Ralph A. Wooster, Robert A. Calvert, and Adrian N. Anderson, eds., *Texas Vistas: Selections from the* Southwestern Historical Quarterly (Austin: Texas State Historical Association, 2006); Charles Swanlund and Kirk Bane, eds., *A Lone Star Reader* (Dubuque, Iowa: Kendall Hunt, 2010); Keith J. Volanto, ed., *Texas Voices* (Wheaton, Ill.: Abigail Press, 2010).

12. David O'Donald Cullen and Kyle G. Wilkison, eds., *The Texas Left: The Radical Roots of Lone Star Liberalism* (College Station: Texas A&M University Press, 2010); Bruce A. Glasrud and James C. Maroney, eds., *Texas Labor History* (College Station: Texas A&M University Press, 2013).

13. Walter L. Buenger and Robert A. Calvert, eds., *Texas through Time: Evolving Interpretations* (College Station: Texas A&M University Press, 1991); Walter L. Buenger and Arnoldo De León, eds., *Beyond Texas through Time: Breaking Away from Past Interpretations* (College Station: Texas A&M University Press, 2011).

14. Laura L. McLemore, *Inventing Texas: Early Historians of the Lone Star State* (College Station: Texas A&M University Press, 2004); Richard B. McCaslin, *At the Heart of Texas: One Hundred Years of the Texas State Historical Association, 1897–1997* (Austin: Texas State Historical Association, 2007).

15. Robert M. Utley, *Lone Star Justice: The First Century of the Texas Rangers* (New York: Oxford University Press, 2002); Robert M. Utley, *Lone Star Lawmen: The Second Century of the Texas Rangers* (New York: Oxford University Press, 2007); Mike Cox, *The Texas Rangers: Wearing the Cinco Paso, 1821–1900* (New York: Tom Doherty Associates, 2008); Mike Cox, *Time of the Rangers: From 1900 to the Present* (New York: Tom Doherty Associates, 2009); Bruce A. Glasrud and Harold J. Weiss, Jr., *Tracking the Texas Rangers: The Nineteenth Century* (Denton: University of North Texas Press, 2012); Bruce A. Glasrud and Harold J. Weiss, Jr., *Tracking the Texas Rangers: The Twentieth Century* (Denton: University of North Texas Press, 2013).

Part I

Topical Essays

CHAPTER 1

Native Americans

Matthew M. Babcock

According to a scholar writing in the late 1980s, "Texas Indian Historiography has dealt too exclusively with military campaigns and too little with tribal histories and ethnohistorical studies."[1] The same could hardly be said today. Over the past two decades scholars in multiple disciplines have produced tribal histories of every major Native American tribe in Texas and cutting-edge ethnohistorical studies. Archaeologists and anthropologists have simultaneously been uncovering the rich precontact history of indigenous groups in the region. By placing Indians at the center rather than on the margins of Texas history and adopting hemispheric and global perspectives in their work, scholars have both been influenced by and contributed to larger trends in the "new Indian history" as well as borderlands, colonial, Latin American, world, and environmental history.[2] This essay examines scholarship on Texas Indians written since 1988 from Native and Euro-American perspectives. It includes works treating multiple Native groups, tribal histories, and biographies of individual chiefs.

David La Vere's *Texas Indians* should be the starting point for anyone interested in conducting Indian-centered research on Texas in any era. Superseding anthropologist William W. Newcomb's classic *Indians of Texas*, La Vere's comprehensive interdisciplinary study traces the cultural history of Texas Indians and their relations with outsiders from twelve thousand years ago to the present from a Native perspective. He defines Texas Indians broadly to include immigrants such as Cherokees, Choctaws, and Alabama-Coushattas from the Southeast but also emigrants whom Anglo-Texans pushed into Oklahoma in the late nineteenth century, whose lives deserve much further study.[3] The tribal overviews in the *Southwest*, *Plains*, and *Southeast* volumes of the Smithsonian Institution's *Handbook of North American Indians* are also excellent starting points for conducting research on Texas archaeology, pre-Columbian history, and tribal history, and the notes serve as useful guides to the most important anthropological and ethnohistorical literature on each Native group.[4]

Researchers interested in viewing Texas Indians from a European perspective should consult sociologist Thomas D. Hall's sweeping *Social Change in the Southwest, 1350–1880*, the first book-length application of world-system theory to the Southwest. Hall argues that imperial Spain, as a core power, tried to make southwestern Native cultures, including Apaches and Comanches, dependent by integrating their production processes into the world market, or "incorporating" them; however, in contrast to most core nation-states, the Spanish failed to garner a net profit from the peripheral area of the Greater Southwest. Although Hall fails to consider the fact that powerful Native peoples living on the peripheries of European empires could qualify as core powers themselves, his book is important because it reminds scholars to consider global economic push-and-pull factors when examining regional processes of social change on frontiers and borderlands. Randolph B. Campbell's well-conceived one-volume textbook *Gone to Texas: A History of the Lone Star State*, though written primarily from a Euro-American perspective, still offers a balanced assessment of Texas Indians from precontact through the late nineteenth century.[5]

One of the most important trends in Texas historiography in the past twenty years has been the extension of history back to the arrival of the first Paleoindians in the region rather than to the European arrival of Cabeza de Vaca or the Anglo-American arrival of Stephen F. Austin. Important archaeological studies of Texas's precontact era include Susan C. Vehik and Timothy G. Baugh's "Cultural Continuity and Discontinuity in the Southern Prairies and Cross Timbers," Donny L. Hamilton's *Prehistory of the Hustler Hills*, and Timothy K. Perttula's collection of essays in *The Prehistoric Archaeology of Texas*. Archaeologist Noel D. Justice's typological research of chipped-stone projectile points in *Stone Age Spear and Arrow Points of the Southwestern United States* and historian William B. Carter's well-written synthesis of indigenous precontact history in *Indian Alliances and the Spanish in the Southwest, 750–1750* serve as important resources for researchers of the trans-Pecos region of West Texas in multiple disciplines.[6]

Since the late 1990s, ethnohistorians have been completely rewriting Texas's colonial history from the perspectives of its Native inhabitants. Gary Clayton Anderson's *Indian Southwest, 1580–1830* offers a radical reconceptualization of Southern Plains Native and European exchange networks that is critical for understanding how Texas Indians adapted to European colonization. Despite a scathing, inaccurate attack on borderlands historiography in his introduction and a reluctance to examine Apache and Comanche raiding south of the Rio Grande, Anderson breaks new ground in this work by demonstrating that Spanish colonization not only altered and destroyed many Native societies but also opened new opportunities for commerce and economic development for Indians and Europeans alike. Employing the anthropological theory of ethnogenesis, or cultural reinvention, Anderson demonstrates that Jumanos, Coahuiltecans, Apaches, Caddos, Wichitas, and Comanches all successfully adapted to European encroachment and environmental stress through such methods as incorporating remnant bands and captives, consolidating villages, forging new alliances, and diversifying their trade goods. According to Anderson, then, mobile Native societies were not just central players in the region but were collectively more economically powerful than Europeans, Mexicans, and Americans, retaining control of the horse, mule, and buffalo trade and the entire greater Southwest exchange-based political economy for two hundred and fifty years until the opening of the Santa Fe trade in 1830.[7]

Several other authors have followed Anderson's lead by assessing how multiple Native groups negotiated European conquest in colonial Texas. In *The Native Americans of the Texas Edwards Plateau*, archaeologist Maria F. Wade demonstrates through careful archaeological, Spanish archival, ethnohistorical, and environmental research that Native peoples east of the Pecos River, especially Lipan Apaches, not only withstood but successfully challenged Spanish political authority and social control in the region. Expanding on earlier research performed by T. N. Campbell, she also greatly improves scholarly understanding of the diversity of Native cultures and biodiversity of the Edwards Plateau region, including the shifting range of the bison from the sixteenth through eighteenth centuries. Relying on world-system theory, social history, and regional analysis, anthropologist Martha McCollough's *Three Nations, One Place* similarly describes nomadic Comanches and sedentary Hasinais evading Spanish efforts to control them economically and politically by using political alliances, military power, and mobility to assert control over the Southern Plains horse and gun trade. Because of the departure of the French in 1763 and the growing power of the Comanches, however, McCollough argues that the Hasinais, devastated by disease, found themselves cut out of both parts of the trade. Finally, in her award-winning *Peace Came in the Form of a Woman*, historian Juliana Barr maintains that Texas Indians' gendered notions of kinship governed their political, social, and economic relationships with Europeans along the eighteenth-century Texas-Louisiana frontier. According to Barr, this means that Texas Indians, including Apaches, Comanches, Caddos, and Wichitas—not Spanish or French colonists—controlled the region.[8]

Authors seeking a more balanced perspective on Indian-European colonial relations in Texas from a European perspective should consult the classic works of David J. Weber and Donald E. Chipman. Weber's impressive *Spanish Frontier in North America* is the most evenhanded and comprehensive synthesis of the history of Spain's North American frontier from Florida to California written to date. Drawing from traditional Spanish archival sources as well as more recent social, economic, and cultural history of the United States and Latin America, Weber views this region's history as a series of interrelated, multilayered cultural conflicts, exchanges, and transformations between Spaniards, Indians, and Europeans. Putting the ghost of Frederick Jackson Turner to rest, Weber argues that Spain's North American frontiers, just as other frontiers, must be understood as zones of cultural interaction that experienced constant processes of expansion and contraction. In other words, Spaniards, Native Americans, and other European powers affected and were affected by each another. Weber sees contention occurring on two levels on the frontier. People within each frontier society struggle internally for power while engaging in larger patterns of intercultural conflict and exchange. The result is cultural transformation, which in this case was a hybridized Hispanic culture and society consisting of Iberian and Indian elements. Weber concludes that it was not an even synthesis, however. Spain's "technological, economic, and political strength" enabled "the core of Hispanic frontier culture and society" to remain "recognizably Hispanic and clearly intact."[9]

Two other impressive syntheses of Spanish-Indian relations stand out for their perspectives on Texas Indians. Donald E. Chipman and Harriett Denise Joseph's recently revised *Spanish Texas, 1519–1821* is the best single-volume synthesis of Texas's colonial history written to date.[10] Originally written from a Spanish imperial perspective, Chipman and Joseph's revised narrative is even more useful for ethnohistorians because it incorporates the past twenty years of secondary scholarship on Texas Indian peoples, highlighting their ability to adapt to European colonization and act independently. In *Bárbaros*, David J. Weber again views Texas Indians from a Spanish imperial perspective.

Encompassing Spain's entire American empire, the book breaks new ground by placing Native responses to Spanish Indian policy in a comparative hemispheric context and demonstrating that unincorporated Indians on Spanish American frontiers not only retained power over their own lives but still controlled more than half of the land mass in the Americas in the mid-1700s.[11]

Several other recent works treating the Spanish colonial era are potentially useful to ethnohistorians in Texas. Based on Spanish archival sources, Mark Santiago's *Red Captain: The Life of Hugo O'Conor* is a solid source on Spanish-Apache warfare in the 1770s. Jack Jackson's *Imaginary Kingdom: Texas as Seen by the Rivera and Rubí Expeditions, 1727 and 1767* consists of English translations of Spanish documents, which contain information on the ethnology of Texas Indians and Spanish Indian policy in these periods, in particular the Marqués de Rubí's recommendation to wage a war of extermination on Lipan Apaches. *The Presidio and Militia on the Northern Frontier of New Spain*, Vol. 2, Part II: *The Central Texas Corridor and the Texas Corridor, 1700–1765*, edited by Diana Hadley, Thomas H. Naylor, and Mardith K. Shuetz-Miller, offers useful primary source information on mission Indians in Texas from La Bahía to San Sabá and on Lipan and Mescalero Apache raids on Texas ranchos and other provincial settlements bordering the desolate Bolsón de Mapimí, which the Indians used as a region of refuge between offensives. On Spanish missions in Texas, see *Archival Investigations for Mission Nuestra Señora de los Dolores de los Ais*, by Adán Benavides, Jr., and Robert Jackson's *From Savages to Subjects*. On Apache Indian reservations along the Spanish-Apache frontier, see Matthew Babcock's "Rethinking the *Establecimientos*." On Indian slavery in colonial Texas, see Juliana Barr's "A Spectrum of Indian Bondage in Spanish Texas" and James F. Brooks's "'We Betray Our Own Nation': Indian Slavery and Multi-ethnic Communities in the Southwest Borderlands." For the Spanish extradition of Apaches from the Apachería, including parts of what is now Texas, to interior Mexico and Cuba, see Mark Santiago's *Jar of Severed Hands*.[12]

Far fewer works of the past twenty years treat multiple Texas Indian groups in the nineteenth century than in the colonial era. Since the early 1990s, scholars have deepened our understanding of the reasons behind the decline of the bison and the American Indians' own role in it. In "Bison Ecology and Bison Diplomacy," for example, environmental historian Dan Flores maintains that environmental change and increasing pressure to trade bison robes and horses to Euro-American traders prevented Southern Plains tribes from achieving a "dynamic, ecological equilibrium" with bison herds in the early nineteenth century.[13] Some of these same scholars have assessed the ecological and economic impact of horses on equestrian groups and the political economy of the Southern Plains.[14] Two ethnohistorians have assessed the decline of Texas Indians in the nineteenth century. Serving as a worthy sequel to historian Elizabeth A. H. John's classic synthesis of European-Indian relations in the colonial Southwest, *Storms Brewed in Other Men's Worlds*, F. Todd Smith's *From Dominance to Disappearance: The Indians of Texas and the Near Southwest, 1786–1859* thoroughly describes the shifting power relations between Texas Indian tribes and Euro-Americans from the late Spanish period, when Comanches, Caddos, and Wichitas dominated the region, to the 1850s, when the U.S. government unsuccessfully tried to relocate Texas Indians reservations in the state. Although largely a heart-wrenching tale of Native decline, Smith's book at the same time shows how Indians negotiated and adapted to military conquest, exile, and forced acculturation in Texas and the Indian Territory. In *The Conquest of Texas*, Gary Clayton Anderson challenges long-standing romanticized myths of Anglo-Texan exceptionalism by arguing that state authorities pursued a policy akin to ethnic cleansing toward Indians and Tejanos, which Texas Rangers first implemented in the 1830s and the U.S. Army employed again in the 1860s. Anderson defines the twentieth-century European term "ethnic cleansing" as "the forced removal of certain culturally identified groups from their lands," which he distinguishes from genocide or "the intentional killing of nearly all of a racial, religious, or cultural group" and anachronistically applies to the middle nineteenth century.[15] In contrast, historian Brian DeLay's *War of a Thousand Deserts* challenges the prevalent notion that indigenous power declined in Texas and across the continent after 1815 by convincingly demonstrating that Comanches, Kiowas, Apaches, and Navajos influenced the course and outcome of the U.S.-Mexico War and shaped the contest for North America through the mid-nineteenth century.[16]

Anthropologists and ethnohistorians have produced numerous tribal histories over the past two decades that treat a wider range of Texas Indian groups than ever before. Although most scholars quickly recognize mobile Comanches and Apaches as powerful tribes in Texas, how many are aware of the extent of Caddo political and economic dominance or the sheer number of tribes, from the Cherokees to the Black Seminoles, who emigrated to East and South Texas from the Southeast in the early nineteenth century?[17] Linguistic anthropologist Nancy Parrot Hickerson's *The Jumanos: Hunters and Traders of the South Plains* is the first-book length study of this elusive group, whose origins and cultural identity have been highly contested by scholars for decades. According to Hickerson, the Jumanos were a distinctive tribe of Tanoan speakers (rather than Uto-Aztecans) located south and east of the Rio Grande. Relying on primary sources, she persuasively argues that they controlled the political economy of the Southern Plains before the ascendancy of the Apaches in the late 1600s; however, she needs more evidence to support her claim that the Kiowas descended directly from one group of Jumanos.[18]

Two excellent interdisciplinary works on the Karankawas have also helped to revive this long-misunderstood tribe's reputation. In *The Karankawa Indians of Texas*, archaeologist Robert A. Ricklis combines archaeological and ethnohistorical data to provide the first modern narrative history of the Karankawas from pre-Columbian times to their cultural extinction in the nineteenth century. Stressing their ability to adapt to their environment and Hispanic encroachment, Ricklis rescues this Gulf Coast tribe from timeworn Eurocentric depictions as primitive cannibalistic savages. Rather than rely solely on violence, the Karankawas instead incorporated Spanish missions into their regional subsistence strategy and peacefully coexisted with Euro-Americans until the arrival of Anglo-Americans in the early nineteenth century.[19] In *The Conquest of the Karankawas and the Tonkawas*, sociologist Kelly F. Himmel draws on world-system theory and internal colonialism to compare Karankawa and Tonkawa efforts to negotiate conquest and incorporation into the regional and global political economy of Mexico, Texas, and the United States. Filling an important void in nineteenth-century Texas historiography, Himmel explains in vivid detail how Anglo-Americans exterminated the Karankawas by 1859 and drove the few remaining Tonkawas out of Texas to the Indian Territory.[20]

No Texas tribe has drawn more attention from ethnohistorians in recent decades than the Comanches. Texas scholars have long recognized Comanche military might. Indeed, Ernest Wallace and E. Adamson Hoebel dubbed them the "Lords of the South Plains" as early as 1952.[21] But since discovering in the mid-1980s that Wallace and Hoebel's work was laced with errors about Comanche social and political organization, anthropologists and ethnohistorians have increasingly focused on the social, political, and economic dimensions of Comanche power and rewritten the history of the tribe. Combining the ethnohistorical method with oral history interviews and sociolinguistic theory, anthropologist Morris W. Foster's *Being Comanche* offers a compelling reinterpretation of Comanche social organization that stresses the continuities in their intracommunity organization from first European contact to the present. In *Los Comanches*, novelist and poet Stanley Noyes offers an exceptionally well-written narrative history of the Comanches from Spanish contact to the eve of the U.S.-Mexican War in which he argues that Comanches were the dominant indigenous power on the Southern Plains from the mid-eighteenth century until the United States' annexation of Texas in 1845. Standing in stark contrast to Noyes's highly readable prose, anthropologist Thomas W. Kavanagh's encyclopedic *Comanche Political History* is still a handy reference for Comanche specialists, serving in combination with John's *Storms Brewed in Other Men's Worlds* as a published record of every major Comanche political and commercial interaction with Spaniards, French, Mexicans, and Anglo-Americans for more than two and a half centuries. Most controversial, however, is Kavanagh's conclusion that the Comanche sociopolitical system was similar to the "typical" Great Plains pattern, consisting of a series of social units ranging from the elementary family to the tribe, whose primary forms by the mid-nineteenth century were five so-called divisions. Gerald Betty's *Comanche Society* argues that the complex evolution of Comanche society can be explained on the basis of kinship, an argument that could be potentially applied to any indigenous equestrian group in the Western Hemisphere.[22]

In his Bancroft-prize winning *Comanche Empire*, Pekka Hämäläinen offers the most radical ethnohistorical argument to date on any single Texas Indian group. Turning world-system and colonial theories completely on their heads and going beyond all previous conceptions of Comanche power, Hämäläinen argues that Comanches did not simply control the horse, mule, and buffalo trade, they were the core imperial power in the Southwest from 1750 to 1850, exploiting the weaker peripheral Spanish, French, Mexican, and American nation-states. Comanches allegedly maintained their dominance through a "centralized multilevel political system" that incorporated Euro-American and indigenous captives, animals, weapons, and other goods and controlled surrounding markets, while making the conscious choice not to incorporate completely or replace the surrounding nation-states themselves.[23]

If Comanches are the Texas tribe that has drawn the most scholarly attention over the past twenty years, the Caddos are a close second. Based on archaeological, ethnographic, historical, and archival data, archaeologist Timothy K. Perttula's *Caddo Nation* convincingly demonstrates that, in spite of population decline from epidemic disease, the Kadodacho, Hasinai, and Natchitoches Caddoan confederacies were the dominant indigenous political power in the "Four Corners" region of present-day Texas, Oklahoma, Arkansas, and Louisiana until 1800, a finding that complicates and challenges the idea of any Comanche "empire" in the same era. In contrast to Perttula's highly technical language and archaeological emphasis, Caddo cultural liaison and enrolled tribal member Cecile Elkins Carter and historian F. Todd Smith have written three highly readable narrative histories of the tribe. Drawing from oral interviews, archaeological data, and historical documents, Carter's *Caddo Indians: Where We Come From* emphasizes Caddo resiliency and adaptability in the face of numerous obstacles, from epidemic disease to military conquest to forced migration from their homeland. In his award-winning *Caddo Indians: Tribes at the Convergence of Empires*, Smith maintains, in contrast to Perttula, that the Caddos capitalized on their position as middlemen in French- and Spanish-controlled Southern Plains trading networks only until 1763 before becoming more dependent on Spanish, British, Chickasaw, Osage, and Anglo-American economic and military power. Smith then carries on his story of Caddo declension in *The Caddos, the Wichitas, and the United States* by showing how U.S. Indian policy led to the forced relocation of Caddos and Wichitas from Texas and how the Dawes Act destroyed their collective land base, which was a central part of their tribal identity. Finally, in *The Caddo Chiefdoms*, David La Vere combines careful archival research with oral history and archaeological evidence to explain that Caddo leaders effectively relied on kinship and the reciprocal exchange of gifts to enhance their regional economic and political authority until Anglo-Americans encroached on their lands after the Louisiana Purchase of 1803, which places him much closer to Perttula's argument than to Smith's.[24]

After the Comanches and Caddos, scholars have devoted the most attention to the Wichitas, Kiowas, and Lipan Apaches, restoring each of these tribes from relative obscurity to their rightful place in Texas history. Picking up where his two previous works left off, F. Todd Smith uses archival French and Spanish sources and published primary and secondary historical sources in *The Wichita Indians*, a well-written and well-researched narrative history of the little-known Caddoan-speaking Taovaya, Tawakoni, Iscani (Waco), Guchita, and Kichai tribes, whom U.S. officials mistakenly dubbed Wichitas in 1835. According to Smith, because of their lack of access to horses and weapons, the Wichitas were never able to dominate the Southern Plains political economy to the extent that Apaches and Comanches had. In contrast to Smith's fine work, Earl H. Elam's *Kitikiti'sh: The Wichita Indians and Associated Tribes in Texas* is a slightly revised version of his 1971 Texas Tech dissertation, which is based on English-language sources.[25] John R. Wunder's *The Kiowa*, part of the Indians of North America Series, provides a brief overview of this nomadic equestrian group from before contact to the present with a penetrating look at their relationship with the U.S. government. Stan Hoig's *The Kiowas and the Legend of Kicking Bird*, though purporting to be both a Kiowa tribal history and a biography of Kicking Bird is in reality only a biography. Most recently, in *Kiowa Humanity and the Invasion of the State*, Jacki Thompson Rand provides the most thorough tribal history of the Kiowas to date rooted in theories of internal colonialism and gender and ethnohistorical sources. Although Rand underemphasizes the extent of Kiowa violence on Tejanos, Anglo-Texans, and Mexicans before the reservation era, she convincingly demonstrates that Kiowas counteracted U.S. policies of assimilation and individualism from 1867 to 1910 by adopting gendered strategies rooted in tribalism.[26]

Until recently, surprisingly few works in the past twenty years have focused on Apache groups in Texas. Thomas F. Schilz's *Lipan Apaches in Texas*, the first scholarly narrative history of the tribe to 1859, makes a compelling case that the Lipan Apaches were the most important tribe on Texas's southwestern frontier before 1821 and traces their removal from Texas and forced relocation with Tonkawas to Oklahoma and Mescaleros to New Mexico. More comprehensive and more deeply researched than Schilz's study, Thomas A. Britten's *Lipan Apaches* reveals how Lipan Apaches creatively adapted to encroachment from surrounding Euro-American and indigenous powers by negotiating shifting alliances with Spaniards, Comanches, and Anglo-Texans. More important, Britten carries the Lipan story forward beyond the end of Schilz's study to the twentieth century. What sets Lipan tribal historian Nancy McGown Minor's two works apart from the majority of the new tribal histories of Texas Indian groups is her heavy reliance on twentieth-century oral history interviews from Lipan Apaches and purported but unverified Lipan Apache descendants. In *The Light Gray People*, she gives us a historical overview and thorough ethnographic description of the tribe. In *Turning Adversity into Advantage*, she provides a highly detailed narrative history of the Lipan Apaches over two centuries based on extensive research in Spanish and English archival sources but often fails to place Lipan activities in broader regional context. Superseding all of these works as the most thorough interdisciplinary Lipan history to date is journalist Sherry Robinson's engaging *I Fought a Good Fight*, which combines oral history, anthropological sources, and traditional historical sources to tell a compelling story of Lipan survival from pre-contact to the present.[27]

Last but not least, scholars have been working to reduce the deficiency in tribal studies of removed southeastern Indians in Texas. Historian David La Vere provides a penetrating overall look at the contested relations between removed southeastern Indian agriculturalists and equestrian Southern Plains groups in the Indian Territory in the early nineteenth century in *Contrary*

Neighbors, but he devotes little attention to those groups who settled in Spanish and Mexican Texas.[28] One of the few works to address this deficiency, historian Dianna Everett's *Texas Cherokees* examines the tensions between Cherokees and Anglo-Texans and the dichotomy the Cherokees had to negotiate between removal on the one hand and extermination on the other.[29]

Scholars have also produced several works on the experience of immigrant Black Seminoles along the Texas-Coahuila border. In *Freedom on the Border*, Kevin Mulroy reveals the little-known story of African American runaways under John Horse and Seminole Indians under Chief Wild Cat relocating from the Indian Territory through Texas to Coahuila. Although most of these "maroons" remained in Mexico, in the wake of a post–Civil War smallpox epidemic a portion resettled in Texas and served as scouts in the U.S. Army. Going beyond Mulroy's work, *The Black Seminoles*, by historian Kenneth W. Porter, is a deeply researched study based on primary historical sources and twentieth-century oral interviews, which includes further information on the experience of the Black Seminole scouts at Fort Clark in West Texas. Providing an important counterbalance to the usual emphasis on Black Seminole male military prowess, Shirley Boteler Mock's interdisciplinary study *Dreaming with the Ancestors* combines documentary research with extensive oral interviews to reveal how Black Seminole women retained African cultural influences ranging from naming and cooking to family practices and religion.[30]

At the same time, scholars have begun to uncover the little-known history of the Alabama-Coushattas. In *The Alabama-Coushatta Indians*, independent scholar Jonathan B. Hook relies on extensive oral interviews with tribal members to show how the Creek-related Alabama-Coushattas employed processes of regenesis and ethnogenesis to adapt to European intrusions in their culture. Historian Sheri Marie Shuck-Hall's *Journey to the West* describes the diasporic migration of several hundred Alabamas and Coushattas from Alabama to East Texas in 1820 and reveals how they successfully worked together to retain land in the state, in contrast to the vast majority of Texas Indians.[31]

So what remains to be done? Given the sheer number of ethnohistorical studies and tribal histories produced in the past two decades, it would seem that scholars have little left to accomplish in Texas Indian history. Huge gaps remain, however, in our understanding of the precontact history of Texas Indians and of those groups who seemingly "disappeared" from the stresses of European warfare, disease, and slavery in the colonial era. More research also needs to be conducted on Indian captivity and slavery in the colonial era, especially for groups other than Comanches and Apaches. Scholars have made enormous progress, but they have still written only a handful of ethnohistorical works on Mexican-Indian and Anglo-Indian relations in nineteenth-century Texas. Updated tribal histories of the Atakapas (including the Bidais), Kickapoos, Tiguas have not yet appeared, and the twentieth and twenty-first centuries remain wide open for study. David La Vere's *Life among the Texas Indians: The WPA Narratives* suggests that possibilities still exist for conducting oral histories with former Texas Indian groups relocated to Oklahoma. Although only three federally recognized tribes—Alabama-Coushattas, Kickapoos, and Tiguas—remain in the state, Lipan Apaches, Comanches, and other Native Americans still reside here, and their stories also need telling. Historian Jeffrey R. Schulze's "Rediscovery of the Tiguas" is a wonderful start, but it is one of the only recent publications on the Tiguas in the twentieth century.[32] Last but not least, although scholars and popular writers have written a steady stream of biographies on prominent Indian chiefs of varying quality, how many biographies of prominent Indian women in Texas exist? The history of Texas Indians, especially Indian women, from the late nineteenth century to the present remains to be written.

NOTES

1. Thomas F. Schilz, "Native Americans in Texas History," in *A Guide to the History of Texas*, ed. Light Townshend Cummins and Alvin R. Bailey, Jr. (New York: Greenwood Press, 1988), 100.

2. See F. Todd Smith, "Texas through 1845: A Survey of the Historical Literature of Recent Decades," *Southwestern Historical Quarterly* 113 (Jan. 2010): 317–18; Pekka Hämäläinen, "Into the Mainstream: The Emergence of a New Texas Indian History," in *Beyond Texas through Time: Breaking Away from Past Interpretations*, ed. Walter L. Buenger and Arnoldo De León (College Station: Texas A&M University Press, 2011), 50–53. Significantly, the first edition of this book, despite being published three years after Cummins and Bailey, *A Guide to the History of Texas*, lacked a chapter on Texas Indian historiography. This alone shows how far the field has developed over the past two decades. See Walter L. Buenger and Robert A. Calvert, eds., *Texas through Time* (College Station: Texas A&M University Press, 1991).

3. David La Vere, *The Texas Indians* (College Station: Texas A&M University Press, 2004); William W. Newcomb, Jr., *The Indians of Texas: From Prehistoric to Modern Times* (Austin: University of Texas Press, 1961).

4. Alfonso Ortiz, ed., *Southwest*, vol. 9, *The Handbook of North American Indians* (Washington: Smithsonian Institution, 1979); Alfonso Ortiz, ed., *Southwest*, vol. 10, *The Handbook of North American Indians* (Washington: Smithsonian Institution, 1983);

Raymond J. DeMallie, ed., *Plains*, 2 vols., vol. 13, *The Handbook of American Indians* (Washington: Smithsonian Institution, 2001); Raymond Fogelson, ed., *Southeast*, vol. 14, *The Handbook of North American Indians* (Washington: Smithsonian Institution, 2004).

5. Thomas D. Hall, *Social Change in the Southwest, 1350–1880* (Lawrence, Kans.: University Press of Kansas, 1989); Randolph. B. Campbell, *Gone to Texas: A History of the Lone Star State* (New York: Oxford University Press, 2003).

6. Susan C. Vehik and Timothy G. Baugh, "Cultural Continuity and Discontinuity in the Southern Prairies and Cross Timbers," in *Plains Indians, A.D. 150–1500: The Archaeological Past of Historic Groups*, ed. Karl H. Schlesier (Norman: University of Oklahoma Press, 1994), 239–63; Donny L. Hamilton, *Prehistory of the Hustler Hills: Granado Cave* (Austin: University of Texas Press, 2001); Timothy K. Perttula, ed., *The Prehistoric Archaeology of Texas* (College Station: Texas A&M University Press, 2004); Noel D. Justice, *Stone Age Spear and Arrow Points of the Southwestern United States* (Bloomington: Indiana University Press, 2002); William B. Carter, *Indian Alliances and the Spanish in the Southwest, 750–1750* (Norman: University of Oklahoma Press, 2009).

7. Gary Clayton Anderson, *The Indian Southwest, 1580–1830: Ethnogenesis and Reinvention* (Norman: University of Oklahoma Press, 1999).

8. Maria F. Wade, *The Native Americans of the Texas Edwards Plateau, 1582–1799* (Austin: University of Texas Press, 2003); Martha McCollough, *Three Nations, One Place: A Comparative Ethnohistory of Social Change during Spain's Colonial Era, 1689–1821* (New York: Routledge, 2004); Juliana Barr, *Peace Came in the Form of a Woman: Indians and Spaniards in the Texas Borderlands* (Chapel Hill: University of North Carolina Press, 2007). See also Juliana Barr, "A Diplomacy of Gender: Rituals of First Contact in the 'Land of the Tejas,'" *William and Mary Quarterly* 61 (July 2004): 393–434; Juliana Barr, "From Captives to Slaves: Commodifying Indian Women in the Borderlands," *Journal of American History* 92 (June 2005): 19–46; Juliana Barr, "Beyond Their Control: Spaniards in Native Texas," in *Choice, Persuasion, and Coercion: Social Control on Spain's North American Frontiers*, ed. Jesús F. de la Teja and Ross Frank (Albuquerque: University of New Mexico Press, 2005), 149–77.

9. David J. Weber, *The Spanish Frontier in North America* (New Haven, Conn.: Yale University Press, 1992), 333. For a more recent synthesis of Spain's southwestern borderlands, including Texas, written from the Spanish perspective, see John L. Kessell, *Spain in the Southwest: A Narrative History of Colonial New Mexico, Arizona, Texas, and California* (Norman: University of Oklahoma Press, 2002).

10. Donald E. Chipman and Hariett Denise Joseph, *Spanish Texas, 1519–1821*, 2nd ed. (1st ed. 1992; Austin: University of Texas Press, 2010).

11. David J. Weber, *Bárbaros: Spaniards and Their Savages in the Age of Enlightenment* (New Haven, Conn.: Yale University Press, 2005).

12. Mark Santiago, *The Red Captain: The Life of Hugo O'Conor, Commandant Inspector of the Interior Provinces of New Spain*, Muesum Monograph 9 (Tucson: Arizona Historical Society, 1994); Jack Jackson and William C. Foster, eds., *Imaginary Kingdom: Texas as Seen by the Rivera and Rubí Military Expeditions, 1727–1767* (Austin: Texas State Historical Association, 1995); Diana Hadley, Thomas H. Naylor, and Mardith Schuetz-Miller, eds., *The Presidio and Militia on the Northern Frontier of New Spain*, Vol. 2, Part 2: *The Central Corridor and the Texas Corridor* (Tucson: University of

Arizona Press, 1997); Adán Benavides, Jr., *Archival Investigations for Mission Nuestra Señora de los Dolores de los Ais, San Augustine County Texas: A Catalog of Documents and Maps of the Mission Dolores de los Ais Historical Materials Collection* (Austin: Texas Department of Transportation, 1998); Robert H. Jackson, *From Savages to Subjects: Missions in the History of the American Southwest* (Armonk, N.Y.: M. E. Sharpe, 2000); Matthew Babcock, "Rethinking the Establecimientos: Why Apaches Settled on Spanish-Run Reservations, 1786–1793," *New Mexico Historical Review* 84, no. 3 (2009): 363–97; Juliana Barr, "A Spectrum of Indian Bondage in Spanish Texas," in *Indian Slavery in Colonial America*, ed. Allan Gallay (Lincoln: University of Nebraska Press, 2009), 277–318; James F. Brooks, "'We Betray Our Own Nation': Indian Slavery and Multi-ethnic Communities in the Southwest Borderlands," in Gallay, *Indian Slavery*, 319–52; Mark Santiago, *The Jar of Severed Hands: The Spanish Deportation of Apache Prisoners of War, 1770-1810* (Norman: University of Oklahoma Press, 2011).

13. Dan Flores, "Bison Ecology and Bison Diplomacy: The Southern Plains from 1800 to 1850," *Journal of American History* 78 (Sept. 1991): 465–85, quote 483; see also Pekka Hämäläinen, "The First Phase of Destruction: Killing the Southern Plains Buffalo, 1790–1840," *Great Plains Quarterly* 21 (Spring 2001): 99–114.

14. Pekka Hämäläinen, "The Rise and Fall of Plains Indian Horse Cultures," *Journal of American History* 90 (2003); Dan Flores, "Bringing Home All the Pretty Horses: The Horse Trade and the Early American West, 1775–1825," *Montana: The Magazine of Western History* 58 (Summer 2008): 3–21.

15. Elizabeth A. H. John, *Storms Brewed in Other Men's Worlds: The Confrontation of Indians, Spanish, and French in the Southwest, 1540–1795* (College Station: Texas A&M University Press, 1975); F. Todd Smith, *From Dominance to Disappearance: The Indians of Texas and the Near Southwest, 1786–1859* (Lincoln: University of Nebraska Press, 2005); Gary Clayton Anderson, *The Conquest of Texas: Ethnic Cleansing in the Promised Land* (Norman: University of Oklahoma Press, 2005). See also Andrew R. Graybill, *Policing the Great Plains: Rangers, Mounties, and the North American Frontier, 1875–1910* (Lincoln: University of Nebraska Press, 2007).

16. Brian DeLay, *War of a Thousand Deserts: Indian Raids and the U.S.-Mexican War* (New Haven, Conn.: Yale University Press, 2008); Brian DeLay, "Independent Indians and the U.S.-Mexico War," *American Historical Review* 112 (Feb. 2007): 35–68. Several books treating the nineteenth century written from a Mexican perspective are also useful for ethnohistorians; see David J. Weber, *The Mexican Frontier, 1821–1846: The American Southwest under Mexico* (Albuquerque: University of New Mexico Press, 1982); Andrés Reséndez, *Changing National Identitites at the Frontier: Texas and New Mexico, 1800–1850* (New York: Cambridge University Press, 2005); Raúl A. Ramos, *Beyond the Alamo: Forging Mexican Identity in San Antonio, 1821–1861* (Chapel Hill: University of North Carolina Press, 2008).

17. In a recent book chapter, Pekka Hämäläinen omits current scholarship on numerous Texas Indian tribes, including Alabama-Coushattas, Atakapas, Lipan Apaches, and Tiguas; see Hämäläinen, "Into the Mainstream," 50–84.

18. Nancy Parrott Hickerson, *The Jumanos: Hunters and Traders of the South Plains* (Austin: University of Texas Press, 1994).

19. Robert A. Ricklis, *The Karankawa Indians of Texas: An Ecological Study of Cultural Tradition and Change* (Austin: University of Texas Press, 1996).

20. Kelly F. Himmel, *The Conquest of the Karankawas and the Tonkawas, 1821–1859* (College Station: Texas A&M University Press, 1999).

21. Ernest Wallace and E. Adamson Hoebel, *The Comanches: Lords of the South Plains*, Civilization of the American Indian Series (1986; reprint, Norman: University of Oklahoma Press, 1952).

22. Morris W. Foster, *Being Comanche: A Social History of an American Indian Community* (Tucson: University of Arizona Press, 1991); Stanley Noyes, *Los Comanches: The Horse People, 1751–1845* (Albuquerque: University of New Mexico Press, 1993); Thomas W. Kavanagh, *Comanche Political History: An Ethnohistorical Perspective, 1706–1875* (Lincoln: University of Nebraska Press, 1996); Gerald Betty, *Comanche Society: Before the Reservation* (College Station: Texas A&M University Press, 2002). In addition to Comanche tribal histories, scholars have also produced biographies of the prominent nineteenth-century Comanche chiefs Buffalo Hump and Quanah Parker and their relations with the United States; see Jodye Lynn Dickson Schilz and Thomas F. Schilz, *Buffalo Hump and the Penateka Comanches* (El Paso: Texas Western Press, 1989); William T. Hagan, *Quanah Parker: Comanche Chief* (Norman: University of Oklahoma Press, 1993); Bill Neeley, *The Last Comanche Chief: The Life and Times of Quanah Parker* (New York: John Wiley, 1995).

23. Pekka Hämäläinen, *The Comanche Empire*, Lamar Series in Western History (New Haven, Conn.: Yale University Press, 2008). See also Pekka Hämäläinen, "The Western Comanche Trade Center: Rethinking the Plains Indian Trade System," *Western Historical Quarterly* 29 (Winter 1998): 485–513; Hämäläinen, "Rise and Fall," 833–62.

24. Timothy K. Perttula, *The Caddo Nation: Archaeological and Ethnohistorical Perspectives* (Austin: University of Texas Press, 1992); Cecile Elkins Carter, *Caddo Indians: Where We Come From* (Norman: University of Oklahoma Press, 1995); F. Todd Smith, *The Caddo Indians: Tribes at the Convergence of Empires, 1542–1854* (College Station: Texas A&M University Press, 1995); F. Todd Smith, *The Caddos, the Wichitas, and the United States: 1846–1901* (College Station: Texas A&M University Press, 1996); David La Vere, *The Caddo Chiefdoms: Caddo Economics and Politics, 700–1835* (Lincoln: University of Nebraska Press, 1998). Herbert Eugene Bolton's classic study on the Hasinais has also been republished; see Bolton, *The Hasinais: Southern Caddoans as Seen by the Earliest Europeans*, ed. Russell M. Magnaghi, The Civilization of the American Indian Series (2002; reprint, Norman: University of Oklahoma Press, 1987).

25. F. Todd Smith, *The Wichita Indians: Traders of Texas and the Southern Plains, 1540–1845* (College Station: Texas A&M University Press, 2000); Earl H. Elam, *Kitikiti'sh: The Wichita Indians and Associated Tribes in Texas, 1757–1859* (Hillsboro, Tex: Hill College Press, 2008).

26. John R. Wunder, *The Kiowas*, ed. Frank W. Porter, Indians of North America Series (New York: Chelsea House, 1989); Stan Hoig, *The Kiowas and the Legend of Kicking Bird* (Niwot: University Press of Colorado, 2000); see also Charles M. Robinson, *Satanta: The Life and Death of a War Chief*, ed. William H. Leckie (Austin: State House Press, 1998). Jacki Thompson Rand, *Kiowa Humanity and the Invasion of the State* (Lincoln: University of Nebraska Press, 2008).

27. Thomas F. Schilz, *Lipan Apaches in Texas* (El Paso: Texas Western Press, 1987); Thomas A. Britten, *The Lipan Apaches: People of Wind and Lightning* (Albuquerque: University of New Mexico Press, 2009); Nancy McGown Minor, *The Light Gray People: An Ethno-History of the Lipan Apaches of Texas and Northern Mexico* (Lanham, Md.: University Press of America, 2009), and *Turning Adversity into Advantage: A History of the Lipan Apaches of Texas and Northern Mexico, 1700–1900* (Lanham, Md.: University Press of America, 2009); Sherry R. Robinson, *I Fought a Good Fight: A History of the Lipan Apaches* (Denton: University of North Texas Press, 2013). See also William Chebahtah and Nancy McGown Minor, *Chevato: The Story of the Apache Warrior Who Captured Herman Lehmann* (Lincoln: University of Nebraska Press, 2007).

28. David La Vere, *Contrary Neighbors: Southern Plains and Removed Indians in Indian Territory* (Norman: University of Oklahoma Press, 2000).

29. Dianna Everett, *The Texas Cherokees: A People between Two Fires, 1819–1840*, The Civilization of the American Indian Series 203 (Norman: University of Oklahoma Press, 1990).

30. Kevin Mulroy, *Freedom on the Border: The Seminole Maroons in Florida, the Indian Territory, Coahuila, and Texas* (Lubbock: Texas Tech University Press, 1993); Kenneth W. Porter, *The Black Seminoles: History of a Freedom-Seeking People* (Gainesville: University Press of Florida, 1996); Shirley Boteler Mock, *Dreaming with the Ancestors: Black Seminole Women in Texas and Mexico* (Norman: University of Oklahoma Press, 2010).

31. Jonathan B. Hook, *The Alabama-Coushatta Indians* (College Station: Texas A&M University Press, 1997); Sheri Marie Shuck-Hall, *The Alabama and Coushatta Indians* (Norman: University of Oklahoma Press, 2008).

32. David La Vere, *Life among the Texas Indians: The WPA Narratives* (College Station: Texas A&M University Press, 1998); Jeffrey M. Schulze, "The Rediscovery of the Tiguas: Federal Recognition and Indianness in the Twentieth Century," *Southwestern Historical Quarterly* 105 (July 2001): 14–39.

CHAPTER 2

Mexican Americans

Arnoldo De León

In historical discourse, the study of Mexican Americans in Texas is generally called Tejano history. As is the case with other histories, its definition might vary. Generally speaking, and for the purposes of this essay, it concerns the history of ethnic Mexicans in Texas from about the year 1836 (when citizens of Mexico became citizens of the Republic of Texas and subsequently of the United States) to the present. It is a relatively young area of study, not having been explored by professionally trained historians until around the early 1970s. If Tejanos, or Mexican-origin persons living in Texas, have been part of the state's population since 1836 (obviously, they inhabited the region long before then), then why had historians ignored their presence until recent times? Consensus and ethnocentric perspectives dominated works in Texas history throughout much of the twentieth century, and such standpoints saw the Texas saga as one of white people, and white males in particular; consequently, the narrative did not allow for agency among Texas women or Texans of color. Until after World War II, and even into the 1960s, Mexican Americans constituted only a small percentage of the overall Texas population, with many working in menial jobs, including migrant labor; most scholars thus dismissed them as people having little historical impact worthy of study.

Beginning in the early 1970s, however, Tejano history flowered and since then has developed into what some historians today consider among the most innovative and vibrant fields within Texas history.[1] Impulses behind the attention given to Mexican Americans in Texas during the 1970s included the New

Left movement throughout the United States (which directed notice to the importance of ordinary people in history) as well as the nationwide Chicano movement. It was during that decade that the first wave of Chicano history works (mainly articles) saw publication, written primarily, but not only, by Mexican American historians specifically attracted to a topic familiar to them by personal connection or experience. Literally scores of writings have poured forth since, penned by a cadre that includes scholars of every racial and ethnic background, trained in the most rigorous Ph.D. programs in Texas and the nation.[2]

The literature of the 1970s and 1980s has been discussed elsewhere, but a synopsis of at least some of the books published during that era might be helpful here, because they influenced later scholarship.[3] In *Desert Immigrants*, Mario T. García introduced what came to be termed the generational model to describe the immigrant experience in a border city (El Paso) for the period 1880–1920. He more fully fleshed out this concept in *Mexican Americans*. For him, twentieth-century Mexican American history unfolded in a succession of discernible phases: the Immigrant Generation (1900–1930), the Mexican American Generation (1930–1960), and the Chicano Generation (post-1960 to circa the 1980s). The Mexican American Generation, García declared, was more politicized than the Immigrant Generation because of Americanizing processes. From this group derived the leadership that between the 1930s and early 1960s undertook, as members of advocacy organizations like the League of United Latin American Citizens (LULAC) and the American G.I. Forum (AGIF), many legal, unionist, journalistic, and even literary campaigns on behalf of Mexican Americans. Significant also from the 1980s was David Montejano's *Anglos and Mexicans in the Making of Texas*, which earned the prestigious Frederick Jackson Turner Award for 1988. A study in historical sociology focused mainly on South Texas, it embraced the sweep of Tejano history from 1836 to 1986, deemphasizing but not altogether abandoning race as a significant determinant in Anglo-Tejano relations and instead accentuating class restructuring over time. Montejano divided the making of Texas between Anglos and Mexicans into epochs, arguing that economic or political transformations during these discrete time periods begot new class societies, generally with Anglos at the top (either as ranchers, farmers, or industrialists) and Mexicans at the bottom (as ranch *peones*, migratory field hands, or unskilled or semiskilled workers in post–World War II urban manufacturing).[4]

In 1991, Richard A. Garcia reinforced the thesis of generational divisions in Mexican American history. His much acclaimed book, *The Rise of the Mexican American Middle Class: San Antonio, 1929–1941*, asked why there was a transformation from a Mexican to a Mexican American consciousness during the Depression era, and how. Garcia posited that in San Antonio (as elsewhere) by the 1930s, Americanization pressures had influenced the immigrants and their children into identifying with American culture and institutions. Such an acculturation manifested itself in the emergence of an Americanized middle-class element. Showing equal interest in class formation, Garcia identified two other classes coexisting with the middle class: the laboring poor and the wealthy exiled Mexican Revolution refugees, or *ricos*. Within the Mexican American community, or *colonia*, *lo mexicano* (a worldview represented by the rico exiles through instruments such as the newspaper *La Prensa*) vied for ethnic and ideological preeminence with *lo Americano*. The latter prevailed and became evident in a new consciousness, actually a dual consciousness, Garcia explained, but Mexican American loyalty had now shifted to U.S. principles. This allegiance was best exemplified in the sentiments of LULAC and its middle-class leadership, which stressed fidelity to the nation of their birth (the United States), called on Tejanos to contribute constructively to their country's well-being, and worked dutifully to earn Tejanos a place in the American mainstream.[5]

In the 1990s, two major monographs expanded upon earlier historiographical constructions by moving beyond Texas historical writings' penchant for parochialism, setting Tejano history within currents unfolding outside state boundaries.[6] Award-winning historian Emilio Zamora, in *The World of the Mexican Worker in Texas*, did so by ascribing greater credit to transnational forces in the making of Tejano history. Whereas previous works had shown demonstrable cultural and ideological ties to Mexico, Zamora, through the prism of the "new labor history," offered evidence that in Texas exiles from Mexico and union activists with ties to both countries and alienated by Texas racism and rejection by U.S. institutions carried on spirited labor-organizing initiatives in the Lone Star State. Because of such groups, unionist ideologies, tactics, and strike strategies from Mexico decidedly shaped Tejano views toward their own labor situation and prompted ethnic Mexicans to join struggles undertaken by Mexico-born organizers, Tejano activists, as well as mainstream U.S. unions such as the American Federation of Labor. Moreover, this connection with Mexico's unionism as well as U.S.-based movements motivated Mexicans in Texas to join labor causes in the early decades of the twentieth century at a time when immigrants, according to the generational model, were inclined to be politically passive and indifferent to their social condition because they expected to return to Mexico someday.[7] A few years later, Julie Leininger Pycior in *LBJ and Mexican Americans* amplified Zamora's beyond-state-borders thesis by noting that Mexican American politics, especially during the 1960s, reached U.S. levels, influenced by Washington on the one hand but intent upon political concessions for Mexican Americans on the other.[8] In making such an assertion, Pycior contributed to a nascent premise in 1990s Texas historiography—that what happened in Texas redounded nationally. For Pycior, organizations such as the AGIF and LULAC made unprecedented inroads into national politics by developing ties to the John F. Kennedy administration via the Viva Kennedy Clubs and strengthening contacts with President Lyndon B. Johnson, whom many middle-class Tejanos had known since the 1940s. In the end, these leaders became disillusioned with LBJ, with many of his Great Society programs failing to benefit disadvantaged Mexican Americans as the activists expected. But their efforts at the national stage on behalf of Mexican Americans buttressed Pycior's case: Tejano history connected with the outside world, as did Texas history.

Anticipating forthcoming publications on Tejano history at the same time that Pycior published her enlightening study was Neil Foley in his Frederick Jackson Turner Prize winner *The White Scourge*.[9] Using a comparative, multiethnic, and gendered analysis, Foley examined shifts in class and racial formation in the Central Texas Blackland Prairie—a mecca of cotton sharecropping and tenant-farming arrangements that included whites, blacks, and Mexicans—and discovered that class trumped race in social categorization. As Montejano had done a decade earlier, Foley acknowledged that class largely determined Tejano social status, but for Foley class was a determinant of racial categorization as well—and thus extended to all three ethnic groups, including whites. Applying the perspective of whiteness studies then coming into vogue, Foley thus argued that the idea of whiteness operated as a social construct that categorized landless Anglos essentially as nonwhite, as people no higher in the social hierarchy than blacks and Mexican Americans. In line with the work of scholars using gender frameworks, *The White Scourge* concluded that agrarian society oppressed women (among them Tejanas) even more than it did male tenant farmers and sharecroppers. Such rural-based thinking consigned women (Mexican, black, or white) to no more than auxiliary characters, both at home and in the fields, sustaining the male figure in his role as family head. On Texas farms, Mexican women fared worse socially and materially than Mexican males.[10]

Works published in the first decade of the 2000s disclosed a continued interest in persistent debates and older subjects and a confidence in the validity of older approaches yet also a determination to research new topics, expand outlooks, and introduce imaginative methods of investigation. In following this course, Mexican American scholarship harmonized with general Texas history patterns.[11] As some students of Texas publications have noted, historians in the early twenty-first century still studied older topics and still relied on time-tested habits in writing Texas history. But coexisting with this historiographical state was a new trajectory, as historians launched new inquiries into heretofore neglected fields (Native Americans, gender, etc.), turned to alternative modes of analysis to study them, and discovered new truths in Texas history. Tejano history kept pace and, to some observers, at this juncture even began giving direction to the broader field of Texas history, setting standards for it, and establishing trends in the use of methodologies, techniques, and approaches.[12]

An approach still holding validity in Tejano history was one applied to the study of Mexican Americans within a transnational backdrop. In *Desert Immigrants*, García had placed the Mexicans of El Paso in such a binational context, and two years later Emilio Zamora (in *The World of the Mexican Worker in Texas)* had similarly positioned his subjects in space that crossed borders. Expectedly, sequels were more elaborate methodologically and analytically than these pioneer works. In *Catarino Garza's Revolution on the Texas-Mexico Border*, Elliott Young focused beyond region (South Texas) and expanded his scope to encompass an international landscape.[13] For Young, local events such as those instigated by Catarino Garza, a Tejano from the border region who led a rebellion on behalf of Mexican rights in both Texas and Mexico in 1891, in some cases reflected larger historic movements and thus necessitated the use of more inventive methodologies such as transnational analysis to understand them. In the 1890s, movements similar to Garza's campaign erupted throughout parts of Latin America; these were drives against the enemies of liberalism, such as imperialism and authoritarianism. Garza's concerns included the oppression of Mexicans not only in Texas but also in Mexico and, upon crossing the border to topple Mexico's dictator Porfirio Díaz, he linked up to movements international in scale. Chased from Texas by authorities, Garza made this way to Cuba and then Central America to join struggles akin to those he had initially waged in South Texas and Mexico—against land grabbers, state power, and the disruptive impact of progress and modernization. Young further attributed international forces to Garza's end, for U.S. influence on affairs in the Western Hemisphere led to Garza's killing in Panama in 1895.[14]

In *Claiming Rights and Righting Wrongs in Texas*, Emilio Zamora followed the interpretive device he had formulated—and became his trademark—almost twenty years earlier.[15] Zamora saw Tejano history as intertwined with Mexico's history during the World War II years; indeed, his protagonists were Mexico and LULAC, cooperating in a struggle to claim rights and right wrongs for Tejanos and Mexican immigrant laborers. Mexican consuls and LULAC leaders stressed upon the U.S. government the need for federal agencies such as the Fair Employment Practices Committee (FEPC) to hear complaints of discrimination raised on the job by both Mexican Americans workers and those *en el estranjero* (Mexicans living in the United States). Mexico, for its part, refused to allow *braceros* to Texas until the state lifted its policy of segregation and discrimination against ethnic Mexicans. Moreover, it continued testing the Good Neighbor Policy even after the U.S. broadened it to cover Mexican Americans. LULAC, of course, continued its own labor and civil rights crusade on behalf of Mexican-origin people for years after World War II.

As in the realm of transnational history, the literature on politics during the 1990s and the first years of the twenty-first century indicated a chain between old and new ways for writing Tejano history. Several features stamped works relying on previous historical forms. For one, they reflected the imprint of the "new social history" of the 1970s and 1980s; thus, these studies obligingly emphasized agency among Tejanos and Tejanas. Works of this genre further tended to follow a narrative/interpretive format and did not necessarily advance new insights. Tied to the earlier years of Tejano historical writings, this strand placed politics within the context of conflict; it focused on events wherein Tejanos clashed with the Anglo power structure using militant protest, ethnic nationalism to provoke white Texans, and daring tactics to confront Texas Rangers.[16] At odds with these older approaches and judgments were ones that yielded somewhat divergent conclusions. Ignacio García, in *Viva Kennedy*, for one, deemphasized confrontation; to him Mexican American civic activists after World War II were not necessarily engaged in resistance politics questioning their oppression; rather, they were astute operators who, with an unbendable confidence in their rights as citizens, sought to "accommodate" themselves to the national stage and by so doing hitch Mexican American destiny to the administrations of Kennedy and Johnson.[17]

Writing five years later, Craig A. Kaplowitz took a position that paralleled Garcia's. In *LULAC: Mexican Americans and National Policy*, Kaplowitz argued that LULAC did indeed perceive prospects for success on behalf of Mexican Americans in a symbiotic relationship with national policymakers.[18] For Kaplowitz, LULAC was not set on tactics, agendas, or post–World War II issues (as its critics during the 1960s had contended) but changed with time. For instance, whereas during the 1930s and into the 1960s LULAC had insisted on the categorization of "white" for Mexican Americans (as certain privileges presumably accompanied whiteness), as national currents shifted so did the League's position; in the 1970s it emphasized ethnicity and the particular needs of Mexican Americans. It succeeded by the mid-1970s in persuading national power brokers to support bilingual education, ensure voting rights, and extend Great Society programs to Mexican Americans. Anthony Quiroz posited the thesis of "consensual politics" in his contribution to Tejano political history, *Claiming Citizenship*, which argued that Tejano faith in the guarantees of American citizenship traditionally determined Mexican American strategies for self and community improvement in Victoria, Texas.[19]

In the field of biography, Tejano writings have mirrored the wider Texas scholarship, reflecting both its defects and merits.[20] Indicating shortcomings, but perhaps also conventions characteristic of first ventures toward producing biography (as did the first crop of biographies that came from the pens of Texas historians during the 1920s through the 1950s), these Tejano academic tomes tend to be male-centered. Taking front stage were men of middle-class standing such as Raymond Telles, Reynaldo Garza, Felix Tijerina, Manuel B. Bravo, and José Antonio Navarro. Though well researched with primary sources, these Tejano biographies inclined toward the approbatory, celebrating the lofty contributions of a hero's traits, among them perseverance, determination, resourcefulness, and belief in their cause. In *Mexican American Odyssey*, Thomas H. Kreneck showed how Felix Tijerina, the Houston entrepreneur, intent on improving education for Tejanos, ultimately convinced the Texas legislature in 1959 to enact his brainchild, the Little School of the 400.[21] The structure of these Tejano biographies often tended to follow a narrative/interpretive style, and though expanding our understanding of the complexity of the person under study the field fell short of inaugurating new approaches or unveiling new trends.[22]

Notwithstanding its flaws, Tejano biography manifested facets that exhibited compliance with newer developments in Texas scholarship. Because some of the subjects came from the ranks of nonelites, as for example nineteenth-century personalities such as Juan Cortina, Petra Vela Kenedy, and Catarino Garza, Tejano biography succeeded in integrating overlooked Tejano historical figures into the larger Texas chronicle. In *Petra's Legacy*, Jane Clements Monday and Frances Brannen Vick not only realize this goal by rescuing Petra Vela (credited for extending philanthropic assistance to the poor and to the Catholic Church) from oblivion but buttressed the notion that Tejanas also deserve consideration in history.[23] Displaying themes found in the wider study of Texas biography, Tejano writings showed how twentieth-century movements among Tejanos at the state level connected to the course of events outside the state, and more significantly to the national stage. Like other Texans of privileged status, Tejanos such as Dr. Hector P. García and Professor Carlos Eduardo Castañeda developed links to national officials and used those connections to help improve conditions within Tejano communities.[24] Some of the fresher themes introduced in Tejano biography have allowed the genre to move away from a reliance on race as a causal factor driving Tejano history. J. Gilberto Quezada, in *Border Boss*, for instance, emphasized geography, demography, and human wants as determining politics in Zapata County.[25] For him, historic circumstances in the region accounted for Bravo's bossism, which spanned the late Depression years to the late 1950s, not ethnic or racial needs as an earlier historiography would have explained. The focus on the twentieth century, and generally the post–World War II era, also permitted scholars to expand on the theme of Texas modernization, which connoted the state's integration into the political mainstream of the nation.[26] All in all, this first real wave of biographies acquitted itself honorably.

Whereas the application of transnational paradigms, approaches toward interpreting politics, and the writings on biography indicated a mix of old and new, historians took on newer topics and produced impressive nuanced studies that harmonized or, as previously mentioned, led the way with trends in the larger Texas historiography. Patrick J. Carroll, in *Felix Longoria's Wake*, for instance, availed himself of theory to a greater degree than had earlier scholars engaged in writing Tejano history. Carroll took interest in what is known historically as the Felix Longoria affair, an episode in Three Rivers, Texas, involving a funeral home owner's refusal to hold services for a Tejano World War II hero. Historians already knew this 1949 episode well, but Carroll wondered how such an event, which paralleled similar ones occurring almost daily in South Texas, took on the dimensions it did. He explained it by relying on a mélange of theoretical postulations. The rational structuralist perspective accounted for the historical conditions that could lead aggrieved parties to rise in rebellion against an injustice, and antistructuralist thought (which incorporates emotive factors) provided for the behavioral force (bereavement for Longoria) that produced social drama (Dr. Hector P. García of the AGIF and Sen. Lyndon B. Johnson sought compromise to solve the crisis and bring redress to the aggrieved). Relying on Victor Turner's concept of *communitas*, which submits that two groups can find a mutual bonding ground (in this case, patriotism following the nationalist passion that World War II unleashed), Carroll explained how the actions taken by Dr. García and LBJ recast Tejanos from people regarded as outsiders to ones being truly loyal Americans—as attested in Longoria's heroism. This negotiation (Turner's accommodative model) facilitated the Mexican American integration into U.S. society without the rejection of a bicultural way of life. As per Glifford Geertz's "interest theory" and "strain theory," Tejanos used ideology—one grounded in their abiding conviction as patriotic Americans—to challenge their status and the Anglo consideration of them as foreigners. For Carroll, a synthesis of such interdisciplinary frameworks explained how the snub by the funeral home director galvanized people, led them to open protest, and turned the affront into a controversy that reached unanticipated proportions.[27]

Validating the interdisciplinary approach in the writing of Tejano history was Cynthia Orozco's *No Mexicans, Women, or Dogs Allowed*. To seal her revisionist argument that the Tejano civil rights movement began in the 1920s (and not after World War II, as convention generally held), Orozco embraced several social science schema, although favoring social movement theory. By the 1920s, she maintained, a Mexican American consciousness had developed among male middle-class individuals who asserted their rights to U.S. citizenship. That this group's advocacy of equal rights qualified as an opportunity for individual and community improvement could be demonstrated by applying a social movement framework. To Orozco, a social movement featured "collective organized actions by a significant number of people with a shared identity and outside organizations representing a group (social category) with a collective identity seeking to assert its will as historical actors to challenge an existing status quo or status for the purpose of a collective goal over a specific time or era."[28]

Certainly, the 1920s movement for equality contained such traits. Because gender functions as an organizing factor under social movement theory, Orozco then utilized a gender analysis to document how Tejanas advanced the cause for la raza's self-preservation. Like Carroll earlier, thus, Orozco illustrated how useful interdisciplinary models could be as vehicles to interpret Tejano history, or, like Foley, to present Tejana history.

Earlier, Roberto R. Treviño, studying Catholicism and the Catholic Church in Houston, had also made inroads in gender studies. In *The Church in the Barrio*, Treviño argued that Mexican American women used ethno-Catholicism (Catholicism as understood and practiced by Mexican Americans and shaped by their historical experiences in Mexico and the United States) to contest Mexican American patriarchy and to achieve self-empowerment.[29] Prayer, appeals, and self-sacrifice earned women recognition as the family's bulwark in spiritual matters. *Altarcitos* (home altars), furthermore, gave women a sense of self-reliance, individuality, and personal uplift. These personalized home grottos offered private spaces where women (in a gendered domain) could reenergize and obtain gender affirmation. But altarcitos were not the sole source of women's empowerment; so too were *tamaladas* (gatherings for making tamales for fundraisers), women's religious clubs, and women's prayer groups. Treviño further explained that during the Chicano movement nuns found forms of self-fulfillment in various kinds of civic involvement (in opposition to the church's tradition of trying to restrict them to the role of priest helpmates) and, even more in violation of gender norms, in assuming leadership roles in politically oriented organizations like Las Hermanas.

Alongside their ambitious efforts to apply gender analysis to Tejano history during this period historians revisited the confounding topic of ethnic identity, but now they offered more complicated explanations for its creation and development. Richard A. Garcia, Mario T. García, and others during the 1980s had looked at stages of identity progression and class structuring, concentrating on pre–World War II years.[30] Guadalupe San Miguel, in *Brown, Not White,* extended that scope to the 1960s and 1970s. Immediately, San Miguel laid out his argument: "The general thesis of this study is that in the early 1970s the diverse responses to educational discrimination [forced integration that classified Mexican Americans as whites, a subterfuge to avoid integrating Anglos into predominantly black schools] by Mexican-origin activists reflected a shift in the community's identity from one based on the politics of the Mexican Generation to one based primarily on those of the Chicano Generation. The shift in consciousness was reflected in the community's rejection of whiteness, gradual social change, and conventional methods of struggle, and in its acceptance of a nonwhite racial status."[31] Though San Miguel downplayed identity, or the search for it, as a force propelling the struggle for educational equality, arguing instead that the movement was against discrimination, he positioned the events transpiring in Houston within the framework of the generational model, which posited the evolution of identities. Thus, he noted that the self-image of the "Chicano Generation" (they were brown) clashed with that of the Mexican American Generation (they were white). By linking the process of identity change to the generational model, San Miguel's study revealed how scholars could explain identity transformation through the use of models still trusted decades later.

But historians by this time were utilizing other historiographic approaches and integrating them into the larger Texas historical narrative in further efforts to unravel the processes behind identity development. Additionally, they introduced new themes into the conversation, such as cultural construction, ideology, ethnic consciousness, ethos, and citizenship. These works attributed ethnic transformation to racial and cultural conflict occurring among competing groups.[32] Leading the way in this school was Benjamin Heber Johnson, who, as opposed to San Miguel, was more absorbed with events occurring in the early twentieth century. In *Revolution in Texas*, Johnson studied the Plan de San Diego (PSD)—a proclamation believed to have originated in the South Texas town of San Diego calling for a rebellion of Tejanos against Anglo oppression—to determine "how a forgotten rebellion and its bloody suppression turned Mexicans into Americans." Placing his study within the transnational approach, as studies on Tejano history were doing at that time, Johnson examined conflict as an agent of identity creation. The PSD—which pitted Mexicans (living on both sides of the border) against whites—put what Johnson labeled the Tejano Progressives in a quandary. An elite group of Tejano landowners, businesspersons, and professionals in the Valley, the Progressives had envisioned the uplifting of la raza in the modernization being carried out at the turn of the century by Anglos founding new farms, expanding railroad lines, and introducing other innovations such as a progressive educational system. In this new world of Anglo South Texas, the Tejano Progressives hoped to achieve equality even as they retained their Mexican ethnicity. But the PSD disrupted their expectations, as those behind it, the Sediciosos, or Seditionists, kindled a campaign of destruction and retaliation against whites that undermined the Progressives' hopes for equality as Anglos reacted by labeling all Tejanos seditionists. In the end, however, the PSD episode proved serendipitous for Tejano Progressives when U.S. military units intervened to quell the disturbance and protect the rights of Mexicans as U.S. citizens. "What they had endured during the PSD and its aftermath convinced them [the Tejano Progressives] of the dangers of statelessness and their risk of becoming a people belonging to no nation." Government intervention had shown them the benefits of becoming Americans, an identity middle-class Tejanos chose, as indicated by the civil rights advocacy organizations they launched during the 1920s in efforts to build the society they had visualized before the PSD troubles.[33] For Johnson, cultural identity emanated from conflict caused by the PSD clashes, persuading a leading Texas scholar to categorize Johnson's work as part of the cultural constructionist school of thought that surfaced in Texas history during the 1990s.[34]

Cynthia Orozco, in her aforementioned *No Mexicans, Women, or Dogs Allowed*, agreed with Johnson that a Mexican American identity was apparent by the 1920s. But her work concerned itself less with the matter of identity formation than it did with ascertaining the origins of civil rights campaigns. It was a group of middle-class leaders conscious of themselves as Mexican Americans—due to such 1910s influences as the Mexican Revolution,[35] the PSD, World War I, and various Americanizing stimuli—who were responsible for launching *the* Mexican American civil rights movement in Texas during the 1920s, she argued strenuously, not a later generation of acculturated Tejanos, as previous studies supposed.[36]

Several other studies published by Tejano historians qualified as "new" histories because of techniques used, themes emphasized, and historiographic trends cast. Roberto R. Treviño's previously mentioned *Church in the Barrio*, for one, added to the emerging field of religion and spirituality at a time when the topic had gained considerable attention in the national historiography. This "new religious history" addressed the manner by which religion affects life experiences, and Treviño found that ethno-Catholicism in the Houston barrios shaped ethnic identity, community development, cultural adjustment, social distinctions, and even views regarding gender. But as per the cultural resistance theory and anthropological models he used, he determined that, though pressured into accommodation by the church and American institutions, Mexican American Houstonians compromised to accept "accommodation without assimilation."[37] José A. Ramírez's *To the Line of Fire* similarly exhibited the manner in which Tejano history complemented the new scholarship under way in mainstream historiography. Ramírez's tome nourished the "new military history" —a developing field emphasizing how military mobilization at the national level commonly impacts society, but also how it influences community consciousness and loyalty to nation. Ramírez's interests lay in connecting life in the barrios and ranchos (mainly in South Texas) to the broader national front. Though some Tejanos resisted, communities by and large provided soldiers to fight the Central powers, used Spanish-language newspapers to support war efforts, bought liberty bonds, provided critical agricultural work to feed millions at home and overseas, and in other ways contributed to helping out their country in the moment of need.[38]

In an impressive award-winning monograph titled *Smeltertown*, Monica Perales skillfully blended an array of approaches and techniques then available in historical studies, including Tejano history, to portray the components of Mexican American life in an El Paso barrio called La Esmelda, so named by its inhabitants, most of whom worked at the local smelter, the American Smelting and Refining Company.[39] Perales used to good effect perspectives from the new social history of the 1960s and 1970s, analytical techniques that studied Tejanos in a transnational context, and the existent knowledge base about migration, biculturalization, and labor organizing. But she structured her study along interdisciplinary avenues, drawing upon anthropology, ethnography, sociology, cultural geography, environmental history, and other fields. By doing so, Perales provided a template for the "new community history," as she elaborated more fully on community experiences (e.g., language, religion, or family life) yet ably expanded on topics like gender or perceptively introduced new ones like space. Gender, indeed, pervaded much of the discussion in *Smeltertown*, in which Perales not only recreated the lives of women at the domestic front but depicted them as agents in the barrio's development; some assumed leadership capacities in drives to improve the material condition and moral well-being of their community. By using insights from environmental and urban studies and heeding lessons from the new social history, she examined La Esmelda as a geographic setting wherein residents adapted to an autonomous zone and forged a way of life that was wholesome in most aspects and for which many of its inhabitants retained fond memories despite its poverty. Perales's worked emerged as genuinely innovative, refreshing, and "cutting edge."

In a quest to "bridge the fields of black and Mexican American history," Brian D. Behnken in *Fighting Their Own Battles* turned to an approach that departed from the one commonly used in writing Texas Mexican history—that of isolating the Mexican American experience from a larger history. Although actually consistent with trends already pursued in Tejano scholarship, ones that studied interactions among groups, Behnken applied a "comparative theoretical framework" more stridently in examining the African American and Mexican American push for civil rights. The comparative model allowed Behnken to examine the two movements, both of which struggled against similar problems: racism, segregation, educational inequality, disfranchisement, police brutality, stereotypes, and poverty. Despite their common difficulties, civil rights leaders could not muster a united front against their Anglo adversaries. Separate geographies, Mexican American emphasis on whiteness, distrust, disagreements over issues, and competition for concessions from Anglo society drove the movements toward different paths. New answers thus obtained from Behnken's comparative analysis, but he also had effectively placed the Texas civil rights movement in a broader context, had integrated three groups into the same Texas story, had underscored the lingering effects of race sentiments, and, significantly, had furthered the momentum that incorporated Tejano history into the greater U.S. narrative.[40]

Of the same age as the history on Native Americans, African Americans, and women in Texas—but much younger than the histories published by mainstream academic Texas historians—the literature on Texas Latinos today flourishes. My own works, published over a forty-year career, evince this florescence. *The Tejano Community* and *They Called Them Greasers*, which I published early, addressed Tejano history's initial concerns: determining what explained the subordinate position of Tejanos in the nineteenth century and discovering how Tejanos resisted their condition (these books remain standards today, especially the latter one).[41] Subsequent monographs dealing with subjects such as urban history and scholarly essays on topics as varied as biography, regionalism, and class formation helped advance the field. Scholarship on Tejanos poured out in such a quantity through the years that I synthesized it in three editions of *Mexican Americans in Texas*.[42] Continuous production of studies further sparked me to update and sum up the literature through catalogues, bibliographies, collections of essays, book reviews, and historiographic pieces. My association with an assemblage responsible for this boom has been personally rewarding and gratifying.

As of this writing, students of Tejano history continue to reinforce their record of credible and substantial works. They have done so by maintaining stride with the scholarship in its companion fields of Texas and Chicano history, but in many fronts, by being at the vanguard of these areas of study. They have effectively tied Tejano history to the national epic and enlarged it to transnational borders. Methodologically, they have made constructive use of interdisciplinary concepts; of approaches effective in analyzing gender, ethnicity, or ethno-religions; and of findings reached by researchers engaged in associated specialties such as cultural studies. The prospects appear bright for Tejano history to continue its recognition as among the best branches of Texas history as a new generation of young scholars build on the work of those who blazed new trails years ago.

NOTES

1. Nancy Beck Young, "Beyond Parochialism: Modernization and Texas Historiography," in *Beyond Texas through Time: Breaking Away from Past Interpretations*, ed. Walter L. Buenger and Arnoldo De León (College Station: Texas A&M University Press, 2011), 262.

2. Those needing a convenient reference to this literature should consult Bruce Glasrud and Arnoldo De León, *Bibliophiling Tejano Scholarship: Secondary Sources on Hispanic Texans* (Alpine, Tex.: Center for Big Bend Studies, 2003). The *Southwestern Historical Quarterly* reports Tejano history publications for the year in its October issue (section titled "Southwestern Collection").

3. Arnoldo De León, "Texas Mexicans: Twentieth-Century Interpretations," in *Texas through Time: Evolving Interpretations*, ed. Walter L. Buenger and Robert A. Calvert (College Station: Texas A&M University Press, 1991), 20–49; Arnoldo De León, "Whither Tejano History: Origins, Development, and Status," *Southwestern Historical Quarterly* 106 (Jan. 2003): 349–64.

4. Mario T. García, *Desert Immigrants, The Mexicans of El Paso, 1880–1920* (New Haven, Conn.: Yale University Press, 1981), and *Mexican Americans: Leadership, Ideology, and Identity, 1930–1960* (New Haven, Conn.: Yale University Press, 1989); David Montejano, *Anglos and Mexicans in the Making of Texas, 1836–1986* (Austin: University of Texas Press, 1987).

5. Richard A. Garcia, *Rise of the Mexican American Middle Class: San Antonio, 1929–1941* (College Station: Texas A&M University Press, 1991), 3–5, 9–11, 46–53, 71–102, chap. 9. Garcia had been developing (along with others) such an argument through the 1980s, as evident in writings such as "The Mexican American Mind: A Product of the 1930s," in *History, Culture, and Society: Chicano Studies in the 1980s*, ed. Mario T. García (Ypsilanti, Mich.: Bilingual Press/Editorial Bilingüe, 1983), 67–93.

6. Young, "Beyond Parochialism," 262.

7. Emilio Zamora, *The World of the Mexican Worker in Texas* (College Station: Texas A&M University Press, 1993), 8, 56, 59–66, 72–81, 200, 207–208.

8. Julie Pycior, *LBJ and Mexican Americans: The Paradox of Power* (Austin: University of Texas Press, 1997).

9. Neil Foley, *The White Scourge: Mexicans, Blacks, and Poor Whites in Texas Cotton Culture* (Berkeley: University of California Press, 1997).

10. At the same that Tejano history assumed innovative turns, scholars retained interest in topics that earlier had preoccupied researchers, among them land loss, racism, and conflict. Armando C. Alonzo's *Tejano Legacy*, for instance, sought to debunk some of the myths associated with those matters. Alonzo contended, forcefully, that Tejano land dispossession in the Lower Rio Grande Valley did not occur as swiftly and as extremely as historians formerly posited, that Tejanos did not suffer open racism as once declared, and that racial conflict did not typify relations as assumed in the past, that instead a spirit of cooperation and accommodation existed between Anglos and Mexicans in South Texas; see *Tejano Legacy: Rancheros and Settlers in South Texas, 1734–1900* (Albuquerque: University of New Mexico Press, 1998), 6–12, 279, 282.

11. Keith J. Volanto, "Strange Brew: Recent Texas Political, Economic, and Military History," in Buenger and De León, *Beyond Texas through Time*, 85–124.

12. Young, "Beyond Parochialism," 262.

13. Elliott Young, *Catarino Garza's Revolution on the Texas Mexico Border* (Durham, N.C.: Duke University Press, 2004); see also Volanto, "Strange Brew," 86–87.

14. Also qualifying as transnational history is Benjamin Heber Johnson, *Revolution in Texas: How a Forgotten Rebellion and Its Bloody Suppression Turned Mexicans into*

Americans (New Haven, Conn.: Yale University Press, 2003), but his monograph is discussed later in the essay in a different context.

15. Emilio Zamora, *Claiming Rights and Righting Wrongs in Texas: Mexican Workers and Job Politics during World War II* (College Station: Texas A&M University Press, 2009).

16. As examples, see Ignacio M. García, *United We Win: The Rise and Fall of the Raza Unida Party* (Tucson: MASRC, University of Arizona Press, 1989), and *Chicanismo: The Forging of a Militant Ethos among Mexican Americans* (Tucson: University of Arizona Press, 1997).

17. Ignacio M. García, *Viva Kennedy: Mexican Americans in Search of Camelot* (College Station: Texas A&M University Press, 2000), 62–63, 79, 175–76.

18. Craig A. Kaplowitz, *LULAC: Mexican Americans and National Policy* (College Station: Texas A&M University Press, 2005). Obviously studies such as these, which connected Tejanos to national politics, conformed to Pycior's model in *LBJ and Mexican Americans*. But Pycior's subject was LBJ and less so the AGIF and LULAC.

19. Anthony Quiroz, *Claiming Citizenship: Mexican Americans in Victoria, Texas* (College Station: Texas A&M University Press, 2005).

20. Volanto, "Strange Brew," 87–88.

21. Thomas H. Kreneck, *Mexican American Odyssey: Felix Tijerina, Entrepreneur and Civic Leader, 1905–1965* (College Station: Texas A&M University Press, 2001).

22. An exception might be Young's monograph on Catarino Garza. See the discussion above under the topic of "transnational history."

23. Jane Clements Monday and Frances Brannen Vick, *Petra's Legacy: The South Texas Ranching Empire of Petra Vela and Mifflin Kenedy* (College Station: Texas A&M University Press, 2007).

24. Ignacio M. García, *Hector P. García: In Relentless Pursuit of Justice* (Houston: Arte Público Press, 2002); and Félix D. Almaráz, *Knight Without Armor: Carlos Eduardo Castañeda, 1896–1958* (College Station: Texas A&M University Press, 1999).

25. J. Gilberto Quezada, *Border Boss: Manuel B. Bravo and Zapata County* (College Station: Texas A&M University Press, 1999).

26. Young, "Beyond Provincialism," 242–52.

27. Patrick J. Carroll, *Felix Longoria's Wake: Bereavement, Racism, and the Rise of Mexican American Activism* (Austin: University of Texas Press, 2003), 195–213. Certainly, before Carroll other writers had used theoretical approaches. Examples include Montejano, *Anglos and Mexicans;* Manuel Peña, *The Texas-Mexican Conjunto: History of a Working-Class Music* (Austin: University of Texas Press, 1985); and Benjamin Márquez, *LULAC: The Evolution of a Mexican American Political Organization* (Austin: University of Texas Press, 1993). However, with the exception of Mario T. García, who applied the generational model to Mexican American history, these scholars were in allied fields, respectively, historical sociology, anthropology, and political science.

28. Cynthia E. Orozco, *No Mexicans, Women, or Dogs Allowed: The Rise of the Mexican American Civil Rights Movement* (Austin: University of Texas Press, 2009), 185.

29. Roberto R. Treviño, *The Church in the Barrio: Mexican American Ethno-Catholicism in Houston* (Chapel Hill: The University of North Carolina Press, 2006). Though other works during the 1990s and early 2000s appeared on Mexican American

women in Texas, few took Tejana history in any particularly groundbreaking direction. As indicated earlier (see note 20), most took a narrative form and tended to celebrate Tejanas' contribution to the larger Mexican American construct. An overview of Texas Mexican women is the much cited: Teresa Palomo Acosta and Ruthe Winegarten, eds., *Las Tejanas: 300 Years of History* (Austin: University of Texas Press, 2003).

30. Scholars who harked back to times earlier than the twentieth century found attachments to sovereignty or region more accurate indices of allegiance. To them, identity could be fluid; Tejanos identified with whichever sovereignty controlled Texas or exerted economic sway over that hinterland. Andrés Reséndez maintained that Tejanos adopted or rejected cultural identities according to which nation actually held political and economic authority over Texas (Tejanos modified their national identity, he showed, as American economic influence became more pervasive in the province by the 1820s); see *Changing National Identities at the Frontier: Texas and New Mexico, 1800–1850* (Cambridge: Cambridge University Press, 2005), 3–6, chap. 5, and 267–68. Raúl Ramos maintained that during three imperial epochs—the colonial era (Spain), 1821–1836 (Mexico), and the post-1836 (the American) period—Tejanos substituted one nationalist identity for another, depending on the historical moment (they maintained "their Mexican identity as an ethnic group in the new American political context"); see *Beyond the Alamo: Forging Mexican Ethnicity in San Antonio, 1821–1861* (Chapel Hill: University of North Carolina Press, 2008), 6–14, 233–35. Elliott Young, *Catarino Garza's Revolution*, 7, took a slightly different position, maintaining that, since transnational events shaped the psyche of people in South Texas, they maintained a "hybrid borderland identity," resisting interference from both Mexico and the United States as *libres fronterizos* (free border people).

31. Guadalupe San Miguel, *Brown, Not White: School Integration and the Chicano Movement in Houston* (College Station: Texas A&M University Press, 2001), xii.

32. Walter L. Buenger, "Three Truths in Texas," in Buenger and De León, *Beyond Texas through Time*, 3–4.

33. Benjamin Heber Johnson, *Revolution in Texas: How a Forgotten Rebellion and Its Bloody Suppression Turned Mexicans into Americans* (New Haven, Conn.: Yale University Press, 2003), 189.

34. Buenger, "Three Truths," 4, 18–19.

35. Concerning the impact that the Mexican Revolution had on Texas Mexicans, see Arnoldo De León, ed., *War Along the Border: The Mexican Revolution and Tejano Communities* (College Station: Texas A&M University Press, 2012).

36. The identity Tejanos gave themselves often clashed with that given them by outsiders. Richard R. Flores delved into the relatively newer subject of historical memory, borrowing from cultural studies, anthropology, geography, urban studies, social history, and other fields. He contended that Anglo-American recollections about the Alamo, which myths and legends distorted and embellished, had by the late nineteenth century produced contrasting identities for Anglos and Mexicans—that of dominant figures for the former and subordinate and inferior laboring classes for the latter. Cultural memory produced rigid ideas about racial differences; see Flores, *Remembering the Alamo: Memory, Modernity, and the Master Symbol* (Austin: University of Texas Press, 2002).

37. Timothy Matovina, in *Tejano Religion and Ethnicity: San Antonio, 1821–1860* (Austin: University of Texas Press, 1995), had earlier argued that religious heritage shaped ethnic identity.

38. José A. Ramírez, *To the Line of Fire: Mexican Texans and World War I* (College Station: Texas A&M University Press, 2009). Other studies on the ordinary experiences of soldiers may be found in several edited works by Maggie Rivas-Rodríguez; see, for example, Maggie Rivas-Rodríguez and Emilio Zamora, eds., *Beyond the Latino WWII Hero: The Social and Political Legacy of a Generation* (Austin: University of Texas Press, 2009).

39. Monica Perales, *Smeltertown: Making and Remembering a Southwest Border Community* (Chapel Hill: University of North Carolina Press, 2010).

40. Brian D. Behnken, *Fighting Their Own Battles: Mexican Americans, African Americans, and the Struggle for Civil Rights in Texas* (Chapel Hill: University of North Carolina Press, 2011), 3; see also William S. Clayson, *Freedom Is Not Enough: The War on Poverty and the Civil Rights Movement in Texas* (Austin: University of Texas Press, 2010).

41. Arnoldo De León, *The Tejano Community, 1836–1900* (Albuquerque: University of New Mexico Press, 1982), and *They Called Them Greasers: Anglo Attitudes toward Mexicans in Texas, 1821–1900* (Austin: University of Texas Press, 1983).

42. Arnoldo De León, *Mexican Americans in Texas: A Brief History* (Wheeling, Ill.: Harlan Davidson, 1993, 1999, 2009).

CHAPTER 3

African Americans

Alwyn Barr

In the past two decades African American history in Texas has attracted a growing number of historians who have expanded our knowledge by exploring new topics and employing new approaches to research and analysis. Two general histories have appeared. A second edition of an earlier volume by Alwyn Barr includes a new chapter on the period 1970–1995. *Texans All*, a new series on ethnic groups, includes a shorter volume on African Texans by Alwyn Barr with greater discussion of social and cultural history. A brief overview of black history in Texas has been authored by Quintard Taylor.[1] Collections of essays by several authors provide another general approach. David A. Williams wrote and edited a history with emphasis on biographies and education, supplemented with eight essays by other authors on aspects of nineteenth- and twentieth-century events. A balanced anthology of eighteen chapters on major topics has been edited by Bruce A. Glasrud and James M. Smallwood. Minorities and women in Texas are the focus of a volume, edited by Stephen Curley and Donald Willett, that contains five essays about African Americans.[2] Three volumes of essays on different regions in the Lone Star State—West, East, and South Texas—have been edited by Glasrud with coeditors.[3] African American women's history has been explored in a book by Ruthe Winegarten and in a volume of chronological essays edited by Glasrud and Merline Pitre.[4] The most comprehensive guide to writings on African American history in Texas up to 2000 was edited by Glasrud and Laurie Champion.[5]

New histories of racial ideas continue to expand our understanding of prejudice and discrimination. Some authors employ an approach referred to as "whiteness" studies. Although Martha Menchaca is an anthropologist, she presents similar analyses about Europeans and Anglo-Americans shaping laws well into the twentieth century to exclude Mexican Americans with recognizable American Indian or African ancestry. Historian Neil Foley explores the construction of "whiteness" by Anglo employers in the Central Texas cotton farming region, with the more successful Mexican American workers gaining a degree of white status while less successful poor whites might lose such advantages and African Americans remained outside the pale. Michael Phillips applies the same concept to Dallas, where Jews and Mexican Americans were not part of nineteenth-century white society. He concludes that in the twentieth century economic success and the idea, popular among some Christians, that Jews would play a part in the return of Jesus made some of them acceptable in white society. To a lesser extent, upwardly mobile Mexican Americans with no strong Indian or African traits might gain acceptance as "white."[6]

Another new concept that offers valuable insights into racial ideas is the comparison of history and popular memory. Applications of such analysis to Texas public memories are brought together in a volume of essays edited by Gregg Cantrell and Elizabeth Hayes Turner. Several contributing authors explore how historical memory was shaped by white authors and monument builders in the nineteenth and early twentieth centuries to ignore or distort the images and roles of African Americans and Mexican Americans. Two essays consider the positive public memories developed by the two minority groups, and a third analyzes the different generational views among African Americans. A different approach to historical memory is Naomi Mitchell Carrier's published plays, which offer mildly Afrocentric views of slavery, the Civil War, emancipation, and postwar race relations.[7]

Since the appearance of Randolph Campbell's general history of slavery in Texas, some new insights have been contributed. Although the number of slaves in Spanish colonial Texas was small, Douglas Richmond has written a detailed study of their lives and chances for freedom. He found that interracial relations including marriage led to complexities in the racial hierarchy. That led to individual emancipation of some slaves, whereas others bought their freedom or ran away. Slaves sought to keep families together despite opposition from some owners. Spanish laws limited trade by slaves and mulattoes, but exceptions increased over time. Free Afro-Tejanos engaged in ranching and joined the militia. As slavery declined, living conditions improved in the Mexican independence period.[8]

Two volumes have focused attention on new perspectives in the nineteenth century. Some German immigrants in the 1840s and 1850s established a slave plantation in Fayette County, explains James C. Kearney, an act that differed from the reluctance of other German settlers about slavery. Sean M. Kelley describes slavery along the lower Brazos River as a borderland environment, which differed with more slaves from Africa and less stability under Mexico to 1836. Thereafter, slaveholders continued to fear slave escapes across the Rio Grande. He also found some differences in attitude between Anglo and German immigrant settlers in the region. In a broader study of the slave trade into the United States, Ernest Obadele-Starks devotes a chapter to the smuggling of slaves into Texas and at times on into the United States.[9]

Specific aspects of slavery have received more detailed investigation in articles, especially using the interviews with former slaves conducted in the 1930s. Slaves' food and its preparation are considered by T. Lindsay Baker. The lives of children and their sense of family are clarified by Elizabeth R. Rabe. A study of urban slavery in Galveston by Robert. S. Shelton shows the greater range of occupations and a more fluid social setting for bondsmen, which resulted in greater restrictions by the town government. Joanna Labor has written a comparable essay on slavery in Austin.[10]

Sources on slavery have been expanded or clarified in new volumes. T. Lindsay Baker and Julie P. Baker have edited Federal Writers Project interviews collected in Oklahoma from former slaves from Texas who described diverse aspects of their lives. An analysis of legal agreements involving slaves in Guadalupe County offers insight into the value of local records about slavery by Mark Gretchen, who provides extensive information about how slaveholders used slaves and about the slaves including their names that emphasize their humanity.[11]

In a chapter of his book on the political and social aspects of the Texas Revolution, Paul Lack clarifies the reactions of slaves who sought to escape amid the chaos of war as well as slaves, and free blacks, who tried to gain freedom by aiding the Texas war for independence. The life of free black William Goyens, who assisted Sam Houston during the Texas Revolution, is reviewed by Linda Devereaux.[12]

Don E. Reynolds has written the most thorough and thoughtful account of the slave revolt fears aroused among many Anglo-Texans by a series of fires in the summer of 1860. Although drought and faulty matches seemed the probable cause, secessionist editors blamed slaves and abolitionists. Vigilante groups gathered to execute or whip numerous slaves and some Northerners in the state at that time.[13]

The Civil War brought some changes in the lives of slaves and slaveholders, as Alwyn Barr explains. Owners from nearby states brought slaves into Texas to avoid Union armies that might free bondsmen. Some slaves had to labor for the Confederate Army. Others sought greater control of their lives as supervision declined when slaveholders went off to war. Limited numbers of bondsmen attempted escape to Mexico, or to Union ships in the gulf, or to federal forces in the Indian Territory. The religious lives of slaves in Houston evolved from attending services in white churches, usually in separate sections before the war, to separate but supervised meetings and buildings by the beginning of the conflict. Charles A. Israel carefully analyzes the process that led to independent congregations during Reconstruction.[14]

The Reconstruction period in Texas can be more clearly understood because Carl Moneyhon has provided a new general history of events that is especially strong on politics and government. Essays by Barry Crouch have been collected in a single volume that includes studies about black views of freedom, white reactions, African American family patterns and politics, as well as the Freedmen's Bureau.[15]

Nancy Cohen-Lack argues that in 1865 Texas planters sought to retain control of slave labor despite emancipation, while slaves resisted to gain control over their lives and labor, with hopes for land to protect their freedom. The U.S. Army first emphasized labor for wages, but the Freedmen's Bureau shifted to protection of labor contracts for the freed people, although planters continued to dominate in many areas. As former slaves tried to establish their status as free workers, they faced opposition that is clarified by Kenneth M. Hamilton in his study of Harrison County. Whites sought to control property, wealth, and black labor with the aid of state laws, county government, and violence. Barry Crouch analyzes the support for planter power under the Texas black code. African Americans who did acquire small plots of farm land in Brazoria County in the late 1860s are described by Sean Kelley as a "Caribbean style reconstituted peasantry" who worked as families but in many cases lost their property before 1900.[16]

Anti-black violence by whites for economic and political reasons continued through much of Reconstruction across most of the state. These actions by individuals as well as groups including the Ku Klux Klan have been analyzed by James Smallwood in three volumes, two with coauthors. Significant numbers of African American soldiers in the U.S. Army helped limit the violence from 1865 to 1867 despite hostility from former Confederates. David Work explains that they also helped the United States pressure France to withdraw its troops from Mexico, and in many cases soldiers saved their pay and acquired an education for their future. William A. Dobak also discusses the border activities of black troops. Two general studies of the Freedmen's Bureau in Texas differ to some extent in their conclusions. Barry A. Crouch finds that despite some lapses the Bureau agents tried to protect African Americans from violence and injustice and to promote their education. Both efforts met opposition from white Texans that limited the results. William L. Richter is more critical of Bureau leaders and sees less impact from agency efforts. Assessing the Bureau in Marshall, Texas, Christopher Bean agrees that agents made positive efforts. Yet lack of manpower and the federal view of the agency as temporary limited its success.[17]

Social developments during Reconstruction included black urbanization as freedmen sought greater safety, a wider range of jobs, and more control over their lives. Migration into Houston is described by Scott Stabler, who recounts the development of a hospital, a park, churches, mutual aid societies, sports teams, and political activities. African American women during Reconstruction did not accept dependent roles based on race or gender. Instead they favored individual freedom, according to Mary Farmer-Kaiser in a book based on Freedmen's Bureau records from four states including Texas. They wanted Bureau assistance to stay home with small children and resisted efforts to apprentice older children to white employers. Black women also sought justice when they were abandoned or abused by a husband or employer. Randolph Campbell found that by 1880 African Americans lived in two-parent families, one-third of the families with children had a child in school, and about 20 percent had acquired property or skilled jobs.[18]

With passage of the 1867 Reconstruction Acts, African Americans could vote and participate in politics in Texas as in other former Confederate states. Based on statistical analysis, Gregg Cantrell states that violence directed at blacks spiked in reaction to adoption of the Reconstruction Acts and again during the first election involving black voters in 1868. Randolph B. Campbell explains that the first blacks to hold public office served as voter registrars in 1867. Campbell also has compared local politics in six diverse counties across Texas and found that the two with the largest black populations sent African American delegates to the state constitutional convention in 1868 and elected Republicans to most local offices in 1869 and on up to 1876. By 1880 only one retained black officeholders and Republican leadership. The career of Joshua Houston, a black political leader in Walker County during Reconstruction, is described by Patricia Smith Prather and Jane Clements Monday.[19]

Reconstruction ended in Texas when the Democratic Party, led by former Confederates, regained control of state government in the mid-1870s. African Americans in the late nineteenth century tried to maintain a strong role in the state Republican Party and in counties with large black populations. Douglas Hales has written the most extensive account of the Cuney family, centered around Galveston alderman and labor organizer Norris Wright Cuney, who became leader of the state Republican Party in the late 1880s and early 1890s. Gregg Cantrell explores the roles of African Americans in the state prohibition campaign of 1887. In the 1890s the Populist Party emerged to challenge Democrats in Texas. Cantrell clarifies the role of John B. Rayner in a biography of the most important black campaigner for the new third party. In a history of disfranchisement efforts by Democrats in the South from 1888 to 1908, Michael Perman analyzes the impact of the white primary and the poll tax in Texas. He concludes that together they reduced black voting by 85 percent as well as white voting by 50 percent, mostly the urban workers and tenant farmers who had voted Populist. Alicia E. Rodriguez found that local Democrats in Dallas lost elections for mayor to an independent candidate in the 1880s. The Democrats turned to the state legislature and courts, dominated by Democrats, in successful efforts to disfranchise working-class voters including many African Americans in 1890s mayor's races.[20]

Beyond political struggles, African Americans faced problems in the legal system. Dale Baum analyzes the lengthy and unsuccessful efforts of a black woman to retain a plantation willed to her by the white father of her son, in the face of legal challenges from white relatives and poor representation by white attorneys. By gerrymandering judicial districts, Democrats in the legislature limited the number of Republican district judges, who were likely to call blacks as well as whites for jury duty and to treat African Americans more fairly than Democratic judges. Alwyn Barr also explains that when three urban counties each had enough population for two judicial districts in the early 1890s two geographical districts were created in each county. By the late 1890s, however, the state had shifted to at-large elections of district judges in each county to limit the chance that Republicans with black support might win election.[21]

Violence remained a greater threat to African Americans compared to Anglos. More detailed accounts of lynching offer new insights into such acts. In a broad study, William D. Carrigan explores eighty years of vigilante activities across

Central Texas. He concludes that Anglos developed a positive memory and tradition of extralegal violence directed at Native Americans, Mexican Americans, and African Americans as well as some whites. Cynthia Skove Nevels focuses on five lynchings of blacks in Brazos County that involved Czech, Italian, and Irish immigrants. She argues that the immigrants sought to establish their "white" identity through their roles in these events. Journalist Gary B. Borders describes the Nacogdoches hanging of an African American man who had confessed to murder; he faced a "legal lynching" after a trial without an attorney under mob pressure amid the intense politics of the 1890s. In a book exploring similar events across the nation, Elliott Jaspin recounts the 1886 mob action in Comanche County in which a black man was seized and executed for the murder of a white woman. The vigilantes then threatened the forty or more African Americans in the county if they did not leave. Some Anglos opposed the threat, but blacks quickly departed, leaving an all-white "sundown" community.[22]

Problems of legal harassment carried over into the efforts of African Americans in Texas who pursued economic opportunities, including land for homes. Dale Baum offers insightful analysis of blacks in Bryan struggling to acquire property and retain ownership in the face of discriminatory law enforcement. The goal of property acquisition by freedmen is explored in an important book by Thad Sitton and James H. Conrad on the development of numerous small black farming communities across eastern Texas on land unattractive to whites, a strategy that allowed some African Americans to avoid everyday domination by Anglos and to form their own churches and schools. Black sharecroppers and laborers often needed credit from white store owners. According to Linda English, owners kept separate records of black purchases and wanted successful African Americans to "secure" the accounts of other blacks but did not discriminate on prices.[23]

In Galveston black dock workers went on strike in 1877 and 1898 seeking equal pay. Robert S. Shelton concludes that some white workers refused to replace the strikers, but the city government used police to aid the shipping company in ending the strikes. To discuss the growing problems of segregation and discrimination, as well as possible solutions, African Texan leaders held several conventions from the late 1860s to the 1890s. These efforts to organize are explored by Alwyn Barr.[24]

Black cowboys formed a smaller but more visible group in the late nineteenth-century Texas economy, as ranching spread from the coastal plains and South Texas into West Texas. Sara R. Massey has edited a volume of biographical essays about individual African Americans who herded cattle, tamed wild horses, and in a few cases became ranchers. Bruce G. Todd provides a more detailed biography of "Bones" Hooks, a respected bronc buster and horse wrangler in the Panhandle who later became a railroad porter and black community leader in Amarillo. In a volume that focuses on class and masculine status in ranching, Jacqueline M. Moore offers insights into the status, numbers, and roles of black cowboys. Michael Searles adds the story of how African American bronc busters might keep a good horse for their own by making the horse seem only partly tamed.[25]

Black soldiers formed four regiments in the U.S. Army on the western frontier of Texas and its Rio Grande border. William A. Dobak and Thomas D. Phillips studied the daily lives of these enlisted men, on and off duty, and conclude that the army did not officially discriminate against them, which has led to some debate. A collection of essays on African American soldiers edited by Bruce A. Glasrud and Michael Searles includes chapters on events in Texas. Paul H. Carlson carefully analyzes a search for Comanches by black cavalry in the Panhandle during a drought that placed the troops in danger for lack of water. He finds the officer in command primarily at fault for their problem. Charles M. Robinson III has written two accounts of the military trial of Lieutenant Henry O. Flipper that led to his dismissal in 1882. The longer second account is more critical of Flipper but seems less analytical of the army's case against him. Jane Eppinga has written the only complete biography of Flipper. An expanded volume of Flipper's memoirs and later writings has been edited by Theodore D. Harris. Tensions related to race, economic change, and politics that resulted in conflict between black soldiers and white cowboys, gamblers, and hunters at San Angelo are explored by Bruce J. Dinges.[26]

Several books offer more detailed accounts of the African Americans who lived at Brackettville and provided scouts for the army. Kenneth Porter's narrative history follows the group from Florida to the Indian Territory, Mexico, and Texas. Kevin Mulroy provides an analytical account of these Seminole maroons. Thomas Britten offers a briefer study focused on their military service for the U.S. Army. Shirley Boteler Mock adds the family memories, African influences, and female perspective of black Seminole women. Frank N. Schubert devotes a chapter to the scouts in his volume on African Americans who received the Medal of Honor in this period. Charles M. Neal, Jr., also includes the black Medal of Honor winners in his book on all who earned that medal in Texas. Eric Strong explores the possibility of a lost treaty promising land to the black Seminoles.[27]

During the Spanish-American War black volunteers from Texas formed majorities in two infantry companies sent to Cuba as part of an African American regiment presumed to be immune to tropical diseases. Roger D. Cunningham explains that they generally served successfully despite discrimination and white criticism. Art T. Burton provides a biography of another African American serving the federal government, deputy marshal Bass Reeves, who worked primarily in the Indian Territory and Oklahoma as well as Paris, Texas.[28]

The social and cultural life of African Americans in late nineteenth-century Texas has begun to receive more attention in recent years. Two books open windows on black urban life. Ellen Beasley explores the history of buildings that faced alleys in Galveston and the African Americans and other working-class people who lived in them. The development of the several black neighborhoods in Austin is the focus of Michelle M. Mears, who discusses day-to-day life and the emergence of schools and churches as well as increased segregation in the twentieth century. Alwyn Barr considers health and housing problems and black responses in Houston and San Antonio.[29]

Churches provided community centers for African Americans in the post–Civil War period. Clyde McQueen brings together in one volume brief histories of 374 black churches established in the nineteenth century in Texas; William E. Montgomery offers broader perspective in the introduction. Marvin C. Griffin has narrated the development of the Baptist General Convention of Texas. Leaders among black Baptists are the focus of two essays by Joe Early, Jr. One provides a biographical account of Israel Campbell, who organized congregations and associations in Texas. Richard Henry Boyd, the central figure in the other article, helped form churches and worked in mission efforts as well as publishing Sunday school literature. An essay by Alwyn Barr explores the development and importance of black urban churches in Houston and San Antonio as well as Little Rock and Shreveport. Evidence that African Americans wore pierced coins as informal charms to protect against harm emerged from archaeological study of burials discovered in downtown Dallas and described by James M. Davidson.[30]

In the early twentieth century most African Americans struggled to maintain their families as sharecroppers. The U.S. Department of Agriculture began to offer some aid in 1914 when it created a Negro Division of its extension services. Debra A. Reid analyzes those efforts by underfunded black agents to explain new farming methods, organize 4-H clubs, and develop canning projects to generate food preservation. In a separate essay Reid also explains the economic and racial factors that led to loss of farms by African Americans in the twentieth century. An additional study by Reid explores the efforts by black farm families to limit their losses when in debt. Eddie Stimpson, Jr., provides a memoir of everyday life for a black sharecropper during the 1930s. Black women are included in the thoughtful study by Rebecca Sharpless of the lives and work of Texas farm women up to 1940.[31]

During this period a growing black urban labor force began to organize unions in Houston and especially in Galveston. Ernest Obadele-Starks offers a broad view of African American organizing in the segregated late nineteenth and early twentieth centuries that included efforts by dock workers, railroad employees, laborers in the oil industry, and men in the steel industry. He emphasizes increased success in the period from the Depression to World War II. A greater focus on Galveston by Clifford Farrington finds some cooperation between black and white unions during strikes for improved wages. Gregg Andrews analyzes the success of the City Party in Galveston during 1919–1920 based on support from black and white dock workers, followed by a failed strike and decline in union influence. Joseph Abel analyzes the efforts of African Americans to gain skilled positions in the Fort Worth aircraft production plants during World War II. He finds some limited success with support from the Fair Employment Practices Commission and white unions seeking to strengthen their own bargaining status. African American women filled an important role in Texas and southern society as cooks in upper-class white homes. Rebecca Sharpless sets aside stereotypes to consider their influence on food patterns, amid the complexities and problems of white domination. A Beaumont example of black domestic servants' work for a wealthy and paternalistic family, by Judith W. Linsley, suggests respectable social status for the servants within the black community. Employer-employee relations included both tension and positive bonds.[32]

An urban black middle class that included business and professional figures also emerged in growing numbers. Emmett J. Scott, who published a black newspaper in Houston, then became the personal secretary of Booker T. Washington. Maceo C. Dailey clarifies Scott's efforts to promote the National Negro Business League and more specific banking and commercial firms. Shennette Garrett-Scott analyzes the founding of a black-operated cotton mill in Dallas and the economic and racial complications that led to its failure. Keith Volanto explores the medical career of Dr. Beadie Eugene Conner in Waco, Cameron, and Austin that included experimenting with contract medicine and seeking to overcome hospital segregation and to promote African American economic development.[33]

The expanding black middle class also sought improved residential areas. William H. Wilson considers the planned creation of Hamilton Park in mid-twentieth-century Dallas, separate from white areas and allowing African Americans to develop a community with schools, churches, and consumer businesses. A broader study of black urbanization in San Antonio is presented by Kenneth Mason, who discusses economic, social, and political efforts. Howard Beeth and Cary D. Wintz have edited a book on African Americans in Houston that includes essays about business and social activities in this period. A photographic presentation of African Americans in Fort Worth from the 1940s to the 1990s, including businesses, social events, schools, and entertainment, is provided by Bob Ray Sanders.[34]

Family life ranked with economic status for understanding African Americans in Texas. Historians in recent years have established that after the Civil War most African Americans lived in two-parent families. Some educated sons of prewar interracial relationships emerged as leaders in the Texas black community. A further clarification about the legal status of such relationships is presented by Charles F. Robinson II, who presents court cases in Texas during Reconstruction that held interracial marriage as well as long-term cohabitation to be legal. Texas Democrats revived laws against intermarriage in the 1870s, however, although they did not apply to informal interracial relationships.[35]

Hopes for education formed another important goal for black Texans. Peggy B. Gill provides a case study of a rural school in East Texas that overcame funding problems to achieve a degree of success as a result of broad community support. The quality of education in private black colleges is considered in three articles by Gail Beil. One discusses the Wiley College debate team that achieved national attention in the 1930s. A second describes the career of James L. Farmer, the earliest black professor in Texas with a doctorate, who taught at Wiley and Samuel Huston colleges from the 1920s to the 1950s. The third focuses on Prof. Melvin Tolson at Wiley, a fine poet who also sought to organize black workers and support civil rights.[36]

Churches continued to be central institutions in small towns and rural areas in the early twentieth century. The first historical account of the black Church of Christ in Texas has been written by Edward J. Robinson. It focuses on the beginnings of congregations, important ministers who led the expansion of the denomination, and the development of church-related schools. Early congregations and a school of the Church of God in Christ are described by Karen Kossie-Chernyshev.[37]

Within segregated black society sports and music provided recreation and entertainment. Rob Fink offers insights into several aspects of black Texas baseball: the influence of famous players from Texas and the importance of its semipro teams and leagues, its African American professional minor league, and the Houston team at the highest level of Negro League baseball. The black Texas pitcher and key figure in the creation of the Negro National League, "Rube" Foster, is the subject of a biography by Robert C. Cottrell. The life of a star shortstop from Texas, Willie Wells, has been recorded by Bob Luke. Jerry Craft adds his thoughtful memories of being the only white player on a black semipro team in the 1950s before desegregation. Rob Fink has expanded his focus on African American sports in Texas by exploring the social and cultural importance of black college football during the second decade of the twentieth century.[38]

The history of black music has been clarified in both general and biographical volumes. In his study of Texas music, Gary Hartman's chapter on black music discusses African influences, gospel, blues, electrical equipment, rock and roll, ragtime and jazz, and more recent styles such as rap. The sources of Texas jazz and its contributions to national music development are presented by Dave Oliphant. The interaction of African American musicians along Deep Ellum and Central Track in Dallas is described by Alan B. Govenar and Jay F. Brakefield. A lesser known style of Texas dance music, Zydeco, is discussed by Roger Wood. The autobiography of bluesman Mance Lipscomb has been edited by Glen Alyn. Kip Lornell and Charles Wolfe explore the life of country blues artist Huddie Ledbetter (better known as Leadbelly). The life of another important country blues figure, Blind Lemon Jefferson, is considered by Govenar.[39]

Writers, artists, and photographers also contributed to African American culture in Texas. Francis E. Abernethy edited a volume on black folklore in Texas. Discussion of gender roles in *Sepia*, a Fort Worth magazine for African Americans, is analyzed by Sherilyn Brandenstein. Black female authors are considered by Lou Halsell Rodenberger in a volume on women in Texas literature. Bernice Love Wiggins published a book of poetry in 1925 at El Paso that has been reprinted with a new introduction by Maceo C. Dailey, Jr., and Ruthe Winegarten. William Loren Katz analyzes the work of Sutton E. Griggs, who wrote novels about different approaches to African American problems at the beginning of the twentieth century. Gabriel Briggs views Sutton Griggs as representative of the New Negro in black southern literature. Maria Karafalis explores Griggs's view of U.S. citizenship in his *Imperium in Imperio*.[40]

The work of artist John Biggers, who painted Texas and African scenes, is considered by Alvia J. Wardlaw. The contributions of black photographers who preserved a sense of African American life in Texas are discussed by Alan B. Govenar.[41]

Bessie Coleman provided a different type of entertainment as the first female stunt pilot. Two biographies by Elizabeth A. H. Freydberg and Doris L. Rich describe her accident-shortened career.[42]

Despite advances in education and culture, and the development of a middle class, African Americans in the early twentieth century continued to face segregation, discrimination, and violence. The Waco lynching and burning of Jesse Washington in 1916 attracted national attention and strengthened the growth of the National Association for the Advancement of Colored People, according to a detailed study by Patricia Bernstein. At Kirven, Texas, in 1922 Anglos burned to death three black men accused of killing a white woman, although two white men probably were guilty and the sheriff tried in vain to head off mob violence; Monte Akers analyzes the murders in an era influenced by Ku Klux Klan activity, followed by decline of the town. Lynch mobs continued into the 1930s, with one in Colorado County, described by Bill Stein, defending its actions as protecting women and fearing limited punishment of two black teenagers accused of rape and murder. Conflicting memories and views lingered for years. Robert Perkinson presents a harsh picture of black and white convicts caught up in the Texas prison system that included convict lease until 1911, followed by agricultural labor on state prison farms. Patricia E. Gower discusses more subtle discrimination in Dallas, where use of at-large elections allowed Anglos to control city government and employ zoning policy to limit city services for African Americans.[43]

Black U.S. soldiers returned to assignments along the Rio Grande after service in the Spanish-American war only to face discrimination and conflicts with police and civilians in the years up to World War I. Garna Christian presents the first general analysis of these events, in which investigations seldom seemed entirely fair to the troops. Taking a broader view from the end of the Civil War to World War I, James N. Leiker explores race relations along the Texas-Mexico border and suggests that African American soldiers fought other ethnic minorities in wartime to gain acceptance by Anglos, and Mexican Americans might harass black troops for similar reasons. The 1970s exoneration of black troops dismissed after unproved charges against them at Brownsville in 1906 is described by John D. Weaver.[44]

African Texans responded to violence and discrimination by looking for ways to organize and challenge those problems. Houston efforts by black leaders in the 1920s seeking to develop unified support for political and economic progress are considered by Howard Beeth. Conflicting approaches of reform or communism in Houston in that period also are explored by Beeth. The alternative of black nationalism among black Texans is analyzed by Bruce A. Glasrud. Theodore M. Lawe discusses the development of business, fraternal, and social organizations that created a middle-class base that later pressed for a role in Dallas politics. The biography of Lulu B. White by Merline Pitre provides insights into NAACP leadership and growth, especially in Houston, as well as the important roles of women. Pitre later expanded on the efforts of black women in Houston. The activities of Juanita Craft of Dallas, who also played an important role in the NAACP, are discussed by Stefanie Decker. Another organization formed to increase black suffrage, the Progressive Voters League, is discussed by W. Marvin Dulaney.[45]

Crucial challenges in the courts to disfranchisement became the basis for a major advance in voting rights. In a new edition of her study about the several legal struggles over the white primary, Darlene Clark Hine is joined by Steven F. Lawson and Merline Pitre in offering new insights into the efforts by a broad range of black men and women to regain the right to vote. The final successful case against the white primary, *Smith v. Allwright*, is given new attention by Charles L. Zelden, who carefully considers court arguments and the resulting enforcement of the decision ending that restriction.[46]

Once African Americans regained voting rights in the 1940s, some began to seek opportunities to represent their communities in local, state, and national government. Barbara Jordan, through hard work and learning the system, became a successful state senator and member of Congress. Mary Beth Rogers has written the first complete biography of Jordan. Jordan's intellectual ideas about government are presented in a volume of her speeches edited by Max Sherman. Other black political leaders are included in a biographical volume by Nancy Baker Jones and Ruthe Winegarten on women in the Texas legislature.[47]

The national Voting Rights Act of 1965 called for an end to at-large elections, which led to districts that allowed African Americans and other minorities to run successfully for local offices. That process in Dallas is described by Ruth P. Morgan, who also explores the charges that some minority representatives engaged in corruption, including the debate over whether their acts differed from previous Anglo activities.[48]

Equal opportunity for education became the next goal of black Texans. Gary M. Lavergne provides an analytical study of the Sweatt case, which desegregated the University of Texas law school in 1950. He carefully discusses the conflicts between Carter Wesley and Lulu White about whether the goal should be equality or desegregation. John Hargis integrated the undergraduate programs of the University of Texas in 1955 in a case described by Richard B. McCaslin. The longer process of moving toward racial equality on the University of Texas campus is explored by Dwonna Goldstone. A broader discussion of desegregation at other colleges and universities in the state is presented by Amilcar Shabazz, who clarifies the problems of harassment and isolation faced by successful plaintiffs. Ronald E. Marcello focuses on attitudes and events in the integration of North Texas State College, which later became the University of North Texas.[49]

Following the Brown decision in 1954–1955, Texas school districts began to desegregate, with some resisting longer than others. Robin Duff Ladino explores the influence of politics in early state opposition to desegregation at Mansfield. Some districts with larger black populations in eastern Texas went through lengthy court proceedings over several years. Glenn Linden and Gerald S. McCorkle describe that process in Dallas, and William Henry Keller considers the stages in Houston. A few smaller districts elsewhere also have been the focus of studies: Ector County by Bryan L. Smith, Port Arthur by Tina M. Kibbe, and Baytown by Chris Danielson. Baptist views on school desegregation are considered at the state level by Blake Killingsworth and David K. Chrisman, in East Texas by Blanche Henderson Brick, and in West Texas by Estelle Owens.[50]

With school desegregation beginning, black Texans turned their attention to desegregation of public places, using negotiations, varied forms of peaceful protest, and court cases. The complex nature of segregation on Texas railroads is carefully analyzed by William S. Osburn. He explains early exceptions in Pullman cars and declining enforcement after World War II, resulting from costs and court cases. Robert J. Robertson considers one of the early instances, at Beaumont, when six African American golfers requested the use of city courses. When rejected, they successfully went to court to gain access. Louis A. Bedford, Jr., a black Dallas attorney and advisor to civil rights activists, is the subject of a biography by Darwin Payne. Peaceful protests in Dallas often pushed white business leaders to negotiate integration and head off possible negative images of white violence, according to Brian D. Behnken. He suggests that pattern as more common in Texas than violent opposition. Thomas Cole focuses on protest leader Eldrewey Stearns in Houston. F. Kenneth Jensen also explores the sit-ins in the Bayou City. Austin protests receive attention from Martin Kuhlman, who focuses on direct action around the University of Texas, and Carolyn Jones, who presents the career of Volma Overton, president of the local NAACP chapter. Donald Seals, Jr., explores the lunch counter sit-ins at Marshall by students from Wiley and Bishop colleges and the resistance by the local white community that temporarily put off desegregation. Gail K. Beil discusses the positive influence of four people from Marshall on adoption of the Civil Rights Act of 1964: James Farmer, leader of the Congress of Racial Equality; Bill Moyers on the staff of President Lyndon Johnson; Lady Bird Johnson; and Zephyr Wright, the president's cook.[51]

Treatment by Anglos dominating law enforcement and courts reflected another concern for African Americans. Dwight Watson describes the Houston police department as defending segregation while the city grew and changed during the twentieth century. He then recounts changes beginning with the appointment of a black police chief.[52]

Economic discrimination also led to challenges during the civil rights movement. Michael R. Botson, Jr., describes efforts by the Hughes Tool Company to limit labor unions and desegregation. He also considers the conflicting views in the Houston black community about separate or integrated unions and the decision of the National Labor Relations Board against segregated unions in 1964. The development of unions and later integration of African American theater workers from the 1930s to the 1960s in Dallas and Houston are discussed by Ernest Obadele-Starks. Lyndon Johnson's War on Poverty aimed at increasing economic opportunity for minorities while also aiding poor whites, in part to increase public and political support. William S. Clayson explores the interaction of that program with civil rights in Texas, primarily through its effort to include local residents in planning Community Action Programs. He concludes that learning to organize may have been more valuable than the declining program funds in the late 1960s. Wesley G. Phelps describes the development and decline of the Community Action Program in Houston.[53]

Sports segregation also faced challenges during the years of the civil rights movement. Charles S. Martin has analyzed its development and decline at the college level, especially in football and basketball, across the South including Texas. He explains why integration occurred earlier at schools like Texas Western College (which became the University of Texas at El Paso) and Texas A&I College. Francine Sanders Romero offers a shorter study of desegregation in boxing.[54]

Two books explore the question of why African Americans and Mexican Americans conducted separate civil rights movements with only limited cooperation. With a focus on the 1940s and 1950s issues of jobs and school segregation in Texas and California, Neil Foley argues that Mexican Americans sought to be considered white and accepted Anglo racial views of African Americans, who in turn allowed anti-immigrant attitudes and concern about job competition to shape their views. Brian Behnken also covers the earlier years and continues into the 1970s to show that Mexican Americans shifted from claiming whiteness to describing themselves as a brown minority. Recent studies by Emilio Zamora and Cynthia E. Orozco claim more black-brown cooperation.[55]

Overlapping the civil rights era, African American music evolved new variations that are discussed by Roger Wood, who focuses on Houston and covers the influence of country blues men such as Sam "Lightnin" Hopkins as well as the interaction with Creole jazz, gospel, and rhythm and blues. The contributions of women are included along with the importance of Duke-Peacock Records.[56]

Two essays explore the impact of wars and military service. Alwyn Barr offers a broad survey of conflicts and black participation from the Spanish colonial military into the post-Vietnam era. Ronald E. Goodwin considers the attitudes and actions of African Texans from the 1990s to the 2000s.[57]

Writers from other fields have provided accounts of lingering problems for African Americans in Texas. Journalist Nate Blakeslee describes the overturning of black drug convictions in Tulia because the only witness proved unreliable. Psychologist Ricardo Ainslie has sought to understand the mind of the lead figure convicted of the dragging death of a black man, James Byrd, Jr., near Jasper in 1998.[58]

Clearly African American history has attracted greater attention from historians, both professional scholars and amateurs, who have increased our understanding of numerous events and topics that previously had not received attention. Others have applied new approaches that add insights into better known topics. The best general histories of the state often are textbooks used in college Texas history classes and certainly include improved treatment of African American history.[59] The most recent period after the civil rights movement will no doubt attract further study, as will urbanization, fraternal organizations, social and cultural activities, and family patterns. At the local level, black history in many counties and towns still awaits exploration.

NOTES

1. Alwyn Barr, *Black Texans: A History of African Americans in Texas, 1528–1995*, 2nd ed. (Norman: University of Oklahoma Press, 1996), and *The African Texans* (College Station: Texas A&M University Press, 2004); Quintard Taylor, "Texas: The South

Meets the West, the View through African American History," *Journal of the West* 44 (Fall 2010): 44–52.

2. David A. Williams, *Bricks without Straw: A Comprehensive History of African Americans in Texas* (Austin: Eakin Press, 1997); Bruce A. Glasrud and James M. Smallwood, eds., *The African American Experience in Texas* (Lubbock: Texas Tech University Press, 2007); Donald Willett and Stephen Curley, eds., *Invisible Texans: Women and Minorities in Texas History* (Boston: McGraw-Hill, 2005).

3. Bruce A. Glasrud, Paul H. Carlson, and Tai D. Kreidler, *Slavery to Integration: Black Americans in West Texas* (Abilene, Tex.: State House Press, 2007); Bruce A. Glasrud and Archie P. McDonald, eds., *Blacks in East Texas History* (College Station: Texas A&M University Press, 2008); Bruce A. Glasrud, *African Americans in South Texas History* (College Station: Texas A&M University Press, 2011).

4. Ruthe Winegarten, *Black Texas Women: 150 Years of Trial and Triumph* (Austin: University of Texas Press, 1994); Bruce A. Glasrud and Merline Pitre, eds., *Black Women in Texas History* (College Station: Texas A&M University Press, 2008).

5. Bruce A. Glasrud and Laurie Champion, eds., *Exploring the Afro-Texas Experience: A Bibliography of Secondary Sources about Black Texans* (Alpine, Tex.: Center for Big Bend Studies, Sul Ross State University, 2000).

6. Martha Menchaca, *Recovering History, Constructing Race: The Indian, Black, and White Roots of Mexican Americans* (Austin: University of Texas Press, 2001); Neil Foley, *The White Scourge: Mexicans, Blacks, and Poor Whites in Texas Cotton Culture* (Berkeley: University of California Press, 1997); Michael Phillips, *White Metropolis: Race, Ethnicity, and Religion in Dallas, 1841–2001* (Austin: University of Texas Press, 2006).

7. Gregg Cantrell and Elizabeth Hayes Turner, eds., *Lone Star Pasts: Memory and History in Texas* (College Station: Texas A&M University Press, 2007); Naomi Mitchell Carrier, *"Go Down, Old Hannah": The Living History of African American Texans* (Austin: University of Texas Press, 2010).

8. Douglas W. Richmond, "Africa's Initial Encounter with Texas: The Significance of Afro-Tejanos in Colonial Texas, 1528–1821," *Bulletin of Latin American Research* 26, no. 2 (2007): 200–21.

9. James C. Kearney, *Nassau Plantation: The Evolution of a Texas-German Slave Plantation* (Denton: University of North Texas Press, 2010); Sean M. Kelley, *Los Brazos de Dios: A Plantation Society in the Texas Borderlands 1821–1865* (Baton Rouge: Louisiana State University Press, 2010); prior to his book, Kelley had published articles on aspects of slavery along the Brazos in the *Journal of Social History* 37 (Spring 2004): 709–23; and in *Civil War History* 54 (Dec. 2008): 406–23. Ernest Obadele-Starks, *Freebooters and Smugglers: The Foreign Slave Trade in the United States after 1808* (Fayetteville: University of Arkansas Press, 2007).

10. T. Lindsay Baker, "More than Just 'Possum 'n Taters': African-American Foodways in WPA Slave Narratives," in *Juneteenth Texas: Essays in African-American Folklore*, ed. Francis E. Abernethy, Carolyn Fiedler Satterwhite, Patrick Mullen, and Alan B. Govenar, 95–128, Publications of the Texas Folklore Society 54 (Denton: University of North Texas Press, 1996); Elizabeth R. Rabe, "Slave Children of Texas: A Qualitative and Quantitative Analysis," *East Texas Historical Journal* 42, no. 1 (2004): 10–24;

Robert S. Shelton, "Slavery in a Texas Seaport: The Peculiar Institution in Galveston," *Slavery and Abolition* 28 (Aug. 2007): 155–68; Joanna Labor, "A History of Slavery in Austin and Surrounding Areas," *Lone Star Legacy: African American History in Texas* 1 (2011): 73–79.

11. T. Lindsay Baker and Julie P. Baker, eds., *Till Freedom Cried Out: Memories of Texas Slave Life* (College Station: Texas A&M University Press, 1997); Mark Gretchen, *Slave Transactions of Guadalupe County, Texas* (Santo Maria, Calif.: Janaway, 2009); Randolph Campbell, ed., William S. Pugsley and Marilyn P. Duncan, comps., *The Laws of Slavery in Texas* (Austin: University of Texas Press, 2010).

12. Paul D. Lack, *The Texas Revolutionary Experience: A Political and Social History of the Texas Revolution, 1835–1836* (College Station: Texas A&M University Press, 1992), chap. 12; Linda Devereaux, "William Goyens: Black Leader in Early Texas," *East Texas Historical Journal* 45, no. 1 (2007): 52–57.

13. Donald E. Reynolds, *Texas Terror: The Slave Insurrection Panic of 1860 and the Secession of the Lower South* (Baton Rouge: Louisiana State University Press, 2007).

14. Alwyn Barr, "Black Texans during the Civil War," in *Invisible Texans: Women and Minorities in Texas History*, ed. Donald Willett and Stephen Curley (Boston: McGraw-Hill, 2005), 86–93; Charles A. Israel, "From Biracial to Segregated Churches: Black and White Protestants in Houston, Texas, 1840–1870," *Southwestern Historical Quarterly* 101 (Apr. 1998): 429–58.

15. Carl H. Moneyhon, *Texas after the Civil War: The Struggle of Reconstruction* (College Station: Texas A&M University Press, 2004); Barry Crouch, *The Dance of Freedom: Texas African Americans during Reconstruction* (Austin: University of Texas Press, 2007).

16. Nancy Cohen-Lack, "A Struggle for Sovereignty: National Consolidation, Emancipation, and Free Labor in Texas, 1865," *Journal of Southern History* 58 (Feb. 1992): 57–98; Kenneth M. Hamilton, "White Wealth and Black Repression in Harrison County, Texas, 1865–1868," *Journal of Negro History* 84 (Fall 1999), 340–59; Barry A. Crouch, "'All the Vile Passions': The Texas Black Code of 1866," *Southwestern Historical Quarterly* 97 (July 1993): 13–34; Sean Kelley, "A Texas Peasantry? Black Smallholders in the Texas Sugar Bowl, 1865–1890," *Slavery and Abolition* 28 (Aug. 2007): 193–209.

17. James M. Smallwood, Barry A. Crouch, and Larry Peacock, *Murder and Mayhem: The War of Reconstruction in Texas* (College Station: Texas A&M University Press, 2003); James M. Smallwood, Kenneth W. Howell, and Carol C. Taylor, *The Devil's Triangle: Ben Biggerstaff, Northeast Texans, and the War of Reconstruction in Texas* (Lufkin: East Texas Publishers, 2007); James M. Smallwood, *The Feud That Wasn't: The Taylor Ring, Bill Sutton, John Wesley Hardin, and Violence in Texas* (College Station: Texas A&M University Press, 2008); David Work, "United States Colored Troops in Texas during Reconstruction, 1865–1867," *Southwestern Historical Quarterly* 109 (Jan. 2006): 337–57; William A. Dobak, *Freedom by the Sword: The U.S. Colored Troops, 1862–1867* (Washington, D.C.: U.S. Army Center of Military History, 2011); Barry A. Crouch, *The Freedmen's Bureau and Black Texans* (Austin: University of Texas Press, 1992); William L. Richter, *Overreached on All Sides: The Freedmen's Bureau Administrators in Texas, 1865–1868* (College Station: Texas A&M University Press, 1991); Christopher

Bean, "A Most Singular and Interesting Attempt: The Freedmen's Bureau at Marshall, Texas," *Southwestern Historical Quarterly* 110 (Apr. 2007): 465–85.

18. Scott Stabler, "Free Men Come to Houston: Blacks during Reconstruction," *Houston Review* 3 (Fall 2005): 40–43, 73–76; Mary Farmer-Kaiser, *Freedwomen and the Freedmen's Bureau: Race, Gender and Public Policy in the Age of Emancipation* (New York: Fordam University Press, 2010); Randolph B. Campbell, *Grass-Roots Reconstruction in Texas, 1865–1880* (Baton Rouge: Louisiana State University Press, 1997); Alwyn Barr, "Reconstruction Change and Continuity in Brazoria County, Texas," *Houston Review* 18, no. 2 (1996): 114–23.

19. Gregg Cantrell, "Racial Violence and Reconstruction Politics in Texas, 1867–1868," *Southwestern Historical Quarterly* 93 (Jan. 1990): 333–55; Randolph B. Campbell, "The First African-American Public Officials in Texas: Voter Registrars in 1867," in Willett and Curley, *Invisible Texans*, 94–105; and *Grass-Roots Reconstruction;* Patricia Smith Prather and Jane Clements Monday, *From Slave to Statesman: The Legacy of Joshua Houston, Servant to Sam Houston* (Denton: University of North Texas Press, 1993).

20. Douglas Hales, *A Southern Family in White and Black: The Cuneys of Texas* (College Station: Texas A&M University Press, 2003); Gregg Cantrell, "'Dark Tactics': Black Politics in the 1887 Texas Prohibition Campaign," *Journal of American Studies* 25 (Apr. 1991): 85–93, *Kenneth and John B. Rayner and the Limits of Southern Dissent* (Urbana: University of Illinois Press, 1993), and *Feeding the Wolf: John B. Rayner and the Politics of Race, 1850–1918* (Wheeling, Ill.: Harlan Davidson, 2001); Michael Perman, *Struggle for Mastery, Disfranchisement in the South, 1888–1908* (Chapel Hill: University of North Carolina Press, 2001); Alicia E. Rodriguez, "Disfranchisement in Dallas: The Democratic Party and the Suppression of Independent Political Challenges in Dallas, Texas, 1891–1894," *Southwestern Historical Quarterly* 108 (July 2004): 42–64.

21. Dale Baum, *Counterfeit Justice: The Judicial Odyssey of Texas Freedwoman Azeline Hearne* (Baton Rouge: Louisiana State University Press, 2009); Alwyn Barr, "The Impact of Race in Shaping Judicial Districts, 1876–1907," *Southwestern Historical Quarterly* 108 (Apr. 2005): 423–39.

22. William D. Carrigan, *The Making of a Lynching Culture: Violence and Vigilantism in Central Texas, 1836–1916* (Urbana: University of Illinois Press, 2004); Cynthia Skove Nevels, *Lynching to Belong: Claiming Whiteness through Racial Violence* (College Station: Texas A&M University Press, 2007); Gary B. Borders, *A Hanging in Nacogdoches: Murder, Race, Politics, and Polemics in Texas' Oldest Town, 1870–1916* (Austin: University of Texas Press, 2006); Elliott Jaspin, *Buried in Bitter Waters: The Hidden History of Racial Cleansing in America* (New York: Basic Books, 2007).

23. Dale Baum, "Burdens of Landholdings in a Freed Slave Settlement: The Case of Brazos County's 'Hall Town,'" *Southwestern Historical Quarterly* 113 (Oct. 2009): 184–204; Thad Sitton and James H. Conrad, *Freedom Colonies: Independent Black Texans in the Time of Jim Crow* (Austin: University of Texas Press, 2005); Linda English, "Recording Race: General Stores and Race in the Late Nineteenth-Century Southwest," *Southwestern Historical Quarterly* 110 (Oct. 2006): 193–217.

24. Robert Shelton, "'Which Ox Is in the Mire': Race and Class in the Galveston Longshoremen's Strike of 1898," *Southwestern Historical Quarterly* 110 (Oct. 2006):

218–39, and "'Built by the Irishmen, the Negro and the Mule': Labor Militancy across the Color Line in Post-Reconstruction Texas," *East Texas Historical Journal* 46, no. 2 (2008): 15–26; Alwyn Barr, "Early Organizing in the Search for Equality: African American Conventions in Late Nineteenth Century Texas," in *Seeking Inalienable Rights: Texans and Their Quest for Justice*, ed. Debra A. Reid (College Station: Texas A&M University Press, 2009), 1–16.

25. Sara R. Massey, ed., *Black Cowboys of Texas* (College Station: Texas A&M University Press, 2000); Bruce G. Todd, *Bones Hooks: Pioneer Negro Cowboy* (Gretna, La.: Pelican, 2005); Jacqueline M. Moore, *Cow Boys and Cattle Men: Class and Masculinities on the Texas Frontier* (New York: New York University Press, 2010); Michael N. Searles, "Taking Out the Buck and Putting in a Trick: The Black Cowboys' Art of Breaking and Keeping a Good Cow Horse," *Journal of the West* 44 (Spring 2005): 53–60.

26. William A. Dobak and Thomas D. Phillips, *The Black Regulars, 1866–1898* (Norman: University of Oklahoma Press, 2001); Bruce A. Glasrud and Michael N. Searles, eds., *Buffalo Soldiers in the West: A Black Soldier Anthology* (College Station: Texas A&M University Press, 2007); Paul H. Carlson, *The Buffalo Soldier Tragedy of 1877* (College Station: Texas A&M University Press, 2002); Charles M. Robinson III, *The Court Martial of Lieutenant Henry Flipper* (El Paso: Texas Western Press, 1994), and *The Fall of a Black Army Officer: Racism and the Myth of Henry O. Flipper* (Norman: University of Oklahoma Press, 2008); Jane Eppinga, *Henry Ossian Flipper: West Point's First Black Graduate* (Plano: Republic of Texas Press, 1996); Theodore D. Harris, ed., *Black Frontiersmen: The Western Memoirs of Henry O. Flipper* (Fort Worth: Texas Christian University Press, 1997); Bruce J. Dinges, "The San Angelo Riot of 1881: The Army, Race, Politics, and Settlement on the Frontier," *Journal of the West* 41 (Summer 2002): 35–45.

27. Kenneth W. Porter, *The Black Seminoles: History of a Freedom-Seeking People* (Gainesville: University Press of Florida, 1996); Kevin Mulroy, *Freedom on the Border: The Seminole Maroons in Florida, the Indian Territory, Coahuila, and Texas* (Lubbock: Texas Tech University Press, 1993); Thomas A. Britten, *A Brief History of the Seminole Negro Indian Scouts* (Lewiston, N.Y.: Mellen Press, 1999); Shirley Boteler Mock, *Dreaming with the Ancestors: Black Seminole Women in Texas and Mexico* (Norman: University of Oklahoma Press, 2010); Frank N. Schubert, *Black Valor: Buffalo Soldiers and the Medal of Honor, 1870–1898* (Wilmington, Del: Scholarly Resources, 1997); Charles M. Neal, Jr., *Valor across the Lone Star: The Congressional Medal of Honor in Frontier Texas* (Austin: Texas State Historical Association, 2003); Eric Emmerson Strong, "The Lost Treaty of the Black Seminoles," *West Texas Historical Association Year Book* 75 (1999): 120–30.

28. Roger D. Cunningham, "'A Lot of Fine, Sturdy Black Warriors': Texas's African American 'Immunes' in the Spanish-American War," *Southwestern Historical Quarterly* 108 (Jan. 2005): 344–67; Art T. Burton, *Black Gun, Silver Star: The Life and Legend of Frontier Marshal Bass Reeves* (Lincoln: University of Nebraska Press, 2006).

29. Ellen Beasley, *The Alleys and Back Buildings of Galveston: An Architectural and Social History* (College Station: Texas A&M University Press, 2001); Michelle M. Mears, *And Grace Will Lead Me Home: African American Freedmen Communities of Austin, Texas* (Lubbock: Texas Tech University Press, 2009); Alwyn Barr, "African-American Housing and Health Patterns in Southwestern Cities, 1865–1900," in *This Corner of*

Canaan: Essays on Texas in Honor of Randolph B. Campbell, ed. Richard B. McCaslin, Donald E. Chipman, and Andrew J. Torget (Denton: University of North Texas Press, 2013), 265–91.

30. Clyde McQueen, *Black Churches in Texas: A Guide to Historic Congregations* (College Station: Texas A&M University Press, 2000); Marvin C. Griffin, *Texas African American Baptists: The Story of the Baptist General Convention of Texas* (Austin: Publisher's Marketing House, 1994); Joe Early, Jr., "Israel Campbell: The Father of Black Texas Baptists," *Baptist History and Heritage* 39 (Summer-Fall 2004): 98–102, and "Richard Henry Boyd: Shaper of Black Baptist Identity," *Baptist History and Heritage* 42 (Summer-Fall 2007): 91–104; Alwyn Barr, "Black Urban Churches on the Southern Frontier, 1865–1900," *Journal of Negro History* 82 (Fall 1997): 368–83; James M. Davidson, "Rituals Captured in Context and Time: Charm Use in North Dallas Freedman's Town (1869–1907), Dallas, Texas," *Historical Archaeology* 38, no. 2 (2004): 22–54.

31. Debra A. Reid, *Reaping a Greater Harvest: African Americans, the Extension Service, and Rural Reform in Jim Crow Texas* (College Station: Texas A&M University Press, 2007); "Racism and Sexism in Rural Texas: The Contested Nature of Progressive Rural Reform, 1870s–1910s," in Reid, *Seeking Inalienable Rights*, 37–57; "African Americans and Land Loss in Texas: Government Duplicity and Discrimination Based on Race and Class," *Agricultural History* 77 (Spring 2003): 258–92; and "Furniture Exempt from Seizure: African American Farm Families and Their Property in Texas," *Agricultural History* 80 (Summer 2006): 336–57; Eddie Stimpson, Jr., *My Remembers: A Black Sharecropper's Recollections of the Depression*, ed. James W. Byrd (Denton: University of North Texas Press, 1996); Rebecca Sharpless, *Fertile Ground, Narrow Choices: Women on Texas Cotton Farms, 1900–1940* (Chapel Hill: University of North Carolina Press, 1998).

32. Bernadette Pruitt, "'For the Advancement of the Race': The Great Migration to Houston, Texas, 1914–1941," *Journal of Urban History* 31 (May 2005): 435–78; Ernest Obadele-Starks, *Black Unionism in the Industrial South* (College Station: Texas A&M University Press, 2000); Clifford Farrington, *Biracial Unions on Galveston's Waterfront, 1865–1925* (Austin: Texas State Historical Association, 2007); Gregg Andrews, "Black Working-Class Political Activism and Biracial Unionism: Galveston Longshoremen in Jim Crow Texas, 1919–1921," *Journal of Southern History* 74 (Aug. 2008): 627–68; Joseph Abel, "African American Labor Unions and the Struggle for Fair Employment in the Aircraft Manufacturing Industry of Texas, 1941–1945," *Journal of Southern History* 77 (Aug. 2011): 595–638; Rebecca Sharpless, *Cooking in Other Women's Kitchens: Domestic Workers in the South, 1865–1960* (Chapel Hill: University of North Carolina Press, 2010); Judith W. Linsley, "Main House, Carriage House: African-American Domestic Employees at the McFaddin-Ward House in Beaumont, Texas, 1900–1950," *Southwestern Historical Quarterly* 103 (July 1999), 17–51.

33. Maceo Crenshaw Dailey, Jr., "The Business Life of Emmett Jay Scott," *Business History Review* 77 (Winter 2003): 667–86; Shennette Garrett-Scott, "'The Hope of the South': The New Century Cotton Mill of Dallas, Texas, and the Business of Race in the New South, 1902–1907," *Southwestern Historical Quarterly* 116 (Oct. 2012): 139–66; Keith Volanto, "The Life and Work of Dr. Beadie Eugene Conner: African American Physician in Jim Crow Texas," *Southwestern Historical Quarterly* 115 (Jan. 2012): 259–80.

34. William H. Wilson, *Hamilton Park: A Planned Black Community in Dallas* (Baltimore: Johns Hopkins University Press, 1998); Kenneth Mason, *African Americans and Race Relations in San Antonio, Texas, 1867–1937* (New York: Garland, 1998); Howard Beeth and Cary D. Wintz, eds., *Black Dixie: Afro-Texan History and Culture in Houston* (College Station: Texas A&M University Press, 1992); Bob Ray Sanders, *Calvin Littlejohn: Portrait of a Community in Black and White* (Fort Worth: Texas Christian University Press, 2009).

35. Charles F. Robinson II, "Legislated Love in the Lone Star State: Texas and Miscegenation," *Southwestern Historical Quarterly* 108 (July 2004): 65–86; see also Robinson, *Dangerous Liaisons: Sex and Love in the Segregated South* (Fayetteville: University of Arkansas Press, 2003).

36. Peggy B. Gill, "Community, Commitment, and African American Education: The Jackson School of Smith County, Texas, 1925–1954," *Journal of African American History* 87 (Spring 2002): 256–68; Gail Beil, "Wiley College: The Great Debaters," *East Texas Historical Journal* 46, no. 1 (2008): 18–26; "James Leonard Farmer: Texas' First African American Ph.D.," *East Texas Historical Journal* 36, no. 1 (1998): 18–25; and "Melvin Tolson: Texas Radical," *East Texas Historical Journal* 40 (Spring 2002): 26–36.

37. Edward J. Robinson, *The Fight Is on in Texas: A History of African American Churches of Christ in the Lone Star State, 1865–2000* (Abilene: Abilene Christian University Press, 2008); Karen Kossie-Chernyshev, "Constructing Good Success: The Church of God in Christ and Social Uplift in East Texas, 1910–1935," *East Texas Historical Journal* 44 (Spring 2006): 49–55.

38. Rob Fink, *Playing in Shadows: Texas and Negro League Baseball* (Lubbock: Texas Tech University Press, 2010); Robert Charles Cottrell, *The Best Pitcher in Baseball: The Life of Rube Foster, Negro League Giant* (New York: New York University Press, 2001); Bob Luke, *Willie Wells: "El Diablo" of the Negro Leagues* (Austin: University of Texas Press, 2007); Jerry Craft and Kathleen Sullivan, *Our White Boy* (Lubbock: Texas Tech University Press, 2010); Rob Fink, "Community Pride, the 'New Negro' and Black College Football in the 1920s," in *Lone Star Legacy: African American History in Texas*, ed. Delitia Daniels (Houston: Aquarius Press, 2011), 92–100.

39. Gary Hartman, *The History of Texas Music* (College Station: Texas A&M University Press, 2008); Dave Oliphant, *Texan Jazz* (Austin: University of Texas Press, 1996); Alan B. Govenar and Jay F. Brakefield, *Deep Ellum and Central Track: Where the Black and White Worlds of Dallas Converged* (Denton: University of North Texas Press, 1998); Roger Wood, *Texas Zydeco* (Austin: University of Texas Press, 2006); Glen Alyn, *I Say Me for a Parable: The Oral Autobiography of Mance Lipscomb, Texas Bluesman* (New York: Da Capo Press, 1993); Kip Lornell and Charles Wolfe, *The Life and Legend of Leadbelly* (New York: HarperCollins, 1992); Alan B. Govenar, "That Black Snake Moan: The Music and Mystery of Blind Lemon Jefferson," in *Bluesland: Portraits of Twelve Major African American Blues Masters*, ed. Pete Welding and Toby Bryon (New York: Penguin, 1991), 16–37.

40. Francis E. Abernethy, ed., *Juneteenth Texas: Essays in African-American Folklore.* Publications of the Texas Folklore Society 54 (Denton: University of North Texas Press, 1996); Sherilyn Brandenstein, "Prominent Roles of Black Womanhood in *Sepia Record,*

1952–1954" (Master's thesis, University of Texas at Austin, 1989); Lou Halsell Rodenberger, "A Developing Tradition: African-American Writers," in *Texas Women Writers: A Tradition of Their Own*, ed. Sylvia Ann Grider and Lou Halsell Rodenberger (College Station: Texas A&M University Press, 1997), 247–52; Bernice Love Wiggins, *Tuneful Tales*, 2nd ed. (Lubbock: Texas Tech University Press, 2002); William Loren Katz, "Sutton E. Griggs: A Black Son of Texas Lifts His Pen," in *Black People Who Made the Old West* (Trenton, N.J.: African World Press, 1992), 170–74; Gabriel Briggs, "Imperium In Imperio: Sutton Griggs, the New Negro of the South," *Southern Quarterly* 45 (Spring 2008): 153–76; Maria Karafalis, "Oratory, Embodiment, and U.S. Citizenship in Sutton E. Griggs' *Imperium in Imperio*," *African American Review* 40 (Spring 2006): 125–43.

41. Alvia J. Wardlaw, *The Art of John Biggers: View from the Upper Room* (Houston: Museum of Fine Arts, 1995); Alan B. Govenar, *Portraits of Community: African-American Photography in Texas* (Austin: Texas State Historical Association, 1996).

42. Doris L. Rich, *Queen Bess: Daredevil Aviator* (Washington, D.C.: Smithsonian Institution Press, 1993); Elizabeth A. H. Freydberg, *Bessie Coleman: The Brownskin Lady Bird* (New York: Garland, 1994).

43. Patricia Bernstein, *The First Waco Horror: The Lynching of Jesse Washington and the Rise of the NAACP* (College Station: Texas A&M University Press, 2005); Monte Akers, *Flames after Midnight: Murder, Vengeance, and the Desolation of a Texas Community* (Austin: University of Texas Press, 1999); Bill Stein, "Colorado County Protects Womanhood: The Murder of Geraldine Kollman and the Subsequent Lynching of the Accused," *Southwestern Historical Quarterly* 108 (Apr. 2005): 440–66; Robert Perkinson, *Texas Tough: The Rise of America's Prison Empire* (New York: Metropolitan, 2010); Patricia E. Gower, "The Price of Exclusion: Dallas Municipal Policy and the Impact on African Americans," *East Texas Historical Journal* 39, no. 1 (2001): 43–54.

44. Garna L. Christian, *Black Soldiers in Jim Crow Texas, 1899–1917* (College Station: Texas A&M University Press, 1995); James N. Leiker, *Racial Borders: Black Soldiers along the Rio Grande* (College Station: Texas A&M University Press, 2002); John D. Weaver, *The Senator and the Sharecropper's Son: Exoneration of the Brownsville Soldiers* (College Station: Texas A&M University Press, 1997).

45. Howard Beeth, "A Black Elite Agenda in the Urban South: The Call for Political and Racial Economic Solidarity in Houston during the 1920s," *Essays in Economic and Business History* 10 (June 1992): 41–55, and "How to Resist? Reformism or Communism in Houston's Black Press during the 1920s," in *Bringing the World Together: Proceedings of the National Association of African American Studies* (1996): 62–82; Bruce A. Glasrud, "Early Black Nationalist Movements in Texas," *Journal of Big Bend Studies* 11 (1999): 159–69; Theodore M. Lawe, "Racial Politics in Dallas in the Twentieth Century," *East Texas Historical Journal* 46, no. 2 (2008): 27–41; Merline Pitre, *In Struggle against Jim Crow: Lulu B. White and the NAACP, 1900–1957* (College Station: Texas A&M University Press, 1999), and "Texas and the Master Civil Rights Narrative: A Case Study of Black Females in Houston," *Southwestern Historical Quarterly* 116 (Oct. 2012): 125–37; Stefanie Decker, "Women in the Civil Rights Movement: Juanita Craft versus the Dallas Elite," *East Texas Historical Journal* 39, no. 1 (2001): 33–42; W. Marvin Dulaney, "The Progressive Voters' League: A Political Voice for African Americans in Dallas," *Legacies* 3 (Spring 1991), 27–35.

46. Darlene Clark Hine, *Black Victory: The Rise and Fall of the White Primary in Texas*, 2nd ed. (Columbia: University of Missouri Press, 2003); Charles L. Zelden, *The Battle for the Black Ballot: Smith v. Allwright, and the Defeat of the Texas All-White Primary* (Lawrence: University Press of Kansas, 2004).

47. Mary Beth Rogers, *Barbara Jordan: American Hero* (New York: Bantam Books, 1998); Max Sherman, ed., *Barbara Jordan: Speaking the Truth with Eloquent Thunder* (Austin: University of Texas Press, 2007); Nancy Baker Jones and Ruthe Winegarten, *Capitol Women: Texas Female Legislators, 1923–1999* (Austin: University of Texas Press, 2000).

48. Ruth P. Morgan, *Governance by Decree: The Impact of the Voting Rights Act in Dallas* (Lawrence: University Press of Kansas, 2004).

49. Gary M. Lavergne, *Before Brown: Heman Marion Sweatt, Thurgood Marshall, and the Long Road to Justice* (Austin: University of Texas Press, 2010); Richard B. McCaslin, "Steadfast in His Intent: John W. Hargis and the Integration of the University of Texas at Austin," *Southwestern Historical Quarterly* 95 (July 1991): 21–41; Dwonna Goldstone, *Integrating the 40 Acres: The 50-Year Struggle for Racial Equality at the University of Texas* (Athens: University of Georgia Press, 2006); Amilcar Shabazz, *Advancing Democracy: African Americans and the Struggle for Access and Equity in Higher Education in Texas* (Chapel Hill: University of North Carolina Press, 2004); Ronald E. Marcello, "Reluctance versus Reality: The Desegregation of North Texas State College, 1954–1956," *Southwestern Historical Quarterly* 100 (Oct. 1996): 153–85.

50. Robin Duff Ladino, *Desegregating Texas Schools: Eisenhower, Shivers, and the Crisis at Mansfield High* (Austin: University of Texas Press, 1996); Glenn Linden, *Desegregating Schools in Dallas* (Dallas: Three Forks Press, 1995); Gerald S. McCorkle, "Busing Comes to Dallas Schools," *Southwestern Historical Quarterly* 111 (Jan. 2008): 304–33; William Henry Keller, *Make Haste Slowly: Moderates, Conservatives, and School Desegregation in Houston* (College Station: Texas A&M University Press, 1999); Bryan L. Smith, "Desegregation in West Texas: The United States v. Ector County ISD Case," *West Texas Historical Association Year Book* 69 (1993): 59–73; Tina M. Kibbe, "School Desegregation in Port Arthur: The Battle between the Community, the Board, and the Justice Department," *East Texas Historical Journal* 44, no. 2 (2006): 3–16; Chris Danielson, "Doing as Little as the Law Requires: School Desegregation in Baytown, Texas," *Southern History* 24 (Spring 2003): 16–28; Blake Killingsworth, "'Here I Am, Stuck in the Middle with You': *The Baptist Standard*, Texas Baptist Leadership, and School Desegregation, 1954–1956," *Baptist History and Heritage* 41 (Spring 2006): 78–92; David K. Chrisman, "Religious Moderates and Race: The Texas Christian Life Commission and the Call for Racial Reconciliation, 1954–68," in Reid, *Seeking Inalienable Rights*, 97–121; Blanche Henderson Brick, "William Morris Ford, "Pastor of First Baptist Church, Longview, Texas and the Southern Baptist View of Race Relations, 1945–1971," *East Texas Historical Journal* 41 (Spring 2003): 53–60; Estelle Owens, "Maximum Christianity, Applied as well as Advocated, One Good Man vs. Racism," *Baptist History and Heritage* 38 (Summer/Fall 2003): 35–40.

51. William S. Osburn, "Curtains for Jim Crow: Law, Race, and the Texas Railroads," *Southwestern Historical Quarterly* 105 (Jan. 2002): 393–427; Robert J. Robertson, *Fair Ways: How Six Black Golfers Won Civil Rights in Beaumont, Texas* (College Station: Texas A&M University Press, 2005); Darwin Payne, *Quest for Justice: Louis A. Bedford Jr.*

and the Struggle for Equal Rights in Texas (Dallas: Southern Methodist University Press, 2009); Brian D. Behnken, "The 'Dallas Way': Protest, Response, and the Civil Rights Experience in Big D and Beyond," *Southwestern Historical Quarterly* 111 (July 2007): 1–29; Thomas Cole, *No Color Is My Kind: The Life of Eldrewey Stearns and the Integration of Houston* (Austin: University of Texas Press, 1997); F. Kenneth Jensen, "The Houston Sit-In Movement of 1960–61," in Beeth and Wintz, *Black Dixie*, 211–22; Martin Kuhlman, "Direct Action at the University of Texas during the Civil Rights Movement, 1960–1965," *Southwestern Historical Quarterly* 98 (Apr. 1995): 550–66; Carolyn Jones, *Volma . . . My Journey: One Man's Impact on the Civil Rights Movement in Austin, Texas* (Austin: Eakin Press, 1998); Donald Seals, Jr., "The Wiley-Bishop Student Movement: A Case Study in the 1960 Civil Rights Sit-Ins," *Southwestern Historical Quarterly* 106 (Jan. 2003): 419–40; Gail K. Beil, "Four Marshallites' Roles in the Passage of the Civil Rights Act of 1964," *Southwestern Historical Quarterly* 106 (July 2002): 1–29.

52. Dwight Watson, *Race and the Houston Police Department, 1930–1990* (College Station: Texas A&M University Press, 2005).

53. Michael R. Botson, Jr., *Labor, Civil Rights, and the Hughes Tool Company* (College Station: Texas A&M University Press, 2005); Ernest Obadele-Starks, "Black Texans and Theater Crafts Unionism: The Struggle for Racial Equality," *Southwestern Historical Quarterly* 106 (Apr. 2003): 533–48; William S. Clayson, *Freedom Is Not Enough: The War on Poverty and the Civil Rights Movement in Texas* (Austin: University of Texas Press, 2010); Wesley G. Phelps, "National Ideal Meets Local Reality: The Grassroots War on Poverty in Houston," in McCaslin, Chipman, and Torget, *This Corner of Canaan*, 385–402.

54. Charles S. Martin, *Benching Jim Crow: The Rise and Fall of the Color Line in Southern College Sports, 1890–1980* (Champaign: University of Illinois Press, 2010); Francine Sanders Romero, "'There Are Only White Champions': The Rise and Demise of Segregated Boxing in Texas," *Southwestern Historical Quarterly* 108 (July 2004): 27–41.

55. Neil Foley, *Quest for Equality: The Failed Promise of Black-Brown Solidarity* (Cambridge: Harvard University Press, 2010); Brian D. Behnken, *Fighting Their Own Battles: Mexican Americans, African Americans, and the Struggle for Civil Rights in Texas* (Chapel Hill: University of North Carolina Press, 2011); Emilio Zamora, *Claiming Rights and Righting Wrongs: Mexican Workers and Job Politics during World War II* (College Station: Texas A&M University Press, 2009); Cynthia E. Orozco, *No Mexicans, Women, or Dogs Allowed: The Rise of the Mexican American Civil Rights Movement* (Austin: University of Texas Press, 2009).

56. Roger Wood, *Down in Houston: Bayou City Blues* (Austin: University of Texas Press, 2003).

57. Alwyn Barr, "The Influence of War and Military Service on African Texans," in *Texans and War: New Interpretations of the State's Military History*, ed. Alexander Mendoza and Charles David Grear (College Station: Texas A&M University Press, 2012), 97–112; and Ronald E. Goodwin, "Black Paradox in the Age of Terrorism: Military Patriotism or Higher Education?" in Mendoza and Grear, *Texans and War*, 283–99.

58. Nate Blakeslee, *Tulia: Race, Cocaine, and Corruption in a Small Texas Town* (New York: Public Affairs, 2005); Ricardo Ainslie, *Long Dark Road: Bill King and Murder in Jasper, Texas* (Austin: University of Texas Press, 2004).

59. Among the better Texas history textbooks and general histories are these: Rupert N. Richardson, Adrian Anderson, Cary D. Wintz, and Ernest Wallace, *Texas: The Lone Star State*, 10th ed. (Upper Saddle River, N.J.: Prentice Hall, 2010); Robert A. Calvert, Arnoldo De León, and Gregg Cantrell, *The History of Texas*, 5th ed. (Wheeling, Ill.: Harlan Davidson); Jesús F. de la Teja, Paula Marks, and Ron Tyler, *Texas: Crossroads of North America* (Boston: Houghton Mifflin, 2003); Randolph B. Campbell, *Gone to Texas: A History of the Lone Star State*, 2nd ed. (New York: Oxford University Press, 2012); Kenneth Howell, Keith J. Volanto, Charles D. Grear, James M. Smallwood, and Jennifer S. Lawrence, *Beyond Myths and Legends: A Narrative History of Texas*, 2nd ed. (Wheaton, Ill.: Abigail Press).

CHAPTER 4

Texas Women

Rebecca Sharpless

The field of Texas women's history has matured significantly since the late 1980s. As Ann Patton Malone predicted in a 1988 essay about women in Light Cummins and Alvin Bailey's *Guide to the History of Texas*, research has continued in familiar historiographical paths but with increased vigor and sophistication. The best of Texas women's history reflects the larger trends in women's history in general, based in theory and with increased analysis of the complexity of women's experiences. Fane Downs, writing in 1991, titled her historiographical essay "Texas Women: History at the Edges," but even then women's history was beginning to command increased attention in the Lone Star State. The Texas State Historical Association (TSHA) spurred interest in women's history for the revised edition of the *Handbook of Texas*, sponsoring a conference, "Women and Texas History," in 1990. The conference, with thirty-two paper sessions and a keynote address by historian Elizabeth Fox-Genovese, resulted in a volume, *Women and Texas History*. Generally clustered around the themes of women and reform, work, and literature, the thirteen essays constituted the first collection written by professionally trained historians. In 1992 the TSHA, at the behest of Ellen Clarke Temple, created the Liz Carpenter Award for the best book on Texas women's history, and it has been awarded annually since, testifying to the growing interest in and vibrancy of the field.[1]

Since the Malone and Downs essays, historiographical studies of Texas women have increased. The TSHA issued *Women and Texas History: An Archival Bibliography* in conjunction with a 1990 conference. In 1995 Elizabeth Snapp and

Harry F. Snapp compiled a 1,000-page bibliography, *Read All about Her! Texas Women's History*, from newspaper articles and collections of papers. Women are included in Michael Phillips's chapter "Why Is Big Tex Still a White Cowboy?" in *Beyond Texas through Time*. Linda Hudson's "Uppity Women Rise Up and Have Breakfast" documents women's experience in the East Texas Historical Association. Susie Kelly Flatau's "Texas Women" profiles the work of historians Cindy Weigand, Lou Halsell Rodenberger, and Ruthe Winegarten. Judith McArthur and Harold Smith examine the twentieth century in *Texas through Women's Eyes*, with documents and extensive bibliography. Two female historians, Llerena Friend and Ruthe Winegarten, appear in *Writing the Story of Texas*.[2]

Native, Spanish, and Mexican women in Texas have received rare but excellent attention. Juliana Barr looks at the ways French, Spanish, and Native men traded women as slaves to cement their diplomatic relationships in "From Captives to Slaves." Barr's monograph *Peace Came in the Form of a Woman* argues that gender constituted the crux of Spanish-Indian diplomacy in eighteenth-century Texas. Work on the Spanish colonial period highlights the unique position of women under Spanish law. In *Notable Men and Women of Spanish Texas*, Donald Chipman and Harriett Denise Joseph present an overview of women's "rigors, responsibilities, and rights" in the Spanish colonial era. Patricia Garza de León, whose family settled the town of Victoria, is included in *De León: A Tejano Family History* by Ana Carolina Castillo Crimm. Jean Stuntz, in *Hers, His, and Theirs* and "Spanish Laws for Texas Women," contrasts the legal rights of women under Spanish law with those under English common law. Amy Meschke Porter argues that local conditions (such as high rates of widowhood) led to changes in gender roles in Spanish Texas. Mary L. Scheer edited *Women in the Texas Revolution*, a collection of eight essays investigating the activities of groups of women during the war.[3]

During the transitional period between Mexican independence and the end of the Civil War, women from the American South found themselves in unknown physical and emotional territory in Texas. Mark Carroll in *Homesteads Ungovernable* uses the evolving body of law to examine power in families and households. Robin C. Sager compares Texas women's conditions with those in other regions in "States of Suffering: Marital Cruelty in Antebellum Virginia, Texas, and Wisconsin." Angela Boswell finds that southern ideals regarding womanhood came with the settlers, both black and white, in Colorado County in *Her Act and Deed*. Adrienne Caughfield's *True Women and Westward Expansion* considers the transmission of domesticity to Texas and concludes that

Anglo women benefited from notions of manifest destiny whereas Indians, Hispanics, and African American women almost always suffered from it. Harriette Andreadis also looks at the emotional impact of migration as seen in women's diaries, finding boredom, loneliness, and depression in her article "True Womanhood Revisited."[4]

Little exists on slave women in Texas, the exception being Angela Boswell's "Black Women in Slavery to 1865" in *Black Women in Texas History*. Three biographies—Paula Mitchell Marks, *Turn Your Eyes toward Texas*; Linda S. Hudson, *Mistress of Manifest Destiny;* and Light Townsend Cummins, *Emily Austin of Texas*—personalize the events of this period through well-connected Anglo women. Institution building also receives attention. M. Monica LaFleur's article "They Ventured to Texas: The European Heritage of Women Religious in the Nineteenth Century," describes the activities of European Roman Catholic nuns from 1847 to 1882, including nursing the sick during outbreaks of yellow fever and the establishment of schools, hospitals, orphanages, and homes for the elderly. Angela Boswell, in "The Meaning of Participation," examines the role of piety in both constraining and liberating white women.[5]

The topic of women in Civil War Texas is just beginning to receive its scholarly due, with a dissertation and book of essays in progress. The impact of Reconstruction on women has also received little attention save for James M. Smallwood and Barry A. Crouch's essay "Texas Freedwomen during Reconstruction" in *Black Women in Texas History.*[6]

Several studies portray social change in the mid-nineteenth century. Florence C. Gould and Patricia N. Pando, in *Claiming Their Land*, present a "first picture" of 1,481 female heads of families and single women who claimed homesteads in Texas between 1845 and 1898. In *Women and the Creation of Urban Life*, Elizabeth York Enstam reveals the importance of Dallas women's work in creating the social and cultural infrastructure and public institutions and agencies. Margaret Breashears in her 1996 dissertation argues that, with regard to immigration and employment, the status of women in Texas showed no dramatic changes between 1860 and 1920. Sally Kitch in *This Strange Society of Women* analyzes the Belton Sanctificationists, a group of fifty women who banded together for religion and economic benefit. Beverly Rowe examines the increasing access of women to education, club work, employment, leisure, and health care in Texarkana between 1880 to 1920. An essay by Rebecca Sharpless, "'Us Has Ever Lived de Useful Life,'" examines the lives and work of late nineteenth-century African American women as Jim Crow laws solidified.[7]

In the last quarter of the nineteenth century, Texas women, like their counterparts everywhere else in the United States, began to unite in common cause to reform the excesses of the period. Women often started their public careers in women's clubs, became outspoken during the Progressive Era, and ended up as suffragists because of their frustration with being disfranchised. Much of the writing of Texas women's history began with this period, due in no small part to the thorough record keeping by the women themselves. An important early overview was Megan Seaholm's "Earnest Women: The White Woman's Club Movement in Progressive Era Texas, 1880–1920." Audrey Crawford's article on African American clubwomen in Houston presents an overview of the Bayou City. Cynthia Morales examines religious groups and benevolent organizations for women in San Antonio as well as professional and labor groups. Adriana Ayala considers the cooperation between Mexican American and Anglo women in San Antonio during the 1920s. Ruth Karbach's "The Modern Woman" examines the Fort Worth Federation of Women's Clubs.[8]

Women banded together for a wide variety of purposes. Kelly McMichael Stott researched the United Daughters of the Confederacy for "From Lost Cause to Female Empowerment." Women in Texas worked diligently for birth control, particularly through Planned Parenthood, as detailed in Harold L. Smith's article on the origins of the movement in Texas in the 1930s and 1940s. Pam Wille studied the early twentieth-century development of the Young Women's Christian Association in Houston. Kate S. Kirkland focused on the philanthropic efforts of Houstonian Ima Hogg. In *Call Her a Citizen*, Kelley King documents the career of tireless Austin clubwoman Anna J. H. Pennybacker. Two essays in *Grace and Gumption* consider the topic of philanthropy: Ruth McAdams's "Mudholes, Fairy Godmothers, and Choir Bells," and Sherrie S. McLeRoy's "In the Interest of the Children."[9]

In the late nineteenth and early twentieth centuries, large numbers of tireless American women took part in wide-ranging organized discussions and activities to improve society. As elsewhere in the United States, Texas women moved from their volunteer activities into lobbying for social reform. In *Creating the New Woman*, Judith N. McArthur details female-inspired efforts to improve conditions for women and children through a variety of avenues. In *Women, Culture, and Community*, Elizabeth Hayes Turner examines ways that Galveston women worked from the 1880s to the 1920s through their homes and churches into civic activism and then suffrage, with added impetus from the Great Storm of 1900. Bruce Glasrud's article "Time of Transition" considers the ways that African American women coped with the deep racism of the period. Elizabeth York Enstam focuses on Dallas in "They Called It 'Motherhood'" and "The Forgotten Frontier: Dallas Women and Social Caring, 1895–1920," as does Jackie McElhaney in "Save the Babies: Blanche Greenburg and the Milk Stations."[10]

Other studies have detailed the activities of individual Progressive women. James D. Ivy examines the divisive effects of suffragist Frances Willard's tour of the state on Texas prohibitionists. Sylvia Hunt writes about schoolteacher and feminist Sue Huffman Brady in "Throw Aside the Veil of Helplessness." Jacquelyn Masur McElhaney outlines in *Pauline Periwinkle and Progressive Reform in Dallas* the influence of journalist Isadore Miner Callaway, as she does in an article, "Pauline Periwinkle: Prodding Dallas into the Progressive Era," in *Women and Texas History*. Other articles in that volume outline women's work in combating particular social ills: Paul M. Lucko on women prison reformers and Judith N. McArthur on women against child labor. Ann R. Gabbert considers the existence of prostitution in El Paso from 1890 until 1920. Ruth Karbach analyzes Fort Worth women in the temperance movement, and Hollace Ava Weiner analyzes the efforts of Jewish Fort Worth women to help immigrants.[11]

From reform efforts, moving into politics was an easy step for women. Marion Barthelme introduced and annotated the letters of one group in *Women in the Texas Populist Movement*. A larger number became involved with the struggle for the vote. Kevin Motl investigated the suffrage movement in its rural manifestations in "A Time for Reform." Jessica Brannon-Wranosky contextualizes the Texas movement in "Southern Promise and Necessity." Local studies include Elizabeth York Enstam's "Dallas Equal Suffrage Association"; Elizabeth Hayes Turner's "'White-Gloved Ladies' and 'New Women' in the Texas Woman Suffrage Movement"; Janelle D. Scott's "Local Leadership in the Woman Suffrage Movement," on Houston; and Jessica Brannon-Wranosky's "Investing in Urban," a study of Corpus Christi. In "From Antisuffragism to Anti-Communism," Elna C. Green looks at Ida Darden, who edited a conservative newspaper from her Fort Worth home.[12]

Besides the well-documented labor struggles, little exists on women in the Great Depression save for Yolanda Chavez Leyva, "Faithful Hard-Working Mexican Hands," and Rebecca Sharpless, "Women and Work in Texas during the Great Depression."[13] World War II is better documented. Tanya Kraus Randall's article on Texas ranch women explains the hardships the war caused females working in the Texas livestock industry. Investigations of women in

Texas industry during the war include Gary Rabalais's article dealing with female refinery workers at Baytown and Sandra D. Harvey's dissertation on women as war workers in Waco. Clarice F. Pollard's "WAACs in Texas during the Second World War" provides a good overview of military activity.[14]

Texas women played important roles in the long civil rights movement. An overview is Stefanie Decker's essay "African American Women in the Civil Rights Era, 1954–1974." Three articles focus on the work of Roman Catholic women and the establishment of schools for African Americans: Anne M. Butler, "Building Justice," which details the work of a Catholic philanthropist in San Antonio; Richard Fossey and Stephanie Morris, "Courage under Fire," examining the response of the Sisters of the Blessed Sacrament to the Ku Klux Klan; and Amanda Bresie, "One Bread, One Body," considering the challenge by the Sisters of the Blessed Sacrament to established racial norms. June M. Steele's "Edward Struggs and Mae Simmons" outlines the struggles for equality on the Llano Estacado.[15]

Merline Pitre analyzes the life of Houston activist Lulu B. White, who was instrumental in two key Supreme Court cases, in *In Struggle against Jim Crow* and "Lulu B. White and the Civil Rights Movement in Houston." Richard W. Byrd's "Interracial Cooperation in a Decade of Conflict" examines the joint work of African American and white women in the 1960s. Rachel Northington Burrow considers the life of Juanita Craft. Lewis L. Gould and Melissa R. Sneed wrote about Barbara Smith, who was denied by the University of Texas the lead role in an opera because of her race. Two essays by Mary Ellen Curtin about the career of Barbara Jordan examine the ongoing difficulties of the first African American woman to serve in the Texas legislature. Anna Victoria Wilson and William E. Seagall, in *Oh! Do I Remember*, chronicles the desegregation of the Austin Independent School District.[16]

Gabriela González explores political activism across the Rio Grande in "Two Flags Entwined," and Cynthia E. Orozco analyzes gender and women's political participation in *No Mexicans, Women, or Dogs Allowed* and "Regionalism, Politics, and Gender in Southwest History." Mary Ann Villareal's article on Marta Cotera examines the work of the author and activist. The social ministry of religious women to Mexican Texans is the topic of Roberto R. Treviño's "Facing Jim Crow."[17]

In Texas, as elsewhere, women provide the backbone of most Christian churches and their work. A dissertation by Eve Carr examines Methodist women's missionary work to bring health care to El Paso. In "Like Water to the Body," Lois E. Myers considers the importance of women to the survival of rural churches. Elizabeth H. Flowers's *Into the Pulpit* analyzes the roles of Southern Baptist women in the struggle over fundamentalism.[18]

The women's movement in Texas has received slight scholarly attention. Rob Fink's article on Hermine Tobolowsky considers the topic of equal rights and the fight for legislation to implement it. Sherilyn Brandenstein examines the *Sepia Record*, a Texas-based periodical and its prescriptions for African American women. Christopher Bean examines the role of Earl Rudder in admitting female students to Texas A&M University.[19]

Nineteenth-century courtship and marriage have been documented through correspondence and official records. Marilyn Ferris Motz, in "Thou Art My Last Love," examines the courtship of two Brazos Valley residents; the letters on which the article is based appear in the same issue of the *Southwestern Historical Quarterly*. Vicki Howard, with "The Courtship Letters of an African American Couple," considers the concerns of two African American schoolteachers in Brenham and Round Top.[20]

Works focusing on women within their families demonstrate the complexity of gender roles in Texas. In *I Would Rather Sleep in Texas*, Mary Margaret McAllen Amberson examines the roles of women in amassing land. In *Petra's Legacy*, Jane Clements Monday and Francis Brannen Vick detail the life and times of Petra Vela Kenedy. Lois E. Myers's *Letters by Lamplight* analyzes the life of Anna Louisa Wellington Stoner in Refugio and Victoria Counties. Francelle Pruitt Blum, conversely, focuses on how marriages could sour in "When Marriages Fail: Divorce in Nineteenth-Century Texas."[21]

Women holding elected office in Texas have received little scholarly attention. Shelley Sallee, in "The Woman of It," looks at the 1924 election of the first female governor in Texas, Miriam A. Ferguson, as does Nancy Beck Young in her article "Me for Ma." Democratic activist Minnie Fisher Cunningham is the topic of Patricia Ellen Cunningham's "Bonnet in the Ring"; Judith N. McArthur's "Minnie Fisher Cunningham's Back Door Lobby in Texas"; and McArthur and Harold L. Smith's *Minnie Fisher Cunningham*. Oveta Culp Hobby, the second woman to hold a federal cabinet-level position, is the subject of doctoral dissertations by Kelli Walsh and Robert T. Pando. Kate S. Kirkland, in "For All Houston's Children," looks at Ima Hogg's only elected office during a time of overcrowding and racial tension in the Houston schools. The life and career of federal judge Sarah Tilghman Hughes are the topic of Darwin Payne's *Indomitable Sarah*. The career of Ann Richards is documented in Sue Tolleson-Rinehart and Jeanie R. Stanley's *Claytie and the Lady*; Celia Morris's *Storming the Statehouse*; and Jan Reid's *Let the People In*.[22]

With "The Significance and Impact of Women on the Rise of the Republican Party in Twentieth Century Texas," Kristi Strickland looks at gender and party changes over time. *Capitol Women*, by Nancy Baker Jones and Ruthe Winegarten, features eighty-six biographical sketches of female legislators. Women in the statehouse are also the focus of Terry L. Gilmour's "A Difference" and of *Chicanas in Charge* by José Angel Gutiérrez and coauthors. Sharon A. Navarro has written on San Antonio legislator Letitia Van de Putte in *Latina Legislator*. Cindy C. Smolovik summarizes women's political activities in Fort Worth in her article "Braving the Smoke."[23]

Studies of women's work, either for wages or not, and their relationships to organized labor have ranged far and wide. Sylvia Hunt studies attitudes of teachers in "Challenging Patriarchy and Domesticity" and "Women Educators in Texas, 1840–1920" and looks at their family lives in "To Wed and to Teach." Debbie Mauldin Cottrell has documented the contributions of Annie Webb Blanton, the first woman elected to statewide office, in *Pioneer Woman Educator* and "Professional, Feminine, and Feminist." Brenda Taylor Matthews analyzes the roles of the Sisters of Saint Mary of Namur in Fort Worth education in "Ladies of Victory." Virginia Spurlin describes the career of African American teacher and home economist Jeffie O. A. Conner. Gloria Duarte, in "Eva Camuñez's Teaching Career," looks at the experiences of a Hispanic woman on the Edwards Plateau.[24] Other aspects of women and work include varying experiences in the oil fields. With "Domesticity and the Texas Oil Fields," Diana Davids Olien explores women's more traditional roles, and Cynthia Devlin's "Twice Through the Glass Ceiling" considers petroleum "landman" and stockbroker Sue Birdwell-Alves. David C. Humphrey's "Prostitution in Texas" provides an overview from the 1830s to the 1960s. Richard F. Selcer's article "Fort Worth and the Fraternity of Strange Women" is a localized study of prostitution.[25]

Judith W. Linsley investigates the domestic workers of one of Beaumont's wealthiest families in "Main House, Carriage House." Rebecca Sharpless, in *Fertile Ground, Narrow Choices*, discusses the lives of women on Texas cotton farms and considers oral history interviews with them in "The Southern Majority." Deborah Wing-Leonard's "Figs, Flappers, and Fignolias" analyzes women's work in Angleton. Julia Kirk Blackwelder's *Stylin' Jim Crow* emphasizes the professional training of women in Houston.[26]

Women in the professions spread across Texas in the twentieth century. In "Medicine on the Blackland Prairie," Michelle M. Mears details the career of Temple physician Claudia Potter. Mary Lynn Irving's "Texas Women in Military Medicine" describes the careers of female veterans serving in the Temple veteran's hospital beginning in 1940. Ann R. Gabbert examines public health and the role on women in El Paso from 1881 to 1941. Troy Ainsworth describes the built environment in "Mabel Welch: El Paso's First Woman Architect," and Jennifer Ross-Nazzal explores women in the space program, including the first female astronauts. Carol Roark summarizes Fort Worth leaders in "Cracking the Glass Ceiling," and Katie Sherrod analyzes female journalists in "High-Heeled Times in the Newsroom."[27]

Labor struggles, particularly among Latinas, have been well documented. The textile industry is the topic of Irene Ledesma in her "Unlikely Strikers" and "Texas Newspapers and Chicana Workers' Activism" and in dissertations by Isaias McCaffery and Benjamin Marquez. The Farah strike in El Paso is covered by Emily Honig in "Women at Farah Revisited" and in Jennifer Rebecca Mata's "Creating a Critical Chicana Narrative." The Tex-Son strike of 1959 in San Antonio is examined by Lori A. Flores in "An Unladylike Strike Fashionably Clothed." The textile industry in Dallas is the focus of Robert S. Shelton's "Yankee Devils in Paradise?" and Patricia Evridge Hill's "Real Women and True Womanhood." In "Carolina Munguía and Emma Tenayuca," Gabriela González looks at the 1930s activities of women volunteers and union leaders in San Antonio. Other works on Tenayuca include Zaragosa Vargas's "Tejana Radical" and Julia Kirk Blackwelder's "Emma Tenayuca."[28]

Women on cattle ranches have enjoyed more attention than those on farms in the eastern part of the state. Sara R. Massey edited sixteen essays in *Texas Women on the Cattle Trails*, demonstrating that women's experiences varied from following their husbands to trailing their own cattle. Georgellen Burnett's *We Just Toughed It Out* depicts the lives of eight women on the Llano Estacado. The *West Texas Historical Association Yearbook* has published over time several articles on West Texas and ranch women, both as a group and as individuals. In "Ranch Women, Cowgirls, and Wildcatters," Judy Alter examines women in nontraditional western roles near Tarrant County.[29]

Writing on women and sport in Texas has been limited. Susan E. Cayleff's *Babe* provides an overview of the notable career of Babe Didrikson Zaharias. Mary Lou LeCompte's *Cowgirls of the Rodeo* and "Home on the Range" examine the professionalization of women's rodeo events, as does Renee Laegreid's *Riding Pretty*.[30]

Some studies focus on women with ethnicity as the primary lens. Ruthe Winegarten, in *Black Texas Women*, gives an overview from the 1840s. Phyllis Wonjou Allen summarizes the roles of African American women in Fort Worth in "These Women Lived!" Teresa Palomo Acosta and Ruthe Winegarten provide a survey of Tejanas from the colonial period to 2000 in *Las Tejanas*, and Julie Leininger Pycior's "Tejanas Navigating the 1920s" considers that decade. Sandra Guerra-Cline examines Mexican American women in one Fort Worth neighborhood in "The North Side, La Fundición, and El TP." German women are the subject of Lauren Ann Kattner's "Growing Up Female in New Braunfels," and Mary Fehler Knarr looks specifically at Lutheran German women in "Faith, Frauen, and the Formation of an Ethnic Identity." In *Undaunted*, Charles H. Russell chronicles the life of Elise Waerenskjold, who immigrated to East Texas from Scandinavia in 1847. Marc Sanders and Ruthe Winegarten trace the story of African American women in Dallas from slavery through the civil rights movement in *The Lives and Times of Black Dallas Women*.[31]

In the future, research on women and Texas will entail a continued search for sources and creative readings of known sources. The topics that merit further exploration are numerous, and the ongoing theorization and analysis will presumably expand. Women's experiences in Texas, as elsewhere, are complex and deserve careful consideration.

NOTES

1. Ann Patton Malone, "Women in Texas History," in *A Guide to the History of Texas*, ed. Light Townsend Cummins and Alvin R. Bailey, Jr. (Westport, Conn.: Greenwood Press, 1988), 123–36; Fane Downs, "Texas Women: History at the Edges," in *Texas through Time: Evolving Interpretations*, ed. Walter L. Buenger and Robert A. Calvert (College Station: Texas A&M University Press, 1991), 81–101; Fane Downs and Nancy Baker Jones, eds., *Women and Texas History: Selected Essays* (Austin: Texas State Historical Association, 1993).

2. Nancy Baker Jones and Debbie Mauldin Cottrell, *Women and Texas History: An Archival Bibliography* (Austin: Texas State Historical Association, 1990); Elizabeth Snapp and Harry F. Snapp, comps., *Read All about Her! Texas Women's History: A Working Bibliography* (Denton: Texas Woman's University Press, 1995); Michael Phillips, "Why Is Big Tex Still a White Cowboy? Race, Gender, and the 'Other Texans,'" in *Beyond Texas through Time: Breaking Away from Past Interpretations*, ed. Walter L. Buenger and Arnoldo De León (College Station: Texas A&M University Press, 2011), 125–78; Linda Hudson, "Uppity Women Rise Up and Have Breakfast: The East Texas Historical Association's Women's History Breakfast," *East Texas Historical Journal* 48 (2009): 48–60; Susie Kelly Flatau, "Texas Women: Their Work, Their Worth: Profiles of Cindy Weigand, Lou Halsell Rodenberger, and Ruthe Winegarten," *Sound Historian* 13 (2009): 13–22; Judith McArthur and Harold Smith, *Texas through Women's Eyes: The Twentieth-Century Experience* (Austin: University of Texas Press, 2010); Kenneth E. Hendrickson, Jr.,

"Llerena Friend," in *Writing the Story of Texas*, ed. Patrick L. Cox and Kenneth E. Hendrickson, Jr. (Austin: University of Texas Press, 2013), 85–98; and Nancy Baker Jones, "Ruthe Winegarten," in Cox and Hendrickson, *Writing the Story*, 223–60.

3. Juliana Barr, "From Captives to Slaves: Commodifying Indian Women in the Borderlands," *Journal of American History* 92 (June 2005): 19–46; Juliana Barr, *Peace Came in the Form of a Woman: Indians and Spaniards in the Texas Borderlands* (Chapel Hill: University of North Carolina Press, 2007); Donald Chipman and Harriett Denise Joseph, *Notable Men and Women of Spanish Texas* (Austin: University of Texas Press, 1999); Ana Carolina Castille Crimm, *De León: A Tejano Family History* (Austin: University of Texas Press, 2003); Jean Stuntz, *Hers, His, and Theirs: Community Property Law in Spain and Early Texas* (Lubbock: Texas Tech University Press, 2005); Jean Stuntz, "Spanish Laws for Texas Women: The Development of Marital Property Law to 1850," *Southwestern Historical Quarterly* 104 (Apr. 2001): 543–59; Amy Meschke Porter, "Women's Lives through Women's Wills in the Spanish and Mexican Borderlands, 1750–1846" (Ph.D. diss., Southern Methodist University, 2005); Mary L. Scheer, *Women in the Texas Revolution* (Denton: University of North Texas Press, 2012); the essays are by Lindy Eakin on Native women, Jean Stuntz on Tejanas, Angela Boswell on African American women, Scheer on Anglo-American women, Dora Guerra on women at the Alamo, Light Cummins on the Runaway Scrape, Jeffrey Dunn on the Battle of San Jacinto, and Laura McLemore on women and the commemoration of the revolution.

4. Mark Carroll, *Homesteads Ungovernable: Families, Sex, Race, and the Law in Frontier Texas, 1826–1860* (Austin: University of Texas Press, 2001); Robin C. Sager, "States of Suffering: Marital Cruelty in Antebellum Virginia, Texas, and Wisconsin" (Ph.D. diss., Rice University, 2012); Angela Boswell, *Her Act and Deed: Women's Lives in a Rural Southern County, 1837–1873* (College Station: Texas A&M University Press, 2001); Adrienne Caughfield, *True Women and Westward Expansion* (College Station: Texas A&M University Press, 2005); Harriette Andreadis, "True Womanhood Revisited: Women's Private Writing in Nineteenth-Century Texas," *Journal of the Southwest* 31 (Summer, 1989): 179–204.

5. Angela Boswell, "Black Women in Slavery to 1865," in *Black Women in Texas History*, ed. Bruce Glasrud and Merline Pitre (College Station: Texas A&M University Press, 2008), 13–37; Paula Mitchell Marks, *Turn Your Eyes toward Texas: Pioneers Sam and Mary Maverick* (College Station, Texas A&M University Press, 1989); Linda S. Hudson, *Mistress of Manifest Destiny: A Biography of Jane McManus Storm Cazneau, 1807–1878* (Austin: University of Texas Press, 2001); Light Townsend Cummins, *Emily Austin of Texas, 1795–1851* (Fort Worth: Texas Christian University Press, 2009); M. Monica LaFleur, "They Ventured to Texas: The European Heritage of Women Religious in the Nineteenth Century," *Catholic Southwest* 8 (1997): 45–64; Angela Boswell, "The Meaning of Participation: White Protestant Women in Antebellum Houston Churches," *Southwestern Historical Quarterly* 99 (July 1995): 26–47.

6. James M. Smallwood and Barry A. Crouch, "Texas Freedwomen during Reconstruction," in Glasrud and Merline Pitre, *Black Women in Texas History*, 38–72.

7. Florence C. Gould and Patricia N. Pando, *Claiming Their Land: Women Homesteaders in Texas* (El Paso: Texas Western Press, 1991); Elizabeth York Enstam,

Women and the Creation of Urban Life, Dallas, Texas, 1843–1920 (College Station: Texas A&M University Press, 1998); Margaret Breashears, "An Analysis of Status: Women in Texas, 1860–1920" (Ph.D. diss., University of North Texas, 1999); Sally Kitch, *This Strange Society of Women: Reading the Letters and Lives of the Woman's Commonwealth* (Columbus: Ohio State University Press, 1992); Beverly Rowe, "Changes in the Status of Texarkana, Texas, Women, 1880–1920" (Ph.D. diss., University of North Texas, 1999); Rebecca Sharpless, "'Us Has Ever Lived de Useful Life': African American Women in Texas, 1874–1900," in Glasrud and Pitre, *Black Women in Texas History*, 73–98.

8. Megan Seaholm, "Earnest Women: The White Woman's Club Movement in Progressive Era Texas, 1880–1920" (Ph.D. diss., Rice University, 1988); Audrey Crawford, "To Protect, to Feed, and to Give Momentum to Every Effort: African American Clubwomen in Houston, 1880–1910," *Houston Review of History and Culture* 1 (2003):15–23; Cynthia Morales, "A Survey of Leadership, Activism, and Community Involvement of Mexican American Women in San Antonio, 1920–1940," *Journal of South Texas* 13 (Fall 2000): 193–206; Adriana Ayala, "Negotiating Race Relations through Activism: Women Activists and Women's Organizations in San Antonio, Texas during the 1920s" (Ph.D. diss., University of Texas at Austin, 2006); Ruth Karbach, "The Modern Woman," in *Grace and Gumption: Stories of Fort Worth Women*, ed. Katie Sherrod (Fort Worth: Texas Christian University Press, 2007), 63–86.

9. Kelly McMichael Stott, "From Lost Cause to Female Empowerment: The Texas Division of the United Daughters of the Confederacy, 1896–1966" (Ph.D. diss., University of North Texas, 2001); Harold L. Smith, "'All Good Things Start with the Women': The Origin of the Texas Birth Control Movement, 1933–1945," *Southwestern Historical Quarterly* 114 (Jan. 2011): 253–85; Pam Wille, "'More than Classes in Swimming and Making Hats': The YWCA and Social Reform in Houston, Texas, 1907–1977" (Ph.D. diss., Texas Tech University, 2004); Kate S. Kirkland, "A Wholesome Life: Ima Hogg's Vision for Mental Health Care," *Southwestern Historical Quarterly* 104 (Jan. 2001): 417–47; Kelley King, *Call Her a Citizen: Progressive-Era Activist and Educator Anna Pennybacker* (College Station: Texas A&M University Press, 2010); Ruth McAdams, "Mudholes, Fairy Godmothers, and Choir Bells," in Sherrod, *Grace and Gumption*, 87–102; Sherrie S. McLeRoy, "In the Interest of the Children," in Sherrod, *Grace and Gumption*, 103–24.

10. Judith N. McArthur, *Creating the New Woman: The Rise of Southern Women's Progressive Culture in Texas, 1893–1918* (Urbana: University of Illinois Press, 1998); Elizabeth Hayes Turner, *Women, Culture, and Community: Religion and Reform in Galveston, 1880–1920* (New York: Oxford University Press, 1997); Bruce Glasrud, "Time of Transition: Black Women in Early Twentieth-Century Texas, 1900–1930," in Glasrud and Pitre, *Black Women and Texas History*, 99–128; Elizabeth York Enstam, "They Called It 'Motherhood': Dallas Women and Public Life, 1895–1918," in *Hidden Histories of Women in the New South*, ed. Virginia Bernhard et al. (Columbia: University of Missouri Press, 1994), 71–95; Elizabeth York Enstam, "The Forgotten Frontier: Dallas Women and Social Caring, 1895–1920," *Legacies* 1 (1989): 20–28; Jackie McElhaney, "Save the Babies: Blanche Greenburg and the Milk Stations," *Legacies* 13 (2001): 19–29.

11. James D. Ivy, "'The Lone Star State Surrenders to a Lone Woman': Frances Willard's Forgotten 1882 Texas Temperance Tour," *Southwestern Historical Quarterly* 102 (July 1998): 45–61; Sylvia Hunt, "'Throw Aside the Veil of Helplessness': A Southern Feminist at the 1893 World's Fair," *Southwestern Historical Quarterly* 100 (July 1996): 49–62; Jacquelyn Masur McElhaney, *Pauline Periwinkle and Progressive Reform in Dallas* (College Station: Texas A&M University Press, 1998); Jacquelyn Masur McElhaney, "Pauline Periwinkle: Prodding Dallas into the Progressive Era," Paul M. Lucko, "The Next 'Big Job': Women Prison Reformers in Texas, 1918–1930," and Judith N. McArthur, "Saving the Children: The Women's Crusade against Child Labor, 1902–1918," in *Women and Texas History: Selected Essays*, ed. Fanes Downs and Nancy Baker Jones (Austin: Texas State Historical Association, 1993), 42–66, 72–87, 157–71; Ann R. Gabbert, "Prostitution and Moral Reform in the Borderlands: El Paso, 1890–1920," *Journal of the History of Sexuality* 12 (2003): 575–604; Ruth Karbach, "Duchesses with Hearts of Love and Brains of Fire," in Sherrod, *Grace and Gumption*, 29–46; Hollace Ava Weiner, "The Jewish Women's Americanization School," in Sherrod, *Grace and Gumption*, 139–56.

12. Marion Barthelme, *Women in the Texas Populist Movement: Letters to the Southern Mercury* (College Station: Texas A&M University Press, 1997); Kevin Motl, "A Time for Reform: The Woman Suffrage Campaign in Rural Texas, 1914–1919" (Ph.D. diss., Texas A&M University, 2006); Jessica Brannon-Wranosky, "Southern Promise and Necessity: Texas, Regional Identity, and the National Woman Suffrage Movement, 1868–1920" (Ph.D. diss., University of North Texas, 2010); Elizabeth York Enstam, "The Dallas Equal Suffrage Association, Political Style, and Popular Culture: Grassroots Strategies of the Woman Suffrage Movement, 1913–1919," *Journal of Southern History* 68 (2002): 817–48; Elizabeth Hayes Turner, "'White-Gloved Ladies' and 'New Women' in the Texas Woman Suffrage Movement," in *Southern Women: Histories and Identities*, ed. Virginia Bernhard et al. (Columbia: University of Missouri Press, 1992), 71–95; Janelle D. Scott, "Local Leadership in the Woman Suffrage Movement: Houston's Campaign for the Vote, 1917–1918," *Houston Review* 12 (1990): 3–22; Jessica Brannon-Wranosky, "Investing in Urban: The Woman's Monday Club and the Entrepreneurial Elite of Corpus Christi, Texas," in *This Corner of Canaan: Essays on Texas in Honor of Randolph B. Campbell*, ed. Richard B. McCaslin, Donald E. Chipman, and Andrew J. Torget (Denton: University of Texas Press, 2013), 311–31; Elna C. Green, "From Antisuffragism to Anti-Communism: The Conservative Career of Ida M. Darden," *Journal of Southern History* 65 (May 1999): 287–316.

13. Yolanda Chavez Leyva, "'Faithful Hard-Working Mexican Hands': Mexicana Workers during the Great Depression," in *Mexican American Women: Changing Images*, ed. John R. Garcia and Thomas Gelsinon (Tucson: Mexican American Research Center, University of Arizona, 1995), 63–77; Rebecca Sharpless, "Women and Work in Texas during the Great Depression," in *Invisible Texans: Women and Minorities in Texas History*, ed. Donald Willett and Stephen Curley (New York: McGraw Hill, 2005), 144–55.

14. Tanya Kraus Randall, "Texas Ranch Women Remember World War II," *Sound Historian* 13 (2011): 41–57; Gary Rabalais, "Humble Women at War: The Case of Humble's Baytown Refinery, 1942–1945," *Houston Review* 2 (2005): 33–36, 58, 69–70; Sandra D. Harvey, "Working for Change: Working Class Women in Waco, Texas War Industrites during World War II" (Ph.D. dissertation, Texas Tech University, 2009); Clarice F.

Pollard, "WAACs in Texas during the Second World War," *Southwestern Historical Quarterly* 93 (July 1989): 61–74; see also Sharon Smith, "Female Home Front Soldiers and Their Food for Freedom Campaign during the Second World War" (M.A. thesis, Texas Woman's University, 1996).

15. Stefanie Decker, "African American Women in the Civil Rights Era, 1954–1974," in Glasrud and Pitre, *Black Women in Texas History*, 159–76; Anne M. Butler, "Building Justice: Mother Margaret Murphy, Race, and Texas," *Catholic Southwest* 13 (2002): 13–36; Richard Fossey and Stephanie Morris, "Courage under Fire: St. Katharine Drexel and the Sisters of the Blessed Sacrament Confront the Texas Ku Klux Klan," *Catholic Southwest* 21 (2010): 7–22; Amanda Bresie, "One Bread, One Body: The Sisters of the Blessed Sacrament in Southeast Texas," *Catholic Southwest* 22 (2011): 21–38; June M. Steele, "Edward Struggs and Mae Simmons: Two African American Educators and the Provisions for Black Schools in Lubbock, Texas, 1930–1970," *West Texas Historical Association Yearbook* 77 (2001): 86–98.

16. Merline Pitre, *In Struggle against Jim Crow: Lulu B. White and the NAACP* (College Station: Texas A&M University Press, 1999), and "Lulu B. White and the Civil Rights Movement in Houston, Texas, 1939–1957," in Willett and Curley, *Invisible Texans*, 192–203; Richard W. Byrd, "Interracial Cooperation in a Decade of Conflict: The Denton (Texas) Christian Women's Inter-Racial Fellowship," *Oral History Review* 19 (Spring-Autumn 1991): 31–53; Rachel Northington Burrow, "Juanita Craft: Desegregating the State Fair of Texas," *Legacies* 16 (Spring 2004): 17–24; Lewis L. Gould and Melissa R. Sneed, "Without Pride or Apology: The University of Texas at Austin, Racial Integration, and the Barbara Smith Case," *Southwestern Historical Quarterly* 103 (July 1999): 67–87; Mary Ellen Curtin, "Reaching for Power: Barbara C. Jordan and Liberals in the Texas Legislature, 1966–1972," *Southwestern Historical Quarterly* 108 (Oct. 2004): 211–31, and "Barbara Jordan: The Politics of Insertion and Accommodation," *Critical Review of International Social and Political Philosophy* 7 (Winter 2004): 279–303; Anna Victoria Wilson and William E. Seagall, *Oh! Do I Remember: Experiences of Teachers during the Desegregation of Austin's Schools, 1964–1971* (Albany, N.Y.: SUNY Press, 2001).

17. Gabriela González, "Two Flags Entwined: Transborder Activists and the Politics of Race, Ethnicity, Class, and Gender in South Texas, 1900–1950" (Ph.D. diss., Stanford University, 2005); Cynthia E. Orozco, *No Mexicans, Women, or Dogs Allowed: The Rise of the Mexican American Civil Rights Movement* (Austin: University of Texas Press, 2009), and "Regionalism, Politics, and Gender in Southwest History: The League of United Latin American Citizens' Expansion into New Mexico from Texas, 1929–1945," *Western Historical Quarterly* 29 (Winter 1998): 459–83; Mary Ann Villareal, "The Synapses of Struggle: Martha Cotera and Tejana Activism," in *Las Obreras: Chicana Politics of Work and Family*, ed. Vicki Ruiz (Los Angeles: UCLA Chicano Research Center, 2000), 273–96; Roberto R, Treviño, "Facing Jim Crow: Catholic Sisters and the 'Mexican Problem' in Texas," *Western Historical Quarterly* 34 (Summer 2003): 139–64; see also Patrick J. Carroll, *Felix Longoria's Wake: Bereavement, Racism, and the Rise of Mexican American Activism* (Austin: University of Texas Press, 2003).

18. Eve Carr, "Missionaries and Motherhood: Sixty-Six Years of Public Health Work in South El Paso" (Ph.D. diss., Arizona State University, 2003); Lois E. Myers, "'Like Water to the Body': Women and the African American Rural Church," *Sound Historian* 10 (2007): 26–38; Elizabeth H. Flowers, *Into the Pulpit: Southern Baptist Women and Power since World War II* (Chapel Hill: University of North Carolina Press, 2012).

19. Rob Fink, "Hermine Tobolowsky, the Texas ELRA, and the Political Struggle for Women's Equal Rights," *Journal of the West* 42 (Summer 2003): 52–57; Sherilyn Brandenstein, "*Sepia Record* as a Forum for Negotiating Women's Roles," in Downs and Jones, *Women and Texas History*, 143–57; Christopher Bean, "'We Want Aggies, Not Maggies': James Earl Rudder and the Coeducation of Texas A&M University," *East Texas Historical Journal* 44 (2006), 17–27.

20. Marilyn Ferris Motz, "'Thou Art My Last Love': The Courtship and Remarriage of a Rural Texas Couple in 1892," *Southwestern Historical Quarterly* 93 (April 1990): 457–74; Vicki Howard, "The Courtship Letters of an African American Couple: Race, Gender, Class, and the Cult of True Womanhood," *Southwestern Historical Quarterly* 100 (July 1996): 65–80.

21. Mary Margaret McAllen Amberson, *I Would Rather Sleep in Texas: A History of the Lower Rio Grande Valley and the People of the Santa Anita Land Grant* (Austin: Texas State Historical Association, 2003); Jane Clements Monday and Francis Brannen Vick, *Petra's Legacy: The South Texas Ranching Empire of Petra Vela and Mifflin Kenedy* (College Station: Texas A&M University Press, 2007); Lois E. Myers, *Letters by Lamplight: A Woman's View of Everyday Life in South Texas, 1873–1883* (Waco, Tex.: Baylor University Press, 1991); Francelle Pruitt Blum, "When Marriages Fail: Divorce in Nineteenth-Century Texas" (Ph.D. diss., Rice University, 2008).

22. Shelley Sallee, "'The Woman of It': Governor Miriam Ferguson's 1924 Election," *Southwestern Historical Quarterly* 100 (July 1996): 1–16; Nancy Beck Young, "'Me for Ma': Miriam Ferguson and Texas Politics in the 1920s," in *We Have Come to Stay: American Women and Political Parties, 1880–1960*, ed. Melanie Gustafson et al. (Albuquerque: University of New Mexico Press, 1999), 121–30; Patricia Ellen Cunningham, "Bonnet in the Ring: Minnie Fisher Cunningham's Campaign for Governor in 1944," in Downs and Jones, *Women and Texas History*, 102–15; Judith N. McArthur, "Minnie Fisher Cunningham's Back Door Lobby in Texas: Political Maneuvering in a One-Party State," in *One Woman, One Vote: Rediscovering the Woman Suffrage Movement*, ed. Marjorie Spruill Wheeler (Troutdale, Ore: New Sage Press, 1995), 315–32; Judith N. McArthur and Harold L. Smith, *Minnie Fisher Cunningham: A Suffragist's Life in Politics* (New York: Oxford University Press, 2003); Kelli Walsh, "Oveta Culp Hobby: A Transformational Leader from the Texas Legislature to Washington, D.C." (Ph.D. diss., University of South Carolina, 2006); Robert T. Pando, "Oveta Culp Hobby: A Study of Power and Control" (Ph.D. diss., Florida State University, 2008); Kate S. Kirkland, "For All Houston's Children: Ima Hogg and the Board of Education, 1943–1949," *Southwestern Historical Quarterly* 101 (Apr. 1998): 460–95; Darwin Payne, *Indomitable Sarah: The Life of Judge Sarah T. Hughes* (College Station: Texas A&M University Press, 2004); Sue Tolleson-Rinehart and Jeanie R. Stanley, *Claytie and the Lady: Ann Richards, Gender, and Politics in Texas* (Austin: University of Press, 1994); Celia Morris,

Storming the Statehouse: Running for Governor with Ann Richards and Dianne Feinstein (New York: Charles Scribner's Sons, 1992); Jan Reid, *Let the People In: The Life and Times of Ann Richards* (Austin: University of Texas Press, 2012).

23. Kristi Strickland, "The Significance and Impact of Women on the Rise of the Republican Party in Twentieth Century Texas" (Ph.D. diss., University of North Texas, 2000); Nancy Baker Jones and Ruthe Winegarten, *Capitol Women: Texas Female Legislators, 1923–1999* (Austin: University of Texas Press, 2000); Terry L. Gilmour, "A Difference: Women in the Texas Legislature" (Ph.D. diss., Texas Tech University, 1999); José Angel Gutiérrez, Michelle Melendez, and Sonia Norola, *Chicanas in Charge: Texas Women in the Electoral Arena* (Lanham, Md.: Altamira Press, 2006); Sharon A. Navarro, *Latina Legislator: Letitia Van de Putte and the Road to Leadership* (College Station: Texas A&M University Press, 2008); Cindy C. Smolovik, "Braving the Smoke," in Sherrod, *Grace and Gumption*, 207–28; see also Sonia R. García, Valerie Martinez-Ebers, Irasema Coronado, Sharon A. Navarro, and Patricia Jaramillo, *Políticas: Latina Public Officials in Texas* (Austin: University of Texas Press, 2008).

24. Sylvia Hunt, "Challenging Patriarchy and Domesticity: Women Educators in Texas, 1840–1940, an Interdisciplinary Study" (Ph.D. diss., University of Texas at Arlington, 1992), "Women Educators in Texas, 1840–1920: Were They Feminists?" *East Texas Historical Journal* 27 (Spring 1989): 16–30, and "To Wed and to Teach: The Myth of the Single Teacher," in Downs and Jones, *Women and Texas History*, 127–42; Debbie Mauldin Cottrell, *Pioneer Woman Educator: The Progressive Spirit of Annie Webb Blanton* (College Station: Texas A&M University Press, 1993), and "Professional, Feminine, and Feminist: Annie Webb Blanton and the Founding of Delta Kappa Gamma," in Downs and Jones, *Women and Texas History*, 88–101; Brenda Taylor Matthews, "Ladies of Victory," in Sherrod, *Grace and Gumption*, 13–28; Virginia Spurlin, "The Conners of Waco: Black Professionals in Twentieth Century Texas" (Ph.D. diss., Texas Tech University, 1991); Gloria Duarte, "Eva Camuñez's Teaching Career, 1932–1942," *West Texas Historical Association Yearbook* 85 (2009): 96–107.

25. Diana Davids Olien, "Domesticity and the Texas Oil Fields: Dimensions of Women's Experience, 1920–1950," in Downs and Jones, *Women and Texas History*, 116–28; Cynthia Devlin, "Twice through the Glass Ceiling: Sue Birdwell-Alves," *East Texas Historical Journal* 49 (Fall 2011): 24–43; David C. Humphrey, "Prostitution in Texas: From the 1830s to the 1960s," *East Texas Historical Journal* 33 (1995): 27–43; Richard F. Selcer, "Fort Worth and the Fraternity of Strange Women," *Southwestern Historical Quarterly* 96 (July 1992): 55–86.

26. Judith W. Linsley, "Main House, Carriage House: African-American Domestic Employees at the McFaddin-Ward House in Beaumont, Texas, 1900–1950," *Southwestern Historical Quarterly* 103 (July 1999): 17–51; Rebecca Sharpless, *Fertile Ground, Narrow Choices: Texas Farm Women, 1900–1940* (Chapel Hill: University of North Carolina Press, 1999), and "The Southern Majority: Interviews with Rural Texas Women," *Sound Historian* 2 (1994): 2–11; Deborah Wing-Leonard, "Figs, Flappers, and Fignolias: Working Women of the 1920s Gulf Coast," *Sound Historian* 11 (2008): 49–67; Julia Kirk Blackwelder, *Stylin' Jim Crow: African American Beauty Training during Segregation* (College Station: Texas A&M University Press, 2003).

27. Michelle M. Mears, "Medicine on the Blackland Prairie: The Story of Dr. Claudia Potter," *Sound Historian* 2 (1994): 36–46; Mary Lynn Irving, "Texas Women in Military Medicine," *Sound Historian* 4 (1997): 44–50; Ann R. Gabbert, "Defining the Boundaries of Care: Local Response to Global Concerns in El Paso Public Health Policy, 1881–1941" (Ph.D. diss., University of Texas at El Paso, 2006); Troy Ainsworth, "Mabel Welch: El Paso's First Woman Architect," *West Texas Historical Association Yearbook* 85 (2009): 139–52; Jennifer Ross-Nazzal, "Pioneering Women of Today: Space Travelers," *Sound Historian* 13 (2009): 23–32; Carol Roark, "Cracking the Glass Ceiling," in Sherrod, *Grace and Gumption*, 229–56; Katie Sherrod, "High-Heeled Times in the Newsroom," in Sherrod, *Grace and Gumption*, 257–86.

28. Irene Ledesma, "Unlikely Strikers: Mexican American Women in Strike Activity in Texas, 1919–1974" (Ph.D. diss., Ohio State University, 1992), and "Texas Newspapers and Chicana Workers' Activism," *Western Historical Quarterly* 26 (1995): 309–31; Isaias McCaffery, "Organizing Las Costureras: Life, Labor and Unionization among Mexicana Garment Workers in Two Borderlands Cities, Los Angeles and San Antonio, 1933–1941" (Ph.D. diss., University of Kansas, 1999); Benjamin Marquez, "Organizing Mexican-American Women in the Garment Industry: La Mujer Obrera," *Women and Politics* 15 (1995): 65–88; Emily Honig, "Women at Farah Revisited: Political Mobilization and Its Aftermath among Chicana Workers in El Paso, Texas, 1972–1992," *Feminist Studies* 22 (Summer 1996): 425–52; Jennifer Rebecca Mata, "Creating a Critical Chicana Narrative: Writing the Chicanas at Farah into Labor History" (Ph.D. diss., Washington State University, 1992); Lori A. Flores, "An Unladylike Strike Fashionably Clothed: Mexicana and Anglo Women Garment Workers against Tex-Son, 1959–1963," *Pacific Historical Review* 78 (Aug. 2009): 367–402; Robert S. Shelton, "Yankee Devils in Paradise? Unionizing Efforts among Dallas Garment Workers, 1933–1935," *Legacies* 6 (1994): 12–19; Patricia Evridge Hill, "Real Women and True Womanhood: Grassroots Organizing among Dallas Dressmakers in 1935," *Labor's Heritage* 5 (1994): 4–17; Gabriela González, "Carolina Munguía and Emma Tenayuca: The Politics of Benevolence and Radical Reform," *Frontiers* 24 (June–Sept. 2003): 200–29; Zaragosa Vargas, "Tejana Radical: Emma Tenayuca and the San Antonio Labor Movement during the Great Depression," *Pacific Historical Review* 66 (1997): 553–80; Julia Kirk Blackwelder, "Emma Tenayuca: Vision and Courage," in *The Human Tradition in Texas*, ed. Ty Cashion and Jesús F. de la Teja (Wilmington, Del.: Rowman and Littlefield, 2001), 191–208.

29. Sara R. Massey, *Texas Women on the Cattle Trails* (College Station: Texas A&M University Press, 2006); Georgellen Burnett, *We Just Toughed It Out: Women in the Llano Estacado* (El Paso: Texas Western Press, 1990); Delmar Hayter, "Pioneer Women of West Texas in the Early Twentieth Century," *West Texas Historical Association Yearbook* [WTHAY] 65 (1989): 78–92; Harry F. Snapp, "West Texas Women: A Diverse Heritage and a Succession of Frontiers," WTHAY 72 (1996): 21–38; Lou Rodenberger, "West Texas Pioneer Women: The Wilder, Stronger Breed," WTHAY 77 (2001): 38–53; Tracy Stewart, "Founding Mothers of Deaf Smith County," WTHAY 84 (2008): 85–94; Jean Stuntz, "West Texas Women in Ranching: Myth and Reality," WTHAY 84 (2008): 49–83; Darlene Bellinghausen, "Dora Merrell Stroup: A Panhandle Pioneer," WTHAY 68 (1992): 147–56, "Mildred Diller and the Diller Ranch," WTHAY 69 (1993): 151–63, and

"A German Ranchwoman on the Brazos," WTHAY 72 (1996): 171–76; Becky Matthews, "Pearl Nance, A Remarkable Ranchwoman," WTHAY 74 (1998): 122–27; June M. Steele, "Mollie Abernathy: Rancher of the South Plains of West Texas, 1900–1919," WTHAY 75 (1999): 102–109; Jack Becker, "Mattie B. Morris Miller: Matriarch, Ranch Woman, and Benefactor," WTHAY 80 (2004): 126–36; Judy Alter "Ranch Women, Cowgirls, and Wildcatters," in Sherrod, *Grace and Gumption*, 47–62.

30. Susan E. Cayleff, *Babe: The Life and Legend of Babe Didrikson Zaharias* (Urbana: University of Illinois Press, 1995); Mary Lou LeCompte, *Cowgirls of the Rodeo: Pioneer Professional Athletes* (Urbana: University of Illinois Press, 1993), and "Home on the Range: Women in Professional Rodeo, 1929–1947," *Journal of Sport History* 17 (1990): 318–46; Renee Laegreid, *Riding Pretty: Rodeo Royalty in the American West* (Lincoln: University of Nebraska Press, 2006).

31. Ruthe Winegarten, *Black Texas Women: 150 Years of Trial and Triumph* (Austin: University of Texas Press, 1995); Phyllis Wonjou Allen, "These Women Lived!" in Sherrod, *Grace and Gumption*, 193–206; Teresa Palomo Acosta and Ruthe Winegarten, *Las Tejanas: 300 Years of History* (Austin: University of Texas Press, 2003); Julie Leininger Pycior, "Tejanas Navigating the 1920s," in *Tejano Epic*, ed. Arnoldo De León (Austin: Texas State Historical Association, 2005), 71–86; Sandra Guerra-Cline, "The North Side, La Fundición, and El TP," in Sherrod, *Grace and Gumption*, 125–38; Lauren Ann Kattner, "Growing Up Female in New Braunfels: Social and Cultural Adaptation in a German-Texan Town," *Journal of American Ethnic History* 9 (Spring 1990): 49–72; Mary Fehler Knarr, "Faith, Frauen, and the Formation of an Ethnic Identity: German Lutheran Women in South and Central Texas, 1831–1890" (Ph.D. diss., Texas Christian University, 2009); Charles H. Russell, *Undaunted: A Norwegian Woman in Frontier Texas* (College Station: Texas A&M University Press, 2006); Marc Sanders and Ruthe Winegarten, *The Lives and Times of Black Dallas Women* (Austin: Eakin Press, 2002).

CHAPTER 5

European Immigrant History in the Nineteenth Century

James C. Kearney

A full synthetic study of European immigration in Texas during the entire nineteenth century has yet to appear except for one very general introductory survey and another analysis that considers only the post–Civil War period.[1] Instead, most published studies tend to focus on individual nationalities or on themes associated with a specific nationality. This essay focuses on the nationalities that proved to be the most important in establishing sustainable, recognizable communities in Texas in which the native languages and customs have persisted over the generations. Preeminent among these communities are the German settlements in Texas. There is an enormous and ever-expanding literature on nineteenth-century German immigration to Texas, which dwarfs the immigration of all the other European nationalities to Texas combined during the period. Nonetheless, Czech, Polish, Wendish, Irish, and English immigrants as well as other national groups added greatly to diversity in Texas.

European immigration to Texas occurred in two substantial waves during the nineteenth century: the first during the three decades preceding the Civil War, the second in the last two decades of the century. Roughly two-thirds of all these immigrants hailed from the present-day Central European countries of Germany, the Czech Republic, Slovakia, and Austria and from France's German-speaking provinces, Alsace and Lorraine.[2] Smaller numbers of immigrants came from Scandinavia, Poland, and Great Britain, which at the time included Ireland. An even smaller contingent hailed from Europe's Mediterranean countries.

Two Irish empresarios, John McMullen and James McGloin, were responsible for the first organized European immigration to Texas after 1824. About two hundred families, mostly of Irish descent, eventually settled in a colony along the lower Nueces River in present-day Refugio and San Patricio Counties during 1828 and 1829. Despite many setbacks and hardships—occasioned above all by the outbreak of the Texas Revolution in 1835—the colony took root and maintained a distinct Irish character for several generations. Well-known ranching families of South Texas, such as the O'Conners of Victoria and Bee Counties, trace their origins back to this colony. Several studies have been published about the Irish in Texas.[3]

Friedrich Ernst (1796–1848) is considered the father of German emigration to Texas by virtue of a letter he wrote back to his friends and family in the Grand Duchy of Oldenburg in 1832. He wrote from his homestead on Mill Creek in present-day Austin County while Texas was still part of Mexico. Ernst's letter also inspired another northern German, Detlef Thomas Friedrich Jordt, to travel to Texas to see for himself if Ernst's glowing depictions were true. The result was *Reise nach Texas* (Journey to Texas), the first book written in German exclusively about Texas from a firsthand perspective.[4]

The Ernst letter fed a peculiar state of mind that came to be known as the "Texas Fever"; once in its grip, many in Germany felt powerless to resist the allure. In contrast to the later Hill Country settlements, German immigration into south-central Texas was largely unorganized; individuals and extended families made the decision to move and financed it on their own penny through a process that is often referred to as "chain" immigration. These immigrants tended to settle in small communities such as Cat Spring, Industry, Shelby, New Ulm, Cummins Creek (Frelsburg), and Milheim.

As opposed to chain immigration, politically sponsored European emigration to Texas on a massive scale began in earnest during Sam Houston's second term as president of the republic (1841–1844); this influx was largely the result of policies he championed. Two European empresarios, Henry Francis Fisher and Henri Castro, received contracts under the new colonization laws sponsored by Houston. Together the two contractors encouraged the eventual introduction of nearly ten thousand Germans and German-speaking Alsatians into the areas west and north of San Antonio.[5] This effort also resulted in the establishment of several towns such as New Braunfels, Fredericksburg, and Castroville, all of which grew quickly in size and importance while maintaining their Germanic character well into the twentieth century. The best entry into the study of German settlements in Texas, whether in south-central Texas or the

Hill Country, remains Rudolph L. Biesele's *History of the German Settlements in Texas.* His method is straightforward, addressing one community at a time. The book is well documented and based on exhaustive research.[6]

For an overview of how Texas fit into the larger picture of German immigration in North America, a study by John Hawgood is indispensable: *The Tragedy of German-America.*[7] More recent studies of the Texas experience begin with Terry G. Jordan's *German Seed in Texas Soil.* This ranks as one of the best books on the subject and reflects the author's broad perspective and training in cultural geography. An additional important survey is Glen E. Lich's *German Texans,* which offers a compendium of documents and monograms. It is part of a series of books on the various ethnic groups in the state published by the Institute of Texan Cultures in San Antonio.[8] The papers presented at a 1980 seminar on German culture in Texas have been published as a book, as well. This volume contains excellent articles by Terry Jordan, Gilbert Jordan, Patrick McGuire, and Hubert Heinen, among others, on the cultural contributions of Texas Germans to the state.[9] Also available are published histories of various German communities, especially Fredericksburg, New Braunfels, Industry, and Comfort.[10]

Several bibliographies of Texas Germania have been published. Two recent ones are Steven M. Benjamin's "The Texas-Germans, a Working Bibliography" and Selma Raunick's "A Survey of German Literature in Texas." In 2005, Thomas Adams edited *Germany and the Americas,* which offers an encyclopedia of Germans in America that can be quite helpful as a quick reference on specific issues.[11] Both Louise Stoehr, wife of Friedrich Ernst, and Caroline Ernst von Hinueber, her daughter, have provided gripping accounts of hardship and perseverance from a woman's perspective. Crystal Sasse Ragsdale has translated and reproduced both accounts in *The Golden Free Land.* The collected correspondence of the extended von Rosenberg family is also quite valuable.[12] This family immigrated to Texas from East Prussia in 1850 and settled in the Round Top area. The letters of Amanda Fallier von Rosenberg, especially, speak eloquently from a woman's point of view to the difficulties, physical and emotional, of beginning a new life on the Texas frontier.

The Fisher Miller Grant, originally issued in 1842 and subsequently extended, was purchased by a corporation of German noblemen in 1845 who adopted the rather long and cumbersome official name Society for the Protection of German Emigrants in Texas. The purposes of the SPGET, which have been the subject of considerable controversy and speculation, are clearly spelled out in many official reports as well as the extensive correspondence contained in archives in several libraries in Texas. Most studies concentrate on the activities of the Society in Texas. Manfred Kossok addresses the politics of immigration from the German side in "Prussia, Bremen, and the 'Texas Question.'" Contemporary works by German immigrants and from officials in Texas of historical importance, either directly or indirectly associated with the SPGET, have been translated into English.[13] James C. Kearney discusses the goals of the organization at length in his book *Nassau Plantation*.[14]

The so-called *Lateiner* (educated) settlements in Texas as well as the communistic commune of Bettina, established by the SPGET in 1847, have received considerable scholarly attention.[15] Several important biographies and studies on personalities associated with the SPGET have been published.[16] A recent book by Jefferson Morgenthaler, *Promised Land*, has made a valuable contribution to our understanding of the SPGET by exploring the diplomatic and personal correspondence of the period. His study sheds light on the international politics behind this early phase of organized European immigration.[17]

With settlement well under way by the time of the Civil War, it was impossible for the German immigrants to escape the pressures of the conflict. They nourished values and attitudes that often contrasted and sometimes clashed with the predominant southern mentality of the Anglo-American majority in the Confederacy. Opposition to slavery and Unionist sentiment among the German settlers in Texas, both preceding and during the war, has provided a fertile field for scholarly interest and controversy. The starting point for a discussion about Texas Germans' relationship to slavery begins in German-language sources, which remain beyond the scope of this chapter because many of them have not been translated from the language in which they were written. Among English sources, Rudolph Biesele's "The Texas State Convention of Germans in 1854" gives a good sense of the intense internal debate within the German communities at the time. For a firsthand account, Charles Nagel has written *A Boy's Civil War Story*. His father, a staunch Unionist, fled to Mexico, leaving his wife and younger children behind but taking the young Charles along. Many of his father's letters, which complement the narrative of his son, have been reproduced in *Germans in the Civil War*. This volume is not restricted to Texas, but the Nagel letters, among others, offer an excellent window into German attitudes in the state. The introduction provides, moreover, an excellent discussion of primary and secondary sources and the strands of disagreement.[18] Walter Kamphoefner has also authored a 1999 article, "New Perspectives on Texas Germans and the Confederacy," that contends that the Germans were not quite as anti-slavery and pro-Union as they are generally made out to be.[19] Several studies deal with dissent in Texas during the war, thus commenting on the German areas.[20]

On August 10, 1862, sixty-two German Unionists from the Hill Country on their way to Mexico were overtaken and ambushed on the Nueces River about sixty miles southwest of present Kerrville by a larger and better armed Confederate force under the command of a Lieutenant McRae. A study by Mary Jo O'Rear provides an overview of the primary and secondary literature about this event as well as an excellent account of the battle itself.[21] Published firsthand accounts of the battle include David R. Hoffmann's "A German-American Pioneer Remembers" and R. H. Williams and John W. Sansom's *The Massacre on the Nueces River.* The latter book is interesting because it contains the testimony of a participant from each side of the conflict, both of whom agree that the actions of the Confederates were illegal, unwarranted, and constituted war crimes. Guido Ransleben's earlier mentioned book, *A Hundred Years of Comfort*, reproduces a firsthand account of the battle written by Jacob Küchler, who led the Fredericksburg contingent of Germans at the battle.[22]

Texas experienced much hardship and violence during Reconstruction.[23] Although the violence was directed against the freedmen in the first instance, it sometimes also affected immigrant communities adversely, especially in the Hill Country. The so-called Hoo Doo War, or Mason County War, for instance, can be understood only in the context of the hard feelings that lingered here between the largely Unionist Germans and the Confederate Anglos.[24]

Immigration to Texas from Europe all but stopped during the war and did not resume in force until several years after the cessation of hostilities. A general economic slump that gripped the whole country and reached its peak in 1872 also retarded European immigration. Once immigration resumed, however, it did so with a fury, driven above all by the spread of railroads across the state. One of the best descriptions of the railroads' influence is Lawrence H. Konecny and Clinton Machann's *Perilous Voyages.*[25] Older immigrants of their new country saw exciting business opportunities in renewed immigration. They flocked to the new towns that were sprouting up and down the new railroads like mushrooms after a spring rain. Here they set up all sorts of businesses—lumberyards, cotton gins, hardware and dry good stores—that catered primarily to the fresh immigrants. Terry Jordan has taken up this subject in "The German Settlement of Texas after 1865," but it is an area that begs for further scholarly examination.[26]

The post–Civil War years witnessed a Czech immigration that further increased the number of new arrivals to Texas from Europe. A pioneering Czech settler in Cat Spring (Austin County), Rev. Ernst Bergmann, wrote a series of glowing letters back to his friends in Moravia in 1849. These letters were widely circulated and published in regional newspapers. One of these letters came to the attention of Josef Lesikar, who subsequently organized the first group of sixteen families to make the journey to a new home and life in Texas. They arrived in 1851 after many struggles. In 1852, Lesikar organized another group and this time made the trip with his own family. Most of these families also settled in Austin County. These two groups formed the vanguard of Czech immigration into the state. Immigration from Bohemia and Moravia resumed significantly after 1880, now actively encouraged and promoted by the Texas railroads, principally the Galveston, Harrisburg, and San Antonio Railroad. It was along this railroad corridor between Houston and San Antonio that a majority of newcomers settled. There are studies of this Czech immigration, which also occurred elsewhere in the United States at the time.[27]

By far the most prolific scholars in reference to the Czechs in Texas have been the team of Clinton Machann and James W. Mendl. Together they have authored two indispensable studies: *The Czechs in Texas* and *Krásná Amerika*. They also collaborated in translating and editing accounts by early settlers, travelers, and journalists in their book *Czech Voices*, which offers special insight into the trials and adjustments of Czech settlers in Texas.[28] Although never published, William Philip Hewitt has written an excellent Ph.D. dissertation on Czech immigration to the Lone Star State.[29] Robert Skrabanek has provided an excellent firsthand account of farm life in the Czech community of Snook in Burleson County, where most of the families were members of the Moravian Protestant Church (Moravian Brethren).[30] Mary Frances Chupick Bennett's recent *Invitation to Cat Spring* is a historical novel that traces the fortunes of a Czech immigrant family from their home in Moravia to the settlement of Cat Spring, one of the original German communities in Austin County but also a destination for Czech immigrants. The novel does a wonderful job of conveying the factors that drove the Czech immigrants from their homeland as well as the powerful attractions Texas offered.[31] In proportion to their numbers and significance, the Czechs in Texas have not received the scholarly attention they deserve, but this is changing. The recent construction of a beautiful Czech Heritage and Cultural Center in La Grange will do much to further a broader awareness of Czech heritage in Texas and keep the legacy alive.

The Wends, sometimes called Serbs, are another nineteenth-century group that came to Texas along with Germans and Czechs. The Wends were the remnants of a Slavic people who once inhabited the lands east of the Elbe River. By the second half of the nineteenth century, nationalism was on the rise throughout Europe, and the Wends felt pressured to abandon their language and customs and become more German. Many saw emigration as the only hope for survival. Hundreds made the move to two principal colonies—one in Australia, the other in Texas. Two studies deal with background history of the Wends in Europe, and two specialized treatments examine their immigration to Texas.[32]

The arrival of the Poles, the next largest contingent of immigrants, can be attributed to the influence and organizational efforts of Leopold Moczygemba (1824–1891), a Polish priest who ministered originally to the spiritual needs of German settlers in the Hill Country. He wrote back to family and friends in the Upper Silesia region of Poland, encouraging them to come to Texas as well. Some did come, and most settled at a place established by the priest in newly organized Karnes County. Moczygemba named the site Panna Maria, Polish for "Virgin Mary." Other Silesians settled at Bandera and San Antonio. T. Lindsay Baker examines this immigration in *The First Polish Americans* and has also written an article about Moczygemba. Joseph Swastek has written a biography of the Polish priest.[33] One other study of Polish Texans remains to be mentioned, Jacek Przygoda's *Texas Pioneers from Poland.* The book, although somewhat chaotic in organization, does document the important role of the Catholic Church as the center of community life. In this respect the book has significance beyond the Polish communities in giving a powerful sense of the determinative role churches often played for all the European immigrant communities in Texas.[34]

Although Swedish immigration remained relatively small compared to other groups, it nevertheless represented the largest population of Scandinavian immigrants in the South in the nineteenth century. Swedish immigration can be traced, above all, to the influence and example of one remarkable man, Swante Magnus Swenson (1816–1896). Swenson arrived in Texas in 1836 and settled in Houston. After various business successes, he developed the fabled SMS ranches in West Texas, which are still in existence today. He inspired others of his countrymen to make the move as well. Swenson often helped underwrite these new immigrants by paying their fares and offering them startup capital. His family established the town of Stamford in the Panhandle in 1899 after he convinced a railroad to lay a line through the town. Many of his countrymen subsequently settled in that area. Swenson has received considerable scholarly attention, especially Mary Whatley Clarke's *The Swenson Saga and the SMS Ranches.*[35] There is a historical literature on the Swedes in Texas in spite of their small numbers. Three studies offer good overviews of the Swedish immigrants.[36]

Danes and Norwegians also established communities in the state, but their numbers were even smaller than the Swedes. The Danes settled in three areas concentrated enough to become ethnic communities in northern Lee County, Gillespie County, and southern Wharton County. For a discussion of the Danes, see *The Danish Texans* by John L. Davis. The Danes in Wharton County have received attention in an article by Thomas P. Christensen, "Danevang, Texas." The Norwegians mostly concentrated in Bosque County prior to the Civil War and were farmers. Theodore Christian Blegen discusses Norwegian immigration in his *Norwegian Migration to America*, as does Richard L. Hooverson in "Midnight Sun to Lone Star: Norwegians in Texas." The Institute of Texan Cultures also has published a booklet, *The Norwegian Texans*. The best scholarly treatment in condensed form has been provided by Lyder L. Unstad, "Norwegian Migration to Texas."[37]

Jewish immigration to Texas is very closely connected with the boom era of the 1880s and 1890s. Many Jewish immigrants with roots in Germany and Eastern Europe arrived during this period. They specialized in setting up small clothing stores and retail shops and eventually came to dominate this aspect of small-town Texas. A recent doctoral dissertation explores this tendency.[38] Though their numbers were limited, Jewish immigrants often contributed disproportionately to the cultural and intellectual development of these fledgling communities through generous support of libraries, literary clubs, and such. A large and growing body of scholarly work exists on Jewish immigrants in Texas. Two books that deal with Jewish pioneers are Natalie Ornish's *Pioneer Jewish Texans* and Bryan F. Stone's *The Chosen Folks*. Earlier works include a photographic history by Cathy Schechter and Ruthe Winegarten, and, more recently, Hollace Weiner's *Lone Stars of David*, a collection of essays on the history and culture of Texas Jews and winner of the Texas Historical Foundation's Doelece Parmelee Award for historical research and writing.[39]

In 1907 several prominent Jewish leaders in Galveston organized what has become known as the "Galveston Movement," an enterprise that has been the focus of considerable scholarly attention. This was a concentrated effort to provide a safe haven for mainly Russian Jews victimized by growing anti-Semitism in Eastern Europe and the alarming resurgence of pogroms. Between 1907 and 1914 the Jewish Immigrants' Information Bureau sponsored more than ten thousand refugees who entered the United States through Galveston. Most of these, however, eventually dispersed across the South and West and did not remain in Texas. This movement is the subject of a dissertation by Bernard Marinbach and also the focus of an article by Gary Dean Best.[40]

Immigration is a major theme in Texas history, which, with proper adjustments to time and place, is just as topical and relevant in the present as it was in the nineteenth century. For the nineteenth century, it is a story of epic dimensions, a narrative littered with myriad accounts of disillusionment and tragedy but also marked by extraordinary successes. Death, disease, misfortune were constant companions on the journey in search of new opportunities in a faraway land. The net result, however, was a process that enriched this state economically, culturally, and socially. Despite all that has been written, much remains to be done about nineteenth-century immigration to Texas, even on the Germans. But it is time for more attention to other nationalities, and this is beginning to happen. It is also time for broader approaches that go beyond the narrow focuses of individual nationalities to address systematically such issues as the contribution of European immigrants in the nineteenth century to the economic, cultural, and social development of the state. For the young scholar, much remains to be done.

NOTES

1. Terry Jordan, *Immigration to Texas* (Boston: American Press, 1980). Historian Barbara Rozek has written a survey history of immigration into Texas for the late nineteenth century: *Come to Texas: Attracting Immigrants, 1865–1915* (College Station: Texas A&M University Press, 2003).

2. Ethel H. and Chester Geue, *A New Land Beckoned: German Immigration to Texas, 1844–1847* (Waco, Tex.: Texian Press, 1966), and *New Homes in a New Land: German Immigration to Texas, 1847–1861* (Waco, Tex.: Texian Press, 1970). For the German immigrants, the most complete compilation of ship lists is a self-published study by Charles Kleinecke: *1844–1846, Fisher-Miller Grant and G.E.C. Forever* (Corsicana, Tex.: C. W. Kleinecke, Jr., 1994). The Galveston County Genealogical Society published a helpful compilation: *Ships Passenger Lists: Port of Galveston, Texas 1846–1871* (Easley, S.C.: Southern Historical Press, 1984). W. M. Von-Maszewski has also compiled a list: *German Emigration Ships to New Orleans, 1865–1869* (Pasadena, Tex.: self-published, 1997).

3. John Brendan Flannery, *The Irish Texans* (San Antonio: University of Texas Institute of Texan Cultures, 1980); Rachel Bluntzer Hébert, *The Forgotten Colony: San Patricio de Hibernia* (Burnet, Tex.: Eakin Press, 1981).

4. The full title is *Reise nach Texas, nebst Nachrichten von diesem Lande: für Deutsche, welche nach Amerika zu gehen beabeabsichtigen* [Travel to Texas with Information about this Country for Germans Intending to go to America] (Bremen: Carl W. Wiehe, 1834). The book has been translated and annotated by James Kearney and Geir Bentzen and is scheduled for publication by the University of Texas in spring 2015.

5. Ollie Solon Loving, "A History of the Fisher-Miller Land Grant from 1842–1860" (M.A. thesis, University of Texas, 1934); Bobby D. Weaver, *Castro's Colony: Empresario Development in Texas, 1842–1865* (College Station: Texas A&M University Press, 2005); Cornelia E. Crook, *Henry Castro: The Story of Early Colonization in Texas* (San Antonio, Tex.: St. Mary's University Press, 1987).

6. Rudolph L. Biesele, *The History of the German Settlements in Texas, 1831–1861* (Austin: Von Boeckmann-Jones, 1930; rpt. 1964); Earlier works that are still relevant and valuable are Gilbert Giddings Benjamin, *The Germans in Texas: A Study in Immigration* (Philadelphia, 1909, rpt. Austin: Jenkins, 1974); Moritz Tilling, *The History of the German Element in Texas* (Houston, 1913); and Don H. Biggers, *German Pioneers in Texas* (Fredericksburg, Tex.: Fredericksburg Publishing, 1925).

7. John Hawgood, *The Tragedy of German-America: The Germans in the United States of America during the Nineteenth Century and After* (New York, 1940; rpt., New York: Arno Press, 1970).

8. Terry G. Jordan, *German Seed in Texas Soil: Immigrant Farmers in Nineteenth-Century Texas* (Austin: University of Texas Press, 1966); Glen E. Lich, *The German Texans* (San Antonio: Institute of Texan Cultures, 1981).

9. Glen E. Lich and Dona B. Reeves, eds., *German Culture in Texas* (Boston: Twayne, 1980).

10. *Fredericksburg, TX: The First Fifty Years* (Fredericksburg, Tex.: Fredericksburg Publishing, 1971, rpt. and trans. of Robert Penninger's 50th anniversary Festival Edition, originally published May 8, 1896, in the German language); Oscar Haas, *History of New Braunfels and Comal County, Texas, 1844–1946* (Austin: Steck, 1968); William Richter and Ann and James Lindemann, *Historical Accounts of Industry, Texas, 1831–1986* (New Ulm, Tex., 1986); Guido Ransleben, *A Hundred Years of Comfort: A Centennial History* (San Antonio, Tex.: Naylor, 1974).

11. Steven M. Benjamin, "The Texas-Germans, a Working Bibliography," *Occasional Papers of the Society for German American Studies* 8 (1980): 91–116; Selma Raunick, "A Survey of German Literature in Texas," *Southwestern Historical Quarterly* 33, no. 2 (Oct. 1929): 135–59; Thomas Adams, ed., *Germany and the Americas: Culture, Politics and Tradition* (New York: ABC-Clio, 2005).

12. Crystal Sasse Ragsdale, ed., *The Golden Free Land: The Reminiscences and Letters of Women on an American Frontier* (Austin: Landmark, 1976). For the von Rosenberg correspondence, see Walter Otto Wupperman, trans., *Emigration of the Von Rosenbergs to Texas, 1849: From the Diary of the Pioneer Mother* (self-published by P.A. Meerscheidt, 1976).

13. Manfred Kossok, "Prussia, Bremen, and the 'Texas Question,' 1835–1845," trans. and with an introduction by Glenn G. Gilbert, *Texana* 3, no. 3 (Fall 1965): 227–69. Other works include "W. Steinert's View of Texas in 1849," Gilbert J. Jordan, ed. and trans. in five installments: *Southwestern Historical Quarterly* 80, no. 1 (July 1976): 57–78; vol. 80, no. 2 (Oct. 1976): 177–200; vol. 80, no. 3 (Jan. 1977): 282–301; vol. 80 no. 4 (Apr. 1977): 399–416; and vol. 81, no. 1 (July 1977): 45–72; Hermann Seele, *The Cypress and Other Writings of a German Pioneer in Texas*, trans. Edward C. Breitenkamp (Austin: University of Texas Press, 1979); *The Diary of Hermann Seele*, trans., introduction,

and notes by Theodore Gish (Austin: German-Texas Heritage Society, 1995); Viktor Bracht, *Texas im Jahre 1848* (Elberfeld u. Iserlohn: Bädeker, 1849), reissued as *Texas in 1848*, Charles Schmidt, trans. with an introduction by Theodore Gish (San Marcos, Tex.: German-Texas Heritage Society, 1991); Alwin H. Sörgel, *Neuste Nachrichten aus Texas* (Leipzig: Expedition des Herold, 1847), reissued as A *Sojourn in Texas, 1846–1847*, trans. and ed. by W. M. Von-Maszewski (San Marcos, Tex.: German Heritage Society, 1992); Carl, Prinz von. Solms-Braunfels, *Texas, Geschildert in Beziehung auf seine geographischen, socialen und übrigen Verhältnissen mit besonderer Rücksicht auf die deutsche Colonisation* (Frankfurt am Main: Johann Davis Sauerländer, 1846), reissued as *Voyage to North America, 1844–45: Prince Carl of Solms's Texas Diary of People, Places, and Events*, trans. by W. M. Von-Maszewski (Denton, Tex.: German-Texan Heritage Society and University of North Texas Press, 2000); Ferdinand Roemer, *Texas* (Bonn: Marcus, 1849), reissued as *Roemer's Texas*, trans. Oswald Mueller (San Antonio, Tex.: Standard, 1935; rpt., Waco, Tex.: Texian Press, 1976).

14. James C. Kearney, *Nassau Plantation: The Evolution of a Texas German Slave Plantation* (Denton: University of North Texas Press, 2010).

15. Among the studies are Ernest G. Fischer, *Marxists and Utopias in Texas* (Burnet: Eakin Press, 1980); Guido E. Ransleben, *A Hundred Years of Comfort in Texas: A Centennial History* (San Antonio: Naylor, 1954; rev. and enl., 1974); Adalbert Regenbrecht, "The German Settlers of Millheim (Texas) before the Civil War," *Southwestern Historical Quarterly* 20, no. 1 (July 1916): 28–34; and Louis Reinhardt, "The Communistic Colony of Bettina," *Southwestern Historical Quarterly* 3, no. 1 (July 1899): 33–40. The most recent (and most informative study) is by German scholar Andreas V. Reichstein: *German Pioneers on the American Frontier: The Wagners in Texas and Illinois* (Denton: University of North Texas Press, 2001).

16. These include Irene Marshall King, *John O. Meusebach, German Colonizer in Texas* (Austin: University of Texas Press, 1967); Henry B. Dielmann, "Dr. Ferdinand Herff, Pioneer Physician and Surgeon," *Southwestern Historical Quarterly* 57, no. 3 (Jan. 1954): 265–84; and Miriam Korff York, *Friedrich Ernst of Industry* (Giddings, Tex.: Nixon Printing, 1989).

17. Jefferson Morgenthaler, *Promised Land* (College Station: Texas A&M University Press, 2009).

18. Rudolph Biesele, "The Texas State Convention of Germans in 1854," *Southwestern Historical Quarterly* 33 (April 1930): 247–61; Charles Nagel, *A Boy's Civil War Story* (St. Louis: Eden, 1935); Walter Kamphoefner and Wolfgang Helbich, eds., Susan Carter Vogel, trans., *Germans in the Civil War* (Chapel Hill: University of North Carolina Press, 2006).

19. Walter Kamphoefner, "New Perspectives on Texas Germans and the Confederacy," *Southwestern Historical Quarterly* 102, no. 4 (April 1999): 441–46.

20. Alwyn Barr, "Records of the Confederate Military Commission in San Antonio, July 2–October 10, 1862," *Southwestern Historical Quarterly* 71, no. 2 (Oct. 1967): 247–78; Bill Stein, "Distress, Discontent, and Dissent: Colorado County, TX, during the Civil War," in *The Seventh Star of the Confederacy*, ed. Kenneth W. Howell (Denton: University of North Texas Press, 2009), 301–16; Walter Buenger, "Texas and the Riddle of

Secession," *Southwestern Historical Quarterly* 87, no. 2 (Oct. 1983): 151–82; Buenger, "Secession Revisited: The Texas Experience," *Civil War History* 30 (Winter 1984): 293–305; Buenger, "Unionism on the Texas Frontier, 1859–61," *Arizona and the West* 22 (Autumn 1980): 237–54; Buenger, "Secession and the Texas German Community: Editor Lindheimer vs. Editor Flake," *Southwestern Historical Quarterly* 82, no. 4 (Apr. 1979): 379–402.

21. Mary Jo O'Rear, "Reckoning at the River: Unionist and Secessionist on the Nueces, August 10, 1862," in Howell, *Seventh Star*, 85–109. See also Claude Elliot, "Union Sentiment in Texas, 1861–1865," *Southwestern Historical Quarterly* 50, no. 4 (April 1947): 449–77; Robert W. Shook, "The Battle of the Nueces," *Southwestern Historical Quarterly* 66, no. 1 (July 1962): 31–42; Stanley S. McGowen, "Battle or Massacre: The Incident on the Nueces," *Southwestern Historical Quarterly* 104, no. 1 (July 2000): 65–90; and Rodman L. Underwood, *Death on the Nueces: German Texans, Treue der Union* (Austin: Eakin Press, 2000).

22. David, R. Hoffmann, "A German-American Pioneer Remembers," *Southwestern Historical Quarterly* 102, no. 4 (Apr. 1999): 487–512; R. H. Williams and John W. Sansom, *The Massacre on the Nueces River: The Story of a Civil War Tragedy* (Grand Prairie, Tex.: Frontier Times Publishing, n.d.).

23. For a discussion of the violence, see James Smallwood, "When the Klan Rode: Terrorism in Reconstruction Texas," in *Still the Arena of Civil War: Violence and Turmoil in Reconstruction Texas, 1865–1874*, ed. Kenneth W. Howell (Denton: University of North Texas Press, 2012), 214–42.

24. David Johnson, *The Mason County "Hoo Doo" War, 1874–1902* (Denton: University of North Texas Press, 2006).

25. Lawrence H. Konecny and Clinton Machann, *Perilous Voyages: Czech and English Immigrants to Texas in the 1870s* (College Station: Texas A&M University Press, 2004).

26. Terry Jordan, "The German Settlement of Texas after 1865," *Southwestern Historical Quarterly* 73, no. 2 (Oct. 1969): 193–212.

27. *The Czech Texans* (San Antonio, Tex.: Institute of Texan Cultures, 1972). Jan Habenicht, *History of Czechs in America* (St. Paul, Minn.: Czechoslovak Genealogical Society International, 2000), places Czech immigration in Texas into the larger context of Czech immigration in America. Eva Eckert addressed the sociology of Czech immigration in *Stones on the Prairie: Acculturation in America* (Bloomington, Ind.: Slovakia, 2006).

28. Clinton Machann and James W. Mendl, *The Czechs in Texas* (College Station: Texas A&M University Department of English, 1979), *Krásná Amerika: A Study of the Texas Czechs, 1851–1939* (Austin: Eakin Press, 1983), and *Czech Voices: Stories from Texas in the Amerikán Národni Kalendář* (College Station: Texas A&M University Press, 2002).

29. William Philip Hewitt, "The Czechs in Texas: A Study of the Immigration and Development of Czech Ethnicity, 1850–1920" (Ph.D. diss., University of Texas at Austin, 1978).

30. Robert L. Skrabanek, *We're Czechs* (College Station: Texas A&M University Press, 1988).

31. Mary Frances Chupick Bennett, *Invitation to Cat Spring* (Bloomington, Ind.: AuthorHouse, 2007).

32. Gerald Stone, *The Smallest Slavonic Nation: The Sorbs of Lusatia* (London: Athlone Press of the University of London, 1972); George Charles Engerrand, *The So-called Wends of Germany and Their Colonies in Texas and in Australia*, University of Texas Bureau of Research in the Social Sciences 7 (Austin, 1934). For book-length treatment of the Wends in Texas, see Anne Blasig, *The Wends of Texas* (San Antonio, Tex.: Naylor, 1954; rpt., Brownsville, Tex.: Springman-King Printing, 1981); and Sylvia Ann Grider, *The Wendish Texans* (San Antonio: University of Texas Institute of Texan Cultures, 1982).

33. T. Lindsay Baker, *The First Polish Americans: Silesian Settlements in Texas* (College Station: Texas A&M University Press, 1979), and "The Reverend Leopold Moczygemba, Patriarch of Polonia," *Polish American Studies*, Spring 1984, 80–86; Joseph Swastek, *Priest and Pioneer: Rev. Leopold Moczygemba* (Detroit, Mich.: Conventual, 1951).

34. Jacek Przygoda, *Texas Pioneers from Poland: A Study in Ethnic History* (Waco, Tex.: Texian Press, 1971).

35. Mary Whatley Clarke, *The Swenson Saga and the SMS Ranches* (Austin: Jenkins, 1976). See also Harry Hunt Ransom, "A Renaissance Gentleman in Texas: Notes on the Life and Library of Swante Palm," *Southwestern Historical Quarterly* 53, no. 3 (Jan. 1950): 225–38; and Carl T. Widén, trans. and ed., *Johannes Swenson: A Journey from Sweden to Texas in 1867* (Austin: self-published, 1954).

36. Magnus Morner, *The Swedish Migrants to Texas* (Chicago: Swedish-American Historical Society, 1987); Carl Martin Rosenquist, *Swedes of Texas* (Austin, 1942); Larry E. Scott, *The Swedish Texans* (San Antonio: University of Texas Institute of Texan Cultures, 1990).

37. John L. Davis, *The Danish Texans* (San Antonio: University of Texas Institute of Texan Cultures, 1979; 2d ed., 1983); Thomas P. Christensen, "Danevang, Texas," *Southwestern Historical Quarterly* 32, no. 1 (July 1928): 67–73; Theodore Christian Blegen, *Norwegian Migration to America* (New York: Haskell House, 1969); Richard L. Hooverson, "Midnight Sun to Lone Star: Norwegians in Texas," *Stirpes* 30 (March 1990): 4–13; Institute of Texan Cultures, *The Norwegian Texans* (San Antonio, Tex.: Encino, 1970); Lyder L. Unstad, "Norwegian Migration to Texas," *Southwestern Historical Quarterly* 43, no. 2 (Oct. 1939): 176–95.

38. Allison Schottenstein, "Jewish Immigration in Small Town Texas" (Ph.D. diss., University of Texas at Austin, 2011).

39. Natalie Ornish, *Pioneer Jewish Texans* (College Station: Texas A&M University Press, 2011); Bryan F. Stone, *The Chosen Folks: Jews on the Frontiers of Texas* (Austin: University of Texas Press, 2012); Cathy Schechter and Ruthe Winegarten, *Deep in the Heart: The Lives and Legends of Texas Jews* (Galveston: Texas Jewish Historical Society, 1989); Hollace Weiner, ed., *Lone Stars of David: The Jews of Texas* (Waltham, Mass: Brandeis University, and Austin: Texas Jewish Historical Society, 2007).

40. Bernard Marinbach, "The Galveston Movement" (Ph.D. diss., Jewish Theological Seminary of America, 1976); Gary Dean Best, "Jacob H. Schiff's Galveston Movement: An Experiment in Immigration Deflection, 1907–1914," *American Jewish Archives* 30 (Apr. 1978): 43–79.

CHAPTER 6

Literature, the Visual Arts, and Music in Texas

Victoria H. Cummins and Light Townsend Cummins

Texas has a vibrant and rich literary, artistic, and musical heritage that began before the era of European contact. A great tradition of creative expression started with Native American residents of what would eventually become Texas. Across all periods of the state's history, hosts of writers, artists, and musicians have made their home in Texas. This chapter traces the development of Texas literature, art, and music, although it must be stressed that the volume of important work on these three topics precludes noting anything more than a representative sampling of authors, artists, and musicians.

LITERATURE IN TEXAS

A variety of compendiums, critical works, and anthologies survey Texas literature with special emphasis on fiction and poetry. Davis Foute Eagleton, a professor of English at Austin College, began systematically surveying Texas writers and poets in the 1890s with the objective of assembling a guide to their work for students and interested readers. His *Writers and Writings of Texas*, published in 1913, has itself become a classic.[1] Texas literary production greatly accelerated in the opening decades of the twentieth century, thus giving rise to other, more modern compendiums of writers and literature. In the mid-1920s, Goldie Capers Smith published a biographical dictionary of writers, composers, and artists working in Texas. In all she provided entries for just over two hundred Texans, some who earned enduring reputations and some who have remained obscure.[2] Florence Alberta Barns was an academic with a doctorate in literature who published *Texas Writers of Today* in 1935. She attempted to provide a short biography for every important living writer in the state along with representative samplings of work by each of them.[3] Writing fifty years later, A. C. Greene's *The Fifty + Best Books on Texas* compiles from the perspective of the 1980s a list of authors and their most important books.[4] In that same vein, *Classics of Texas Fiction*, edited by James Ward Lee in 1987, covers some forty authors who wrote from the late nineteenth century to the late 1980s.[5] Don Graham's *Lone Star Literature* presents excerpts from Texas authors from the late nineteenth century to the present day, providing a sampling of their work.[6] A 1989 volume edited by Craig Clifford and Tom Pilkington, *Range Wars*, contains a series of essays on the nature and character of Texas literature by a group of well-known writers from around the state.[7] Tom Pilkington's *State of Mind: Texas Literature and Culture* is a cogent and finely reasoned critical survey of writing in Texas from the Spanish colonial era to the late twentieth century. Pilkington examines the subtle influences that cultural change has had on the literary expression rooted in the state.[8]

The Spanish and Mexican eras of Texas history witnessed a measured literary production, mostly in the form of memoirs, memorials, and written reports about Texas by various individuals who passed through the region. The best-known work from the Spanish colonial era remains the memorial of Alvar Nuñez Cabeza de Vaca, who was shipwrecked on the Texas coast in 1528 and wandered a good part of its geography until finally returning to New Spain (Mexico) in 1536. First published in 1542, the memoirs of his experiences have been standard reading for generations and have been published in numerous English-language editions.[9] In the 1770s a Spanish priest named Fray Juan Augustín Morfi wrote a long narrative of his travels in Texas that some readers have characterized as the first history of Texas. José Cortes, another Spaniard who passed through Texas, wrote a long report of his trip in the 1790s.[10]

It should also be noted that Prof. Nicolás Kanellos of the University of Houston founded the Recovering the U.S. Hispanic Literary Heritage Project for the purpose of identifying and publishing works from the Spanish-language heritage of the Southwest, including Texas. Although the focus of this project now includes all aspects of Spanish-language literature produced in the United States up to the year 1960, it has recovered obscure works from the Spanish and Mexican eras of Texas history, making them available to the public in either published or online digitized form.[11] The era of Mexican Texas from 1821 to 1836 witnessed the continued writing of reports by Spanish speakers in the province along with the appearance of Anglo-American writers who came from the United States. Manuel Mier y Terán made an inspection tour of Texas in 1828 for the purpose of reporting to his superiors in Mexico City about conditions in the province.[12] Mary Austin Holley, a cousin of Stephen F. Austin, enjoys the distinction of being the first major English-language author to write about Texas. She visited Texas several times in the 1830s and 1840s and wrote popularly oriented books—part travelogue, part public relations—in an effort to spur immigration from the United States. Her 1833 book, *Texas: Observations Historical, Geographic, and Descriptive,* continues to be considered a literary classic of the period.[13]

The period of the Republic and of the antebellum era failed to produce much enduring literature, perhaps because Texans were preoccupied with economic development along with the political problems that would eventually result in secession. Mirabeau B. Lamar, president of the Republic of Texas, wrote poetry. His book, *Verse Memorials*, was published in 1857.[14] However, his poetry is today considered to have very little, if any, literary merit. Melinda Rankin, a Presbyterian missionary who lived in Texas at various times during the 1840s and 1850s, wrote two books about the state. Her first, *Texas in 1850*, is considered to be of marked literary quality in its descriptions of the state in the antebellum period.[15] The architect and urban planner Frederick Law Olmstead traveled through Texas in the decade before the Civil War. His impressions were published in 1857 as *A Journey through Texas*, a dark work that highlighted the evils of slavery in the Lone Star State.[16] As would also be the case in painting and art, some literary work flowed from European immigrants who came to Texas in that era. Victor Considerant wrote about his Reunion Colony in *Au Texas*.[17]

A flowering of Texas literature came in the three decades after the Civil War as the population of the state expanded and its cities grew. William Sidney Porter, known by his pen name O. Henry, lived for more than a decade in Texas during the 1880s and 1890s, first on a ranch, then at Austin, and finally in Houston. Several of his works had Texas settings, although he did most of his writing after later settling in New York City.[18] Not surprisingly, cowboy and frontier literature became a major genre of Texas writing from the post–Civil War decades into the early twentieth century, some of it fiction and some in the form of memoirs. Much of this literature placed Texas within a larger context of the American West. Cowboy and western fiction as a literary genre is the subject of William T. Pilkington's *Critical Essays on the Western*

Novel, which contains chapters by various authorities who deal with Texas authors along with those from elsewhere.[19] One of the best of the cowboy-frontier authors of the late nineteenth and early twentieth centuries was Charles A. Siringo, who wrote *A Texas Cowboy*.[20] Andy Adams, who spent much of the 1880s living in Texas, became a prolific writer of western theme books, highlighted in 1903 by *The Log of a Cowboy*.[21] John C. Duval, who some critics have called the best Texas writer of his era, published his *Early Times in Texas* as a magazine serial in the late 1860s; but it did not become a book until 1892. Duval's masterpiece will remain *The Adventures of Big-Foot Wallace: The Texas Ranger and Hunter*.[22]

Texas literature flourished during the early years of the twentieth century, an era when regional viewpoints in literature became popular across the nation. The rise of regionalism witnessed the arrival of the author who would be for decades thereafter the best-known and most widely read Texas writer, J. Frank Dobie. An English instructor at the University of Texas during the early decades of his career and a folklorist by practice, Dobie collected tales of the Southwest from the early twentieth century to his death in 1964.[23] Most of his books found their way to best-seller lists. His publisher, the Little-Brown Company of Boston and its successors, has kept many of his books in print to date. Dobie is the subject of three full biographies.[24] The 1930s and 1940s also witnessed the appearance of high-quality Texas fiction based on the state's southern heritage. George Session Perry's *Hold Autumn in Your Hand*, published in 1941, remains the best Texas fiction dealing with the lives of sharecroppers.[25] Laura Krey's 1938 *And Tell of Time* looks at the state and its culture through the prism of its Confederate heritage.[26] Edward Everett Davis also wrote from the viewpoint of the South. His novel, *The White Scourge*, painted the state's heritage in a very uncomplimentary manner, as did *Land Without Moses* by Charles Curtis Munz.[27] The greatest writer of the era to see Texas from a southern perspective, however, was Katherine Anne Porter, who hailed from the small town of Kyle. Although Porter went to great lengths to obscure her Texas background once she became an internationally significant writer, much of her early work was steeped in the southern culture of the state. Although she moved away from Texas in 1918 while in her early twenties and never again made it her residence, some of her best short story fiction is set in the Lone Star State.[28]

In the years after World War II, Fred Gipson emerged as an acclaimed Texas author largely because of his first book, *Hound Dog Man*. He continued to write fiction for several decades, achieving commercial success with *Old Yeller*, which the Walt Disney Company made into a popular motion picture.[29] One of the more curious, yet significant works of Texas fiction to emerge during this era is Madison Cooper's novel *Sironia, Texas.*[30] A Waco native, Cooper had been writing quietly since the 1920s without much public notice while he operated his family's central Texas grocery business. Few people realized he was a writer until Houghton Mifflin published this book in 1952, the result of more than a decade's work by Cooper.

Three fiction writers during the 1940s and 1950s continued the southern rural perspective that had long been popular as a Texas genre. William Goyen, a graduate of Rice Institute, wrote *House of Breath* and *Ghost and Flesh*, both of which established his reputation as an important author.[31] Much of his work centered on life and labor in East Texas. William Humphrey, writing in the tradition of Mississippian William Faulkner, set his novels in the northeastern part of the state. Several of his books gained wide readership, including *Home from the Hill* and *The Ordways.*[32] Like Goyen and Humphrey, William A. Owens set much of his fiction in rural East Texas, where he had spent his youth. An academic who taught for many years at Columbia University, Owens used his personal experiences to inform his writing in ways that were heavily autobiographical, including in *This Stubborn Soil*, *A Season of Weathering*, and *Tell Me a Story, Sing Me a Song.*[33]

The 1960s and 1970s saw the appearance of new Texas writers and poets, many of whom are still living and actively involved in their careers. Patrick Bennett interviewed a dozen Texas writers who were active during the 1970s in his book *Talking with Texas Writers: Twelve Interviews.*[34] Betsy Feagan Colquitt's *A Part of Space: Ten Texas Writers* provides an introduction to some Texas authors who emerged in these decades, including John Howard Griffin, Edwin "Bud" Shrake, John Graves, and Larry McMurtry.[35] McMurtry has been the most widely read and commercially successful at the national level. The winner of a 1985 Pulitzer Prize for *Lonesome Dove*, he began to establish his preeminence as a Texas author with the publication of *Horseman, Pass By* in 1961, which became the motion picture *Hud.*[36] McMurtry's work has been the subject of an ever-expanding number of critical and literary assessments; a good place to begin is Mark Busby's *Larry McMurtry and the West.*[37] Busby concentrates his analysis on how Texas and its culture influenced McMurtry. Less known nationally than McMurtry, but also widely read, is Elmer Kelton, who wrote dozens of novels set in the cattle country of West Texas. Although many of these appeal only to readers of the western genre, some of his novels, including *The Time It Never Rained*, are considered classics of Texas fiction. His acclaimed 1971 novel

The Day the Cowboys Quit is based on a strike that occurred in the ranch country during the 1880s.[38]

Texas has also been fertile ground for poets. Phillip Graham provided numerous examples of verse written during the antebellum era in his 1936 book *Early Texas Verse, 1835–1850*.[39] The compendium *A Century with Texas Poets and Poetry*, edited by Vaida Stewart Montgomery, highlights those individuals writing in the first three decades of the twentieth century.[40] The heritage of poetry in the state can be further appreciated in Peggy Z. Lynch's *Behold Texas* and Margaret R. Edwards's *The Poets Laureate of Texas*.[41] A modern survey edited by Billy Bob Hill, *Texas in Poetry 2*, provides examples of Texas poems from the early nineteenth century to the present day.[42]

One of the first widely known Texas poets was William Lawrence Chittenden. A native of New Jersey, he moved to West Texas in the 1890s and became a poet of note with publication of his ever popular verse "The Cowboy's Christmas Ball," which celebrates a holiday tradition in the West Texas town of Anson.[43] A Swedish immigrant to Texas, John Peter Sjolander, lived at Cedar Bayou and began to publish poetry in the late 1870s. Many of his poems became features in national magazines and the newspapers of Texas, thus making him perhaps the best-known poet in the Lone Star State, often being called the "Dean of Texas Poets" during his lifetime.[44] In the first half of the twentieth century, the poet Hilton R. Greer enjoyed acclaim, although few people remember him today. He was instrumental in organizing the Texas Poetry Society in 1921 and also assembled a compendium of Texas poetry in 1923, *Voices of the Southwest*.[45] Houston's Vassar Miller published her first volume of poetry, *Adam's Footprint*, in 1956, opening a career that eventually made her poet laureate of Texas before her death in 1998.[46] San Antonio's Naomi Shihab Nye wrote her first book of poems, *Different Ways to Pray*, in 1980 and is still writing award-winning poetry.[47]

African American writers have been active in the state from the time of Sutton E. Griggs, who published his novel *Imperium in Imperio* in 1899. Griggs continued writing into the twentieth century, and his life is chronicled by Finnie D. Coleman.[48] The folklorist J. Mason Brewer emerged as one of the first widely read African American authors in Texas, as analyzed by James Byrd in his biographical study. Brewer's *The Word on the Brazos* became a classic when published in 1953.[49] In the modern era, the African American playwright and author J. California Cooper has been writing since the 1980s, authoring plays, short stories, and novels.[50] Reginald McKnight won an O.

Henry Award and published several novels including *The Kind of Light That Shines on Texas.*[51]

Texas has also produced talented women writers, especially in the realms of fiction and poetry. A useful and solid overview of female authors in Texas can be found in *Texas Women Writers*, edited by Sylvia A. Grider and Lou Halsell Rodenberger.[52] It contains biographical essays on prominent women writers in the state from the time of Mary Austin Holley to the present era, with attention given to the authors of prose, poetry, and drama, including a special section dealing with Tejana and African American writers. This volume also has an extensive bibliography that notes works by the writers themselves along with publications that provide critical commentary on their work. Although space precludes discussing most of these female writers, it should be noted that Dorothy Scarborough's fiction gained an international following in the early twentieth century. Her 1926 book *The Wind*, which examines the hardships faced by women on the Texas frontier, guaranteed her reputation when Metro-Goldwyn-Mayer Studios filmed this powerful novel as a blockbuster 1928 motion picture starring Lillian Gish, a film still considered today as a classic of the silent screen.[53]

Tejano writers have developed a diverse literature in recent decades; for a survey, see Dagoberto Gilb's *Hecho: An Anthology of Texas-Mexican Literature.* Gilb, a faculty member at Texas State University in San Marcos, is the author of several fiction works.[54] Rolando Hinojosa has become one of the most prolific Tejano writers of the modern era; for an assessment of his work, see Joyce Glover Lee's *Rolando Hinojosa and the American Dream.*[55] Tomás Rivera, a Texas native, graduated from what is now Texas State University and then earned a Ph.D. from the University of Oklahoma before becoming a university administrator. He wrote short stories, essays, and fiction.[56] An Alamo City author, Sandra Cisneros, is a prolific writer of essays, short stories, and poetry; her work is examined in Carmen Haydée's *Border Crossings and Beyond.* A 1984 novel, *The House on Mango Street*, is among Cisneros's best-known works.[57] Carmen Tafolla of San Antonio has written over fifteen books of fiction and poetry, capturing much about the lives of Spanish-speaking Texans in her work.[58]

Current writers are featured in a book of oral interviews with Texas authors edited by Frances Leonard and Ramona Crowley. Their *Conversations with Texas Writers* contains edited interview transcripts of fifty male and female writers from widely diverse backgrounds and literary orientations across the state, most of whom are still active. It also provides a short biography of each author along with a selected bibliography of his or her work.[59] Leonard and Crowley's book is a good introduction to Texas writers active in the early twenty-first century, a large and expanding group who are continuing to add to the Texas literary tradition.

THE VISUAL ARTS IN TEXAS

As in the case for literature, Texas has enjoyed a lively and enduring tradition in the visual arts. The study of the history of art in Texas must begin with a small number of general references used by all scholars. Goldie Capers Smith's previously noted 1926 compendium was a biographical reference to the creative community in Texas targeting an audience of library patrons, students, clubwomen, and general readers interested in living Texas writers, composers, and artists. Though two-thirds of the entries were devoted to literary figures, sixty Texas-born or Texas-resident painters and sculptors were also included. Two years later, prominent clubwoman Frances Battaile Fisk published her groundbreaking *History of Texas Artists and Sculptors*, which is still a standard reference work on artists active before 1930.[60] Fisk's book, written to help clubwomen research information on current and past Texas art and artists, was the first attempt to survey systematically the visual arts in the Lone Star State. Fisk employed a three-phase periodization of art history in Texas (early 1888–1900; middle 1900–1917; present 1917–1927) with biographical vignettes of artists, subdivided loosely by specialty, artistic medium, and geographic area. Unlike Smith, Fisk addressed printmaking and ceramics, although the coverage was thin. Though not comprehensive, the book included painters and sculptors prominent in the late 1920s and identified some emerging artists. It mentioned more than 350 visual artists and craftspeople. In 1935, Esse Forrester-O'Brien published *Art and Artists of Texas*, which expanded the scope of Fisk's work.[61] O'Brien's book was almost purely biographical, with little attempt at art history, but covered not just painters and sculptors but printmakers, craftspeople, architects, wood carvers, fashion and stage designers, and cartoonists as well. Her opening chapter on art in Texas highlighted organizations and institutions important to the promotion of the visual arts in the state. She also included chapters on pioneer art and artists, the art works in the Texas capitol, and the artists of the just-completed Public Works of Art Project. All three of these reference volumes contained information about a significant number of female artists but included few Hispanics and no African Americans.

Two more recent art reference works, Paula and Michael Grauer's *Dictionary of Texas Artists, 1800–1945* and John and Deborah Powers's *Texas Painters, Sculptors and Graphic Artists*, are more comprehensive. Exhaustively researched, each gives shorter entries on a large number of artists of all genres, listing basic biographical data, information about participation in shows and exhibits, awards and prizes won by the artists, and museums that hold their work.[62]

There are no equivalently comprehensive reference works for post–World War II Texas. However, Michael Grauer's article in *Twentieth Century Texas: A Social and Cultural History* briefly traces the history of artists and art teachers in the state to the early twenty-first century.[63] The catalog of a 1971/72 exhibit, *Texas Painting and Sculpture*, is notable for a series of brief but much-cited essays on the development of the visual arts in Dallas, San Antonio, Houston, Austin, and Fort Worth.[64] The *Handbook of Texas Online* is an excellent source of articles on a variety of art topics including art schools and institutions, art teachers and critics, biographies of specific artists, and art history.[65]

The story of art in Texas begins with Native Americans. Their work remains visible today in unique forms of artistic expression—petroglyphs (pictures carved on rock) and pictographs (painting on rock). In the 1930s, Dallas artist Forrest Kirkland became the first person to study this Native American form of expression systematically. For almost a decade, he traveled Texas to sketch and reproduce in exact rendition the thousands of pictographs scattered across the state. Kirkland's reproductions were eventually edited by Native American expert W. W. Newcomb, Jr., and later published after the artist's death.[66]

In the Spanish and Mexican periods, missionaries and settlers introduced European-style art into Texas. Their work was mostly religious in theme. In *The Art and Architecture of Texas Missions*, Jacinto Quirarte uses information from archival documents, drawings, and photos to reconstruct what the decoration and altar pieces in Texas's mission churches would have looked like; he also analyzes the iconography of the altar pieces.[67] Little secular art was produced before the arrival of Anglo-Americans in the 1820s and 1830s. A notable exception is a mid-eighteenth-century oil painting titled "The Destruction of Mission San Sabá in the Province of Texas and the Martyrdom of the Fathers Alonso Giraldo de Terreros, Joseph Santiesteban," by an unknown Mexican artist. This painting depicts the 1758 massacre of friars at the San Sabá mission near present-day Menard. Sam DeShong Ratcliffe analyzes this work in *Painting Texas History to 1900*.[68]

In the period from the 1820s to 1900, Anglo-American settlement brought artists to Texas from other parts of the nation and from Europe. Pauline A.

Pinckney has documented these artists, who included Thomas Jefferson Wright, George R. Allen. William M. G. Samuel, and George Catlin, all of whom painted oil portraits of leading citizens and made engravings of the flora and fauna of the Texas frontier.[69] An influx of European colonists at mid-century brought painters with continental training like Richard Petri, Carl Iwonski, Hermann Lungkwitz, and Theodore Gentilz. They also painted settler portraits, Indians, and landscapes and documented the lives of German-speaking immigrants in Texas. The previously cited Ratcliffe work, *Painting Texas History*, is the definitive work on late nineteenth-century Texas artwork. Ratcliffe traces the careers of these immigrant artists who helped to delineate and interpret the Texas experience on canvas, additionally including Henry Arthur McArdle, William Henry Huddle, Samuel Chamberlain, and Sarah Hardinge.

The scope and concept of "Texas art" is open to interpretation and contention; for some views of the concept, see William Goetzmann's introductory essay in *Texas Images and Visions*, which considers artists' depictions of Texas from the earliest eastern adventurers to artists working in the 1980s, or Alison de Lima Greene's *Texas: 150 Works from the Museum of Fine Arts Houston*, which celebrates the centenary of that institution, tracing its history and focusing on artists' works from its permanent collection that have depicted the state through the century.[70]

Two Texas artists achieved enduring reputations during the late nineteenth and early twentieth centuries: painters Frank Reaugh and Robert Jenkins Onderdonk. Reaugh was particularly enamored of Longhorn cattle, producing hundreds of pastels, oils, and watercolors of them throughout his career.[71] Onderdonk was a native of Maryland who moved first to Dallas in 1889, and then to San Antonio in the 1890s, where he spent the remainder of his life, painting local color in the Alamo City and helping to found the San Antonio Art League. Two of his children, Julian and Eleanor, later became important to Texas art. Julian became accomplished in painting colorful South Texas landscapes, especially those that featured bluebonnets. The younger sister, Eleanor, who served for many decades as curator of art at the Witte Museum in San Antonio, was one of the greatest proponents of Texas art in the state.[72] The influence of impressionism on Texas artists during the late nineteenth and early twentieth centuries is highlighted in Michael Grauer's *Texas Impressionism*.[73]

The period between the world wars saw the flowering of Texas regionalist art. William E. Reaves addresses in *Texas Art and a Wildcatter's Dream* the short-lived (1927–1929) but influential Texas Wildflower competitions, whose rich prizes stimulated interest in the Texas landscape by painters in and outside of the state.[74] Regionalism emerged full blown in the 1930s, centering in Dallas. Rick Stewart's book on the subject presents biographical information about the artists who were active in this movement.[75] Francine Carraro's biography of artist and art educator Jerry Bywaters is a thoroughly researched volume that provides an enormous amount of contextual information about the art world in Dallas in the regionalist era.[76] Susie Kalil's biography of artist Alexandre Hogue examines the life and work of this important Texas regionalist.[77] Philip Parisi has documented the location of the regionalist post office murals in Texas painted during the 1930s and 1940s, providing information about both the works and their creators.[78]

Regionalism died away in the 1940s as nonobjective art came into vogue. This proved the case in Fort Worth, where a group of artists including Bror Utter, Cynthia Brants, and Bill Bomar began working in ways different from the earlier regionalists.[79] The contemporary arts movement proved especially successful in Houston starting in the 1950s when museum director Jermayne MacAgy and art patron Dominique de Menil worked hard to advance its cause in the Bayou City. Houston artists active in this movement included Robert Preusser, Carden Bailey, Gene Charlton, Joseph Glasco, and Charles Shorre.[80] More recently, no one city has dominated Texas in the visual arts.[81] An unlikely center for modern art in Texas took shape in 1971 when New York City artist Donald Judd moved to Marfa in the Big Bend Country. He took the facilities of a military post, Fort D. A. Russell, and made then into a center for the arts, calling it the Chinati Foundation.[82]

In the first half of the twentieth century a small number of Hispanic artists, most of them foreign born, participated in the Texas art community and exhibited in the same shows as Anglo artists. Figures in this group, which included José Arpa, Xavier Gonzalez, Antonio García, Porfirio Salinas, and Octavio Medellín, were covered in the works already mentioned about the first half of the twentieth century. However, Mexican American artists born in Texas did not find this kind of acceptance. In the post–World War II era a younger group of artists came of age feeling marginalized and neglected by the arts community. As a product of the push for civil rights and cultural recognition by the Mexican American community at large by the late 1960s, artists began to organize networks to gain notice and appreciation for their work. Art historians and curators have approached the study of the art created by Texans of Hispanic heritage from several perspectives, varying in the scope and breadth of artists included. The broadest perspective, manifested in works such as *Houston Hispanic Artists: New Views*, groups together artists of varied Hispanic backgrounds, including foreign-born artists from Latin America and Spain as well as Mexican Americans.[83] Art historian Jacinto Quirarte's pioneering work *Mexican American Artists* addresses the work of artists of Mexican descent whether born in the United States or Mexico.[84] He profiles the careers of more than twenty Mexican American artists working in Texas, New Mexico, and California in the twentieth century. The narrowest focus is found in books and catalogues devoted to Mexican American artists who have self-identified as Chicano/a. General works about Chicano art that include Texas artists are Shifra Goldman and Tomás Ybarra-Frausto's *Arte Chicano*, Jacinto Quirarte's *Chicano Art History*, and Richard Griswold del Castillo, Teresa McKenna, and Yvonne Yarbro-Bejarano's edited *Chicano Art.*[85] *Con Safo: The Chicano Art Group and the Politics of South Texas*, by Ruben C. Cordova, chronicles the origins, activities, and decline of one of the earliest and most important Chicano art networks in Texas.[86]

Hispanic women also created activist networks, notably Mujeres Artistas de Suroeste (MAS), founded in Austin in 1977. Santa Barraza was one of the founders of MAS and has remained a forceful advocate for Chicana art. María Herrera-Sobek edited *Santa Barraza, Artist of the Borderlands*, a collection autobiographical, biographical, and critical articles on Barraza's life and work.[87] Miguel Juárez's *Colors on Desert Walls* presents a unique aspect of El Paso's Chicano artistic heritage, mural painting.[88] This bilingual volume includes interviews with ten mural artists, color photos of the murals, and a list of all known murals, whether extant or not. A few other Hispanic artists have works that focus individually on their lives and art, including Porfirio Salinas, Dionicio Rodríguez, and Luís Jiménez.[89]

Women artists have been working in Texas since the nineteenth century, and their output is represented in the exhibition catalogs and general books about Texas artists mentioned above, as well as in general works on western artists. In the 1970s, Patricia D. Hendricks published *20th Century Women Artists in Texas* to accompany an exhibit of the same name.[90] Sylvia Moore's *No Bluebonnets, No Yellow Roses* is a brief volume containing ten essays mostly concerned with contemporary women artists in the Lone Star State.[91] Two of its essays address women artists before 1936 and another discusses two women who founded privately funded art museums some thirty years apart. Susan Landauer and Becky Duval Reese's chapter in *Independent Spirits: Women Painters of the American West* gives information about the lives and careers of several Texas women artists and fits them into trends on the national and regional level.[92] A more general reference work, Kovinick and Kovinick's *Encyclopedia of Women*

Artists of the American West, is also a useful resource.[93] A recent look at women artists is Kippra D. Hopper and Laurie J. Churchill's *Art of West Texas Women*, which looks at the work of twenty contemporary artists.[94]

Fewer works deal exclusively with African American art and artists. The Centennial Celebration held in Dallas during 1936 was one of the first Texas events to feature African American art. The celebration of African American culture was confined to a special building at Fair Park called the Hall of Negro Life. This edifice exhibited the works of nationally known African American painters including Aaron Douglass. The paintings of Texas artists Samuel A. Countee of Houston and Frank Sheinall of Galveston were also on display.[95] In *Black Art in Houston*, John Biggers and Carroll Simms, along with John Edward Weems, surveyed an African American art community nurtured by the art department founded by Biggers at Texas Southern University in the late 1940s.[96] Biggers himself became a major Texas artist, known especially for his murals; several books have been published about his art.[97] In the past decade, the Museum of Fine Arts Houston sponsored a symposium and mounted a show of African American art from Houston collections; although *Collecting African American Art* focuses on the nationally known artists, there is also information on some Texas-based professional artists and self-taught "naïve" artists from Houston.[98]

In addition to painting, Texas has always had a strong tradition in sculpture. Patricia D. Hendricks and Becky Duval Reese surveyed Lone Star sculptural history in their *Century of Sculpture in Texas, 1889–1989*.[99] A convenient handbook edited by Carol Morris Little and arranged by city of location lists public sculpture in the state.[100] Elizabet Ney emerged in the 1890s as one of the leading and best-known sculptors in the state and created important statues until her death in 1907; she is the subject of several biographies.[101] Pompeo Coppini, the start of whose career in Texas overlapped Ney's, enjoys the distinction of being perhaps the most prolific sculptor in terms of number of works now spread across the state. He was a classical sculptor in the beaux arts tradition who eagerly sought commissions in Texas for over a half century, sculpting statues of Texas political leaders, educators, military heroes, and individuals as subjects drawn from the history of the state.[102] His student and studio associate, Waldine Tauch, continued his artistic styles and subject matter until her death in 1986.[103]

In the years after World War II, Austin's Charles Umlauf emerged as the state's most innovative sculptor. A faculty member in the art department of the University of Texas until his retirement in the 1980s, Umlauf greatly advanced sculpture in Texas, blending abstraction with representational norms to create a distinctive style.[104] Roy Fridge became active as a sculptor in the alternative art movement of the early 1960s. One of Fridge's associates, Jim Love, excelled at making steel sculptures, using the cutting torch as an instrument of art. Luís Jiménez also developed innovative sculptural forms, using fiberglass and interior lighting to craft beguiling translucent sculptures of great distinctiveness. James Surls, a native Texas sculptor who lived at Splendora for many years before moving to Colorado, became well known for his large wood and metal sculptures, some of which have designs burned into them.[105]

MUSIC IN TEXAS

There are some excellent general reference sources for Texas music. The large number of biographies written about the lives of popular Texas musicians precludes specific mention of them here. Willie Nelson, for example, could be the subject of a very long bibliography. As well, biographies of individual musicians can be easily located by searching the name of the subject. A good place to start research on music topics is *The Handbook of Texas Music*.[106] This handy reference is the product of a multiyear collaborative project that used articles from the *Handbook of Texas Online* as its starting point. Recently updated and expanded in a second edition, its articles cover music venues; institutions such as symphony orchestras, choral societies, and record companies; histories of groups and ensembles; the development of musical genres; music education and music educators; and biographies of composers and individual artists. Biographical articles are limited to deceased artists; however, a detailed index indicates where living performers are referenced in the various articles. Articles have short bibliographies and some include a discography. The website of the Center for Texas Music History at Texas State University is also an excellent source of information.[107] From it can be accessed *Texas Music History Online*, an interactive resource for researchers, educators, and Texas music enthusiasts; and the *Texas Music Bibliography*, last updated in 2005, with published and unpublished sources arranged by genre; it also allows full-text access to articles from the *Journal of Texas Music History*.[108]

For a more synthetic treatment of Texas music before 1950, see Lawrence Clayton and Joe W. Specht's edited *Roots of Texas Music*.[109] The editors assembled a group of specialists who each wrote a chapter on the evolution of eight different genres of Texas music. Gary Hartman contributed an overview of Texas music to begin the book. Each chapter has notes, and there is a general index. These articles are an excellent way to identify the names of groups and individual artists, which can then be studied in more detail using *The Handbook of Texas Music.* Another general work is Larry Willoughby's *Texas Rhythm and Texas Rhyme.*[110] This is a pictorial history written as an introduction for the general public. Its theme is the diversity of Texas popular music as a reflection of the cultural diversity of the state. There is an introduction on nineteenth-century music, and the rest of the book is mostly arranged by genre, covering up to the 1980s. This work includes a bibliographic essay and index.

Early sources on Texas music and musical performances are sparse. In her previously cited 1926 work, *The Creative Arts in Texas,* Goldie Capers Smith included biographies of twenty-three then living composers, including the legendary David Guion. The earliest work wholly devoted to Texas music was written by librarian Lota M. Spell.[111] Published in the year of the Texas Centennial, Spell's reference guide was written for clubwomen, teachers, and the general public interested in music and included examples of sheet music and lyrics as illustrations. After some brief background chapters on the indigenous, Spanish, Mexican, and German roots of Texas music, most of the book dealt with music education, music publishing, and musical institutions from 1910 to the mid-1930s. A final chapter presented folk music and Texas composers.

Austin, El Paso, and Houston have been the object of music-oriented histories. By chronicling the musical groups, solo artists, and theatrical troupes who performed in Austin in the first half of the twentieth century, Mint O. James-Reed documented the firm foundations for serious music and theater in that city.[112] Short chapters in this volume addressed the Austin Civic Opera, music study clubs, the Austin Community Concert Association, music in the public schools, the music department at the University of Texas, and the history of the Austin Symphony Orchestra. Robert M. Stevenson provided similar perspective for El Paso in his book *Music in El Paso, 1919–1939.*[113] He gave short biographies of early El Paso performers, music educators, and composers, with attention to nonnative musician-teachers who brought music to El Paso. He also listed touring soloists and musical ensembles who came though El Paso before World War II. Longtime Houston music critic Hubert Roussel set the symphony orchestra into the context of music in Houston and the establishment of orchestras in Texas.[114] Historian Robert I. Giesberg's two studies of the Houston Grand Opera give an overview of musical performances (particularly opera) in that city before the founding of the opera company in 1956 as well as a discussion of the accomplishments of that institution in its first fifty years.[115]

For country and western music in Texas, one must begin with Bill C. Malone's groundbreaking work on rural and working-class southern music, *Country Music, USA,* which makes numerous references to Texas.[116] Much of his chapter "The Cowboy Image and the Growth of Western Music" is about Texas and Texans. Malone traces the evolution of "hillbilly" music into "western" or cowboy music, highlighting the careers of greats such as Gene Autry, Adolph Hofner, Ernest Tubb, and the Light Crust Doughboys as illustrations. He finds that this genre has eclectic roots including southern rural music, gospel, popular music, blues, jazz, Cajun, and German.

Musicologist Jean A. Boyd studies western swing in *The Jazz of the Southwest.*[117] Based largely on oral history interviews, she presents a cross-section of artists, time periods, and bands, making the case that they were not hillbilly singers or country artists, as generally presumed, but true jazz musicians. Boyd conceptualizes western swing as mainstream swing jazz played on traditional country instruments. Boyd has also done a study of one of Texas's most famous swing groups, the Light Crust Doughboys.[118] Dave Oliphant in his study *Texan Jazz* acknowledges that Texas cities did not serve as centers of development for this musical form, and there is no specifically Texan form of modern jazz. Instead, the book identifies the contributions of many Texans, starting with Scott Joplin, who participated in the recording of jazz in the major urban centers in which it did develop.[119]

Alan B. Govenar has written extensively on the origins and development of the blues in Texas, with particular focus on Dallas and Houston. Since 1981, Govenar has interviewed more than one hundred blues artists in Texas. His works—including *Living Texas Blues; Meeting the Blues; The Early Years of Rhythm and Blues;* and *Texas Blues*—are excellent sources of information on African American blues artists.[120] He has also published, with Jay F. Brakefield, *Deep Ellum: The Other Side of Dallas.*[121] *Texas Blues* is the broadest in scope and most comprehensive of Govenar's works to date, correcting inaccurate and incomplete information, incorporating all of the interview material from his earlier books, and adding new material from interviews done by others.

For additional information on Houston, see Roger Wood's *Down in Houston,* a study of the blues in that city. The author, who teaches English in the Houston Community College system, mixes excerpts from oral history interviews he has conducted with his own reminiscences about the blues scene in Houston over several decades. The book is well illustrated with photos by James Fraher.

Wood highlights lesser-known local performers as well as such nationally recognized stars as Lightnin' Hopkins. Another Wood-Fraher collaboration, *Texas Zydeco*, uses this same approach and makes the case for zydeco as a Texas musical genre.[122] Wood also coauthored a book with Andy Bradley dealing with the history of the Sugar Hill recording studio in Houston. It is heavily based on oral history interviews with musicians and sound engineers who worked at the studios.[123] The book combines a synthetic history of the studio and its impact on popular music in Texas from its founding in 1941 to the present, with stories of the many artists who recorded there. Preston Lauterbach discusses the contributions of black blues musicians in Texas clubs, particularly in Houston, to the evolution of rock 'n' roll, and music journalist Michael Corcoran profiles a number of lesser-known African American solo artists and groups from around the state.[124]

Treatments of the Austin music scene include musicologist Travis D. Stimeling's look at the emergence of the "outlaw" brand of progressive country music in the 1970s, *Cosmic Cowboys and New Hicks*, and ethnographer Barry Shank's examination of the Austin music scene and its devotees in the early 1990s, *Dissonant Identities*.[125] For two insider views, see Johnny Bush's and Vince Bell's autobiographical works.[126] Several works photographically document the popular television show *Austin City Limits*.[127] On Austin's famous music festival, see *SXSW Scrapbook* by Peter Blackstock and Jason Cohen, which highlights in words and pictures the origins and first twenty-five years of this celebrated music festival.[128]

There are several good sources on Mexican American music in Texas. Anthropologist Manuel H. Peña has addressed the music of Hispanic Texans in three scholarly works; the broadest of these, *Música Tejana*, is a study of Texas Mexican, or Tejana, music that analyzes its three major genres, which he identifies as the *corrido*, the *canción*, and the *canción-corrido*. Peña also examines the evolution of two types of ensembles emerging from the Tejano community, the *conjunto* and the *orquesta tejana*. He ties the evolution of this music and the typical groups who played it to changes in Texas Mexican society in the mid-twentieth century.[129] Historian Guadalupe San Miguel, Jr., addresses the evolution of *música tejana* and its reflection of relations between Mexican Texans and Anglos in *Tejano Proud*.[130] Authors Juan Tejada and Avelardo Valdez define the genre and the makeup of the typical *conjunto* group in *Puro Conjunto*.[131] Articles in this volume by a large variety of contributors cover the origins, history, and development of conjunto from its nineteenth-century roots and identify its major figures. For Tejano folk music, see the landmark work on the subject by Amerigo Paredes, a collection of folksongs dating from the 1750s to the 1960s from the Lower Rio Grande Valley between Laredo/Nuevo Laredo and Brownsville/Matamoros.[132] Paredes included transcriptions and lyrics in translation as well as in the original Spanish. Each section has a narrative introduction setting the collected songs in historical and cultural context. Ramiro Burr has produced an additional reference on this subject, *The Billboard Guide to Tejano and Regional Mexican Music*, which has a historical introduction dealing with the origins, influences, and evolution of Texas Mexican music; an A-Z encyclopedia with brief entries on individuals and groups; and a glossary.[133]

Few sources devote themselves exclusively to women and Texas music. Gary Hartman's article "From Yellow Roses to Dixie Chicks" introduces female performers and composers while discussing presentations of gender roles and male-female relations in the various genres of Texas music.[134] In *Women in Texas Music*, Kathleen Hudson interviews more than three dozen women who perform in a wide array of genres about their careers, motivations, and aspirations.[135]

Texas has a long and distinguished history of literary, artistic, and musical production across the state. Today, every major city, and many smaller ones, nurture writers, artists, and musicians contributing to a lively artistic community. They are diverse in their styles and subject matter. Vibrancy is the primary hallmark today in the realms of Texas literature, the visual arts, and music.

NOTES

1. Davis F. Eagleton, *Writers and Writings of Texas* (New York: Broadway, 1913).
2. Goldie Capers Smith, *The Creative Arts in Texas: A Handbook of Biography* (Nashville, Tenn.: Cokesbury, 1926).
3. Florence Alberta Barns, *Texas Writers of Today* (Dallas: Tardy, 1935).
4. A. C. Greene, *The Fifty+ Best Books on Texas* (Denton: University of North Texas Press, 1998, reprint of 1982 edition).
5. James Ward Lee, *Classics of Texas Fiction* (Dallas: E-Heart Press, 1987).
6. Don Graham, ed., *Lone Star Literature: From the Red River to the Rio Grande* (New York: W. W. Norton, 2003).
7. Craig Clifford and Tom Pilkington, eds., *Range Wars: Heated Debates, Sober Reflections, and Other Assessments of Texas Writing* (Dallas: Southern Methodist University Press, 1989).
8. Tom Pilkington, *State of Mind: Texas Literature and Culture* (College Station: Texas A&M University Press, 1998).

9. Roleno Adorno and Patrick Charles Pautz, *The Narrative of Cabeza de Vaca* (Lincoln: University of Nebraska Press, 2003).

10. Elizabeth A. H. John and John Wheat, eds. and trans., *Views from the Apache Frontier Report on the Provinces of New Spain* (Norman: University of Oklahoma Press, 1994).

11. The full extent of this project can be seen on its website: http://artepublicopress.uh.edu/arte-publico-wp/recovery-project/. The Arte Publico Press in Houston has published many titles from this project.

12. For Mier y Terán's diary, see Jack Jackson, ed., *Texas by Terán* (Austin: University of Texas Press, 2000). Jackson has also edited the memorial that resulted from an 1834 inspection report made during a visit to Texas by Juan N. Almonte; see Jackson, ed., *Almonte's Texas* (Austin: Texas State Historical Association, 2003).

13. Mary Austin Holley, *Texas: Observations Historical, Geographic, and Descriptive* (New York: Arno Press, 1973, reprint of 1833 edition). For more information about Holley, see Rebecca Smith Lee, *Mary Austin Holley: A Biography* (Austin: University of Texas Press, 1962); and Light Townsend Cummins, *Emily Austin of Texas, 1795–1851* (Fort Worth: Texas Christian University Press, 2009).

14. Mirabeau B. Lamar, *Verse Memorials* (New York: W. P. Fetridge, 1857).

15. Melinda Rankin, *Texas in 1850* (Boston: Damrell and Moore, 1850).

16. Frederick Law Olmstead, *A Journey through Texas; or, A Winter of Saddle and Camp Life on the Border Country of the United States and Mexico* (New York: Dix, 1857).

17. Victor Considerant, *Au Texas: With the Addition of the Great West, and European Colonization in Texas* (Philadelphia: Porcupine Press, 1975, reprint of 1854 edition).

18. Gerald Langford, *Alias O. Henry: A Biography of William Sidney Porter* (New York: Macmillan, 1957).

19. William T. Pilkington, ed., *Critical Essays on the Western American Novel* (Boston: G. K. Hall, 1980). See also Richard W. Etulain, *Telling Western Stories: From Buffalo Bill to Larry McMurtry* (Albuquerque: University of New Mexico Press, 1999).

20. Charles A. Siringo, *A Texas Cowboy; or, Fifteen Years on the Hurricane Deck of a Spanish Pony* (New York: Sloane, 1950, reprint of 1885 edition); Orlan Sawey, *Charles Siringo* (Boston: Twayne, 1981); Ben E. Pingenot, *Siringo: The True Story of Charles A. Siringo* (College Station: Texas A&M University Press, 1989).

21. Andy Adams, *The Log of a Cowboy: A Narrative of the Old Trail Days* (Lincoln: University of Nebraska Press, 1964, reprint of 1903 edition); Wilson M. Hudson, *Andy Adams: His Life and Writings* (Dallas: SMU Press, 1964).

22. John C. Duval, *Early Times in Texas* (Lincoln: University of Nebraska Press, 1986, reprint of 1882 edition), and *The Adventures of Big-Foot Wallace: The Texas Ranger and Hunter* (Lincoln: University of Nebraska Press, 1966, reprint of 1870 edition).

23. Dobie published his first major book, *Vaquero of the Brush Country*, in 1929, followed by several dozen titles over the next three decades. In the late 1940s and early 1950s he authored a guide to southwestern literature in several editions: J. Frank Dobie, *A Guide to the Life and Literature of the Southwest* (Dallas: SMU Press, 1952).

24. Winston Bode, *J. Frank Dobie: A Portrait of Pancho* (Austin: Steck-Vaughn, 1968); Lon Tinkle, *An American Original: The Life of J. Frank Dobie* (Boston: Little, Brown,

1978); Steven L. Davis, *J. Frank Dobie: A Liberated Mind* (Austin: University of Texas Press, 2009).

25. George Sessions Perry, *Hold Autumn in Your Hand* (Albuquerque: University of New Mexico Press, 1975, reprint of 1941 edition); Garna L. Christian, *George Sessions Perry: The Man and His Words* (Philadelphia: Xlibris, 2009).

26. Laura Krey, *And Tell of Time* (Boston: Houghton Mifflin, 1938).

27. Edward Everett Davis, *The White Scourge* (San Antonio, Tex.: Naylor, 1940); Charles Curtis Munz, *Land Without Moses* (New York: Harper, 1938).

28. The most recent biography of Porter is Darlene Harbour Unrue, *Katherine Anne Porter: The Life of an Artist* (Jackson: University Press of Mississippi, 2005). See also Jane DeMouy, *Katherine Anne Porter's Women: The Eye of Her Fiction* (Austin: University of Texas Press, 1983); Clinton Machann and William Bedford Clark, eds., *Katherine Anne Porter and Texas: An Uneasy Relationship* (College Station: Texas A&M University Press, 1990); and Joan Givner, *Katherine Anne Porter: A Life* (New York: Simon and Schuster, 1982).

29. Fred Gipson, *Hound Dog Man* (Lincoln: University of Nebraska Press, 1980, reprint of 1949 edition), and *Old Yeller* (New York: Harper and Row, 1990, reprint of 1956 edition).

30. Madison Cooper, *Sironia, Texas* (Boston: Houghton Mifflin, 1952).

31. William Goyen, *House of Breath* (New York: Random House, 1975, reprint of 1950 edition), and *Ghost and Flesh* (New York: Random House, 1952).

32. William Humphrey, *Home from the Hill* (New York: Alfred A. Knopf, 1958), and *The Ordways* (Baton Rouge: LSU Press, 1997, reprint of 1964 edition).

33. William A. Owens, *The Stubborn Soil* (New York: Charles Scribner's Sons, 1966), *A Season of Weathering* (New York: Charles Scribner's Sons, 1973), and *Tell Me a Story, Sing Me a Song* (Austin: University of Texas Press, 1983).

34. Patrick Bennett, *Talking with Texas Writers: Twelve Interviews* (College Station: Texas A&M University Press, 1980); the featured writers are Larry McMurtry, A. C. Green, John Graves, Max Apple, Shelby Hearon, Leon Hale, Preston Jones, Elmer Kelton, Frances Mossiker, William Goyen, Larry L. King, and Tom Lea.

35. Betsy Feagan Colquitt, *A Part of Space: Ten Texas Writers* (Fort Worth: Texas Christian University Press, 1969). John Howard Griffin became best known for *Black Like Me* (New York: Houghton Mifflin, 1961). Edwin "Bud" Shrake wrote ten novels and several other works about Texas, including *Blessed McGill* (New York: Popular Library, 1969).

36. Larry McMurtry, *Lonesome Dove* (New York: Simon and Schuster, 1985), and *Horseman, Pass By* (New York: Harper, 1961).

37. Mark Busby, *Larry McMurtry: An Ambivalent Relationship* (Denton: University of North Texas Press, 1995); Charles D. Peavy, *Larry McMurtry* (Boston: Twayne, 1977); John M. Reilly, *Larry McMurtry: A Critical Companion* (Westport, Conn.: Greenwood Press, 2000).

38. Elmer Kelton, *The Time It Never Rained* (Garden City, N.Y.: Doubleday, 1973), and *The Day the Cowboys Quit* (Garden City, N.Y.: Doubleday, 1971).

39. Philip Graham, *Early Texas Verse, 1835–1850* (Austin: Steck, 1936).

40. Vaida Steward Montgomery, *A Century with Texas Poets and Poetry* (Dallas: Kaleidograph Press, 1934).

41. Peggy Z. Lynch, *Behold Texas: As Seen by Texas Poets* (Austin: Nortex Press, 1983); Margaret R. Edwards, *The Poets Laureate of Texas, 1932–1966* (San Antonio, Tex.: Naylor, 1966).

42. Billy Bob Hill, ed., *Texas in Poetry 2* (Fort Worth: Texas Christian University Press, 2002.) This volume updates a 1994 version that Hill edited.

43. William Lawrence Chittenden, *Ranch Verses* (New York: G. P. Putnam's Sons, 1893).

44. John Peter Sjolander, *Salt of Earth and Sea* (Dallas: P. L. Turner, 1928).

45. Hilton Greer, *Voices of the Southwest: A Book of Texas Verse* (New York: Macmillan, 1923).

46. Vassar Miller, *Adam's Footprint* (New Orleans, La.: New Orleans Poetry Journal, 1956).

47. Naomi Shihab Nye, *Different Ways to Pray: Poems* (Portland, Ore.: Breitenbush, 1980).

48. Finnie D. Coleman, *Sutton E. Griggs and the Struggle against White Supremacy* (Knoxville: University of Tennessee Press, 2007).

49. James W. Byrd, *J. Mason Brewer: Negro Folklorist* (Austin: Steck-Vaughn, 1967); J. Mason Brewer, *The Word on the Brazos* (Austin: University of Texas Press, 1953).

50. A representative sampling includes J. California Cooper, *Family: A Novel* (New York: Doubleday, 1991), *The Wake of the Wind* (New York: Doubleday, 1998), and *Life Is Short but Wide* (New York: Doubleday, 2009).

51. Reginald McKnight, *The Kind of Light That Shines on Texas* (Boston: Little Brown, 1992).

52. Sylvia Ann Grider and Lou Halsell Rodenberger, eds., *Texas Women Writers: A Tradition of Their Own* (College Station: Texas A&M University Press, 1997).

53. Dorothy Scarborough, *The Wind* (Austin: University of Texas Press, 1979, reprint of 1925 edition).

54. Dagoberto Gilb, *Hecho en Tejas: An Anthology of Texas-Mexican Literature* (Albuquerque: University of New Mexico Press, 2006). Fiction titles by Gilb include *The Magic of the Blood* (Albuquerque: University of New Mexico Press, 1993), *Woodcuts of Women* (New York: Grove Press, 2001), and *Before the End, After the Beginning* (New York: Grove Press, 2011).

55. Joyce Glover Lee, *Rolando Hinojosa and the American Dream* (Denton: University of North Texas Press, 1967). Books by Hinojosa include *Mi Querido Rafa* (Houston: Arte Publico Press, 1981), *Klail City* (Houston: Arte Publico Press, 1987), and *We Happy Few* (Houston: Arte Publico Press, 2006).

56. Tomás Rivera, *Tomás Rivera: The Complete Works* (Houston: Arte Publico Press, 1992).

57. Carmen Haydée Rivera, *Border Crossings and Beyond: The Life and Works of Sandra Cisneros* (Santa Barbara, Cal.: Preager, 2009); Sandra Cisneros, *The House on Mango Street* (Houston: Arte Publico Press, 1984).

58. Carmen Tafolla, *Curandera* (San Antonio, Tex.: M&A Editions, 1983).

59. Francis Leonard and Ramona Crowley, *Conversations with Texas Writers* (Austin: University of Texas Press, 2005).

60. Frances Battaile Fisk, *A History of Texas Artists and Sculptors* (Abilene, Tex.: Fisk, 1928).

61. Esse Forrester-O'Brien, *Art and Artists of Texas* (Dallas: Tardy, 1935).

62. Paula L. Grauer and Michael R. Grauer, *Dictionary of Texas Artists, 1800–1945* (College Station: Texas A&M University Press, 1999); John E. Powers and Deborah D. Powers, *Texas Painters, Sculptors and Graphic Artists: A Biographical Dictionary of Artists in Texas before 1942* (Austin: Woodmont Books, 2000).

63. Michael Grauer, "Wider than the Limits of Our State: Texas Art in the Twentieth Century," in *Twentieth Century Texas: A Social and Cultural History*, ed. John W. Story and Mary L. Kelley (Denton: University of North Texas Press, 2008), 267–99.

64. *Texas Painting and Sculpture: The 20th Century* (Dallas: Broadnax, 1971).

65. Texas State Historical Association, *The Handbook of Texas Online:* www.tsha-online.org/handbook/online.

66. Forrest Kirkland and William W. Newcomb, *The Rock Art of Texas Indians* (Austin: University of Texas Press, 1967).

67. Jacinto Quirarte, *The Art and Architecture of Texas Missions* (Austin: University of Texas Press, 2002).

68. Sam DeShong Ratcliffe, *Painting Texas History to 1900* (Austin: University of Texas Press, 1992).

69. Pauline Pinckney, *Painting Texas: The Nineteenth Century* (Austin: University of Texas Press for the Amon Carter Museum, 1967).

70. William H. Goetzmann and Becky Duval Reese, *Texas Images and Visions* (Austin: Archer M. Huntington Art Gallery, University of Texas, 1983); Alison de Lima Greene, *Texas: 150 Works from the Museum of Fine Arts Houston* (Houston: Museum of Fine Arts, 2000). For another view of Texas art as concept, see Edmund P. Pillsbury and Richard R. Brettell, eds., *Texas Vision: The Barrett Collection: The Art of Texas and Switzerland* (Dallas: Southern Methodist University Press, 2004).

71. J. Evetts Haley, *F. Reaugh: Man and Artist* (El Paso, Tex.: Hertzog, 1960); Donald L. Weismann, ed., *Frank Reaugh, Painter to the Longhorns* (College Station: Texas A&M University Press, 1985).

72. Cecilia Steinfeldt, *The Onderdonks: A Family of Texas Painters* (San Antonio, Tex.: Trinity University Press, 1976); William Rudolph, *Julian Onderdonk: American Impressionist* (Dallas: Dallas Museum of Art, and New Haven, Conn.: Yale University Press, 2008).

73. Michael Grauer, *Texas Impressionism: Branding with Brushstroke and Color* (Canyon, Tex.: Panhandle Plains Historical Museum, 2012).

74. William E. Reaves, *Texas Art and a Wildcatter's Dream: Edgar B. Davis and the San Antonio Art League* (College Station: Texas A&M University Press, 1998).

75. Rick Stewart, *Lone Star Regionalism: The Dallas Nine and Their Circle, 1928–1945* (Austin: Texas Monthly Press for the Dallas Museum of Art, 1985). For other works on Dallas artists of the 1930s, see Ellen Buie Niewyk, *Jerry Bywaters, Lone Star Printmaker* (Dallas: Southern Methodist University Press, 2007); and Sam DeShong Ratcliffe, *Jerry Bywaters, Interpreter of the Southwest* (College Station: Texas A&M University Press, 2007).

76. Francine Carraro, *Jerry Bywaters: A Life in Art* (Austin: University of Texas Press, 1994).

77. Susie Kalil, *Alexandre Hogue: An American Visionary* (College Station: Texas A&M University Press, 2010).

78. Philip Parisi, *The Texas Post Office Murals: Art for the People* (College Station: Texas A&M University Press, 2004). For additional studies of early twentieth-century art in Texas, see Eleanor Jones Harvey, ed., *In Context: Painting in Dallas, 1889–1945* (Dallas: McKinney Avenue Contemporary and Texas Art Collectors Association, 1999); Michael Grauer, *First Light: Local Art and the Fort Worth Public Library, 1901–1961* (Fort Worth, Tex.: Fort Worth Public Library foundation, 2001); Mark Edward Thistlethwaite, *Celebrating Early Texas Art: Treasures from Dallas-Fort Worth Private Collections, 1900–1960* (San Angelo, Tex.: Center for the Advancement and Study of Early Texas Art, 2005); and William E. Reaves et al., *Houston Art in Houston Collections: Works from 1900 to 1965* (Houston: Heritage Society, 2006). El Paso artist Tom Lea played a significant role in the development of regional art from the 1930s to the 1960s; see Kathleen Hjerter, *The Art of Tom Lea* (College Station: Texas A&M University Press, 1989).

79. Scott Grant Barker and Jane Myers, *Intimate Modernism: Fort Worth Circle Artists in the 1940s* (College Station: Texas A&M University Press, 2008). For a firsthand account of this period in Dallas-Fort Worth, see Donald Vogel, *Memories and Images: the World of Donald Vogel and Valley House Gallery* (Denton: University of North Texas Press, 2000).

80. Barbara Rose and Susie Kalil, *Fresh Paint: The Houston School* (Austin: Texas Monthly Press, 1985); Grauer, "Wider Than the Limits;" Suzanne Weaver and Lane Relyea, *Come Forward: Emerging Art in Texas* (College Station: Texas A&M University Press, 2003).

81. Grauer, "Wider Than the Limits;" Suzanne Weaver and Lane Relyea, *Come Forward: Emerging Art in Texas* (College Station: Texas A&M University Press, 2003).

82. Marianne Stockebrand, *Chinati: The Vision of Donald Judd* (New Haven, Conn.: Yale University Press, 2010).

83. *Houston Hispanic Artists: New Views* (Houston: Glassell School of Art, Museum of Fine Arts, 1987). See also *A Directory of Hispanic American Arts Organizations* (San Antonio, Tex.: Research Center for the Arts and Humanities, 1982).

84. Jacinto Quirarte, *Mexican American Artists* (Austin: University of Texas Press, 1973).

85. Shifra Goldman and Tomás Ybarra-Frausto, *Arte Chicano: A Comprehensive Annotated Bibliography of Chicano Art, 1965–1981* (Berkeley: Chicano Studies Library Publication Unit, University of California, Berkeley, 1985); Jacinto Quirarte, *Chicano Art History: A Book of Selected Readings* (San Antonio: Research Center For the Arts and Humanities, University of Texas at San Antonio, 1984); Richard Griswold del Castillo, Teresa McKenna and Yvonne Yarbro-Bejarano, eds., *Chicano Art: Resistance and Affirmation, 1965–1985* (Los Angeles: Wright Art Gallery, University of California, 1991).

86. Ruben C. Cordova, *Con Safo: The Chicano Art Group and the Politics of South Texas* (Los Angeles: UCLA Chicano Studies Research Center Press, 2009).

87. María Herrera-Sobek, ed., *Santa Barraza, Artist of the Borderlands* (College Station: Texas A&M University Press, 2001).

88. Miguel Juárez, with photographs by Cynthia Weber Farah, *Colors on Desert Walls: The Murals of El Paso* (El Paso: Texas Western Press, University of Texas at El Paso, 1997).

89. Ruth Goddard, *Porfirio Salinas* (Austin: Rock House, 1975); Patsy Pittman Light, *Capturing Nature: The Cement Sculpture of Dionicio Rodríguez* (College Station: Texas A&M University Press, 2008); *Luís Jiménez* (Corpus Christi: Art Museum of South Texas, 2001).

90. Patricia D. Hendricks, *20th Century Women in Texas Art* (Austin: Laguna Gloria Art Museum, 1974).

91. Sylvia Moore, *No Bluebonnets, No Yellow Roses: Essays on Texas Women in the Arts* (New York: Midmarch Arts Press, 1988).

92. Susan Landauer and Becky Duval Reese, "Lone Star Spirits," in *Independent Spirits: Women Painters of the American West, 1890–1945*, ed. Patricia Trenton (Berkeley: University of California Press and the Autry Museum of Western Heritage, 1995), 183–207.

93. Phil Kovinick and Marian Yoshiki-Kovinick, *An Encyclopedia of Women Artists of the American West* (Austin: University of Texas Press, 1998).

94. Kippra D. Hopper and Laurie J. Churchill, *Art of West Texas Women: A Celebration* (Lubbock: Texas Tech University Press, 2010).

95. Jesse O. Thomas, *Negro Participation in the Texas Centennial Exposition* (Boston: Christopher Publishing House, 1938).

96. John Biggers, Carroll Simms, and John Edward Weems, *Black Art in Houston: The Texas Southern University Experience* (College Station: Texas A&M University Press, 1978).

97. Alvia J. Wardlaw et al., *The Art of John Biggers: View from the Upper Room* (Houston: Museum of Fine Arts, 1995); Olive Jensen Theisen, *A Life on Paper: The Drawings and Lithographs of John Thomas Biggers* (Denton: University of North Texas Press, 2006); Olive Jensen Theisen, *Walls That Speak: The Murals of John Thomas Biggers* (Denton: University of North Texas Press, 2010).

98. John Hope Franklin and Alvia J. Wardlaw, *Collecting African American Art: The Museum of Fine Arts Houston* (Houston: Museum of Fine Arts, 2009).

99. Patricia D. Hendricks and Becky Duval Reese, *A Century of Sculpture in Texas, 1889–1989* (Austin: Archer M. Huntington Gallery, 1989).

100. Carol Morris Little, *A Comprehensive Guide to Outdoor Sculpture in Texas* (Austin: University of Texas Press, 1996).

101. Emily M. Fourny, *The Art of the Woman: The Life and Work of Elizabet Ney* (Lincoln: University of Nebraska Press, 1988); Marjory Goar, *Marble Dust: The Life of Elizabet Ney, an Interpretation* (Austin: Eakin Press, 1984); Jan Fortune, *Elizabet Ney* (New York: Alfred A. Knopf, 1943); Bride Neill Taylor, *Elizabet Ney, Sculptor* (New York: Devin-Adair, 1916).

102. Pompeo Coppini, *From Dawn to Sunset* (San Antonio, Tex.: Naylor, 1949).

103. Alice Hutson, *From Chalk to Bronze: A Biography of Waldine Tauch* (Austin: Shoal Creek, 1978).

104. Donald B. Goodall, *Charles Umlauf, Sculptor* (Austin: University Art Museum of the University of Texas, 1967).

105. Roy Fridge, *Heroes, Hermits, Shamans, and Boats: The Works of Roy Fridge, 1959–1984* (Corpus Christi, Tex.: Art Museum of South Texas, 1985); Lynn M. Herbert et al., *Jim Love: From Now On* (New York: Palgrave Macmillan, 2006); Luis Jimenez and Rudolfo N. Anaya, *Man on Fire: Luis Jimenez* (Albuquerque, N.M.: Albuquerque Museum, 1994); Sue Graze, *Visions: James Surls, 1974–1984* (Dallas: Dallas Museum of Art, 1984).

106. Laurie E. Jasinski, ed., *Handbook of Texas Music*, 2nd ed. (Denton: Texas State Historical Association Press, 2012).

107. Texas State University Department of History, Center for Texas Music History: www.txstate.edu/ctmh/.

108. *Journal of Texas Music History* (San Marcos, Tex.: Institute for the History of Texas Music, Texas State University, 2001–).

109. Lawrence Clayton and Joe W. Specht, eds., *The Roots of Texas Music* (College Station: Texas A&M University Press, 2003).

110. Larry Willoughby, *Texas Rhythm and Texas Rhyme: A Pictorial History of Texas Music* (Austin: Texas Monthly Press, 1984; 2nd ed., Ton Kawa Free Press, 1990). Alan Govenar's *Everyday Music* (College Station: Texas A&M University Press, 2012) also stresses the enormous diversity in Texas music.

111. Lotta M. Spell, *Music in Texas: A Survey of One Aspect of Cultural Progress* (Austin, Tex: 1936; reprint New York, AMS, 1973).

112. Mint O. James-Reed, *Music in Austin, 1900–1956* (Austin: Von Boeckmann-Jones, 1957).

113. Robert M. Stevenson, *Music in El Paso, 1919–1939* (El Paso, Tex.: University of El Paso Press, 1970).

114. Hubert Roussel, *The Houston Symphony Orchestra, 1913–1971* (Austin: University of Texas Press, 1972).

115. Robert I. Giesberg, *The Houston Grand Opera: A History* (Houston: Grand Opera Guild, 1981); Robert I. Giesberg, Carl Cunningham, and Alan Rich, *The Houston Grand Opera at Fifty* (Houston: Herring Press, 2005).

116. Bill C. Malone and Jocelyn R. Neal, *Country Music, USA*, 3rd rev. ed. (Austin: University of Texas Press, 2010). For country singers in Texas, see Phil Fry and Jim Lee, *Texas Country Singers* (Fort Worth: Texas Christian University Press, 2008). For traditional Texas songs, see Francis Edward Abernethy, *Singin' Texas*, 2nd ed. (Denton: University of North Texas Press, 1994). Aaron A. Fox, *Real Country: Music and Language in Working Class Culture* (Durham, N.C.: Duke University Press, 2004), studies the music's impact on the people who love it.

117. Jean A. Boyd, *The Jazz of the Southwest: An Oral History of Western Swing* (Austin: University of Texas Press, 1998).

118. Jean A. Boyd, *"We're the Light Crust Doughboys from Burrus Mill": An Oral History* (Austin: University of Texas Press, 2003); see also John Marx Dempsey, *The Light Crust Doughboys Are on the Air: Celebrating Seventy Years of Texas Music* (Denton: University of North Texas Press, 2002). For a work focusing on one of the earliest western

swing bands, see Cary Ginell, *Milton Brown and the Founding of Western Swing* (Urbana: University of Illinois Press, 1994). For a discussion of the influences on and development of country music in West Texas, see Joe Carr and Alan Munde, *Prairie Nights to Neon Lights: The Story of Country Music in West* Texas (Lubbock: Texas Tech University Press, 1995); and Christopher Oglesby, *Fire in the Water, Earth in the Air: Legends of West Texas Music* (Austin: University of Texas Press, 2006).

119. Dave Oliphant, *Texan Jazz* (Austin: University of Texas Press, 1996); see also Oliphant's *Jazz Mavericks of the Lone Star State* (Austin: University of Texas Press, 2007).

120. Alan B. Govenar, *Living Texas Blues* (Dallas: Dallas Museum of Art, 1985), *Meeting the Blues: The Rise of the Texas Sound* (Dallas: Taylor, 1988), *The Early Years of Rhythm and Blues: Focus on Houston* (Houston: Rice University Press, 1990), and *Texas Blues: The Rise of a Contemporary Sound* (College Station: Texas A&M University Press, 2008). Govenar also has written *Lightnin' Hopkins: His Life and Blues* (Chicago: Chicago Review Press, 2010).

121. Alan B. Govenar and Jay Brakefield, *Deep Ellum: The Other Side of Dallas* (College Station: Texas A&M University Press, 2013).

122. Charles Roger Wood, photographs by James Fraher, *Down in Houston: Bayou City Blues* (Austin: University of Texas Press, 2003), and *Texas Zydeco* (Austin: University of Texas Press, 2006).

123. Charles Roger Wood and Andy Bradley, *House of Hits: the Story of Houston's Gold Star/Sugar Hill Recording Studios* (Austin: University of Texas Press 2010).

124. Preston Lauterbach, The *Chitlin' Circuit and the Road to Rock 'n' Roll* (New York: W. W. Norton, 2011); Michael Corcoran, *All Over the Map: True Heroes of Texas Music* (Austin: University of Texas Press, 2005).

125. Travis D. Stimeling, *Cosmic Cowboys and New Hicks: The Countercultural Sounds of Austin's Progressive Country Music Scene* (New York: Oxford University Press, 2011); Barry Shank, *Dissonant Identities: The Rock 'n' Roll Scene in Austin, Texas* (Hanover, N.H.: University Press of New England, 1994); see also Jason Mellard, *Progressive Country: How the 1970s Transformed the Texan in Popular Culture* (Austin: University of Texas Press, 2013).

126. Johnny Bush and Rick Mitchell, *Whiskey River (Take My Mind): The True Story of Honkey-Tonk* (Austin: University of Texas Press, 2007); Vince Bell, *One Man's Music: The Life and Times of Texas Songwriter Vince Bell* (Denton: University of North Texas Press, 2009).

127. These include Clifford Endres, *Austin City Limits* (Austin: University of Texas Press, 1987); and Scott Newton and Terry Lickona, *Austin City Limits: 35 Years in Photographs* (Austin: University of Texas Press, 2010).

128. Peter Blackstock, Jason Cohen, and Andy Smith, *SXSW Scrapbook: People and Things That Went Before* (Austin: Essex Press, 2011).

129. Manuel H. Peña, *Música Tejana: The Cultural Economy of Artistic Transformation* (College Station: Texas A&M University Press, 1999). Two other works by Peña, *The Texas-Mexican Conjunto: History of a Working-Class Music* (Austin: University of Texas Press, 1985), and *The Mexican American Orquesta: Music, Culture, and the Dialectic of Conflict* (Austin: University of Texas Press, 1999), focus in detail on the history of

these ensembles and relate their music and popularity to changes and class divisions in Texas-Mexican society.

130. Guadalupe San Miguel, Jr., *Tejano Proud: Tex-Mex Music in the Twentieth Century* (College Station: Texas A&M University Press, 2002).

131. Juan Tejada and Avelardo Valdez, *Puro Conjunto: An Album in Words and Pictures* (Austin: Center for Mexican-American Studies, University of Texas at Austin, 2001).

132. Amerigo Paredes, *A Texas-Mexican Cancionero: Folksongs of the Lower Border* (Urbana: University of Illinois Press, 1976).

133. Ramiro Burr, *The Billboard Guide to Tejano and Regional Mexican Music* (New York: Billboard Books, 1999).

134. Gary Hartman, "From Yellow Roses to Dixie Chicks: Women and Gender in Texas Music History," in Storey and Kelley, *Twentieth Century Texas*, 196–219.

135. Kathleen Hudson, *Women in Texas Music: Stories and Songs* (Austin: University of Texas Press, 2007).

CHAPTER 7

Texas Urban History

Richard B. Wright

In 1988, two scholars tried to define the parameters of urban history in the *Journal of Architectural Education*. They drew on sources that have equated urban history and social history since at least the 1960s (when the latter was first called the "new social history") and concluded that, "like social history, urban history is whatever the author makes it." They quoted the Sorbonne-trained Americanist Olivier Zunz, who noted for social history that, although such amorphousness contributed to the overall good of expanding history's scholarly reach, it was also the case that a "lack of a clear program" could lead "to a fragmentation and a diminished focus" in research. The concomitant quest for new methods could also lead to the uncritical use of other disciplines. Despite these cautions, the authors of the article generally felt that there should not be a "dominant approach" to urban history.[1]

In the twenty-four years since those words were written, this trend of a diffused and diverse focus for urban history has only increased. A time-honored stop for students of urban history on the Internet is Gilbert Stelter's overview of the subject at the University of Guelph in Canada. Stelter bravely attempts to adumbrate four general themes around which studies cohere in the field: urbanization, urban biography, thematic studies, and cultural studies. In the latter case, the flair for "reading" cities in a theoretically informed, almost para-literary way still seems largely unexplored turf in Texas history. The study of urbanization for Stelter is most typically driven by the rigorous use of structural, behavioral, and other social-scientific analyses of a quantitative nature that are more synchronic in nature than diachronic. Stelter thus reasons that urbanization tends more often to provide evidentiary frameworks for history writing about cities rather than a methodological focus per se (although as in the "new social history" mentioned above, it was in the 1960s that historians first started using quantitative methods to bring the anonymous majority of people in cities to the forefront of inquiry, as opposed to elites and leaders, leading thus to the term "new urban history"). Stelter's "urban biographies," on the other hand, have long been quite plentiful in Texas history and often predate the 1990 starting date of this review. Such biographies can be found for even small towns in Texas, due to the explosion of county-level histories written before and after the bicentennial year of 1976. With the interesting exception of Dallas, though, much of the most worthwhile historical writing on cities since 1990 has instead largely focused on a diverse range of thematic studies, as might be predicted.[2]

Because of the growing diffusion of thematic foci in urban history overall, though, developing an overall command of the literature of urban history in Texas since 1990 can be quite daunting, since it is so unwieldy and cross-disciplinary. In addition, a majority of Texans have lived in cities and towns since the end of World War II, and since 1970 that percentage has been over 80 percent—an amount today totaling well over 20 million people. Thus, most all of Texas history since World War II *is* also urban history by definition (especially when one considers that the U.S. Census Bureau defines as "urban" any town with, in part, a population of 2,500 or more). As a result of these facts, the possibilities for thematic foci are vast; if seen liberally, the number of articles, books, book chapters, and theses that have been written since 1990 on Texas subjects that are rooted in urban contexts reaches quite easily into four figures. The aforementioned lack of any consensus on how urban history can be defined in disciplinary terms is obviously of little help in determining whether a given study can be labeled more as urban-historical than something else, so one is left instead to develop what are essentially interdisciplinary parameters based on the nature of the specific topic and proclivities of the researcher.[3]

In the case of this review, then, it should be obvious that only a small fraction of all the potentially relevant sources for this field can be cited here, unfortunately. Certain decisions (almost arbitrary in some cases) have been made to give some limits to the scope of the essay and the range of sources. Entire subtopics or sources with potential relevancy to cities are not touched (e.g., small guidebooks; archaeological, planning, and preservation reports; pictorial works, archive references, memoirs; educational, religious, health-care, and artistic institutions; most urban biographies, civic-leader biographies, and views of social life and customs that are published in what appear to be non-refereed contexts; undergraduate and master's theses), but not in any way should this be interpreted as a judgment of irrelevance for such themes or works—it is simply that some limits must be established in order to treat the material somewhat consistently across different cities in the state, and to stay within the length requirements for this survey. Titles that may overlap with those in other chapters here are included mostly because their setting is a particular city. Books and dissertations are privileged, because their bibliographies are more extensive and thus more helpful for the student than those found in articles or book chapters. If an author has written about a topic in more than one venue, only the latest publication is included. Reprints and new editions of pre-1990 works are generally not included. Finally, only the largest metropolitan areas can be addressed here—Houston, San Antonio, Dallas—with some brief mention of titles from other cities around the state at the end of the essay. Multiple citations for any one urban setting are selected in part to display the range of different approaches and methods taken in the historical writing on that particular city; because of the diffuse nature of urban history today, breadth of coverage is thus emphasized at the expense of depth.

As a general overview, Amy Bridges's *Morning Glories: Municipal Reform in the Southwest* provides an engagingly written introduction to the interrelationship of twentieth-century cities, politics, and growth in the Southwest. A lot of the time one would spend on conceptualizing can be saved in approaching the subject of modern Texas cities if one understands that their developmental trajectories are not at all unique. Bridges was among the first to show that there are remarkable similarities in the trajectories of Dallas, Houston, San Antonio, and Austin, and between those Texas locales and other southwestern cities like San Diego, Albuquerque, and San José: all were early proponents of political reform; all ended up with nonpartisan political systems of limited participation and even boss rule as a result of that reform; all went through perturbations during the Depression and the interwar years; all experienced tremendous growth up until the early 1970s, before "growth" started to develop less positive connotations and minorities started to press for change (especially via the change from at-large elections to single-district representation), with a concomitant change to today's more open (but also more contentious and factionalized) brand of urban politics. Bridges's work evolved out of the "Sunbelt" interpretive phenomenon that reached its peak in the historical and social-science literature of the 1970s and '80s; although that concept is no longer seen to have as much heuristic efficacy as it once did, Char Miller's 1990 essay "Sunbelt Texas" in the landmark historiographical anthology *Texas through Time* shows the utility of this orientation when applied primarily to one area instead of a broad region. David McComb, one of the most authoritative experts on Texas urban history, embraces an expansive, almost phenomenological perspective on urbanization in the *Portable Handbook of Texas*. Another basic source to consult should be the anthology *Urban Texas*, also published in 1990 and edited by Miller and Heywood Sanders, where themes from Galveston and the three major metropolitan areas of the state are featured. It still appears to be the only anthology exclusively devoted to urban-historical themes in the state twenty-two years later, although, now thirty years old, *Texas: A Geography*, by Terry Jordan and others, is still extremely useful as a historical reference for urbanization-related topics and as an introduction to the state's urban and industrial geography. Each of these last four works provides a good introduction to pre-1990 literature on Texas urban history and urbanization.[4]

The urban-history literature on Houston is quite varied in focus; due to the city's size, importance, and relative proximity of several large universities, this literature is also enhanced by a growing number of dissertations that explore Houston's history in various ways. There is also an active, vital community of public historians in the Bayou City, as well as commentators on design and urban planning who make important contributions to the understanding of the local urban fabric, via the journals *Houston History* (formerly the *Houston Review of History and Culture*), and *Cite* (rhymes with "sight"), respectively. (A website for the former journal gives download access for some issues and a search feature for past tables of content.) Research on the varied ethnic constituencies and heritages that make up an increasingly important part of the city's history may be richer in breadth for Houston at this point than for any other Texas municipality. *Black Dixie*, edited by Howard Beeth and Cary D. Wintz, is a pioneering anthology, not only because of the breadth of topics explored but also because it covers a single urban population of African Americans in the South from slavery into modern times.[5]

Studies of important figures in the ethnic history of the city include Merline Pitre's recent profile of Lulu B. White and the NAACP in Houston up to 1957 and Thomas H. Kreneck's study of the mid-century Mexican American leader and businessman Felix Tijerina. Peg Purser's *Minority Settlement Patterns in the Houston Area* is a potentially useful reference.[6]

Asian communities in Houston and their role in the modern city's development are starting to receive scholarly notice. Roy Vu's University of Houston dissertation breaks ground on the history of the Vietnamese community in the city from 1975 to 2005. An even newer phenomenon in Houston is addressed in Rubén Hernández-León's *Metropolitan Migrants*, which focuses on a working-class neighborhood in the northern Mexican metropolis of Monterrey and how industrial modernization has caused migration of such urban workers (i.e., as opposed to migrant agricultural laborers) to cities like Houston. Environmental aspects are still underaddressed in the urban history of Texas; Martin Melosi and Joseph Pratt focus on this rich topic in the anthology *Energy Metropolis*.[7]

Relatively recent introductory sources on the city include Betty Chapman's *Historic Houston* and Stanley Siegel and John Moretta's *Houston: A Chronicle of the Bayou City*. Nineteenth-century topics are the focus of a variety of works. "The Role of Merchants in Promoting Economic Development in the Houston-Galveston Region, 1836–1860," by Suzanne L. Summers is one; Stephen L. Hardin's *Texian Macabre* provides an engrossing, at times almost surreal account of life in antebellum Houston. A focus on the forgotten or lost historical and urban fabric of the city can be explored in Marguerite Johnston's 1992 study *Houston: The Unknown City, 1836–1946* and in *Houston's Forgotten Heritage*, by Dorothy Houghton.[8]

Other studies focusing on Houston's built environment include *Houston Lost and Unbuilt*, by Steven Strom. Cheryl Ferguson's four-volume University of Delaware dissertation on upscale suburban architecture in Dallas and Houston from 1890 to 1930 came out in 2004. Stephen Fox's award-winning study of the homes designed by John F. Staub was published in 2007. A real treasure-trove anthology of articles selected from the pages of *Cite* was published in 2003, called *Ephemeral City*. Neighborhoods, public housing, governance issues, transportation, architecture, planning and zoning, Houston suburbs, parks, public spaces, specific buildings, even the watery lowland ecology of the city are all explored in these insightful essays about one of the country's most discussed urban environments. Though most of the articles are critical and prescriptive in nature (and many others from past issues of *Cite* related thematically to the ones published in the anthology are cited at the end of each article), the contributions of Stephen Fox probably hold the greatest interest for historians (including his debunking of the myth that Houston has never had any urban planning). Another contributor to that anthology, Joel Warren Barna, published *The See-Through Years*, which the *New York Times* named as its book of the year on architecture for 1992. The book addresses themes in metro areas throughout the state.[9]

In the areas of public housing and redevelopment, the New Deal–era San Felipe Courts project (and the land it sits upon) in Houston's Fourth Ward is discussed in Robert Thomas and Richard Murray's study *Progrowth Politics: Change and Governance in Houston*—a valuable resource for historians that provides a wealth of statistical data about (and historical sketches of) the city's growth policies. Public housing projects like San Felipe (and elsewhere) are also analyzed architecturally in Jay C. Henry's *Architecture in Texas*, a book that is extremely useful for buildings in cities all over the state. The *Ephemeral City* anthology mentioned above also contains work devoted to housing issues.[10]

Important power figures in the Bayou City's modern developmental history are investigated in Kate Kirkland's 2004 dissertation on the philanthropy and urban ideals of the Hogg family across two generations. Steven Fenberg published a much-needed biography titled *Unprecedented Power: Jesse Jones, Capitalism, and the Common Good.* The modern growth of the city is also traced in Paul Levengood's dissertation, "For the Duration and Beyond: World War II and the Creation of Houston, Texas."[11]

San Antonio's urban historiography has some distinctive qualities. There is an especially active local and private publishing tradition in the area, so not as much has made it to peer-reviewed, academic publishing circles as one might expect given the rich history of the city.[12] On the other hand, environmental history and the history of the city's non-Anglo, non-German racial and ethnic communities have developed in rewarding ways since 1990—and the understanding of the city's colonial origins is even deeper today than it was twenty-plus years ago. For environmental history, Char Miller has authored two authoritative, yet highly readable books: *On the Border* and *Deep in the Heart of San Antonio* (which also deals with urban topics other than environmental ones). Laura Anne Wimberley has written a dissertation on the history of San Antonio's relationship with the Edwards Aquifer since the 1890s. More recently, Charles R. Porter has contributed *Spanish Water, Anglo Water*. Books dealing with the nineteenth-century city include Judith Berg-Sobré's work on historic festivals, Teresa Perrin's dissertation "Crime and Order in San Antonio during the Civil War and Reconstruction," and Lawrence Knight's dissertation "Becoming a City and Becoming American."[13]

Kenneth Mason's 1994 doctoral thesis focuses on African Americans and race relations from 1867 to 1937. Mel Brown contributed an award-winning small-press study of the city's Chinese community over a hundred-year period from 1875. Race relations and the role of women activists and women's organizations in San Antonio during the 1920s have been researched in a dissertation by Adriana Ayala.[14]

Adina De Zavala is the focus of a fascinating article by Kenneth Hafertepe, in which he exposes the former's rather imaginative 1920s restoration campaign for the Spanish Governor's Palace. In a similar vein, Lewis F. Fisher has written a book-length study on San Antonio's precarious preservation outlook. Robert Gonzalez has written a chapter in his book, *Designing Pan-America*, that focuses on the 1968 HemisFair; Sterlin Holmesly has also collected several dozen firsthand accounts about HemisFair '68 and its impact on the city in a small-press book. In a somewhat similar vein, Laura Hernández-Ehrisman's *Inventing the Fiesta City* appeared in 2008. The important Texas regionalist architect O'Neil Ford is the subject of two books—one by Mary George, the other by David Dillon.[15]

There is, of course, a rich and growing literature on San Antonio's varied Hispanic roots—Spanish/Canary Islander, Mexican, Mexican American/Tejano—and the role of that heritage in the shaping of the city. Gerald Poyo and Gilberto Hinojosa have contributed an important study of the culture and the roots of Tejano identity in the eighteenth-century town, and this was supplemented a few years later by a work with a somewhat different emphasis, Frank de la Teja's well-known *San Antonio de Béxar*. James Early's study of Spanish colonial architecture and urbanism devotes a whole section to Texas and San Antonio. The Mexican period of the city from 1821 is addressed in several works, including Raúl Ramos's recent book *Beyond the Alamo* and Timothy Matovina's *Tejano Religion and Ethnicity*. Shannon Barker's dissertation addresses the acculturation of Mexican immigrant families to the city from 1880 to 1929, at which point Richard Garcia's oft-cited *Rise of the Mexican American Middle Class* picks up with a related topic, and Richard Buitron published a work on the emergence of Tejano identity in the city from 1913 to 2000. Rodolfo Rosales's work represents a culmination in the study of this sociocultural evolution, as his work *The Illusion of Inclusion* addresses the initial phases of the integration of Mexican Americans into the city's political process (if not into its power structures). *Quixote's Soldiers*, by David Montejano, examines the Chicano movement in the city from 1966 to 1981.[16]

Bucking the trend of urban history studies moving toward increasingly varied strands, Dallas has instead seen a remarkable coalescence of historical writing around more of a meta-topic over the past fifteen years or so: the definition and historical evolution of the city's unique nature, identity, and overall meaning. The varying interpretive aims and thematic foci of books by Robert Fairbanks,

Elizabeth Enstam, Jacquelyn McElhaney, Patricia Hill, and William Wilson, as well as Amy Bridges's *Morning Glories*, mentioned at the beginning of this essay, can all be grasped in a valuable long review essay by Alan Lessoff. More recently, Harvey Graff and Royce Hanson have also added to this fertile discussion on how one should make sense of the city, its identity, political dynamics, and historical patterns of development. Darwin Payne, the author of many books on Dallas, provides a crisply written chronicle of the city's modern history in a small-press publication. Michael Hazel wrote a history of the city for the Texas State Historical Association (TSHA) in 1997. *White Metropolis: Race, Ethnicity, and Religion in Dallas*, by Michael Phillips, has also been a noteworthy addition to this focus on articulating (or redefining) the city's meaning and identity.[17]

African American history in Dallas is analyzed in *Deep Ellum and Central Track*, by Alan Govenar and Jay Brakefield, and in a publication by Marc Sanders and Ruthe Winegarten titled *The Lives and Times of Black Dallas Women*. On topics rooted in the nineteenth century, there is Susanne Starling's TSHA book on Warren Angus Ferris, the founder of Dallas County; Alicia Rodriquez's research findings on the Democratic Party and disfranchisement in Dallas in the 1890s; and Richard Smith's dissertation on the 1850s Dallas-area utopian community of La Réunion. Jewish history in Dallas is the subject of works by Rose Biderman and Gerry Cristol. Patricia Hill has written a study on organizing among Dallas dressmakers in 1935.[18]

Other studies addressing topics from the late nineteenth and twentieth centuries include Cynthia Northrup's dissertation on George Dealey; *John Rosenfield's Dallas*, a small-press publication by Ronald Davis; Mark Morris's "Saving Society through Politics: The Ku Klux Klan in Dallas," a dissertation; and Patricia Gower's dissertation from the year previous to Morris's titled "Dallas: Experiments in Progressivism." Rose-Mary Rumbley, an author of many books on the area, investigated the history of the Dallas Park and Recreation Board in a small-press publication. The history of the city's built environment is the focus of a book published by the Dallas chapter of the American Institute of Architects called *Transformations: The Architects, Buildings, and Events that Shaped Dallas Architecture*. Virginia McAlester and others collaborated on a study of the homes of the Park Cities. Willis Winters and Richard Brettell produced a monograph on the architect Mark Lemmon.[19]

Space limitations dictate that only a few additional sources be cited from each of several other cities. Fort Worth has benefitted from studies by J'Nell Pate (on North Fort Worth), Victoria and Walter Buenger (about the local businessman Marvin Leonard and his involvement with the city), and Carlos Cuéllar (on Mexican Fort Worth). Judith Linsley, Ellen Rienstra, and Jo Ann Stiles have studied the impact of Spindletop on the development of Beaumont. Similarly, the impact of oil on the urban development of Midland is one of the topics addressed in *The Gusher Age*, by Diana Olien and Roger Olien. The leading monograph on El Paso history is by Wilbert Timmons; Allison Tirres has contributed a distinctive perspective on the catalytic contributions made to the historical development of El Paso by the legal community. Charles Harris and Louis Sadler examine the Mexican Revolution from the perspective of that city, and Marcia Daudistel has edited a recent anthology of important women in El Paso history. Monica Perales explores the intersection of environmental, ethnic, and class issues in a 2010 study of the Smeltertown neighborhood of the city. Engaging views of nineteenth-century life in Laredo can be found in Robert Wood's *Life in Laredo*, and John Adams has written a sweeping chronicle of the city's commercial history from 1755 to 1955. Jerry Thompson's *Warm Weather and Bad Whiskey* analyzes the 1886 election riot in Laredo and its pivotal role in the city's political history. In a similar vein, Mary Jo O'Rear has addressed the key role played by Corpus Christi's 1919 hurricane on the political and economic development of the city (and region), and Alan Lessoff has analyzed the lack of historical progress in comprehensive planning for the city and for South Texas.[20]

Similar to O'Rear's work in theme is Patricia Bixel and Elizabeth Turner's book *Galveston and the 1900 Storm*. Turner has also written the frequently cited *Women, Culture, and Community*. A guide to Galveston's history has been written by David McComb. TSHA has published several noteworthy books on Galveston, including Clifford Farrington's interesting study of biracial unions on the Galveston waterfront. Susan Hardwick examines Galveston in *Mythic Galveston*. Stephen Fox has produced an impressively thorough history of the built environment in twentieth-century Brownsville and the Lower Rio Grande Valley. Geographer Daniel Arreola's *Tejano South Texas* looks closely at spatiohistorical dimensions of culture and ethnicity in the region's towns and cities. Kenneth Ragsdale explores the role of aviation and business in the growth of modern Austin. The literature on Waco has broadened with the publication of Patricia Bernstein's book on the rise of the NAACP there and with Virginia Spurlin's dissertation "The Connors of Waco: Black Professionals in Twentieth Century Texas." Paul Carlson develops the history of Amarillo from its cattle-based origins to its more diversified role as a modern regional center; two years later, Carlson and Donald Abbe produced a centennial history of Lubbock. Linda

Scarbrough has demonstrated the rich possibilities of studying the historical transformation from rural to suburbanized realms in Williamson County.[21]

NOTES

1. Zeynip Chelik and Dianne Favro, "Methods of Urban History," *Journal of Architectural Education* 41 (Spring 1988): 4–9, quotes 5, 7.

2. Gilbert A. Stelter, "Part I: General Concepts and Sources. 1. Introduction to the Study of Urban History," http://scale.cs.uoguelph.ca/history/urban/mod01.html. On "new urban history," see also http://en.wikipedia.org/wiki/Urban_history#New_urban_history. Perhaps the book in this review that resonates most harmoniously with the goals of cultural studies is Harvey J. Graff, *The Dallas Myth: The Making and Unmaking of an American City* (Minneapolis: University of Minnesota Press, 2008).

3. Char Miller and David R. Johnson, "The Rise of Urban Texas," in *Urban Texas: Politics and Development*, ed. Char Miller and Heywood T. Sanders (College Station: Texas A&M University Press, 1990), 3–29 (Texas demographic statistics: 3–7, esp. fig. 1.1).

4. Amy Bridges, *Morning Glories: Municipal Reform in the Southwest* (Princeton, N.J.: Princeton University Press, 1997); another useful overview that contextualizes Texas urban growth within the broader setting of the postwar U.S. West is John M. Findlay, *Magic Lands: Western Cityscapes and American Culture after 1940* (Berkeley: University of California Press, 1992), 1–51. Char Miller, "Sunbelt Texas," in *Texas through Time: Evolving Interpretations*, ed. Walter L. Buenger and Robert A. Calvert (College Station: Texas A&M University Press, 1991), 279–309; David G. McComb, "Urbanization," in *The Portable Handbook of Texas*, ed. Roy R. Barkley and Mark F. Odintz (Austin: Texas State Historical Association, 2000), 913–22, and in *The New Handbook of Texas*, ed. Ron Tyler, Douglas E. Barnett, Roy R. Barkley, Penelope C. Anderson, and Mark F. Odintz (6 vols.; Austin: Texas State Historical Association, 1996), 6:669–77, and online: http://www.tshaonline.org/handbook/online/articles/hyunw; the first two iterations of McComb's piece contain illustrations; the second and third contain bibliography. Miller and Sanders, *Urban Texas*; Terry G. Jordan, with John L. Bean, Jr., and William M. Holmes, *Texas: A Geography* (Boulder: Westview Press, 1984), 209–68. For summaries of the lifecycle and denouement of the Sunbelt debate, see Alan Lessoff, "America's City: Dallas and United States Urban History," *Journal of Urban History* 26 (May 2000): 530–44, esp. 530–31, 543 n. 3; and David R. Goldfield and Howard N. Rabinowitz, "Epilogue: The Vanishing Sunbelt," in *Searching for the Sunbelt: Historical Perspectives on a Region*, ed. Raymond A. Mohl (Knoxville: University of Tennessee Press, 1990), 224–33.

5. *Houston History*, past issues: http://houstonhistorymagazine.org/past-issues; Howard Beeth and Cary D. Wintz, eds., *Black Dixie: Afro-Texan History and Culture in Houston* (College Station: Texas A&M University Press, 1992).

6. Merline Pitre, *In Struggle against Jim Crow: Lulu B. White and the NAACP, 1900–1957* (College Station: Texas A&M University Press, 1999); Thomas H. Kreneck, *Mexican*

American Odyssey: Felix Tijerina, Entrepreneur and Civic Leader, 1905–1965 (College Station: Texas A&M University Press, 2001); also by Kreneck is *Del Pueblo: A History of Houston's Hispanic Community* (College Station: Texas A&M University Press, 2012; a revised edition of a 1989 work); Peg Purser, *Minority Settlement Patterns in the Houston Area* (Houston: Center for Public Policy, University of Houston, 1992). Houston (as well as Laredo and the Lower Rio Grande Valley) is studied in the anthology of Emilio Zamora, Cynthia Orozco, and Rodolfo Rocha, eds., *Mexican Americans in Texas History: Selected Essays* (Austin: Texas State Historical Association, 2000).

7. Roy Vu, "Rising from the Cold War Ashes: Construction of a Vietnamese American Community in Houston, 1975–2005" (Ph.D. diss., University of Houston, 2006); Rubén Hernández-León, *Metropolitan Migrants: The Migration of Urban Mexicans to the United States* (Berkeley: University of California Press, 2008); Martin V. Melosi and Joseph A. Pratt, eds., *Energy Metropolis: An Environmental History of Houston and the Gulf Coast* (Pittsburgh: University of Pittsburgh Press, 2007); see also Jan Lin, "Ethnic Places, Postmodernism, and Urban Change in Houston," *Sociological Quarterly* 36 (Fall 1995): 629–47. It should be noted that dissertations today can often be downloaded in moments from most university library databases (although the illustrative material is often of poor quality).

8. Betty Trapp Chapman, *Historic Houston: An Illustrated History and Resource Guide* (San Antonio, Tex.: Historical Publishing Network, 1997); Stanley Siegel and John Moretta, *Houston: A Chronicle of the Bayou City* (Sun Valley, Calif.: American Historical Press, 2005); Suzanne Lynn Summers, "The Role of Merchants in Promoting Economic Development in the Houston-Galveston Region, 1836–1860" (Ph.D. diss., University of Texas at Austin, 1996); Stephen L. Hardin, *Texian Macabre: The Melancholy Tale of a Hanging in Early Houston* (Abilene, Tex.: State House Press, 2007); Marguerite Johnston, *Houston: The Unknown City, 1836–1946* (College Station: Texas A&M University Press, 1992); Dorothy Knox Howe Houghton, *Houston's Forgotten Heritage: Landscape, Houses, Interiors, 1824–1914* (College Station: Texas A&M University, 1998). A similar book to the latter, with coverage of house interiors in cities across the state, is Cynthia Brandimarte, *Inside Texas: Culture, Identity, and Houses, 1878–1920* (Fort Worth: Texas Christian University Press, 1991).

9. Steven Strom, *Houston Lost and Unbuilt* (Austin: University of Texas Press, 2010); Cheryl L. Ferguson, "Upscale Suburban Architecture and Development in Dallas and Houston, Texas, 1890–1930" (Ph.D. diss., University of Delaware, 2004); Stephen Fox and Richard Cheek, *The Country Houses of John F. Staub* (College Station: Texas A&M University Press, 2007); Barrie Scardino, William F. Stern, and Bruce C. Webb, eds., *Ephemeral City:* Cite *Looks at Houston* (Austin: University of Texas Press, 2003); Joel Warren Barna, *The See-Through Years: Creation and Destruction in Texas Architecture and Real Estate, 1981–1991* (Houston: Rice University Press, 1992).

10. Robert D. Thomas and Richard W. Murray, *Progrowth Politics: Change and Governance in Houston* (Berkeley: IGS Press, Institute of Government Studies, University of California at Berkeley, 1991), 371–89; Jay C. Henry, *Architecture in Texas, 1895–1945* (Austin: University of Texas Press, 1993), 284–89; Diane Y. Ghirardo, "Wielding the

HACHet at Allen Parkway Village," in Scardino, Stern, and Webb, *Ephemeral City*, 100–109; see also Beeth and Wintz, *Black Dixie*. For a period survey on public housing in Texas, see Robert B. Fairbanks, "Public Housing for the City as a Whole: The Texas Experience, 1934–1955," *Southwestern Historical Quarterly* 103 (Apr. 2000): 403–24.

11. Kate Sayen Kirkland, "Envisioning a Progressive City: Hogg Family Philanthropy and the Urban Ideal in Houston, Texas, 1910–1975" (Ph.D. diss., Rice University, 2004); Steven Fenberg, *Unprecedented Power: Jesse Jones, Capitalism, and the Common Good* (College Station: Texas A&M University Press, 2011); Paul Alejandro Levengood, "For the Duration and Beyond: World War II and the Creation of Modern Houston, Texas" (Ph.D. diss., Rice University, 1999).

12. For example, Maverick Publishing Company and the *San Antonio Express-News* have published numerous titles on the city's history; three local writers, with many book titles between them, are Lewis F. Fisher, Mel Brown, and John Ogden Leal.

13. Char Miller, *On the Border: An Environmental History of San Antonio* (Pittsburgh: University of Pittsburgh Press, 2001), and *Deep in the Heart of San Antonio: Land and Life in South Texas* (San Antonio: Trinity University Press, 2004); Laura Anne Wimberley, "The 'Sole Source': A History of San Antonio, South Central Texas, and the Edwards Aquifer, 1890s–1990s" (Ph.D. diss., Texas A&M University, 2001); Charles R. Porter, *Spanish Water, Anglo Water: Early Development in San Antonio* (College Station: Texas A&M University Press, 2009); Judith Berg-Sobré, *San Antonio on Parade: Six Historic Festivals* (College Station: Texas A&M University Press, 2003); Teresa Thomas Perrin, "Crime and Order in San Antonio during the Civil War and Reconstruction" (Ph.D. diss., University of Texas at Austin, 2001); Lawrence Phillip Knight, "Becoming a City and Becoming American: San Antonio, Texas, 1848–1861" (Ph.D. diss., Texas A&M University, 1997). See also Dale Baum and Worth Robert Miller, "Ethnic Conflict and Machine Politics in San Antonio, 1892–1899," *Journal of Urban History* 19 (Aug. 1993): 63–84.

14. Kenneth Mason, "Paternal Continuity: African-Americans and Race Relations in San Antonio, Texas, 1867–1937" (Ph.D. diss., University of Texas at Austin, 1994); Mel Brown, *Chinese Heart of Texas: The San Antonio Community, 1875 to 1975* (Austin: Lily on the Water Publications, 2005); Adriana Ayala, "Negotiating Race Relations through Activism: Women Activists and Women's Organizations in San Antonio, Texas during the 1920s" (Ph.D. diss., University of Texas at Austin, 2005).

15. Kenneth Hafertepe, "Restoration, Reconstruction, or Romance? The Case of the Spanish Governor's Palace in Hispanic-Era San Antonio, Texas," *Journal of the Society of Architectural Historians* 67 (Sept. 2008): 412–33; Lewis F. Fisher, *Saving San Antonio: The Precarious Preservation of a Heritage* (Lubbock: Texas Tech University Press, 1996); Robert Alexander Gonzalez, *Designing Pan-America: U.S. Architectural Visions for the Western Hemisphere* (Austin: University of Texas Press, 2011); Sterlin Holmesly, *HemisFair '68 and the Transformation of San Antonio* (San Antonio, Tex.: Maverick, 2003); Laura Hernández-Ehrisman, *Inventing the Fiesta City: Heritage and Carnival in San Antonio* (Albuquerque: University of New Mexico Press, 2008); Mary Carolyn Hollers George, *O'Neil Ford, Architect* (College Station: Texas A&M University Press, 1992); David Dillon, *The Architecture of O'Neil Ford: Celebrating Place* (Austin: University of Texas Press, 1999).

16. Gerald Eugene Poyo and Gilberto Miguel Hinojosa, *Tejano Origins in Eighteenth-Century San Antonio* (Austin: University of Texas Press for the University of Texas Institute of Texas Cultures at San Antonio, 1991); Jesús F. de la Teja, *San Antonio de Béxar: A Community on New Spain's Northern Frontier* (Albuquerque: University of New Mexico Press, 1995); James Early, *Presidio, Mission, and Pueblo: Spanish Architecture and Urbanism in the United States* (Dallas: Southern Methodist University Press, 2004); Raúl A. Ramos, *Beyond the Alamo: Forging Mexican Ethnicity in San Antonio, 1821–1861* (Chapel Hill: University of North Carolina Press, in association with the William P. Clements Center for Southwest Studies, Southern Methodist University, 2010); Timothy M. Matovina, *Tejano Religion and Ethnicity: San Antonio, 1821–1860* (Austin: University of Texas Press, 1995); E. Shannon Barker, "Los Tejanos de San Antonio: Mexican Immigrant Family Acculturation, 1880–1929" (Ph.D. diss., George Washington University, 1996); Richard A. Garcia, *Rise of the Mexican American Middle Class: San Antonio, 1929–1941* (College Station: Texas A&M University Press, 1991); Richard A. Buitron, *The Quest for Tejano Identity in San Antonio, Texas, 1913–2000* (New York: Routledge, 2004); Rodolfo Rosales, *The Illusion of Inclusion: The Untold Political Story of San Antonio* (Austin: University of Texas Press, 2000); David Montejano, *Quixote's Soldiers: A Local History of the Chicano Movement, 1966–1981* (Austin: University of Texas Press, 2010). See also William Clayson, "'The Barrios and the Ghettos Have Organized!': Community Action, Political Acrimony, and the War on Poverty in San Antonio," *Journal of Urban History* 28 (Jan. 2002): 158–83.

17. Bridges, *Morning Glories*; Lessoff, "America's City"; Elizabeth York Enstam, *Women and the Creation of Urban Life: Dallas, Texas, 1843–1920* (College Station: Texas A&M University Press, 1998); Robert B. Fairbanks, *For the City as a Whole: Planning, Politics, and the Public Interest in Dallas, Texas, 1900–1965* (Columbus: Ohio State University Press, 1999); Patricia Evridge Hill, *Dallas: The Making of a Modern City* (Austin: University of Texas Press, 1996); Jacquelyn Masur McElhaney, *Pauline Periwinkle and Progressive Reform in Dallas* (College Station: Texas A&M University Press, 1998); William H. Wilson, *Hamilton Park: A Planned Black Community in Dallas* (Baltimore: Johns Hopkins University Press, 1998); Graff, *Dallas Myth*; Royce Hanson, *Civic Culture and Urban Change: Governing Dallas* (Detroit, Mich.: Wayne State University Press, 2003); Darwin Payne, *Big D: Triumphs and Troubles of an American Supercity in the 20th Century* (Dallas: Three Forks Press, 2000); Michael V. Hazel, *Dallas: A History of "Big D"* (Austin: Texas State Historical Association, 1997); Michael Phillips, *White Metropolis: Race, Ethnicity, and Religion in Dallas, 1841–2001* (Austin: University of Texas Press, 2006). Although barely pre-1990, the following title is important for discussing the Kessler Plan for Dallas as an application of the "City Beautiful" principles once popular among in the Progressive Era nationally: William H. Wilson, *The City Beautiful Movement* (Baltimore: Johns Hopkins University Press, 1989), 254–78.

18. Alan B. Govenar and Jay F. Brakefield, *Deep Ellum and Central Track: Where the Black and White Worlds of Dallas Converged* (Denton: University of North Texas Press, 1998); Marc Sanders and Ruthe Winegarten, *The Lives and Times of Black Dallas Women* (Austin: Eakin Press, 2002); Susanne Starling, *Land Is the Cry: Warren Angus Ferris, Pioneer Texas Surveyor and Founder of Dallas County* (Austin: Texas State Historical

Association, 1998); Alicia E. Rodriquez, "Disfranchisement in Dallas: The Democratic Party and the Suppression of Independent Political Challenges in Dallas, Texas, 1891–1894," *Southwestern Historical Quarterly* 108 (July 2004), 42–64; Richard Allan Smith, "La Réunion—A Utopian Community in Texas 1855–1859" (Ph.D. diss., University of Texas at Arlington, 2000); Rose G. Biderman, *They Came to Stay: The Story of the Jews of Dallas, 1870–1997* (Austin: Eakin Press, 2002); Gerry Cristol, *A Light in the Prairie: Temple Emanu-El of Dallas, 1872–1997* (Fort Worth: Texas Christian University Press, 1998); Patricia Evridge Hill, "Real Women and True Womanhood: Grassroots Organizing among Dallas Dressmakers in 1935," *Labor's Heritage* 5 (Spring 1994) (entire issue); see also Arthur T. Tatman, "La Camara, 1939: A 'Mexican' Chamber of Commerce Forms in Dallas," *Journal of the West* 45 (Fall 2006): 36–47.

19. Cynthia L. Clark Northrup, "George Bannerman Dealey: A Study in Persuasion, Perseverance, and Progressivism" (Ph.D. diss., Texas Christian University, 2003); Ronald L. Davis, *John Rosenfield's Dallas: How the Southwest's Leading Critic Shaped a City's Culture, 1925–1966* (Dallas: Three Forks Press, 2002); Mark N. Morris, "Saving Society through Politics: The Ku Klux Klan in Dallas, Texas in the 1920s" (Ph.D. diss., University of North Texas, 1997); Patricia Ellen Gower, "Dallas: Experiments in Progressivism, 1898–1919" (Ph.D. diss., Texas A&M University, 1996); Rose-Mary Rumbley, *Strolling through the Park: 100 Years of the Dallas Park and Recreation Board* (Austin: Nortex Press, 2005); Marcel Quimby, Dennis Stacy, and Willis Winters, *Transformations: The Architects, Buildings, and Events That Shaped Dallas Architecture* (Dallas: American Institute of Architects, Dallas Chapter, and New York: McGraw-Hill Construction Information Group, 2008); Virginia McAlester, Willis Cecil Winters, Prudence MacKintosh, and Steve Clicque, *Great American Suburbs: The Homes of the Park Cities, Dallas* (New York: Abbeville Press, 2008); Richard R. Brettell and Willis Winters, *Crafting Traditions: The Architecture of Mark Lemmon* (Dallas: Southern Methodist University Press, for Meadows Museum at Southern Methodist University, 2005). See also Henry, *Architecture in Texas*, and Ferguson, "Upscale Suburban Architecture."

20. J'Nell Pate, *North of the River: A Brief History of North Fort Worth* (Fort Worth: Texas Christian University Press, 1994); Victoria L. Buenger and Walter L. Buenger, *Texas Merchant: Marvin Leonard and Fort Worth* (College Station: Texas A&M University, 1998); Carlos E. Cuéllar, *Stories from the Barrio: A History of Mexican Fort Worth* (Fort Worth: Texas Christian University Press, 2003); Judith Walker Linsley, Ellen Walker Rienstra, and Jo Ann Stiles, *Giant under the Hill: A History of the Spindletop Oil Discovery at Beaumont, Texas, in 1901* (Austin: Texas State Historical Association, 2002); Diana Davids Olien and Roger M. Olien, *Oil in Texas: The Gusher Age, 1895–1945* (Austin: University of Texas at Austin, 2002); Wilbert H. Timmons, *El Paso: A Borderlands History*, 2nd ed. (El Paso: Texas Western Press/University of Texas at El Paso, 2004); Allison Brownell Tirres, "Lawyers and Legal Borderlands," *American Journal of Legal History* 50, no. 2 (2008–2010), 156–99; Marcia Hatfield Daudistel, ed., *Grace and Gumption: The Women of El Paso* (Fort Worth: Texas Christian University Press, 2011); Charles H. Harris and Louis R. Sadler, *The Secret War in El Paso: Mexican Revolutionary Intrigue, 1906–1920* (Albuquerque: University of New Mexico Press, 2009); for a complementary perspective, see Miguel Antonio Levario, *Militarizing the Border:*

When Mexicans Became the Enemy (College Station: Texas A&M University Press, 2012). Monica Perales, *Smeltertown: Making and Remembering a Southwest Border Community* (Chapel Hill: University of North Carolina Press, 2010); local historians who have produced many studies on El Paso include Fred M. Morales and Leon Claire Metz. Robert D. Wood, *Life in Laredo: A Documentary History from the Laredo Archives* (Denton: University of North Texas Press, 2004); John A. Adams, Jr., *Conflict and Commerce on the Rio Grande: Laredo, 1755–1955* (College Station: Texas A&M University Press, 2008); Jerry D. Thompson, *Warm Weather and Bad Whiskey: The 1886 Laredo Election Riot* (El Paso: Texas Western Press, 1991); on public housing, see Carlos Valle, "Urban Growth with Limited Prosperity: A History of Public Housing in Laredo, Texas 1938–2006" (Ph.D. diss., University of New Orleans, 2007). Mary Jo O'Rear, *Storm over the Bay: The People of Corpus Christi and Their Port* (College Station: Texas A&M University Press, 2009); Alan Lessoff, "Harland Bartholomew and Corpus Christi: The Faltering Pursuit of Comprehensive Planning in South Texas," *Planning Perspectives* 18 (Apr. 2003): 197–232; also by Lessoff: "A Texas City and the Texas Myth: Urban Historical Identity in Corpus Christi," *Southwestern Historical Quarterly* 100 (Jan. 1997): 305–29.

21. Patricia Bellis Bixel and Elizabeth Hayes Turner, *Galveston and the 1900 Storm: Catastrophe and Catalyst* (Austin: University of Texas Press, 2000); Elizabeth Hayes Turner, *Women, Culture, and Community: Religion and Reform in Galveston, 1880–1920* (New York: Oxford University Press, 1997); David G. McComb, *Galveston: A History and a Guide* (Austin: Texas State Historical Association, 2000); Clifford Farrington, *Biracial Unions on Galveston's Waterfront, 1865–1925* (Austin: Texas State Historical Association, 2007); Susan Wiley Hardwick, *Mythic Galveston: Reinventing America's Third Coast* (Baltimore: Johns Hopkins University Press, 2002); see also Harold M. Hyman, *Oleander Odyssey: The Kempners of Galveston, Texas, 1854–1980s* (College Station: Texas A&M University Press, 1990). Stephen Fox, "Architecture in Brownsville: The 20th Century," in *Studies in Matamoros and Cameron County History*, ed. Milo Kearney, Anthony Knopp, and Antonio Zavaleta (Brownsville: University of Texas at Brownsville and Texas Southmost College, 1997), 283–346. Kearney and Knopp have edited other anthologies on the Lower Rio Grande Valley at their home institution, the University of Texas-Brownsville, and have also written *Border* Cuates: *A History of the U.S.-Mexican Twin Cities* (Austin: Eakin Press, 1995); Stanley C. Green is another professor who has done tending of a similar nature in his adopted hometown fields of Laredo history. Similar in geographic theme to *Border* Cuates (with studies of Brownsville and El Paso): Robin E. Robinson, "Vice and Tourism on the U.S.-Mexican Border: A Comparison of Three Communities in the Era of U.S. Prohibition" (Ph.D. diss., Arizona State University, 2002). Daniel D. Arreola, *Tejano South Texas: A Mexican American Cultural Province* (Austin: University of Texas Press, 2002). Kenneth B. Ragsdale, *Austin, Cleared for Takeoff: Aviators, Businessmen, and the Growth of an American City* (Austin: University of Texas Press, 2004); for a focus more on Austin's political history, see Bridges, *Morning Glories*, 67–70, 79, 83–84, 91–94, 115–18, 143, 193–94; for another perspective on the Tom Miller years in Austin, see L. Patrick Hughes, "To Meet Fire with Fire: Lyndon Johnson, Tom Miller, and Home-Front Politics," *Southwestern Historical Quarterly* 100 (Apr.

1997): 452–76. Patricia Bernstein, *The First Waco Horror: The Lynching of Jesse Washington and the Rise of the NAACP* (College Station: Texas A&M University Press, 2006); Virginia Lee Spurlin, "The Connors of Waco: Black Professionals in Twentieth Century Texas" (Ph.D. diss., Texas Tech University, 1991); Paul H. Carlson, *Amarillo: The Story of a Western Town* (Lubbock: Texas Tech University Press, 2006); Paul H. Carlson and Donald R. Abbe, *The Centennial History of Lubbock: Hub City of the Plains* (Virginia Beach, Va.: Donning, 2008); Linda Scarbrough, *Road, River, and Ol' Boy Politics: A Texas County's Path from Farm to Supersuburb* (Austin: Texas State Historical Association, 2005); see also Mark Friedberger, "Development, Politics, and the Rural-Urban Fringe in North Texas," *Southwestern Historical Quarterly* 109 (Jan. 2006): 358–83. On Abilene, see the recent major study: Robert W. Sledge, *A People, A Place: The Story of Abilene* (2 vols.; Buffalo Gap, Tex.: State House Press, distributed by Texas A&M University Press Consortium, 2008–11).

CHAPTER 8

Texas Military History

Richard B. McCaslin

Those who have sought to write the history of Texas have far too often focused on the vagaries of popular memory, thus failing to produce carefully researched analytical narratives that might convey something far more substantive about the Lone Star State. This is certainly true of many who have written on the military history of Texas. Confined by the outlines of Texas mythology, scholars have, deliberately or not, retold the same stories about the Alamo, Texas Rangers, and the armies of the United States and the Confederate States of America. Rather than undertake new research and apply new analytical frameworks, they have frequently recounted key events in familiar ways, or they have simply ignored many significant subjects altogether. But in the past two decades, much new scholarship on the Lone Star State has emerged, and many recent works offer new perspectives on Texas military history. These scholars seek to replace myths about Texas's military past with analysis based upon careful research. The result is not perfect, but a substantial body of work has emerged of which many Texans can truly be proud.

This essay offers a selection of some of the best work produced in the past twenty years on the military history of Texas. The list is by no means exhaustive, but it does include books that scholars working in the field should know. The focus of course is on Texas: the colony and state itself, Texas units, and Texas institutions. The scope includes operations and events that involved the armed forces of Spain, Mexico, the Republic of Texas, the United States, and the Confederate States of America as well as the state of Texas, though not necessarily all Texans and their many experiences. Because conflict often involves non-combatants, some studies of what has been called the "home front" are included. And because Texas shares a historically volatile border with Mexico, some of the scholarly work on the conflicts in that area are included if they discuss the role of the U.S. Army to a significant degree. Again, the result is a body of work that puts aside myths based upon popular memory and recovers information that helps to explain the evolution of Texas from a frontier colony into a modern state.

Prior to 1995, few attempted to bring all the periods of Texas military efforts together in one coherent survey. This oversight has been partially addressed by the publication of Joseph G. Dawson's *The Texas Military Experience.* Dawson is the editor rather than the author, but under his aegis the writers of this collection put aside myth in favor of more substantive analysis. They cover the usual subjects but also probe into some lesser-known stories, such as the role of women in the U.S. Army in nineteenth-century Texas. A more recent anthology, Alexander Mendoza and Charles D. Grear's *Texans and War*, offers more information on women, Native Americans, and African Americans in Texas, adding perspectives as well on dissent and even prisoners of war. For those interested in visiting the locations where many Texas military events occurred, a well-researched resource is Thomas E. Alexander and Dan K. Utley's *Faded Glory.* Although they focus on events from the war with Mexico to the end of World War II, it can be argued that these are the most important in the development of modern Texas.[1]

Spain defended the Texas frontier for well over a century, and that era has not been overlooked by recent scholars. Robert S. Weddle has produced several fine books on the rivalry between the French and Spanish along the northern coast of the Gulf of Mexico, but in his recent *Texas: After the Massacre* he expands upon his earlier research to provide new insights. A highlight of this work is a translation by Carole Lipscomb of a diary composed during the fateful 1759 expedition. This important resource can be supplemented by several published collections of contemporary maps compiled by two of the best cartographic experts on early Texas: William C. Foster, *Spanish Expeditions into Texas, 1689–1768*; Jack Jackson, *Imaginary Kingdom: Texas as Seen by the Rivera and Rubi Military Expeditions, 1727 and 1767*; and Jackson, *Shooting the Sun: Cartographic Results of Military Activities in Texas, 1689–1829.* Such material helps shift the focus from where the Spanish expeditions may have walked to the impact their experiences and observations had on larger policy decisions.[2]

The Texas fight for independence has clearly captured the imagination of Texans, and they finally have a military history of that event worthy of their attention: Stephen L. Hardin's *Texian Iliad*. Hardin combines thorough research with a fine writing style to provide a new Texas classic. For those interested in a more immediate perspective on the conflict, new editions of some of the Mexican participants have been published. James E. Crisp wrote an interesting introduction for an expanded edition of José Enrique de la Peña's *With Santa Anna in Texas*, translated and edited by Carmen Perry. Jack Jackson edited (and John Wheat translated) *Almonte's Texas*. Wheat also translated *General Vicente Filisola's Analysis of José Urrea's Military Diary*, edited by Gregg J. Dimmick. And lest anyone forget that not all men who fought for Texas were Anglos, Jesús F. de la Teja edited *A Revolution Remembered: The Memoirs and Selected Correspondence of Juan N. Seguín*.[3]

Accounts of the fight for the Alamo have always dominated the military history of the Texas war for independence, and they continue to be a large subset of the writing on the period. William C. Davis uses biography to provide a human perspective in *Three Roads to the Alamo*. A more standard history, informed by new research, can be found in R. Bruce Winders's *Sacrificed at the Alamo*. Phillip T. Tucker offers a new interpretation of the final battle in *Exodus from the Alamo*, arguing that some defenders tried to abandon the position. Such suppositions are based upon a flood of new research, much of which can be found in Todd Hanson's compilation *The Alamo Reader*. James E. Crisp offers an extensive discussion of the most popular debates in *Sleuthing the Alamo*. Thomas R. Lindley makes a similar effort in *Alamo Traces*. For more information from contemporaries, or those who claimed to be, see Bill Groneman's *Eyewitness to the Alamo* and Gary S. Zaboly's *An Altar for Their Sons*.[4]

As any good Texan knows, all of the fighting during the Texas war for independence did not occur at the Alamo, and the struggle in fact did not either begin or end there. Alwyn Barr, in *Texans in Revolt*, provides a detailed account of how San Antonio fell into Texan hands. Stuart Reid offers an intriguing international perspective in *The Secret War for Texas*. Gary Brown has published two interesting books on prominent Anglo participants: *Volunteers in the Texas Revolution*, and *Hesitant Martyr in the Texas Revolution: James Walker Fannin*. Edward L. Miller, in *New Orleans and the Texas Revolution*, provides even more information about that port city's contributions to the Texas cause. Of course, Texas independence was won on April 21, 1836, and the latest work on that final clash is Stephen L. Moore's *Eighteen Minutes: The Battle of San Jacinto and the Texas Independence Campaign*. The impact of that clash and its aftermath cannot, however, be understood properly without Gregg J. Dimmick's *Sea of Mud: The Retreat of the Mexican Army after San Jacinto, an Archeological Investigation*. This literally groundbreaking classic recounts the chaos that prevented an effective Mexican response to the overwhelming but not decisive defeat of their commander, Santa Anna.[5]

The Republic of Texas struggled to defend itself from Mexican and Indian forces alike, but the Texans also could not resist picking a fight themselves. Stephen L. Moore, in *Savage Frontier*, provides four volumes of detailed information on the operations of military and paramilitary organizations on the frontiers of Texas. The tragic Mier expedition has drawn the attention of three authors in the past two decades: Sam W. Haynes, *Soldiers of Misfortune*; Joseph M. Nance, *Dare-Devils All*; and Mary Margaret McAllen Amberson, *A Brave Boy and A Good Soldier*. Another abortive military expedition by Texans is recounted by Paul N. Spellman in *Forgotten Texas Leader: Hugh McLeod and the Texan Santa Fe Expedition*. His subject, McLeod, survived a Mexican prison only to die of disease while serving as a colonel in the Confederate army. Three versions of a similar hard-luck story can be found in Douglas V. Meed's *Fighting Texas Navy*, Jonathan W. Jordan's *Lone Star Navy*, and John Powers's *First Texas Navy*, each of which provides an interesting perspective on Texas's short-lived fleet.[6]

The annexation of Texas by the United States of course led to war with Mexico. R. Bruce Winders, in *Crisis in the Southwest*, properly places Texas in the center of that conflict and its aftermath. Texans played a prominent, and often controversial, role in the war, which is well recounted in Frederick Wilkins's *Texas Rangers in the Mexican War*. In this book, Wilkins expands upon themes established in his earlier work, *The Legend Begins: The Texas Rangers, 1823–1845*. For a brief but useful introduction to primary and secondary sources on the subject, see Charles M. Robinson's *Texas and the Mexican War*.[7]

Victory in the war with Mexico left the U.S. Army with the overwhelming task of defending the southern and western frontiers of Texas. Brian DeLay, in *War of a Thousand Deserts*, offers an impressive survey of the magnitude, and historical roots, of that responsibility. Thomas T. Smith wrote a modern perspective on the antebellum era, *The U.S. Army and the Texas Frontier Economy*, and followed it with *The Old Army in Texas*. Smith argues that military posts were the primary conduit for federal support of frontier development in Texas, providing a pathway for the movement of federal dollars into Texan pockets. Newly published primary sources include Robert Wooster's edited *Recollections of Western Texas . . . by Two of the U.S. Mounted Rifles* and two edited works by Jerry D. Thompson: *Fifty Miles and a Fight: Major Samuel Heintzelman's Journal of Texas and the Cortina War*, and *Texas and New Mexico on the Eve of the Civil War: The Mansfield and Johnston Inspections, 1859–1861*. Interestingly, Smith, Wooster, and Thompson joined with Ben E. Pingenot to edit *The Reminiscences of Major General Zenas R. Bliss*. Such resources allow researchers to move beyond telling stories of bluecoats fighting Indians and explore the broader impact of the army on antebellum Texas, and vice versa.[8]

When the army failed to defend antebellum Texas effectively, a host of Texas volunteers, remembered as Rangers, enlisted for the job. Recent broad surveys of note on this era include these: Thomas W. Knowles, *They Rode for the Lone Star*, Vol. 1; Frederick Wilkins, *Defending the Borders*; Robert M. Utley, *Lone Star Justice*; Michael L. Collins, *Texas Devils*; and Mike Cox, *The Texas Rangers*. All of these are eminently readable, and each provides an interesting perspective on the subject, but Wilkins's is the most thoroughly researched of the lot. Among the recent biographies of the great Ranger captains of this period, Thomas W. Cutrer provides a model for others in *Ben McCulloch and the Frontier Military Tradition*. Diverging from a formula that emphasizes martial glory to the detriment of other aspects of a subject's life, Cutrer's study reveals how military efforts fit into the context of economic and political development in antebellum Texas. This work strongly influenced the approach taken by Richard B. McCaslin in *Fighting Stock: John S. "Rip" Ford of Texas*. And for the other side of the story, at least along the Rio Grande, read Jerry D. Thompson, *Cortina: Defending the Mexican Name in Texas*.[9]

Although Texans leaders have worked hard to define their state as "western" in popular memory, few subjects in Texas history have drawn more scholarly attention than the Civil War. Senior scholar Ralph A. Wooster led the way in the past two decades with his *Texas and Texans in the Civil War*, which closely followed an anthology he edited: *Lone Star Blue and Gray*. Wooster added to the corpus with *Civil War Texas*, then added *Lone Star Generals in Gray* and *Lone Star Regiments in Gray*. All in all, these works together are essential for those interested in Texas's experience in the Civil War. A pair of award-winning anthologies on the subject appeared even more recently: Charles D. Grear's edited *The Fate of Texas* and Kenneth W. Howell's edited *The Seventh Star of the Confederacy*. Both works offer new perspectives and opportunities for replacing myth with history. Perhaps the boldest effort to confront popular memory came in another work from Grear with *Why Texans Fought in the Civil War*. He systematically discusses each group in the Lone Star State, offering explanations that are sure to inspire many future scholarly exchanges.[10]

For those interested in individual campaigns and battles that took place in Texas or on its borders during the Civil War, historians have produced some fine work in the past twenty years. Donald S. Frazier began with a detailed history of the ill-fated New Mexico campaign in *Blood and Treasure*, then produced *Cottonclads!* Two years later, Edward T. Cotham wrote *Battle on the Bay*, which was followed by *Sabine Pass*. All of these works became the standard references on their topics. Most recently, Frazier has undertaken a multivolume history of the Civil War in Louisiana, beginning with *Fire in the Cane Field*. For another scholarly perspective on the Union attempts to invade Texas through southern Louisiana, see Richard G. Lowe's *Texas Overland Expedition of 1863*. When it proved impossible to cross the bayou country and enter the Lone Star State, federal officials tried landing on the Texas coast, a poorly supported failure recounted in Stephen A. Townsend's acclaimed *Yankee Invasion of Texas*. Stephen A. Dupree, in *Planting the Union Flag in Texas*, provides a fuller account by including the disastrous Red River campaign. For the Union forces, the final humiliation came with a stinging defeat at Palmito Ranch in May 1865, after most Confederate forces outside of Texas had surrendered. This story is nicely retold in Jeffrey W. Hunt's *Last Battle of the Civil War: Palmetto Ranch*, though additional details can be found in Phillip T. Tucker's *Final Fury: Palmito Ranch, the Last Battle of the Civil War*.[11]

Recent scholars have produced some well-researched regimental histories for the Civil War period, and they belatedly raised the bar in research and analysis by expanding the focus of their work on Texas units. Anne J. Bailey provides a useful overview of mounted operations in *Texans in the Confederate Cavalry*. For western theater buffs, two books provide information on a pair of regiments that served with distinction in the brigade that bore Lawrence S. "Sul" Ross's name: Douglas Hale, *The Third Texas Cavalry in the Civil War*; and Martha L. Crabb, *All Afire to Fight*. Crabb's work has drawn exceptionally strong reviews for the depth of her research. Those interested in Trans-Mississippi campaigns can find much of interest in Stanley S. McGowen's *Horse Sweat and Powder Smoke* and Thomas Reid's *Spartan Band: Burnett's 13th Texas Cavalry in the Civil War*. The 13th Texas Cavalry actually served mostly as a dismounted unit, and the book on the division to which it was assigned won one of the highest national awards for Civil War history: Richard G. Lowe, *Walker's Texas Division, C.S.A.* Lowe analyzes not only actions and experiences but also the character of the men who followed John G. Walker, providing some compelling new insights into Civil War Texans. This model was followed effectively by John R. Lundberg in *Granbury's Texas Brigade*, which singles out one hard-fighting unit from his earlier work, *The Finishing Stroke: Texans in the 1864 Tennessee Campaign*. The template has thus been established for scholars to continue the task of replacing Lost Cause myths with more accurate word pictures of Confederate Texans.[12]

The Civil War deeply affected people of all kinds, at all levels, and this is reflected in the historical literature on Texas. In addition to the previously mentioned biographies of prominent Confederates Benjamin McCulloch and John S. Ford, by Cutrer and McCaslin, respectively, Carl H. Moneyhon has produced a long-overdue study of a Lone Star unionist, Edmund J. Davis. At the grassroots level, Philip R. Caudill used a variety of sources on William B. Duncan of the 21st Texas Infantry to write *Moss Bluff Rebel*. Jerry D. Thompson expanded upon his earlier research on Tejanos to produce *Vaqueros in Blue and Gray*. And Stephen Chicoine merged military history with local studies in *Confederates of Chappell Hill, Texas*. Of course, the home front has not been overlooked by scholars who write about Texas in the Civil War, but they have focused primarily on violence and disaffection. The almost forgotten role of various state and local units has been admirably recovered in David Paul Smith, *Frontier Defense in the Civil War*. In his second volume of a proposed trilogy on William Quantrill, Paul R. Petersen discusses his Lone Star operations in *Quantrill in Texas*. Not all Texans supported the Confederacy, and many of them paid for their dissent with their lives. How and why this happened is vividly recounted in Richard B. McCaslin's *Tainted Breeze: The Great Hanging at Gainesville, Texas* and David Pickering and Judy Falls's *Brush Men and Vigilantes*. McCaslin in particular digs deep into national, state, and local sources to explain the event and its consequences.[13]

The latest generation of historians have certainly not neglected to share some of the best primary sources they have uncovered in telling the story of Civil War Texas. For Texans who fought in the Army of Northern Virginia, the standard accounts have relied heavily on Joseph B. Polley's *A Soldier's Letters to Charming Nellie*, an expanded and heavily annotated version of which has been produced by Richard B. McCaslin. Polley's comrade in Hood's Texas Brigade, Robert Campbell, wrote the postwar memoir edited by George Skoch and Mark W. Perkins for *Lone Star Confederate: A Gallant and Good Soldier of the 5th Texas Infantry*. A foot soldier in the West provided the material for James M. McCaffrey's edited *Only a Private: A Texan Remembers the Civil War*. Thomas W. Cutrer has edited two useful compilations: *Terry's Texas Ranger Trilogy* and *Our Trust Is in the God of Battles*. For the Trans-Mississippi, Richard G. Lowe produced *A Texas Cavalry Officer's Civil War*, and Jerry D. Thompson edited *Civil War in the Southwest: Recollections of the Sibley Brigade*. Another perspective on the Trans-Mississippi can be found in Thompson's *Tejanos in Gray: Civil War Letters of Captains Jose Rafael de la Garza and Manuel Yturri*. Edward T. Cotham has produced a Union perspective of the fighting at Galveston and Sabine Pass in *The Southern Journey of a Civil War Marine*.[14]

The latest generation of historians has rediscovered the tremendous value of images and artifacts in conveying the impact of the Civil War, and those who write about Texas follow this general rule. A rich trove of photographs, accompanied by substantial biographies, can be found in Carl H. Moneyhon and Bobby Roberts's *Portraits of Conflict*. One of the most effective collectors of nineteenth-century Texas photographs teamed with the one of the best historians of the Rio Grande area to produce a fine book of images: Jerry D. Thompson and Lawrence T. Jones III, *Civil War and Revolution on the Rio Grande Frontier*. Another collector, Richard M. Ahlstrom, photographed hundreds of items for his *Texas Civil War Artifacts*. Taken together, this trio of works provides a visual perspective on Civil War Texas that adds a much-needed dimension to the written records Texans left behind.[15]

The primary military challenge for Texas after the Civil War was forcing a conclusion to long-standing conflicts with Indians, which accelerated as people flooded into the state looking for a new start on the frontier. Most of the recent research focuses on the history of individual posts, although Loyd M. Uglow provides a useful overview in his *Standing in the Gap: Army Outposts, Picket Stations, and the Pacification of the Texas Frontier*. Thomas T. Smith laid the groundwork for some of his later publications with *Fort Inge*. Ty Cashion focused his attention three hundred miles to the north in *A Texas Frontier: The Clear Fork Country and Fort Griffin*, expanding upon the community history offered in *The Frontier World of Fort Griffin*, by Charles M. Robinson III. But the template for future studies of frontier outposts, inside and outside of Texas, has been established by Robert Wooster. Building upon research conducted for a National Park Service site study, he wrote *Fort Davis: Outpost on the Texas Frontier*, then broadened his context to produce *Frontier Crossroads: Fort Davis and the West*. In each of his works, Wooster follows the tenets of the new military history in discussing not just administrative affairs and military operations but also the lifestyles of the soldiers and the impact of the post on the surrounding region and its diverse inhabitants.[16]

Black soldiers, popularly known as "buffalo" soldiers, continue to be of great interest to scholars who study military affairs in Texas. Those who served in the complex ethnic world of South Texas are discussed in James N. Leiker's

Racial Borders. A broader perspective is offered by Garna L. Christian with *Black Soldiers in Jim Crow Texas*, though the stories are no less tragic. Perhaps one of the least known, but no less disturbing, disasters that involved black troopers is recounted by Paul H. Carlson in *The Buffalo Soldier Tragedy of 1877*. Some scant comfort may be found in the number of black soldiers whose stories can be found in Charles M. Neal's *Valor across the Lone Star: The Congressional Medal of Honor in Frontier Texas*. Neal spent years researching the stories of the sixty-seven men, representing a diverse range of backgrounds and ethnicities, who are included in this thick volume, and the result is a highly detailed work that provides much material to replace hollow myths with engaging history.[17]

Biography can be an effective way to convey substantive lessons about history, and some recent scholars have chosen that literary path in exploring the period of the major Indian wars in Texas. The relentless and frequently controversial commander of the 24th U.S. Infantry and later the 4th U.S. Cavalry seems to have drawn the most attention. Three authors produced useful biographies of him in the past twenty years: Michael D. Pierce, *The Most Promising Young Officer*; Charles M. Robinson III, *Bad Hand*; and J'Nell L. Pate, *Ranald Slidell Mackenzie*. Another commander of the 24th Infantry in Texas is discussed by Paul H. Carlson in *"Pecos Bill": A Military Biography of William R. Shafter*. The army relied on the support of the Texas Rangers during the waning days of the Red River War of the 1870s, even as the Rangers were making the transition into a law enforcement organization. A key figure in that shift is the subject of Chuck Parsons and Marianne E. Hall Little's *Captain L. H. McNelly, Texas Ranger*. A veteran of both the Confederate army and Gov. Edmund J. Davis's state police, McNelly led a special force of Rangers that cooperated with U.S. infantry and cavalry along the Rio Grande border before tuberculosis forced him to retire. His true-life exploits overshadow any myths of the period, and his story, like that of his army contemporaries, provides an insightful perspective on the post–Civil War frontier in Texas.[18]

The close of the nineteenth century, and the entry of the United States into the race for overseas colonies, brought a reorganization of both the Texas Rangers and the national armed forces. The former increasingly focused on law enforcement, and the latter absorbed many Texas militia units into the national guard. Either many Texas regiments did not make it into combat, as happened during the Spanish-American War, or those Texans who fought did so as members of units that were not strictly identified with the Lone Star State, such as Theodore Roosevelt's Rough Riders. Some Texans who enlisted in 1898, however, persisted in service in some capacity, and when the border became inflamed in the Mexican Revolution of 1910–1920 they rode south as Rangers or national guard and joined with the army in operations on both sides of the Rio Grande. Three books offer Texas-centric perspectives on the border chaos: James A. Sandos, *Rebellion in the Borderlands*; Benjamin H. Johnson, *Revolution in Texas;* and Charles H. Harris and Louis R. Sadler, *The Texas Rangers and the Mexican Revolution.* Though it is only a small fraction of the entire collection, compelling insights can be gleaned from the images in Frank N. Samponaro and Paul J. Vanderwood's *War Scare on the Rio Grande.* It was certainly not the Rangers' finest hour, and it remains a period that mythmakers often prefer to overlook, but a proper understanding of these events is necessary for a full understanding of the persistent attitudes concerning both the Rangers and the U.S. military in South Texas.[19]

World War I is in many ways a forgotten war in U.S. history. This is true as well for the Texas doughboys who fought overseas, but a few scholars have made some progress in solving this problem. The best is Gregory W. Ball, *They Called Them Soldier Boys.* Bruce L. Brager's *Texas 36th Division* recounts the service of Texas and Oklahoma national guard who fought together in two world wars. A small step in recovering the stories of one of the Lone Star State's long-marginalized populations can be found in José A. Ramírez's *To the Line of Fire: Mexican Texans and World War I.* Published primary sources from Texans who served during World War I are scarce, but George B. Clark edited Warren R. Jackson's 1920s memoirs, titled *His Time in Hell: A Texas Marine in France.* Because many other Texas units, and Texans of all ethnicities and genders, fought in World War I, this field remains open to those interested in recovering all of Texas's past.[20]

World War II transformed Texas into a modern state, converting its economy from one dominated by agriculture to a primarily industrial system and shifting its population from a rural majority to one that is mostly urban. At the same time, the turmoil and inequities of the period led to fundamental changes in civil rights. Perhaps for these reasons, this era has drawn a lot of attention from recent scholars. An interesting overview is offered in an anthology edited by James Ward Lee, *1941: Texas Goes to War.* Joyce Gibson Roach takes a more literary approach, mixing fictional essays with nonfictional recollections, in another edited anthology, *Collective Heart: Texans in World War II.* Louis Fairchild is more straightforward in his presentation of true-life remembrances titled *They Called It the War Effort.*[21]

One of the greatest factors in the transformation of Texas during World War II was the expansion of air power operations, including both production and training. The best surveys of the topic are both written by Thomas E.

Alexander: *The Stars Were Big and Bright*, followed by *The Wings of Change.* Alexander also tried his hand at writing a history of a typical installation, *Rattlesnake Bomber Base: Pyote Army Airfield in World War II.* Not all of these bases were used by U.S. air crews, as Tom Killebrew recounts in *The Royal Air Force in Texas.* But no matter what their purpose was in World War II, most of these installations have now fallen into ruin or have been converted for other uses by the communities adjacent to them. Lasting change, however, is the theme of J'Nell L. Pate in *Arsenal of Defense: Fort Worth's Military Legacy.* Far from just the sleepy cow town of myth, Fort Worth has been transformed by its ongoing military role, from frontier outpost to industrial powerhouse.[22]

Recent scholars have also provided some fine work on World War II military operations that involved Texas or Texans. Starting close to home, an unsettling threat to the Lone Star State is discussed by Melanie Wiggins in *Torpedoes in the Gulf: Galveston and the U-boats.* In addition to the previously mentioned history of the 36th Division, two books have appeared on another hard-fighting unit: James S. Powell, *Learning under Fire: The 112th Cavalry Regiment in World War II;* and Robert P. Wiggins, *Jungle Combat with the 112th Cavalry.* The latter is a compilation of firsthand accounts by veterans. A sad and almost forgotten story is retold by Kelly E. Crager in *Hell under the Rising Sun: Texan POWs and the Building of the Burma-Thailand Death Railway.* Cindy Weigand breaks new ground in her study of more than two dozen female veterans in *Texas Women in World War II.* And for a visual record of the war, many would argue that the best combat artist of World War II came from El Paso. His work is presented in *The Two Thousand Yard Stare: Tom Lea's World War II*, edited by Brendan M. Greeley, Jr.[23]

Texans have continued to fight in the many conflicts in which the United States has become embroiled since the close of World War II. But thanks to modern military organization, they no longer fight in Texas units, and thankfully they no longer fight to defend Texas itself. Their military history has become part of a larger, national whole. So, though their battles do not end in 1945, a distinct military history of Texas gives way to a broader narrative focused on the United States. The engrossing story of almost three centuries of conflict, however, continues to draw the attention of scholar and amateur alike. In sum, during the past two decades historians have greatly expanded scholarly perspectives on the military experience of Texans, beginning with their defense of their own frontiers and continuing through their battles against and later in support of the government whose annexation they welcomed. The result is a richer history that can better serve as a source of regional pride, and self-identity, than any myth.

NOTES

1. Joseph G. Dawson, *The Texas Military Experience: From the Texas Revolution through World War II* (College Station: Texas A&M University Press, 1995); Alexander Mendoza and Charles D. Grear, *Texans and War: New Interpretations of the State's Military History* (College Station: Texas A&M University Press, 2012); Thomas E. Alexander and Dan K. Utley, *Faded Glory: A Century of Forgotten Texas Military Sites, Then and Now* (College Station: Texas A&M University Press, 2012).

2. Robert S. Weddle, *Texas: After the Massacre: The Violent Legacy of the San Saba Mission* (Lubbock: Texas Tech University Press, 2007); William C. Foster, *Spanish Expeditions into Texas, 1689–1768* (Austin: University of Texas Press, 1995); Jack Jackson, *Imaginary Kingdom: Texas as Seen by the Rivera and Rubi Military Expeditions, 1727 and 1767* (Austin: Texas State Historical Association, 1995); Jack Jackson, *Shooting the Sun: Cartographic Results of Military Activities in Texas, 1689–1829* (Dallas: Book Club of Texas, 1998).

3. Stephen L. Hardin, *Texian Iliad: A Military History of the Texas Revolution* (Austin: University of Texas Press, 1994); James E. Crisp, ed., *With Santa Anna in Texas: A Personal Narrative of the Revolution* (College Station: Texas A&M University Press, 1997); Jack Jackson, ed., and John Wheat, trans., *Almonte's Texas: Juan N. Almonte's 1834 Inspection, Secret Report, and Role in the 1836 Campaign* (Austin: Texas State Historical Association, 2005); Gregg J. Dimmick, ed., and John Wheat, trans., *General Vicente Filisola's Analysis of José Urrea's Military Diary: A Forgotten 1838 Publication by an Eyewitness to the Texas Revolution* (Austin: Texas State Historical Association, 2007); Jesús F. de la Teja, ed., *A Revolution Remembered: The Memoirs and Selected Correspondence of Juan N. Seguín* (Austin: State House Press, 1991).

4. William C. Davis, *Three Roads to the Alamo: The Lives and Fortunes of David Crockett, James Bowie, and William Barret Travis* (New York: Harper Collins, 1998); R. Bruce Winders, *Sacrificed at the Alamo: Tragedy and Triumph in the Texas Revolution* (Austin: State House Press, 2004); Phillip T. Tucker, *Exodus from the Alamo* (Havertown, Pa.: Casemate, 2010); Todd Hanson, *The Alamo Reader: A Study in History* (Mechanicsburg, Pa.: Stackpole Books, 2003); James E. Crisp, *Sleuthing the Alamo: Davy Crockett's Last Stand and Other Mysteries of the Texas Revolution* (New York: Oxford University, 2005); Thomas R. Lindley, *Alamo Traces: New Evidence and New Conclusions* (Dallas: Taylor, 2003); Bill Groneman, *Eyewitness to the Alamo* (Plano: Republic of Texas Press, 1996); Gary S. Zaboly, *An Altar for Their Sons: The Alamo and the Texas Revolution in Contemporary Newspaper Accounts* (Abilene, Tex.: State House Press, 2011).

5. Alwyn Barr, *Texans in Revolt: The Battle for San Antonio, 1835* (Austin: University of Texas Press, 1990); Stuart Reid, *The Secret War for Texas* (College Station: Texas A&M University Press, 2007); Gary Brown, *Volunteers in the Texas Revolution: The New Orleans Greys* (Plano: Republic of Texas Press, 1999), and *Hesitant Martyr in the Texas Revolution: James Walker Fannin* (Plano: Republic of Texas Press, 2000); Edward L. Miller, *New Orleans and the Texas Revolution* (College Station: Texas A&M University Press, 2004); Stephen L. Moore, *Eighteen Minutes: The Battle of San Jacinto and the*

Texas Independence Campaign (Plano: Republic of Texas Press, 2004); Gregg J. Dimmick, *Sea of Mud: The Retreat of the Mexican Army after San Jacinto, an Archeological Investigation* (Austin: Texas State Historical Association, 2004).

6. Stephen L. Moore, *Savage Frontier: Rangers, Riflemen, and Indian Wars in Texas*, 4 vols. (Denton: University of North Texas Press, 2006–2010); Sam W. Haynes, *Soldiers of Misfortune: The Somervell and Mier Expeditions* (Austin: University of Texas Press, 1990); Joseph M. Nance, *Dare-Devils All: The Texan Mier Expedition, 1842–1844* (Austin: Eakin Press, 1998); Mary Margaret McAllen Amberson, *A Brave Boy and A Good Soldier* (Austin: Texas State Historical Association, 2006); Paul N. Spellman, *Forgotten Texas Leader: Hugh McLeod and the Texan Santa Fe Expedition* (College Station: Texas A&M University Press, 1999); Douglas V. Meed, *The Fighting Texas Navy, 1832–1845* (Plano: Republic of Texas Press, 2001); Jonathan W. Jordan, *Lone Star Navy* (Dulles, Va.: Potomac Books, 2005); John Powers, *The First Texas Navy* (Austin: Woodmont Books, 2006).

7. R. Bruce Winders, *Crisis in the Southwest: The United States, Mexico, and the Struggle over Texas* (Lanham, Md.: Rowman and Littlefield, 2002); Frederick Wilkins, *Texas Rangers in the Mexican War: The Highly Irregular Irregulars* (Austin: Eakin Press, 2001), and *The Legend Begins: The Texas Rangers, 1823–1845* (Austin: State House Press, 1996); Charles M. Robinson, *Texas and the Mexican War: A History and a Guide* (Austin: Texas State Historical Association, 2004).

8. Brian DeLay, *War of a Thousand Deserts: Indian Raids and the U.S.-Mexican War* (New Haven, Conn.: Yale University, 2008); Thomas T. Smith, *The U.S. Army and the Texas Frontier Economy, 1845–1900* (College Station: Texas A&M University Press, 1999), and *The Old Army in Texas: A Research Guide to the U.S. Army in Nineteenth-Century Texas* (Austin: Texas State Historical Association, 2000); Robert Wooster, ed., *Recollections of Western Texas . . . by Two of the U.S. Mounted Rifles* (Dallas: Book Club of Texas, 1995); Jerry D. Thompson, ed., *Fifty Miles and a Fight: Major Samuel Heintzelman's Journal of Texas and the Cortina War* (Austin: Texas State Historical Association, 1998), and *Texas and New Mexico on the Eve of the Civil War: The Mansfield and Johnston Inspections, 1859–1861* (Albuquerque: University of New Mexico Press, 2001); Ben E. Pingenot et al., ed., *The Reminiscences of Major General Zenas R. Bliss, 1854–1876: From the Texas Frontier to the Civil War and Back Again* (Austin, Texas State Historical Association, 2007).

9. Thomas W. Knowles, *They Rode for the Lone Star: The Saga of the Texas Rangers*, Vol. 1: *The Birth of Texas-Civil War* (Dallas: Taylor, 1999); Frederick Wilkins, *Defending the Borders: The Texas Rangers, 1848–1861* (Austin: State House Press, 2001); Robert M. Utley, *Lone Star Justice: The First Century of the Texas Rangers* (New York: Oxford University Press, 2002); Michael L. Collins, *Texas Devils: Rangers and Regulars on the Lower Rio Grande, 1846–1861* (Norman: University of Oklahoma Press, 2008); Mike Cox, *The Texas Rangers: Wearing the Cinco Peso, 1821–1900* (New York: Forge Books, 2008); Thomas W. Cutrer, *Ben McCulloch and the Frontier Military Tradition* (Chapel Hill: University of North Carolina Press, 1993); Richard B. McCaslin, *Fighting Stock: John S. "Rip" Ford of Texas* (Fort Worth: Texas Christian University Press, 2011); Jerry D. Thompson, *Cortina: Defending the Mexican Name in Texas* (College Station: Texas A&M University Press, 2007).

10. Ralph A. Wooster, *Texas and Texans in the Civil War* (Austin: Eakin Press, 1996); Ralph A. Wooster, ed., *Lone Star Blue and Gray: Essays on Texas in the Civil War* (Austin: Texas State Historical Association, 1995); Ralph A. Wooster, *Civil War Texas: A History and a Guide* (Austin: Texas State Historical Association, 1999), *Lone Star Generals in Gray* (Austin: Eakin Press, 2000), and *Lone Star Regiments in Gray* (Austin: Eakin Press, 2002); Charles D. Grear, ed., *The Fate of Texas: The Civil War and the Lone Star State* (Fayetteville: University of Arkansas Press, 2008); Kenneth W. Howell, ed., *The Seventh Star of the Confederacy: Texas during the Civil War* (Denton: University of North Texas Press, 2009); Charles D. Grear, *Why Texans Fought in the Civil War* (College Station: Texas A&M University Press, 2010).

11. Donald S. Frazier, *Blood and Treasure: Confederate Empire in the Southwest* (College Station: Texas A&M University Press, 1995); Donald S. Frazier, *Cottonclads! the Battle of Galveston and the Defense of the Texas Coast* (Austin: State House Press, 1996); Edward T. Cotham, *Battle on the Bay: The Civil War Struggle for Galveston* (Austin: University of Texas Press, 1998), and *Sabine Pass: The Confederacy's Thermopylae* (Austin: University of Texas Press, 2004); Donald S. Frazier, *Fire in the Cane Field: The Federal Invasion of Louisiana and Texas, January 1861–January 1863* (Abilene, Tex.: State House Press, 2008); Richard G. Lowe, *The Texas Overland Expedition of 1863* (Abilene, Tex.: McWhiney Foundation Press, 1996); Stephen A. Townsend, *The Yankee Invasion of Texas* (College Station: Texas A&M University Press, 2006); Stephen A. Dupree, *Planting the Union Flag in Texas: The Campaigns of Major General Nathaniel P. Banks in the West* (College Station: Texas A&M University Press, 2008); Jeffrey W. Hunt, *The Last Battle of the Civil War: Palmetto Ranch* (Austin: University of Texas Press, 2002); Phillip T. Tucker, *The Final Fury: Palmito Ranch, The Last Battle of the Civil War* (Mechanicsburg, Pa.: Stackpole Books, 2001).

12. Anne J. Bailey, *Texans in the Confederate Cavalry* (Abilene, Tex.: McWhiney Foundation Press, 1998); Douglas Hale, *The Third Texas Cavalry in the Civil War* (Norman: University of Oklahoma Press, 1992); Martha L. Crabb, *All Afire to Fight: The Untold Story of the Ninth Texas Cavalry* (New York: William Morrow, 2000); Stanley S. McGowen, *Horse Sweat and Powder Smoke: The First Texas Cavalry in the Civil War* (College Station: Texas A&M University Press, 1999); Thomas Reid, *Spartan Band: Burnett's 13th Texas Cavalry in the Civil War* (Denton: University of North Texas Press, 2005); Richard G. Lowe, *Walker's Texas Division, C.S.A.: Greyhounds of the Trans-Mississippi* (Baton Rouge: Louisiana State University Press, 2004); John R. Lundberg, *Granbury's Texas Brigade: Diehard Western Confederates* (Baton Rouge: Louisiana State University Press, 2012), and *The Finishing Stroke: Texans in the 1864 Tennessee Campaign* (Austin: State House Press, 2003).

13. Carl H. Moneyhon, *Edmund J. Davis: Civil War General, Republican Leader, Reconstruction Governor* (Fort Worth: Texas Christian University Press, 2010); Philip R. Caudill, *Moss Bluff Rebel: A Texas Pioneer in the Civil War* (College Station: Texas A&M University Press, 2009); Jerry D. Thompson, *Vaqueros in Blue and Gray* (Austin: State House Press, 2000); Stephen Chicoine, *Confederates of Chappell Hill, Texas: Prosperity, Civil War and Decline* (Harrisburg, Pa.: McFarland, 2004); David Paul Smith, *Frontier Defense in the Civil War: Texas Rangers and Rebels* (College Station: Texas A&M

University Press, 1992); Paul R. Petersen, *Quantrill in Texas: The Forgotten Campaign* (Nashville, Tenn.: Cumberland House, 2007); Richard B. McCaslin, *Tainted Breeze: The Great Hanging at Gainesville, Texas, 1862* (Baton Rouge: Louisiana State University Press, 1994); David Pickering and Judy Fall, *Brush Men and Vigilantes: Civil War Dissent in Texas* (College Station: Texas A&M University Press, 2000).

14. Joseph B. Polley, *A Soldier's Letters to Charming Nellie*, ed. Richard B. McCaslin (Knoxville: University of Tennessee Press, 2008); George Skoch and Mark W. Perkins, *Lone Star Confederate: A Gallant and Good Soldier of the 5th Texas Infantry* (College Station: Texas A&M University Press, 2003); James M. McCaffrey, ed., *Only a Private: A Texan Remembers the Civil War—The Memoirs of William J. Oliphant* (Pearland, Tex.: Halcyon Press, 2004); Thomas W. Cutrer, *Terry's Texas Ranger Trilogy* (Austin: State House Press, 1996), and *Our Trust Is in the God of Battles: The Civil War Letters of Robert Franklin Bunting, Chaplain, Terry's Texas Rangers, C.S.A.* (Knoxville: University of Tennessee Press, 2006); Richard G. Lowe, *A Texas Cavalry Officer's Civil War: The Diary and Letters of James C. Bates* (Baton Rouge: Louisiana State University Press, 1999); Jerry D. Thompson, ed., *Civil War in the Southwest: Recollections of the Sibley Brigade* (College Station: Texas A&M University Press, 2001); Jerry Don Thompson, *Tejanos in Gray: Civil War Letters of Captains Jose Rafael de la Garza and Manuel Yturri* (College Station: Texas A&M University Press, 2011); Edward T. Cotham, *The Southern Journey of a Civil War Marine: The Illustrated Note-book of Henry O. Gusley* (Austin: University of Texas Press, 2006).

15. Carl H. Moneyhon and Bobby Roberts, *Portraits of Conflict: A Photographic History of Texas in the Civil War* (Fayetteville: University of Arkansas Press, 1998); Jerry D. Thompson and Lawrence T. Jones III, *Civil War and Revolution on the Rio Grande Frontier: A Narrative and Photographic History* (Austin: Texas State Historical Association, 2004); Richard M. Ahlstrom, *Texas Civil War Artifacts: A Photographic Guide to the Physical Culture of Texas Civil War Soldiers* (Denton: University of North Texas Press, 2008).

16. Loyd M. Uglow, *Standing in the Gap: Army Outposts, Picket Stations, and the Pacification of the Texas Frontier, 1866–1886* (Fort Worth: Texas Christian University Press, 2001); Thomas T. Smith, *Fort Inge: Sharps, Spurs, and Sabers on the Texas Frontier, 1849–1869* (Austin: Eakin Press, 1993); Ty Cashion, *A Texas Frontier: The Clear Fork Country and Fort Griffin, 1849–1887* (Norman: University of Oklahoma Press, 1996); Charles M. Robinson III, *The Frontier World of Fort Griffin: The Life and Death of a Western Town* (Arthur H. Clark, 1992); Robert Wooster, *Fort Davis: Outpost on the Texas Frontier* (Austin: Texas State Historical Association, 994), and *Frontier Crossroads: Fort Davis and the West* (College Station: Texas A&M University Press, 2005).

17. James N. Leiker, *Racial Borders: Black Soldiers along the Rio Grande* (College Station: Texas A&M University Press, 2002); Garna L. Christian, *Black Soldiers in Jim Crow Texas, 1899–1917* (College Station: Texas A&M University Press, 1995); Paul H. Carlson, *The Buffalo Soldier Tragedy of 1877* (College Station: Texas A&M University Press, 2003); Charles M. Neal, *Valor across the Lone Star: The Congressional Medal of Honor in Frontier Texas* (Austin: Texas State Historical Association, 2002).

18. Michael D. Pierce, *The Most Promising Young Officer: A Life of Ranald Slidell Mackenzie* (Norman: University of Oklahoma Press, 1993); Charles M. Robinson III, *Bad*

Hand: A Biography of General Ranald S. Mackenzie (Austin: State House Press, 1993); J'Nell L. Pate, *Ranald Slidell Mackenzie: Brave Cavalry Colonel* (Austin: Eakin Press, 1994); Paul H. Carlson, *"Pecos Bill": A Military Biography of William R. Shafter* (College Station: Texas A&M University Press, 1989); Chuck Parsons and Marianne E. Hall Little, *Captain L. H. McNelly, Texas Ranger: The Life and Times of a Fighting Man* (Austin: State House Press, 2001).

19. James A. Sandos, *Rebellion in the Borderlands: Anarchism and the Plan of San Diego, 1904–1923* (Norman: University of Oklahoma Press, 1992); Benjamin H. Johnson, *Revolution in Texas: How a Forgotten Rebellion and Its Bloody Suppression Turned Mexicans into Americans* (New Haven, Conn.: Yale University Press, 2003); Charles H. Harris and Louis R. Sadler, *The Texas Rangers and the Mexican Revolution: The Bloodiest Decade, 1910–1920* (Albuquerque: University of New Mexico Press, 2004); Frank N. Samponaro and Paul J. Vanderwood, *War Scare on the Rio Grande: Robert Runyon's Photographs of the Border Conflict, 1913–1916* (Austin: Texas State Historical Association, 1992).

20. Gregory W. Ball, *They Called Them Soldier Boys: A Texas Infantry Regiment in World War I* (Denton: University of North Texas Press, 2013); Bruce L. Brager, *The Texas 36th Division: A History* (Austin: Eakin Press, 2002); José A. Ramírez, *To the Line of Fire: Mexican Texans and World War I* (College Station: Texas A&M University Press, 2009); George B. Clark, ed., *His Time in Hell: A Texas Marine in France* (New York: Presidio Press, 2001).

21. James Ward Lee, *1941: Texas Goes to War* (Denton: University of North Texas Press, 1991); Joyce Gibson Roach, *Collective Heart: Texans in World War II* (Austin: Eakin Press, 1996); Louis Fairchild, *They Called It the War Effort: Oral Histories from World War II, Orange, Texas* (Austin: Eakin Press, 1993).

22. Thomas E. Alexander: *The Stars Were Big and Bright: The United States Army Air Forces and Texas during World War II* (Austin: Eakin Press, 2000), *The Wings of Change: The Army Air Force Experience in Texas during World War II* (Abilene, Tex.: McWhiney Foundation Press, 2003), and *Rattlesnake Bomber Base: Pyote Army Airfield in World War II* (Abilene, Tex.: State House Press, 2005); Tom Killebrew, *The Royal Air Force in Texas: Training British Pilots in Terrell during World War II* (Denton: University of North Texas Press, 2003); J'Nell L. Pate, *Arsenal of Defense: Fort Worth's Military Legacy* (Denton: Texas State Historical Association, 2011).

23. Melanie Wiggins, *Torpedoes in the Gulf: Galveston and the U-boats, 1942–1943* (College Station: Texas A&M University Press, 1995); James S. Powell, *Learning under Fire: The 112th Cavalry Regiment in World War II* (College Station: Texas A&M University Press, 2010); Robert P. Wiggins, *Jungle Combat with the 112th Cavalry: Three Texans in the Pacific during World War II* (Harrisburg, Pa: McFarland, 2011); Kelly E. Crager, *Hell under the Rising Sun: Texan POWs and the Building of the Burma-Thailand Death Railway* (College Station: Texas A&M University Press, 2008); Cindy Weigand, *Texas Women in World War II* (Plano: Republic of Texas Press, 2003); Brendan M. Greeley, Jr., ed., *The Two Thousand Yard Stare: Tom Lea's World War II* (College Station: Texas A&M University Press, 2008).

Part II

Chronological Essays

CHAPTER 9

Spanish, Mexican, and Republican Texas to 1845

F. Todd Smith

Between the 1920s and 1960s, historians of the United States, with very few exceptions, explained the era prior to 1846 in terms of the triumph of Anglo-American civilization over supposedly inferior races. Despite the fact that people had inhabited the region for at least 15,000 years, and that Texas was a Spanish colony for more than a century, many historians—as well as most of the public—believed that Texas history did not begin until the appearance of Stephen F. Austin in the early 1820s. Even though Mexico controlled Texas at the time, scholars of the period were interested principally in how Anglos inevitably wrested the region from Hispanics, defeated the indigenous nations, and rightfully attached it to the United States.

During the past two decades, however, the writing of Texas history to 1846 has undergone a dramatic transformation. Many scholars, reflecting historiographical trends concerning other parts of the Americas and the Atlantic World, have portrayed early Texas as a frontier region inhabited by various groups of people—none intrinsically more important than the other—who competed for resources in a relatively equal manner. This new scholarship has sought to present a much fuller picture of the region, demonstrating how dynamic groups of Native Americans, Tejanos, and Anglos competed and interacted until the latter group finally—but not inevitably—established hegemony at the end of the period.

During the first two decades of the twentieth century, scholars produced several groundbreaking studies concerning colonial Texas. Much of the research, like most works on American history written at the time, was influenced by Frederick Jackson Turner's 1893 thesis that placed an emphasis on the frontier, which he defined as being the line between civilization and savagery. According to Turner, U.S. history was primarily the story of English-speaking white Anglo-Saxon Protestants using their superior forms of government, economy, and religion to push the frontier westward across North America from the Atlantic to the Pacific, triumphing over inferior groups of Native Americans and Latin Catholics along the way.[1]

Herbert Eugene Bolton, a young professor who began teaching at the University of Texas at Austin in 1901, sought to expand Turner's thesis by pointing out that Spain had "civilized" parts of the North America long before the westward expansion of white Anglo-Saxon Protestants. Bolton moved on to the University of California at Berkeley in 1911, where he established the field of Spanish borderlands studies, in which he and his numerous graduate students investigated the areas within the boundaries of the United States—from California to Florida—that Spain had explored and colonized between 1500 and 1821. Bolton and his students emphasized that the Spaniards had pushed the frontier northward from Mexico through the civilizing agency of the Franciscan missionaries who had attempted to bring Christianity to the heathen Indians of the Southwest and Florida. The Bolton school, with its emphasis on priests, explorers, and government officials, dominated the field of the Spanish borderlands through the 1960s. Bolton published a series of articles concerning the founding of missions and Indian relations in Spanish Texas during the first two decades of the twentieth century, as did his student, William E. Dunn. In the middle of the century, a few of Bolton's students published valuable annotated translations of Spanish journals, reports, letters, and other documents, and a couple of Catholic scholars continued to focus on the Franciscan missions, praising particularly those located at San Antonio.[2]

Little, however, was written by the Boltonians about the common Hispanic settlers, or Tejanos, who established the communities of San Antonio, La Bahía, and Nacogdoches during the colonial period. They stressed the presumed pure-blooded Spanish conquest over the supposed mixed-blooded Mexican Americans. In large part, this was due to the racial attitudes of their earlier era of scholarship. The number of Mexican Americans in Texas, as well as their political and economic influence in the state, reached its nadir in the early twentieth century, and most Anglo-Texans considered them to be inferior. Therefore, their story—like those of Indians and blacks—was overlooked in the Bolton-inspired history books.[3]

This trend was reinforced by the United States' victories in the two world wars. To many Americans, these hard-fought triumphs over evil states proved what they had long believed—that the United States had been chosen by God to fulfill its inevitable destiny of demonstrating to the rest of the world the proper forms of government, economy, and religion. Many white Anglo-Saxon Protestant Texans—most of whom did not consider that any other group could actually lay claim to being Texan—associated their ancestors' nineteenth-century conquest over Indians and Mexicans on the frontier with American victories in the twentieth century. In their minds, the Lone Star State and its triumphant history constituted the perfect venue to celebrate the successes of the United States. Unsurprisingly, from this viewpoint, the Alamo emerged as Texas's version of Pearl Harbor. Like the United States' triumphs in the two world wars, the Anglo conquest of Texas was not only righteous and just, it was also destined and inevitable.[4]

As a result, most of the mid-twentieth-century scholars who wrote on Texas prior to 1846 did so in a teleological fashion, explaining nearly all events as leading directly to the Anglo triumph. The few historians who paid any attention to the colonial period highlighted the activities of such men as Philip Nolan and Augustus William Magee, who preceded the wave of conquering Anglos during the final years of Spanish Texas.[5] Scholars paid even less attention to the Indians of Texas, who were considered only as barriers to civilization.[6] Historians instead focused on the years 1821–1836, writing in the long shadow of Eugene C. Barker, whose works, including a highly influential biography of Stephen F. Austin, stressed the belief that Texas history during this period represented the westward march of Anglo manifest destiny. Scholars tended to neglect the military aspects of the rebellion, choosing instead to dwell on the battle of the Alamo and the "suffocating power of its heroes." The few works written on the Lone Star Republic focused solely on the Anglo majority—usually the elites rather than the common settlers—and dealt with issues such as politics and the origins of Texas distinctiveness. Scholars during the middle of the twentieth century completely neglected the Tejanos, Indians, and blacks who lived in Texas between 1836 and 1845.[7]

In the 1960s and 1970s, historians of the United States began to back away from the frontier thesis and the inevitability of a triumphant westward expansion and paid more attention to minority groups. Three independent scholars working outside the academy produced important studies of colonial Texas that broke new ground. Newspaperman Robert S. Weddle wrote a series of books on previously unexamined missions in Texas, the French impact on the

Spanish settlement of the colony, as well as Spanish maritime activity.[8] Elizabeth A. H. John published an innovative work that dealt with the Indians of Texas and New Mexico and their interactions with Spaniards and Frenchmen during the colonial period.[9] Rather than view the Europeans as civilizers, John paid close attention to the various tribes as they followed their own self-interests. Illustrator Jack Jackson highlighted the beginnings of Texas's cattle industry in the eighteenth-century Spanish era, offsetting the emphasis previous scholars had placed on Anglo ranching in the 1800s.[10]

Three academic historians also published influential works that challenged commonly held views of Texas in the period prior to 1846. Randolph B. Campbell produced the first general study of slavery in Texas, arguing that the state's experience with bondage fit squarely within the southern tradition.[11] This assertion challenged the belief in the Lone Star State's distinctiveness and its western, ranching tradition. Gilberto M. Hinojosa demonstrated how the Tejano community at Laredo, established in the mid-eighteenth century, responded to the changes wrought by the evolving geopolitical conditions of the nineteenth century.[12] David J. Weber published a highly influential book that included a discussion of the Anglo settlement of Texas and the subsequent rebellion from the viewpoint of the nascent Mexican republic.[13] Seen through this lens, Weber succeeded in placing Texas in a broader international perspective, distant from the simple explanation of the revolt being the inevitable triumph of westward-marching Anglos.

In 1992, Weber followed up this work with the publication of *The Spanish Frontier in North America*, a magisterial synthesis of all the research on the Spanish borderlands that had been undertaken since Bolton began his archival investigations nine decades before.[14] Most important, Weber employed—and popularized for students of early Texas—the new definition of frontier that scholars had been in the process of adopting over the course of the prior two decades.[15] Instead of portraying the frontier as a boundary between civilization and barbarism, Weber defined it as a zone of interaction where different cultures of relatively equal power either contended for resources and control or established an interdependence. He also stressed that contention within the frontier zone powerfully transformed all parties involved. Using this framework, Weber—like colonial historians throughout the Americas—did not privilege the Spaniards or other Europeans but paid equal attention to Native Americans and how both Europeans and the tribes were changed by the process of interaction. The work also examined the fates of the common Hispanic settlers, moving away from the traditional Boltonian focus on priests, explorers, and officials.

Weber's book has been, without a doubt, the most influential work in early Texas history over the course of the past two decades; most scholars, particularly those whose research dealt with Spanish Texas, Native Americans, and Tejanos, eagerly adopted its main precepts. In addition, Weber was able to disseminate this view of Texas as a contested frontier through his position as director of the Clements Center for Southwest Studies, established in 1996 at Southern Methodist University. Over the past dozen years or so, a group of Clements Center research fellows have produced important, groundbreaking works that have provided students with a much deeper understanding of the various forces involved in the history of Texas before 1846. As a result, most historians no longer define early Texas in a teleological deterministic and ethnocentric fashion. Instead, the new scholarship portrays Texas as a frontier zone where various groups, none more powerful or innately superior than the other, contested for resources in a relatively demanding physical environment. The new scholars have produced exciting, dynamic studies of Indians and Tejanos, have critically reexamined the Anglo colonization of the 1820s and 1830s, and have sought to explain the events of the Texas Revolution and its aftermath in terms that differ from the standard explanations of westward expansion and manifest destiny.

The full inclusion of the region's Native Americans—Alabama-Coushattas, Atakapas, Caddos, Cherokees, Coahuiltecans, Comanches, Delawares, Jumanos, Karankawas, Kickapoos, Kiowas, Lipan Apaches, Seminoles, Shawnees, Tonkawas, and Wichitas, among others—has been the most important development in early Texas historiography over the past two decades. The scholars who began writing on Texas Indians in the early 1990s were influenced by innovative studies that examined indigenous peoples elsewhere in North America.[16] These works portrayed the Indians as fully active participants in the European colonization process, who adapted and adjusted in various ways to the whole-scale changes wrought by the intruders. As a result, the surviving reconstituted Native groups remained powerful entities for a much longer period than previously recognized. Although some Indians fought the European settlers, the new scholarship focused on how most of them actually established mutually beneficial relationships with the newcomers, who historians no longer assumed had arrived in America as superior conquerors. Accepting the ideas promoted by this impressive body of work, scholars working on Texas Indians prior to 1845 produced several major general works—as well as many supporting books and articles of narrower focus—that convincingly demonstrate that Native Americans actually dominated Texas and the Southwest during the era of Spanish colonial rule.

At the forefront of this movement were Gary Clayton Anderson and his student David La Vere.[17] Anderson's 1999 book, *The Indian Southwest, 1580–1830*, eschewed the traditional political analysis of the interaction between Indians and Euroamericans in favor of focusing on Native exchange networks and how they adapted over the course of two and a half centuries, innovatively demonstrating the development of the Native political economy outside the sphere of European control.[18] Anderson also introduced the concept of "ethnogenesis," showing how the area's Indians actively altered themselves culturally to forge unity with other groups by abandoning languages, social practices, and economic processes to meet the needs of the new order that began with the arrival of the Spaniards in the sixteenth century. Among other items, Anderson discussed the changing role of women, the climate and environment, and the dynamics of political hierarchies within the various tribes.

Anderson's perspective greatly influenced a new generation of scholars of Native American history, including his protégé La Vere, who published *The Caddo Chiefdoms*, a work that examines the previously overlooked East Texas tribe that played such a vital role in Texas history.[19] Importantly, La Vere emphasized the Caddos' well-developed political system that allowed for great continuity and dominant power well into the nineteenth century, despite the Euroamerican intrusion. Also appearing in 1998, La Vere's *Life among the Texas Indians* presented in organized fashion the oral histories of various Texas tribes that were collected during the Great Depression by the Works Progress Administration.[20] In the forty-five page introduction of this work, La Vere provided the first narrative history of all the Texas Indian tribes in nearly four decades, following them from their arrival through their forced removal to Oklahoma in the late nineteenth century. La Vere's 2004 *Texas Indians* extended this essay to produce a masterful overview of the entire state based upon the voluminous research that had taken place in the prior decade; this work stresses the importance of kinship and political economy outside the scope of Euroamerican intervention.[21] In the same year, archaeologist Timothy K. Perttula edited an important work, *The Prehistory of Texas*, in which the leading archaeologists of Texas employed the wealth of information gathered over the course of the previous half century to summarize clearly the current state of archaeological knowledge in the sixteen different cultural-ecological regions of the state.[22]

In 2007, Juliana Barr published an award-winning book that examines the indigenous tribes of Spanish Texas through the prism of gender, thus providing as deep an understanding of Indian-Euroamerican relations between the Red River and the Rio Grande as scholarship has produced in other, better-studied regions of North America.[23] Barr's work is based on the idea that the various tribes, not the Spaniards, dominated colonial Texas. Therefore, they dictated the terms of engagement with Euroamericans through the networks of kinship that provided the infrastructure for native political and economic systems and codified both domestic and foreign relations. Because the Indians of Texas used gender as the organizing principle of their kin-based social, economic, and political domains, it also functioned as a communication tool for the often nonverbal cross-cultural interaction between the tribes and the intruding Spaniards and Frenchmen.

In 2008, Finnish-born Pekka Hämäläinen published a book that logically concluded what the above works had hinted at without explicitly stating: that the Comanche tribe, through its ability to control the horse trade of the Southern Plains, created an empire in the Southwest that did not just compete with Texas and New Mexico but dominated the two far-flung Spanish colonies to such an extent that, by the turn of the nineteenth century, both were economically dependent upon the group that earlier scholars had considered only as savage barriers to civilization.[24] Hämäläinen's brilliantly argued study should result in a complete rethinking of the way most people have understood the colonial Southwest and Texas for years to come.[25]

Although the just-mentioned works were heavily influenced by recent scholarship concerning Indians in other parts of the Americas, none explicitly compares events in the region with those that took place elsewhere or attempt to place Native American activities in Texas in an international context.[26] In 2005, however, David J. Weber produced yet another landmark study, one that examines the experiences of unincorporated, independent Indians—such as the Comanches in Texas and New Mexico—who successfully resisted subjugation by soldiers and conversion by missionaries throughout the Spanish empire during the late eighteenth and early nineteenth centuries.[27] In doing so, Weber places Texas in its imperial context, as a fringe region on the far northern frontier, having much more in common with undeveloped areas such as south-central Chile, northwestern Argentina, and the Caribbean coast of Central America than with the centers of Spanish power in Mexico and Peru. Weber's work refutes the notion of Texan distinctiveness that had been central to the traditionalists' argument prior to the 1990s while reinforcing the idea that the province epitomized the new definition of a frontier, where power was contested and no one group was hegemonic.

Scholars have continued to show great interest in Spanish explorations of Texas and the Gulf Coast throughout the colonial period. Although many diaries and journals of Spanish exploration and settlement were translated and annotated during the first half of the twentieth century, the later editors who worked with the primary documents have provided commentaries that reflect the new-found respect for, and understanding of, both the Spaniards and the Native Americans they encountered.[28] In addition, chroniclers of the various expeditions place the Texas entradas in their imperial context, thus denying any notion of distinctiveness. More recently, for example, historians have shed interesting new light on Cabeza de Vaca and his travels.[29] In 2007, Andrés Reséndez referenced these works and employed the wealth of research that had been done on the Spaniards in Latin America, as well as the indigenous peoples they encountered, to write a well-informed account of Cabeza de Vaca's journey, expertly placing it within the context of Spanish sixteenth-century exploration and clearly explaining the reactions of the Native Americans he came in contact with.[30] As a result, Cabeza de Vaca no longer seems to be a mythological creature unique to Texas. In fact, by stressing that Cabeza de Vaca later became an official in Paraguay, Reséndez and the others have demonstrated that Texas was just another province within the Spanish empire.

Another group of recent scholars has done a similar job in rescuing the French landing on the Texas Gulf Coast in the late seventeenth century from the fog of the fabulous. At the forefront of this effort is Robert S. Weddle, who in 1992 published the aptly titled *French Thorn: Rival Explorers in the Spanish Sea*, as the second volume in his trilogy on the Spanish Caribbean and the Gulf Coast.[31] Using a wealth of primary documents from France and Spain, Weddle narrates the ill-fated attempt by René Robert Cavelier, sieur de La Salle, to establish a French colony on the Texas coast in the 1680s, which then spurred the Spaniards to explore and settle the coastal region from Tampico to Florida.[32] In 1995 archaeologists from the Texas Historical Commission shed new light on La Salle's efforts along the Gulf Coast by uncovering and excavating the wreck of one of his ships, *La Belle*, in Matagorda Bay. The discovery led Weddle back to the expedition once again, resulting in the publication of *The Wreck of the* Belle in 2001.[33] In this work Weddle convincingly demonstrates that La Salle was not the heroic explorer he had previously been portrayed as. Instead, he characterizes the Frenchman as a deceitful paranoiac who was single-handedly responsible for the failure of the French settlement on the Texas coast.[34] As Reséndez did with Cabeza de Vaca, Weddle ties La Salle's effort in Texas to exploits elsewhere in the Americas, denying any notion of an exclusive focus on Texas.

Weddle also utilized the heretofore untranslated campaign diary of Juan Ángel de Oyarzún, captain of a Mexican company of soldiers, to revise dramatically the interpretation of the 1758 Comanche, Wichita, and Caddo attack on the Spanish mission on the San Saba River, along with the supposedly disastrous expedition to the Red River the following year to punish the Taovayas and their allies. Traditionalist historians had used the so-called massacre at the San Sabá Mission and the presumed defeat of the Spanish forces, led by Diego Ortiz Parrilla, as proof that Spanish Texas was a failed province. Employing a wealth of documents in combination with the campaign diary, Weddle demonstrated that, despite the "bad press" given by rivals (and accepted as truth by historians ever since), the Spanish attack was relatively successful, leading to the Wichitas' suing for peace the following year.[35] Other researchers uncovered documents that further reinforce Weddle's opinion of the Spanish expedition.[36] The whole effort to rescue Ortiz Parrilla's reputation reflects the willingness of present-day scholars to accept the interpretation of Spanish Texas as a frontier region containing different criteria for success than those provinces at the centers of empire.

Other colonial Texas scholars have successfully placed the province within the context of the Spanish empire and the role it played in the diplomacy of the Atlantic world. In 1992, just on the cusp of the new wave of research concerning Native Americans and Hispanics in colonial Texas, Donald E. Chipman produced an overview of Spain's three-hundred-year experience in Texas.[37] Based on archival sources and previously published literature, Chipman's synthesis presented a balanced account of exploration, settlement, missions, and Indian relations. Most important, Chipman used his background in Latin American colonial history to demonstrate just how Texas fit within the Spanish empire while explaining the role such institutions as the Catholic Church played in the conquest of the Americas, and how the missionaries adapted to changing conditions as they advanced northward from central Mexico. The author also expertly showed how events such as Napoleon's invasion of Spain in 1808 and the subsequent Hidalgo Revolt had disastrous results for Texas, a province that was actually thriving in the late eighteenth and early nineteenth centuries.[38] Reflecting the only scholarship available on Texas prior to the 1990s, the work was a top-down look at the colony and, as such, provided a solid, factual narrative of Spanish Texas that had been sorely lacking.

In 1999, Donald Chipman and Harriett Denise Joseph surveyed the story of the colony through fifteen biographical sketches of notable Spaniards and

Frenchmen—explorers, priests, military men, and government officials—who played important roles in the establishment of Spanish Texas.[39] In addition to these men, Chipman and Joseph mined the archival sources to include a chapter on various women in the colony in order to demonstrate the vital, yet overlooked, influence of women in Texas. Jean A. Stuntz provided an in-depth, pioneering examination of Spanish community property law on the frontier of colonial Mexico, particularly in Spanish Texas, during the middle decades of the eighteenth century.[40]

Whereas Chipman's synthesis gave attention to Texas and the international scene, a new generation of scholars have produced a series of fine community studies of Tejano settlements. These important works reflect the recent trend in borderlands historiography that emphasizes a focus on the common Hispanic settlers on Spain's northern frontier.[41] The most important of these works, written by Jesús F. de la Teja, examined the Tejano community at San Antonio de Béxar.[42] Reflecting the influence of David Weber, de la Teja stresses the importance of the frontier on the development of Béxar. The author employs a wealth of archival sources to demonstrate how the three distinct groups of settlers at San Antonio—soldiers, Canary Islanders, and Franciscan missionaries and their indigenous neophytes—eventually formed a single community on the distant frontier as isolation, Indian attacks, and shared religion caused them to intermarry and unify. Most important, de la Teja demonstrates how the three groups, after overcoming their differences in the first half of the century, were able to create a distinct frontier ranching and farming community centered around a thriving, inclusive Catholic Church. The author stresses that San Antonio was successful in its own frontier fashion.

Whereas the Tejano community studies were influenced by recent scholarship on Hispanic settlements throughout the Spanish borderlands and in New Spain, the so-called new Latin American mission history has had little effect on the study of the chain of Franciscan missions in Texas.[43] The new scholarship questions the mid-twentieth-century emphasis on the heroic struggle of the Franciscans to civilize the supposedly heathen savages by combining social history, ethnohistory, and quantitative studies in an effort to understand more fully the generally negative impact the missionaries had upon the Indian societies they dealt with. Adán Benavides published an excellent article dealing with the history of the Hispanic parish church of San Fernando de Béxar, overlooked by earlier historians of the eighteenth century in favor of the Franciscan missions.[44] Two years later, Timothy Matovina demonstrated how the Canary Islanders who established the San Fernando parish incorporated the

Virgin of Guadalupe as their protectress, thus associating the parish with the Mexican character over the subsequent three centuries.[45]

Although scholars in the past two decades have successfully demonstrated how Texas fit within the Spanish Atlantic, they have been less accomplished in pointing out the direct ties the province had with the communities of northern Mexico. In 2001, Leslie Offutt published a community study of Saltillo, the town in Coahuila that was generally the jumping-off point for entering Texas from the south, but did not effectively pursue its commercial bearing on San Antonio.[46] Four years later, however, Jesús F. de la Teja began preliminary work on the subject and ably demonstrated how enterprising San Antonio merchants actively pursued trade at the annual Saltillo Fair in the late eighteenth and early nineteenth centuries, proving that Bexareños were neither victims of an uncaring and incompetent government nor the lazy, insubordinate riffraff portrayed by traditionalist scholars.[47]

Another group of researchers have demonstrated the important role the French Louisiana post of Natchitoches played in the affairs of Spanish Texas during the eighteenth century. In 1998, Patricia R. Lemée demonstrated how the marriage of Louis St. Denis to Manuela Sánchez Navarro helped establish a trade cartel with Spanish relatives in Texas.[48] David La Vere published an article on the commercial ties between St. Denis and other French traders from Natchitoches and Texas Indians.[49] In 2003, F. Todd Smith examined the role played by Athanase de Mézières, son-in-law of St. Denis, in directing the Indian affairs in Texas from Natchitoches after the transfer of Louisiana to Spain in the 1760s.[50] Two years later, H. Sophie Burton published a study of trade workers from Natchitoches and their shift from commercial dealings with the Indians to stock raising along the Louisiana-Texas frontier during the late eighteenth century after the decline in commerce with the Native Americans because of their population losses.[51] And in 2008, Burton and Smith teamed up to produce the first detailed community study of colonial Natchitoches, examining its vital role in the development of the Louisiana-Texas frontier.[52]

The tumultuous final years of Spanish Texas, wracked by rebellion, invasion, and counterrevolution, were once neglected by scholars—except for those interested in Native Americans—as the period continued to be seen as little more than a pause before the arrival of Stephen F. Austin. Jesús F. de la Teja provided a much-needed narrative examining filibusters from the United States.[53] This essay pays particular attention to the complex political and economic forces affecting the residents of San Antonio in an attempt to clarify the reasons they teetered between loyalty and rebellion. David E. Narrett has reexamined the career of Mexican revolutionary José Bernardo Gutiérrez de Lara and his role in association with Augustus William Magee in the filibustering expedition that temporarily overthrew Spanish rule in Texas in 1812–1813.[54] Jeffersonian historians Frank Lawrence Owsley, Jr., and Gene A. Smith place the Gutiérrez-Magee expedition in the context of overall American expansion in the first two decades of the nineteenth century.[55] Despite these efforts, much work remains to be done on the final two decades of Spanish Texas, particularly concerning the activities of common Tejano settlers in the East Texas community of Nacogdoches as well as at La Bahîa, near the coast.[56]

Andrés Reséndez's *Changing National Identities at the Frontier* is the most important work to appear on Mexican Texas during the past twenty years.[57] The author compares the experiences of New Mexico and Texas in the first half of the nineteenth century in order to examine the manner in which each colony eventually became part of the United States. Reséndez challenges the traditional historiography that dealt with the nationalities of Mexicans and Anglos as if they were monolithic identities. Instead he emphasizes that the region was exceedingly fluid, allowing the various Spanish speakers, English speakers, and even indigenous peoples of the area to follow their own self-interest to choose identities based upon the conflicting forces of the Mexican state and the American market.

Stephen F. Austin was one of the most important men who changed identities—from American to Spaniard to Mexican to Texan—several times during the period. To his previous biographer and to most historians of Texas, though, Austin was never anything but an Anglo at the forefront of the westward march of triumphant American civilization. However, in the first biography of Austin written in three quarters of a century, Gregg Cantrell emphasizes that Austin's colony fit into the young Mexican republic's unsuccessful attempt to integrate its frontier provinces into the national economy and polity.[58] Thus, he emphasizes Austin's title of *empresario*, or colonization agent, and the role he played in trying to make this uniquely Mexican project succeed. In addition, Cantrell provides a balanced account of the iconic Austin, portraying him as an obsessively driven and ambitious man who constantly fought an internal battle between his own personal interests and his feelings of obligation toward others.

Peter Ellis Bean, the subject of Jack Jackson's final book, was another Anglo who lived in Mexican Texas and embodied Reséndez's claim that the fluidity of the province allowed great opportunities for changing identities.[59] Jackson mined Spanish and Mexican documents to piece together the fascinating life of Bean, an associate of Philip Nolan, who moved to Texas in 1823 and became the Mexican Indian agent for the eastern part of the state, establishing a reputation for fairness in dealing with the indigenous tribes as well as with recent arrivals such as the Cherokees, who were fleeing from the United States. Jackson used his deep knowledge of the period to place Bean's career in perspective, skillfully showing how he easily maneuvered among the various groups without completely identifying with any of them. Despite the appearance of the important books by Cantrell and Jackson, few other scholars have investigated the thirty thousand or so Anglo-Americans who migrated to Texas before 1835.[60]

On the other hand, three studies have appeared on non-Anglo groups who arrived in Texas during the Mexican era. Dianna Everett produced an innovative work that examines the plight of the immigrant Cherokees who moved to northeastern Texas in 1819 and found themselves squeezed between unwelcoming Comanches and Wichitas and equally hostile Anglo-Texans.[61] Ultimately, the Texans, during the administration of Mirabeau Buonaparte Lamar, violently forced the Cherokees to flee north of the Red River to Indian Territory, where they joined their recently displaced brethren. Graham Davis provided a well-researched book on the Irish empresarios and the San Patricio and Refugio colonies they founded in South Texas in the early 1830s.[62] Ana Carolina Castillo Crimm wrote an excellent study of the heretofore neglected de León family, who founded the only successful colony other than Austin's in Texas during the 1820s.[63] Crimm describes the establishment by Martín and Patricia de León of the Hispanic colony and town of Victoria on the Guadalupe River in 1824 and that colony's survival despite trying circumstances.

For the most part, recent Texas historians have continued to neglect slavery and the large numbers of blacks who were forced to migrate westward with their Anglo masters. Although Campbell's book on slavery in antebellum Texas, *An Empire for Slavery*, had challenged the notion of the state's distinctiveness, his work focused almost entirely on the period after annexation, and his chapters on the Mexican period agreed with Barker's belief that slavery was merely incidental to Anglo colonization and the creation of the Texas Republic. By contrast, Andrew J. Torget followed Reséndez's contention that the key to understanding Texas prior to 1836 is to recognize the overlapping influences of the American economy and the Mexican political system.[64] Drawing from a wide array of sources from both U.S. and Mexican archives, Torget asserts that the creation of a slaveholding society in Texas was achieved only because the federal structure of Mexico's government enabled Tejanos and certain Coahuilans to work with the Anglos to foster cotton agriculture in the region actively.

A few excellent works illuminate their experiences during the tumultuous years between 1821 and 1846. In 1994, Andrés Tijerina published an important work that provides a much-needed overview of the Hispanic population of Texas during the Mexican era.[65] Tijerina emphasizes the political role played by the relatively liberal federalist Tejanos, explaining how the forces of the frontier, the attractions of Anglo-American economic progress, and the partisan dynamics of state and national leaders created a political culture of conflict, particularly in relation to the more conservative forces in Mexico City. The following year, Timothy M. Matovina published a complementary work that stresses how shared religion served to unify a well-defined Tejano community in San Antonio, whose strong leaders worked to defend their values against the overwhelming Anglo power structure that emerged after independence.[66] In 1997, Josefina Zoraida Vázquez detailed the reasons the Mexican government promoted Anglo colonization in the 1820s, and Jesús F. de la Teja explained why Tejanos initially supported immigration from the United States.[67] Eleven years later, Raúl A. Ramos published an excellent study of the Tejanos of San Antonio between Mexican independence and the Civil War that serves as a worthy successor to de la Teja's work on the community of colonial Béxar.[68] Following the call of the new definition of frontier history, Ramos stresses the interaction between the Tejanos and the Anglo immigrants rather than cultural conflict while demonstrating that the Bexareños ultimately used their experience on the frontier to forge a new ethnic identity within the dominant American culture.

Three translated documents clearly demonstrate how Mexican government officials viewed the changing situation in Texas in the 1820s and 1830s. Andrés Tijerina and David J. Weber collaborated to produce a brief but comprehensive report of the state of Coahuila y Tejas in 1824, written by Gov. José Rafael Gonzales.[69] Jack Jackson put forth an annotated edition of the previously unpublished diary kept by Gen. Manuel Mier y Terán on his 1828 inspection of Texas.[70] Although two other accounts of this trip—by Jean Louis Berlandier and José María Sánchez y Tapia—had been published in English, Terán's diary presents a more detailed account of Nacogdoches and the many Indian representatives he met with there than the others. Jackson's excellent annotations, along with a clearly written introduction and background, make this work an extremely valuable source, revealing the significant role Terán played in setting Mexican policy for Texas between 1828 and 1832. Jackson supplemented this excellent work with an equally impressive book that provides the first English translation of a secret report written by Col. Juan N. Almonte, who in 1834 conducted the last inspection of Texas by a Mexican official before the revolution. Almonte's report, along with an assortment of his letters and his diary of Santa Anna's 1836 campaign to Texas, offers crucial new insights on the revolutionary period.[71]

Several excellent works on Indians were published during the past twenty years. The most important book to appear, and certainly the most controversial, is Gary Clayton Anderson's *Conquest of Texas*.[72] In this much-debated work, Anderson indicts the Anglos who flocked to Texas in the 1820s and 1830s with the charge of ethnic cleansing—adopting the term used to describe the situation in late twentieth-century Yugoslavia—as they followed a policy of forced removal of Indians and, to a smaller degree, Tejanos. Anderson savagely attacks the sacrosanct Texas Rangers, calling them a paramilitary group that carried out the whims of the Anglos by attacking Indian villages filled with women and children, killing, robbing, and raping as they fulfilled their goal of spreading terror so that Native groups would leave the state. This denigration of the Texas Rangers flies in the face of the interpretation offered by the stellar western history scholar Robert M. Utley, who presents a balanced account of the citizen soldiers which, while not painting them in a heroic light, does fit more with the traditional viewpoint than with Anderson's screed.[73] Although other scholars of Indian relations are not as strident in their charges against the Anglo-Texans, for the most part their works support Anderson's claims.[74]

Although most scholars tended to portray the Texas Indians as victims in the period after 1821, Brian DeLay's *War of a Thousand Deserts* supports Pekka Hämäläinen's claims concerning the Comanches by demonstrating, through painstaking research in northern Mexican archives, that the tribe and its allies adopted a policy of aggressive war against Mexico in the 1830s that revitalized their horse- and buffalo-based economy.[75] In addition to explaining the economic factors that caused the Comanches to take the offensive, DeLay shows, in opposition to apologists such as Anderson, that the Indians purposefully practiced cruelty against the Mexicans in order to gain revenge and personal prestige. Most important, DeLay convincingly argues that the Anglo-American victories in the Texas Revolution and the U.S.-Mexican War were aided by the constant Comanche onslaught, which weakened the Mexican government to such an extent that it was left nearly defenseless in the face of yet another northern aggression.

It is no surprise that recent scholars have paid almost as much attention to the six-month period of the Texas Revolution as they did for the century and a half of Spanish and Mexican rule. Whereas an excessive amount of the work has been spent on discussions concerning the iconic battle of the Alamo, a few innovative studies appeared that shed new light on the rebellion, providing balanced accounts that moved away from the traditional heroic retelling of the birth of the Republic. In 1992, Paul D. Lack published the most important work of the period concerning the Texas Revolution, offering the first systematic analysis of the revolt as political and social history.[76] Unlike scholars who focused on the cause of the conflict and the military execution of the war, Lack pays attention to the political turbulence and racial and ethnic strife that characterized the period. He undermines the traditional view of the revolution as a heroic triumph for freedom, claiming that victory was due only to incredible good fortune as the Texans entered their quarrel with Mexico as a fragmented people, individualistic, divided from one community to another by rivalries for land, and lacking a consensus about the meaning of political changes in Mexico. Lack also investigates relatively unexamined subjects such as the membership of the volunteer army, Texas Tories, the majority of Texans who refused military service, Tejanos, and black slaves.

Following Lack's lead, Stephen L. Hardin produced a straightforward military history of the Texas Revolution that is free of the parochial chauvinism that often weakened traditional accounts of the conflict.[77] Hardin fairly analyzes the strengths and weakness of the opposing armies, stressing that the contest was not an unequal one won by superior valor and bravery. He also challenges the role, usually depicted in heroic terms, of Sam Houston in the revolution. In 2004, William C. Davis provided a narrative of the military action of the revolution that agrees with Hardin's depiction of Sam Houston while returning to a more heroic interpretation of events.[78] The same year, H. W. Brands, a diplomatic historian who had written on a wide range of topics from the California gold rush to Theodore Roosevelt, brought the argument around full circle with a popular narration of the revolution that places the event once again in the traditional terms of American expansion and manifest destiny.[79] Despite these attempts to broaden the study of the Texas Revolution, historians have continued to pay an inordinate amount of interest in the battle of the Alamo, particularly debating the relatively meaningless issue of the manner in which Davy Crockett died.[80]

All of the attention paid to the Alamo in the past twenty years did not prevent scholars from examining other aspects of the Texas Revolution. Two works, in particular, have added important new information to the subject. Gregg J. Dimmick investigated the Mexican army's actions after the defeat at the battle of San Jacinto.[81] Using documentary evidence and archeological studies, Dimmick explains that Vicente Filisola, second-in-command of the Mexican forces in Texas, decided to stage a tactical withdrawal in order to reconstitute the separate elements of his forces and prepare for a counterstrike. The withdrawal route, however, led the Mexican forces over an alluvial plain which, after two days of heavy rains, turned into a virtual sea of mud. The Mexican army broke down in the sludge, leading to a full-blown retreat which, according to Dimmick, did more to secure Texas independence than other, more recognized, events. Edward L. Miller, looks at the Texas Revolution from the viewpoint of merchants in New Orleans and argues that actors in the Crescent City largely determined the outcome of the war.[82] In this interesting study, Miller asserts that the concerns of the Texan revolutionaries were secondary to the plans of powerful New Orleans commercial interests and their schemes for American territorial expansion. In a related article, James M. Denham discusses the role New Orleans merchants played in the Texas independence movement, claiming that their initial support dissipated once those involved in commerce with Mexico began to suffer financially.[83] In opposition to the traditionalists' triumphalist viewpoint, the new works stress the idea that the Texan victory was neither inevitable nor heroic, nor was it necessarily just.[84]

Following the new trend that pays more attention to Hispanics in Texas, three works have appeared that deal with Tejanos and their experiences in the rebellion. Stephen L. Hardin published an essay in which he argues that the distinctive frontier heritage of the Tejanos influenced the Anglos to incorporate military tactics that helped lead to victory.[85] Jesús F. de la Teja edited Juan N. Seguín's memoirs, which document the career of the most conspicuous Mexican to fight on the side of the rebels in 1835–1836. The work includes de la Teja's substantial introduction, which provides the fullest and most authoritative account of Seguin's life yet published.[86] Margaret Swett Henson wrote a biography of Lorenzo de Zavala, first vice-president of the Republic of Texas, paying particular attention to his previous experiences in Mexico and how this knowledge influenced his activities north of the Rio Grande.[87]

Also in contrast to previous scholarship, a few historians have demonstrated that Texas remained a contested frontier after 1836, emphasizing that Anglo hegemony was not completely achieved until the completion of the U.S.-Mexican War in 1848. Richard Bruce Winders asserts that the so-called Texas Revolution was just one of the many conflicts that took place during the thirty-year struggle between Mexico and the United States for possession of the province. By avoiding the arbitrary periodization that prior historians had accepted, Winders stresses the continuities of the era between 1821 and 1848, emphasizing—like most other historians of the past twenty years—the cooperation between Anglos and Hispanics in the region rather than cultural antagonism.[88] Paul D. Lack investigated the overlooked Córdova revolt, in which Tejanos near Nacogdoches joined disgruntled Indians, Anglos, and a few blacks in the summer of 1838 to rise in rebellion against the Texas Republic.[89] Whereas the few previous works on the revolt had focused on the event as yet another effort by the Mexican government to regain Texas, Lack investigated the affair from the perspective of the rebels themselves. He found that the Tejanos who joined the revolt did so in opposition to the rising Anglo power that isolated them from political and economic opportunity. The controversial Somervell and Mier expeditions of 1842 received a fair account for the first time from Sam W. Haynes.[90] Previous primary and secondary accounts of the ill-fated expedition had portrayed the Texan invaders as martyrs in a glorious cause and had caricatured the Mexicans as inhumane barbarians. They had also placed blame for the expedition's failure upon Sam Houston. Haynes, on the other hand, clearly demonstrates that the affair fit into the Texas president's pragmatic plan for annexation to the United States and portrays Santa Anna and the Mexicans in a sympathetic light.[91]

The relative lack of scholarship concerning the period from 1821 to 1846 demonstrates how the historiography of early Texas changed strikingly over the past two decades. Whereas scholars paid little attention to Native Americans and Tejanos in the middle decades of the twentieth century, Anglos in Texas, except for a few participants in the Texas Revolution, have been grossly neglected more recently. Historians of the colonial period successfully moved away from the previous notion of Texas as being a frontier between civilization and barbarism, overwhelmingly adopting the new definition that emphasized the colony as a region where various groups of equal worth contested for power and resources. More often than not, the different aggregations created an interdependence. Although Hispanic scholars produced an impressive amount of work dealing with the Tejano experience in Texas throughout the period, the full inclusion of Native Americans in the colonial era—to the point that many historians considered them to be the dominant group in the region—has been the most important and dramatic change in the historiography. Except for a few notable exceptions, however, most Anglo scholars of the Texas Revolution and the Republic of Texas have continued to portray the era in semitriumphalist terms of manifest destiny, choosing to pay an inordinate amount of attention to the heroes of the revolution. Ironically, scholars continue to overlook the common Anglo settlers—in addition to their black slaves—who actually established hegemony in Texas by the end of the period.

Although there remains a need for more research to be completed on the colonial period in Texas history, particularly concerning the lives of women, the period 1821–1846 demands the most attention in the immediate future. Scholars of the period should follow the lead of their colonial brethren and recognize that Texas remained a contested frontier during the Mexican and Republic eras, with various groups of Indians, Tejanos, Anglos, and blacks residing in the region in a manner that was generally more interdependent than hostile. Rather than view the installation of Anglo dominance as being inevitable due to superior culture, scholars need to investigate the process by which the establishment of this hegemony took place. Portrayed in this light, a more complete understanding of Texas prior to statehood will come into view, one that will become even more pertinent as the century and a half of Anglo dominance in Texas will probably continue to wane in the twenty-first century.

NOTES

1. Frederick Jackson Turner, "The Significance of the Frontier in History," in *Selected Essays of Frederick Jackson Turner*, ed. Ray Allen Billington (Englewood Cliffs, N.J.: Prentice-Hall, 1961), 37–62.

2. David J. Weber, "Turner, the Boltonians, and the Borderlands," *American Historical Review* 91 (Feb. 1986): 66–81; Donald E. Chipman, "Spanish Texas," in *Texas through Time: Evolving Interpretations*, ed. Walter L. Buenger and Robert A. Calvert (College Station: Texas A&M University Press, 1991), 102–13, 117–18.

3. Arnoldo De León, "Texas Mexicans: Twentieth-Century Interpretations," in Buenger and Calvert, *Texas through Time*, 20–25.

4. One popular writer wrote dramatic histories of both Pearl Harbor and the Alamo; see Walter Lord, *Day of Infamy* (New York: Harper, 1958), and *A Time to Stand* (New York: Harper, 1961).

5. Chipman, "Spanish Texas," 123–25.

6. The best example of this type of writing is Rupert Norval Richardson, *The Comanche Barrier to South Plains Settlement: A Century and a Half of Savage Resistance to the Advancing Frontier* (Glendale, Calif.: Arthur H. Clark, 1933).

7. Paul D. Lack, "In the Long Shadow of Eugene C. Barker: The Revolution and the Republic," in Buenger and Calvert, *Texas through Time*, 134–64.

8. Robert S. Weddle, *The San Sabá Mission: Spanish Pivot in Texas* (Austin: University of Texas Press, 1964), *San Juan Bautista: Gateway to Spanish Texas* (Austin: University of Texas Press, 1968), *Wilderness Manhunt: The Spanish Search for La Salle* (Austin:

University of Texas Press, 1973), and *Spanish Sea: The Gulf of Mexico in North American Discovery, 1500–1685* (College Station: Texas A&M University Press, 1985).

9. Elizabeth A. H. John, *Storms Brewed in Other Men's Worlds: The Confrontation of Indians, Spanish, and French in the Southwest, 1540–1795* (College Station: Texas A&M University Press, 1975).

10. Jack Jackson, *Los Mesteños: Spanish Ranching in Texas, 1721–1821* (College Station: Texas A&M University Press, 1986).

11. Randolph B. Campbell, *An Empire for Slavery: The Peculiar Institution in Texas, 1821–1865* (Baton Rouge: Louisiana State University Press, 1989).

12. Gilberto M. Hinojosa, *A Borderlands Town in Transition: Laredo, 1755–1870* (College Station: Texas A&M University Press, 1983). Two other influential studies appeared that touched upon the Tejano experience prior to 1845: Arnoldo De León, *The Tejano Community, 1836–1900* (Albuquerque: University of New Mexico Press, 1982); and David Montejano, *Anglos and Mexicans in the Making of Texas, 1836–1936* (Austin: University of Texas Press, 1987).

13. David J. Weber, *The Mexican Frontier, 1821–1846: The American Southwest under Mexico* (Albuquerque: University of New Mexico Press, 1982).

14. David J. Weber, *The Spanish Frontier in North America* (New Haven, Conn.: Yale University Press, 1992).

15. For a succinct discussion of this process, see Andrew R. L. Cayton and Frederika J. Teute, "Introduction: On the Connection of Frontiers," in *Contact Points: American Frontiers from the Mohawk Valley to the Mississippi, 1750–1830*, ed. Cayton and Teute (Chapel Hill: University of North Carolina Press, 1998), 1–15.

16. Among the most influential of these works were Francis Jennings, *The Invasion of America: Indians, Colonialism, and the Cant of Conquest* (Chapel Hill: University of North Carolina Press, 1975); Neal Salisbury, *Manitou and Providence: Indians, Europeans, and the Making of New England, 1500–1643* (New York: Oxford University Press, 1982); James H. Merrell, *The Indians New World: Catawbas and Their Neighbors from European Contact to the Era of Removal* (Chapel Hill: University of North Carolina Press, 1989); Richard White, *The Middle Ground: Indians, Europeans, and Republics in the Great Lakes Region, 1650–1815* (New York: Cambridge University Press, 1991); Daniel K. Richter, *The Ordeal of the Longhouse: The Peoples of the Iroquois League in the Era of European Colonization* (Chapel Hill: University of North Carolina Press, 1992); and Daniel H. Usner, Jr., *Indians, Settlers, and Slaves in a Frontier Exchange Economy: The Lower Mississippi Valley before 1783* (Chapel Hill: University of North Carolina Press, 1992).

17. Gary Clayton Anderson, *Kinsmen of Another Kind: Dakota-White Relations, 1650–1800* (Lincoln: University of Nebraska Press, 1984).

18. Gary Clayton Anderson, *The Indian Southwest, 1580–1830: Ethnogenesis and Reinvention* (Norman: University of Oklahoma Press, 1999).

19. David La Vere, *The Caddo Chiefdoms: Caddo Economics and Politics, 700–1835* (Lincoln: University of Nebraska Press, 1998). Other works on the Caddos that appeared in the past two decades and reinforce La Vere's interpretation are Cecile Elkins Carter, *Caddo Indians: Where We Come From* (Norman: University of Oklahoma Press, 1995); F. Todd Smith, *The Caddo Indians: Tribes at the Convergence of Empires, 1542–1854*

(College Station: Texas A&M University Press, 1995); Daniel A. Hickerson, "Hasinai-European Interaction, 1694–1715," *East Texas Historical Journal* 34 (Fall 1996): 3–16, and "Historical Processes, Epidemic Disease, and the Formation of the Hasinai Confederacy," *Ethnohistory* 44 (Winter 1997): 31–52; Sharon McCormick Derrick and Diane E. Wilson, "The Effects of Epidemic Disease on Caddo Demographic Structure," *Bulletin of the Texas Archeological Society* 72 (2001): 91–103.

20. David La Vere, *Life among the Texas Indians: The WPA Narratives* (College Station: Texas A&M University Press, 1998).

21. David La Vere, *The Texas Indians* (College Station: Texas A&M University Press, 2004).

22. Timothy K. Perttula, ed., *The Prehistory of Texas* (College Station: Texas A&M University Press, 2004).

23. Juliana Barr, *Peace Came in the Form of a Woman: Indians and Spaniards in the Texas Borderlands* (Chapel Hill: University of North Carolina Press, 2007). See also Barr, "A Diplomacy of Gender: Rituals of First Contact in the 'Land of the Tejas,'" *William and Mary Quarterly* 61 (July 2004): 393–434, "From Captives to Slaves: Commodifying Indian Women in the Borderlands," *Journal of American History* 92 (June 2005): 19–46, and "Beyond Their Control: Spaniards in Native Texas," in *Choice, Persuasion, and Coercion: Social Control on Spain's North American Frontiers*, ed. Jesús F. de la Teja and Ross Frank (Albuquerque: University of New Mexico Press, 2005), 149–78.

24. Pekka Hämäläinen, *The Comanche Empire* (New Haven, Conn.: Yale University Press, 2008). See also Hämäläinen, "The Western Comanche Trade Center: Rethinking the Plains Indian Trade System," *Western Historical Quarterly* 29 (Winter 1998): 485–513, and "The Rise and Fall of Plains Indian Horse Cultures," *Journal of American History* 90 (Dec. 2003): 833–62.

25. Other important works on the Comanches are Stanley Noyes, *Los Comanches: The Horse People, 1751–1845* (Albuquerque: University of New Mexico Press, 1993); Thomas W. Kavanagh, *Comanche Political History: An Ethnohistorical Perspective, 1706–1875* (Lincoln: University of Nebraska Press, 1996); Gerald Betty, *Comanche Society: Before the Reservation* (College Station: Texas A&M University Press, 2002); David La Vere, "Friendly Persuasions: Gifts and Reciprocity in Comanche-Euroamerican Relations," *Chronicles of Oklahoma* 71 (Fall 1993): 322–37; Michael L. Tate, "Comanche Captives: People between Two Worlds," *Chronicles of Oklahoma* 72 (Fall 1994): 228–63; and Daniel J. Gelo, "'Comanche Land and Ever Has Been': A Native Geography of the Nineteenth-Century Comanchería," *Southwestern Historical Quarterly* 103 (Jan. 2000): 272–300.

26. Most of the excellent studies on the other Indian tribes of Texas over the past twenty years have also been rather narrowly focused. These include William W. Newcomb, Jr., "Historic Indians of Central Texas," *Bulletin of the Texas Archaeological Society* 64 (1993): 1–63; Nancy Parrot Hickerson, *The Jumanos: Hunters and Traders of the South Plains* (Austin: University of Texas Press, 1994); Robert A. Ricklis, *The Karankawa Indians of Texas: An Ecological Study of Cultural Tradition and Change* (Austin: University of Texas Press, 1996); F. Todd Smith, *The Wichita Indians: Traders of Texas and the Southern Plains, 1540–1845* (College Station: Texas A&M University Press,

2000); Maria F. Wade, *The Native Americans of the Texas Edwards Plateau, 1582–1799* (Austin: University of Texas Press, 2003); and Thomas A. Britten, *The Lipan Apaches: People of Wind and Lightning* (Albuquerque: University of New Mexico Press, 2009). Additionally, three innovative, influential works appeared that deal with Native Americans who impacted Texas from the outside: Willard H. Rollings, *The Osage: An Ethnohistorical Study of Hegemony on the Prairie-Plains* (Columbia: University of Missouri Press, 1992); James F. Brooks, *Captives and Cousins: Slavery, Kinship, and Community in the Southwest Borderlands* (Chapel Hill: University of North Carolina Press, 2002); and Kathleen DuVal, *The Native Ground: Indians and Colonists in the Heart of the Continent* (Philadelphia: University of Pennsylvania Press, 2006).

27. David J. Weber, *Bárbaros: Spaniards and Their Savages in the Age of Enlightenment* (New Haven, Conn.: Yale University Press, 2005).

28. Among the many excellent works that deal with early Spanish explorations in Texas are Jack Jackson, *Flags along the Coast: Charting the Gulf of Mexico, 1519–1759: A Reappraisal* (Austin: Book Club of Texas, 1995), and *Shooting the Sun: Cartographic Results of Military Activities in Texas, 1689–1829*, 2 vols. (Lubbock: Book Club of Texas, 1999); Dennis Reinharz and Gerald D. Saxon, eds., *Mapping and Empire: Soldier-Engineers on the Southwestern Frontier* (Austin: University of Texas Press, 2005); Donald E. Chipman, "Alonso Alvarez de Pineda and the Río de las Palmas: Scholars and the Mislocation of a River," *Southwestern Historical Quarterly* 98 (Jan. 1995): 369–85; John Miller Morris, *El Llano Estacado: Exploration and Imagination on the High Plains of Texas and New Mexico, 1536–1860* (Austin: Texas State Historical Association, 1997); Lawrence A. Clayton, Vernon James Knight, Jr., and Edward C. Moore, eds., *The De Soto Chronicles: The Expedition of Hernando de Soto to North America in 1539–1543*, 2 vols. (Tuscaloosa: University of Alabama Press, 1993); Nancy Adele Kenmotsu, James E. Bruseth, and James E. Corbin, "Moscoso and Route in Texas," in *The Expedition of Hernando de Soto West of the Mississippi, 1541–1543*, ed. Gloria A. Young and Michael P. Hoffman (Fayetteville: University of Arkansas Press, 1993), 106–31; Charles Hudson, *Knights of Spain, Warriors of the Sun: Hernando de Soto and the South's Ancient Chiefdoms* (Athens: University of Georgia Press, 1997); and Richard Flint, *No Settlement, No Conquest: A History of the Coronado Expedition* (Albuquerque: University of New Mexico Press, 2008).

29. David A. Howard, *Conquistador in Chains: Cabeza de Vaca and the Indians of the Americas* (Tuscaloosa: University of Alabama Press, 1997); Donald Olson, Marilynn S. Olson, Russell L. Doescher, Lance L. Lambert, David E. Lemke, Angela M. Carl, Ross Johnson, Sandra D. Smith, and Kent H. Trede, "Piñon Pines and the Route of Cabeza de Vaca," *Southwestern Historical Quarterly* 101 (Oct. 1997): 175–86; Maria F. Wade, "Go-Between: The Roles of Native American Women and Alvar Nuñez Cabeza de Vaca in Southern Texas in the Sixteenth Century," *Journal of American Folklore* 112 (Summer 1999): 332–42; Rolena Adorno and Patrick Charles Pautz, *Alvar Nuñez Cabeza de Vaca: His Account, His Life, and the Expedition of Pánfilo de Narvaez*, 3 vols. (Lincoln: University of Nebraska Press, 1999), and *The Narrative of Cabeza de Vaca* (Lincoln: University of Nebraska Press, 2003); Alex D. Krieger, *We Came Naked and Barefoot: The Journey of Cabeza de Vaca across North America* (Austin: University of Texas Press, 2003).

30. Andrés Reséndez, *A Land So Strange: The Epic Journey of Cabeza de Vaca* (New York: Basic Books, 2007).

31. Robert S. Weddle, *The French Thorn: Rival Explorers in the Spanish Sea, 1682–1762* (College Station: Texas A&M University Press, 1992). The excellent third volume of the trilogy focused mainly on Spanish expeditions along the coasts of Florida and Mexico; see Weddle, *Changing Tides: Twilight and Dawn in the Spanish Sea, 1763–1803* (College Station: Texas A&M University Press, 1995).

32. Among the many works that examine primary documents and the early Spanish settlement of Texas are William C. Foster, ed., *Texas and Northeastern Mexico, 1630–1690* (Austin: University of Texas Press, 1997); Brian Imhoff, ed., *The Diary of Juan Domínguez de Mendoza's Expedition into Texas, 1683–1684* (Dallas: Clements Center for Southwest Studies, Southern Methodist University Press, 2002); William C. Foster, *Spanish Expeditions into Texas, 1689–1768* (Austin: University of Texas Press, 1995); William C. Foster and Jack Jackson, eds., "The 1693 Expedition of Gregorio de Salinas Varona to Sustain the Missionaries among the Tejas Indians," *Southwestern Historical Quarterly* 97 (Oct. 1993): 265–311; Jesús F. de la Teja, ed., *Preparing the Way: Preliminary Studies of the Texas Catholic Historical Society* (Austin: Texas Catholic Historical Society, 1997); Debbie S. Cunningham, "The Domingo Ramón Diary of the 1716 Expedition into the Province of the Tejas Indians: An Annotated Translation," *Southwestern Historical Quarterly* 110 (July 2006): 39–67; David McDonald, Kay Hindes, and Kathleen Gilmore, eds. and trans., "The Marqués de Aguayo's Report to the King regarding His Expedition to Restore and Establish Missions and Presidios, 1720–1722," *Bulletin of the Texas Archeological Society* 70 (1999): 59–64; and Jack Jackson and William C. Foster, eds., *Imaginary Kingdom: Texas as Seen by the Rivera and Rubí Military Expeditions, 1727 and 1767* (Austin: Texas State Historical Association, 1995).

33. Robert S. Weddle, *The Wreck of the* Belle, *the Ruin of La Salle* (College Station: Texas A&M University Press, 2001).

34. Works that supplement Weddle's work on La Salle's colony include Curtis Tunnell, "A Cache of Cannons: La Salle's Colony in Texas," *Southwestern Historical Quarterly* 102 (July 1998): 19–43; Kathleen K. Gilmore, "Treachery and Tragedy in the Texas Wilderness: The Adventures of Jean L'Archeveque in Texas (A Member of La Salle's Colony)," *Bulletin of the Texas Archeological Society* 69 (1998): 35–46; and William C. Foster, ed., *The La Salle Expedition to Texas: The Journal of Henri Joutel, 1684–1687* (Austin: Texas State Historical Association, 1998).

35. Robert S. Weddle, *After the Massacre: The Violent Legacy of the San Sabá Mission* (Lubbock: Texas Tech University Press, 2007).

36. Donald E. Chipman and Luis López Elizondo, "New Light on Felipe de Rábago y Terán," *Southwestern Historical Quarterly* 111 (Oct. 2007): 161–81. See also Juan M. Romero de Terreros, "The Destruction of the San Sabá Mission: A Discussion of the Casualties," *The Americas* 60 (Apr. 2004): 617–27; Sam D. Ratcliffe, "'*Escenas de Martirio*': Notes on *The Destruction of Mission San Sabá*," *Southwestern Historical Quarterly* 94 (Apr. 1991): 507–34; and Elizabeth A. H. John, "A Case Study of the Interdependence of Archeology and History: The Spanish Fort Sites on the Red River," *Bulletin of the Texas Archeological Society* 63 (1992): 197–209.

37. Donald E. Chipman, *Spanish Texas, 1519–1821* (Austin: University of Texas Press, 1992). For a shorter overview of Spanish Texas, see Jesús F. de la Teja, "Spanish Colonial Texas," in *New Views of Borderlands History*, ed. Robert H. Jackson (Albuquerque: University of New Mexico, 1998): 107–30.

38. Among the many published primary documents dealing with late Spanish Texas over the past two decades are Donald C. Cutter, ed. and trans., *The Defenses of Northern New Spain: Hugo O'Conor's Report to Teodoro de Croix, July 22, 1777* (Dallas: Southern Methodist University Press, 1994); Elizabeth A. H. John, ed., "Governing Texas, 1779: The Karankawa Aspect," *Southwestern Historical Quarterly* 104 (Apr. 2001): 561–76; Jack Jackson, "The 1780 Cabello Map: New Evidence That There Were Two Mission Rosarios, and a Possible Correction on the Site of El Fuerte del Cíbolo," *Southwestern Historical Quarterly* 107 (Oct. 2003): 203–16; Elizabeth A. H. John, ed., "Inside the Comanchería, 1785: The Diary of Pedro Vial and Francisco Xavier Chaves," *Southwestern Historical Quarterly* 98 (July 1994): 27–56; Elizabeth A. H. John, ed., *Views from the Apache Frontier: Report on the Northern Provinces of New Spain by José Cortés, Lieutenant in the Royal Corps of Engineers, 1799* (Norman: University of Oklahoma Press, 1989); Elizabeth A. H. John, ed., "Views from a Desk in Chihuahua: Manuel Merino's Report on Apaches and Neighboring Nations, ca. 1804," *Southwestern Historical Quarterly* 95 (Oct. 1991): 139–75; and Jesús F. de la Teja, ed., "Ramón de Murillo's Plan for the Reform of New Spain's Frontier Defenses," *Southwestern Historical Quarterly* 107 (Apr. 2004): 501–33.

39. Donald E. Chipman and Harriett Denise Joseph, *Notable Men and Women of Spanish Texas* (Austin: University of Texas Press, 1999).

40. Jean A. Stuntz, *Hers, His, and Theirs: Community Property Law in Spain and Early Texas* (Lubbock: Texas Tech University Press, 2005).

41. For examples of this new scholarship, see the essays in Jackson, *New Views of Borderlands History*, and de la Teja and Frank, *Choice, Persuasion, and Coercion*.

42. Jesús F. de la Teja, *San Antonio de Béxar: A Community on New Spain's Northern Frontier* (Albuquerque: University of New Mexico Press, 1995). Other community studies are Gerald E. Poyo and Gilberto M. Hinojosa, eds., *Tejano Origins in Eighteenth-Century San Antonio* (Austin: University of Texas Press, 1991); Armando Alonzo, *Tejano Legacy: Rancheros and Settlers in South Texas, 1734–1900* (Albuquerque: University of New Mexico Press, 1998); Andrés Tijerina, *Tejano Empire: Life on the South Texas Ranches* (College Station: Texas A&M University Press, 1998); Daniel D. Arreola, *Tejano South Texas: A Mexican Cultural Province* (Austin: University of Texas Press, 2002); Francis Xavier Galán, "Last Soldiers, First Pioneers: The Los Adaes Border Community on the Louisiana-Texas Frontier, 1721–1779" (Ph.D. diss., Southern Methodist University, 2006); and Francis Xavier Galán, "Presidio Los Adaes: Worship, Kinship, Commerce with French Natchitoches on the Spanish-Franco-Caddo Borderlands, 1721–1773," *Louisiana History* 49 (Spring 2008): 191–208.

43. For the background of this movement, see Erick Langer and Robert H. Jackson, eds., *The New Latin American Mission History* (Lincoln: University of Nebraska Press, 1995).

44. Adán Benavides, "Sacred Space, Profane Reality: The Politics of Building a Church in Eighteenth-Century Texas," *Southwestern Historical Quarterly* 107 (July 2003): 1–33.

45. Timothy Matovina, *Guadalupe and Her Faithful: Latino Catholics in San Antonio, from Colonial Origins to the Present* (Baltimore: Johns Hopkins University Press, 2005).

46. Leslie Offutt, *Saltillo, 1770–1810: Town and Region in the Mexican North* (Tucson: University of Arizona Press, 2001).

47. Jesús F. de la Teja, "The Saltillo Fair and Its San Antonio Connections," in *Tejano Epic: Essays in Honor of Félix D. Almaráz Jr.*, ed. Arnoldo De León (Austin: Texas State Historical Association, 2005), 15–27.

48. Patricia R. Lemée, "*Tios* and *Tantes*: Familial and Political Relationships of Natchitoches and the Spanish Frontier," *Southwestern Historical Quarterly* 102 (Jan. 1998): 340–58; see also Lemée, "Ambivalent Successes and Successful Failures: St. Denis, Aguayo, and Juan Rodríguez," in *The French in Texas: History, Migration, Culture*, ed. François Lagarde (Austin: University of Texas Press, 2003), 35–45.

49. David La Vere, "Between Kinship and Capitalism: French and Spanish Rivalry in the Colonial Louisiana-Texas Indian Trade," *Journal of Southern History* 64 (May 1998): 198–206; see also La Vere, ed., "An Expedition to the Kichai: The Journal of François Grappe, September 24, 1783," *Southwestern Historical Quarterly* 98 (July 1994): 58–78.

50. F. Todd Smith, "Athanase de Mézières and the French in Texas, 1750–1803," in Lagarde, *French in Texas*, 46–59.

51. H. Sophie Burton, "'To Establish a Stock Farm for the Raising of Mules, Horses, Horned Cattle, Sheep, and Hogs': The Role of Spanish Bourbon Louisiana in the Establishment of Vacheries along the Louisiana-Texas Borderland, 1766–1803," *Southwestern Historical Quarterly* 104 (July 2005): 98–132.

52. H. Sophie Burton and F. Todd Smith, *Colonial Natchitoches: A Creole Community on the Louisiana-Texas Frontier* (College Station: Texas A&M University Press, 2008).

53. Jesús F. de la Teja, "Rebellion on the Frontier," in *Tejano Journey, 1770–1850*, ed. Gerald E. Poyo (Austin; University of Texas Press, 1996), 15–30.

54. David E. Narrett, "José Bernardo Gutiérrez de Lara: Caudillo of the Mexican Republic in Texas," *Southwestern Historical Quarterly* 106 (Oct. 2002): 195–228.

55. Frank Lawrence Owsley, Jr., and Gene A. Smith, *Filibusters and Expansionists: Jeffersonian Manifest Destiny, 1800–1821* (Tuscaloosa: University of Alabama Press, 1997).

56. Among the other studies dealing with the final two decades of Spanish Texas are Félix D. Almaráz, Jr., "Texas Governor Manuel Salcedo and the Court-Martial of Padre Miguel Hidalgo, 1810–1811," *Southwestern Historical Quarterly* 94 (Apr. 1996): 435–64; R. Dale Olson, "French Pirates and Privateers in Texas," in Lagarde, *French in Texas*, 60–78; Betje Black Klier, "Champ d'Asile," in Lagarde, *French in Texas*, 79–97; Rafe Blaufarb, *Bonapartists in the Borderlands: French Exiles and Refugees on the Gulf Coast, 1815–1835* (Tuscaloosa: University of Alabama Press, 2006); and Ed Bradley, "Fighting for Texas: Filibuster James Long, the Adams-Onís Treaty, and the Monroe Administration," *Southwestern Historical Quarterly* 102 (Jan. 1999): 323–42.

57. Andrés Reséndez, *Changing National Identities at the Frontier: Texas and New Mexico, 1800–1850* (Cambridge: Cambridge University Press, 2005).

58. Gregg Cantrell, *Stephen F. Austin, Empresario of Texas* (New Haven, Conn.: Yale University Press, 1999).

59. Jack Jackson, *Indian Agent: Peter Ellis Bean in Mexican Texas* (College Station: Texas A&M University Press, 2005).

60. Among the few studies that deal with Anglo-Texans are Margaret Swett Henson and Deolece Parmlee, *The Cartwrights of San Augustine: Three Generations of Agricultural Entrepreneurs in Nineteenth-Century Texas* (Austin: Texas State Historical Association, 1993); Mark Carroll, *Homesteads Ungovernable: Families, Sex, Race, and the Law in Frontier Texas, 1823–1861* (Austin: University of Texas Press, 2001); Anne H. Sutherland, *The Robertsons, the Sutherlands, and the Making of Texas* (College Station: Texas A&M University Press, 2006); Light Townsend Cummins, *Emily Austin of Texas, 1795–1851* (Fort Worth: Texas Christian University Press, 2009); and Stephen L. Hardin, *Texian Macabre: the Melancholy Tale of a Hanging in Early Houston* (Abilene, Tex.: State House Press, 2007).

61. Dianna Everett, *The Texas Cherokees: A People between Two Fires, 1819–1840* (Norman: University of Oklahoma Press, 1990).

62. Graham Davis, *Land! Irish Pioneers in Mexican and Revolutionary Texas* (College Station: Texas A&M University Press, 2002).

63. Ana Carolina Castillo Crimm, *De León: A Tejano Family History* (Austin: University of Texas Press, 2003).

64. Andrew J. Torget, "Cotton Empire: Slavery in the Texas Borderlands, 1820–1837," (Ph.D. diss., University of Virginia, 2009).

65. Andrés Tijerina, *Tejanos and Texas under the Mexican Flag, 1821–1836* (College Station: Texas A&M University Press, 1994); see also Tijerina, "Under the Mexican Flag," in Poyo, *Tejano Journey*, 33–47.

66. Timothy M. Matovina, *Tejano Religion and Ethnicity: San Antonio, 1821–1860* (Austin: University of Texas Press, 1995).

67. Josefina Zoraida Vázquez, "The Colonization and Loss of Texas: A Mexican Perspective," in *Myths, Misdeeds, and Misunderstandings: The Roots of Conflict in U.S.-Mexican Relations*, ed. Jaime E. Rodriguez O. and Kathryn Vincent (Wilmington, Del.: Scholarly Resources, 1997): 47–77; Jesús F. de la Teja, "The Colonization and Independence of Texas: A Tejano Experience," in Rodriguez O. and Vincent, *Myths, Misdeeds, and Misunderstandings*, 79–95.

68. Raúl A. Ramos, *Beyond the Alamo: Forging Mexican Ethnicity in San Antonio, 1821–1861* (Chapel Hill: University of North Carolina Press, 2008).

69. Andrés Tijerina and David J. Weber, eds., "The State of Coahuila y Tejas in 1824: A Governor's View from Saltillo," *Southwestern Historical Quarterly* 100 (Oct. 1996): 187–204.

70. Jack Jackson, ed., *Texas by Terán: The Diary Kept by General Manuel de Mier y Terán on His 1828 Inspection of Texas* (Austin: University of Texas Press, 2000).

71. Jack Jackson, ed., *Almonte's Texas: Juan N. Almonte's 1834 Inspection, Secret Report, and Role in the 1836 Campaign* (Austin: Texas State Historical Association, 2003).

72. Gary Anderson, *The Conquest of Texas: Ethnic Cleansing in the Promised Land, 1820–1875* (Norman: University of Oklahoma Press, 2005).

73. Robert M. Utley, *Frontier Justice: The First Century of the Texas Rangers* (New York: Oxford University Press, 2002).

74. These works include H. Allen Anderson, "The Delaware Indians and Shawnee Indians and the Republic of Texas, 1820–1845," *Southwestern Historical Quarterly* 94 (Oct. 1990): 231–60; Donald G. Hunter, "Their Final Years: The Apalachee and Other

Immigrant Tribes on the Red River, 1763–1834," *Florida Anthropologist* 47 (Mar. 1994): 3–45; Jonathan B. Hook, *The Alabama-Coushatta Indians* (College Station: Texas A&M University Press, 1997); Kelly F. Himmel, *The Conquest of the Karankawas and the Tonkawas, 1821–1859* (College Station: Texas A&M University Press, 1999); and F. Todd Smith, *From Dominance to Disappearance: The Indians of Texas and the Near Southwest, 1786–1859* (Lincoln: University of Nebraska Press, 2005).

75. Brian DeLay, *War of a Thousand Deserts: Indian Raids and the U.S.-Mexican War* (New Haven, Conn.: Yale University Press, 2008), "Independent Indians and the U.S.-Mexican War," *American Historical Review* 112 (Feb. 2007): 35–68, and "The Wider Worlds of Handsome Man: Southern Plains Indians Invade Mexico, 1830–1846," *Journal of the Early Republic* 27 (Mar. 2007): 83–103.

76. Paul D. Lack, *The Texas Revolutionary Experience: A Political and Social History* (College Station: Texas A&M University Press, 1992).

77. Stephen L. Hardin, *Texian Iliad: A Military History of the Texas Revolution, 1835–1836* (Austin: University of Texas Press, 1994).

78. William C. Davis, *Lone Star Rising: The Revolutionary Birth of the Texas Republic* (New York: Free Press, 2004).

79. H. W. Brands, *Lone Star Nation: How a Ragged Army of Volunteers Won the Battle for Texas Independence—and Changed America* (New York: Doubleday, 2004).

80. These works include Bill Groneman, *Defense of a Legend: Crockett and the de la Peña Diary* (Plano: Republic of Texas Press, 1994); James E. Crisp, "The Little Book That Wasn't There: The Myth and Mystery of the de la Peña Diary," *Southwestern Historical Quarterly* 98 (Oct. 1994): 261–96; David B. Gracy II, "'Just as I Have Written It': A Study of the Authenticity of the Manuscript of José Enrique de la Peña's Account of the Texas Campaign," *Southwestern Historical Quarterly* 105 (Oct. 2001): 255–91; Jack Jackson and James E. Ivey, "Mystery Artist of the Alamo: José Juan Sánchez," *Southwestern Historical Quarterly* 105 (Oct. 2001): 207–53; Thomas Ricks Lindley, *Alamo Traces: New Evidence and New Conclusions* (Lanham, Md.: Republic of Texas Press, 2003); and James E. Crisp, *Sleuthing the Alamo: Davy Crockett's Last Stand and Other Mysteries of the Texas Revolution* (New York: Oxford University Press, 2004). Other works concerning the Alamo are Crystal Sasse Ragsdale, *Women and Children of the Alamo* (Austin: State House Press, 1994); Timothy Matovina, *The Alamo Remembered: Tejano Accounts and Perspectives* (Austin: University of Texas Press, 1995); Bill Groneman, *Eyewitness to the Alamo* (Plano: Republic of Texas Press, 1996); J. R. Edmonson, *The Alamo Story: From Early History to Current Conflicts* (Plano: Republic of Texas Press, 2000); and Todd Hansen, ed., *The Alamo Reader: A Study in History* (Mechanicsburg, Pa.: Stackpole Books, 2003).

81. Gregg J. Dimmick, *Sea of Mud: The Retreat of Mexican Army after San Jacinto, an Archeological Investigation* (Austin: Texas State Historical Association, 2004).

82. Edward L. Miller, *New Orleans and the Texas Revolution* (College Station: Texas A&M University Press, 2004).

83. James M. Dedham, "New Orleans, Maritime Commerce, and the Texas War for Independence, 1836," *Southwestern Historical Quarterly* 98 (Jan. 1994): 511–34.

84. Among the other studies that appeared concerning the Texas Revolution are Margaret Swett Henson, "Politics and the Treatment of the Mexican Prisoners after the Battle of San Jacinto," *Southwestern Historical Quarterly* 94 (Oct. 1990): 189–230; Clifford

Hopewell, *Remember Goliad: Their Silent Tents* (Austin: Eakin Press, 1998); Gary Brown, *Hesitant Martyr of the Texas Revolution: James Walker Fannin* (Plano: Republic of Texas Press, 2000); Stephen L. Moore, *Eighteen Minutes: The Battle of San Jacinto and the Texas Independence Campaign* (Lanham, Md.: Republic of Texas Press, 2004); and Bill and Marjorie K. Walraven, "The 'Sabine Chute': The U.S. Army and the Texas Revolution," *Southwestern Historical Quarterly* 107 (Apr. 2004): 573–601. Published primary accounts include Joseph Milton Nance, "Abel Morgan and His Account of the Battle of Goliad," *Southwestern Historical Quarterly* 100 (Oct. 1996): 207–33; Paul D. Lack, ed., *The Diary of William Fairfax Gray: From Virginia to Texas, 1835–1837* (Dallas: William P. Clements Center for Southwest Studies, Southern Methodist University, 1997); Louis E. Brister, "The Journal of Col. Edward Harkort, Captain of Engineers, Texas Army, February 8–July 17, 1836," *Southwestern Historical Quarterly* 102 (Jan. 1999): 345–79; Jimmy L. Bryan, Jr., ed., *The Adventures and Recollections of General Walter P. Lane, a San Jacinto Veteran, Containing Sketches of the Texian, Mexican, and Late Wars, with Several Indian Fights Thrown In* (Dallas: William P. Clements Center for Southwest Studies, Southern Methodist University, 2000); and Gregg J. Dimmick, ed., *General Vicente Filisola's Analysis of José Urrea's Military Diary: A Forgotten 1838 Publication by and Eyewitness to the Texas Revolution* (Austin: Texas State Historical Association, 2007).

85. Stephen L. Hardin, "Efficient in the Cause," in Poyo, *Tejano Journey*, 49–71.

86. Jesús F. de la Teja, ed., *A Revolution Remembered: The Memoirs and Selected Correspondence of Juan N. Seguín* (Austin: State House Press, 1991).

87. Margaret Swett Henson, *Lorenzo de Zavala: The Pragmatic Idealist* (Fort Worth: Texas Christian University Press, 1996).

88. Richard Bruce Winders, *Crisis in the Southwest: The United States, Mexico, and the Struggle for Texas* (Wilmington, Del.: Scholarly Resources, 2002).

89. Paul D. Lack, "The Córdova Revolt," in Poyo, *Tejano Journey*, 89–109.

90. Sam W. Haynes, *Soldiers of Misfortune: The Somervell and Mier Expeditions* (Austin: University of Texas Press, 1990).

91. Published primary accounts of the period include Gerald D. Saxon and William B. Taylor, eds., *Narrative of the Texan Santa Fé Expedition*, 2 vols. (Dallas: William P. Clements Center for Southwest Studies, 2004); Andrés Reséndez, trans., *A Texas Patriot on Trial in Mexico: José Antonio Navarro and the Texan Santa Fe Expedition* (Dallas: William P. Clements Center for Southwest Studies, Southern Methodist University, 2005); Sam W. Haynes, ed., *Journal of the Texian Expedition against Mier* (Austin: W. Thomas Taylor, 1993); and Mary Margaret McAllen Amberson, *A Brave Boy and a Good Soldier: John C. C. Hill and the Texas Expedition to Mier* (Austin: Texas State Historical Association, 2006).

CHAPTER 10

Antebellum Texas, 1846–1860

Randolph B. Campbell

Virtually every review of recent Texas historiography begins with the observation that diverse ethnic groups and women are finally taking their rightful place in the story of the Lone Star State. Texas history is no longer the province of heroic Anglo men; instead, in the past twenty-five years those who once dominated the story often appear as at best oppressors or at worst murderous villains. Writings on the history of Texas from statehood to secession have followed the same general trend, making studies of those other than Anglo men the place to begin this essay.

The first people of Texas, the Native Americans, have received more attention than other ethnic groups during the past two and a half decades. David La Vere's 2003 general history of Indians in Texas has replaced the traditional account published by W. W. Newcomb in 1961 as the standard work on the subject.[1] Two other important books focus on Texas Indians during the early and mid-nineteenth century and therefore deal heavily with the late antebellum years. F. Todd Smith has told the story of the Indians' decline in numbers and influence in *From Dominance to Disappearance*, and Gary C. Anderson's *The Conquest of Texas: Ethnic Cleansing in the Promised Land* lives up to the promise of his title by describing in detail the violent racist destruction of the state's first people.[2] Smith's book is sympathetic to the Indians; Anderson's seethes with indignation at their treatment. The latter stands old-fashioned Texas Indian history on its head by portraying the whites as savages and the Indians as victims. Finally, Paul H. Carlson's *Plains Indians* provides a broader context for the major groups of Indians in western Texas in these years.[3]

In addition to works that deal with Indians in general, there are excellent histories of most tribes, especially the Comanches. The most celebrated is Pekka Hämäläinen's *Comanche Empire*, which argues that those fierce warriors controlled western Texas and fought off intruders in a manner that, although not regimented like a European empire, rivaled the power of other such dominant imperial peoples.[4] Three other books, by Thomas W. Kavanagh, Gerald Betty, and Morris W. Foster examine more specific facets of Comanche life and also cover the years 1845–1865.[5] Paul Carlson and Tom Crum offer, in *Myth, Memory, and Massacre: The Pease River Capture of Cynthia Ann Parker*, a persuasive revision of the myths surrounding the recapture of the best known of all the captives (some would now say "adoptees") of the Comanches.[6] Brian DeLay has written a brilliantly researched and argued work that emphasizes the role of Comanche raiders in turning much of the northern reaches of Mexico into a "desert" of destroyed ranches and villages, which proved inviting to expansionist leaders of the United States after the annexation of Texas.[7]

Next to the Comanches in receiving attention from scholars during the past quarter century have been the Caddos of East Texas. The Caddos had declined to a position of minor importance by 1845, but major studies that carried their story to that point and beyond should be mentioned. An archaeologist, Timothy K. Perttula, began the flow of studies with his *Caddo Nation*, and he was soon joined by F. Todd Smith with *The Caddo Indians*. A few years later Perttula and fellow archaeologist James E. Bruseth added *The Native History of the Caddo*. Shortly after completing his study of the Caddos, Smith broadened his approach to write *The Caddos, the Wichitas, and the United States*, which tells the story of both groups as they suffered through the abortive Texas reservation system and were forced from the state. Later, Smith brought the story of the Wichitas up to the late antebellum period in *The Wichita Indians*.[8]

The Apaches, a tribe that remained important in spite of their conquest by the Comanches, finally received a comprehensive history in Thomas A. Britten's *Lipan Apaches*. James L. Haley offered a broader study in *Apaches: A History and Culture Portrait*. Two groups that played an important role earlier in Texas history but would largely disappear during the late antebellum years are discussed in Robert A. Ricklis's *Karankawa Indians of Texas* and Kelly F. Himmel's *Conquest of the Karankawas and the Tonkawas*. Other smaller tribes that survived to remain in contemporary Texas are described in Bill Wright's *Tiguas: Pueblo*

Indians of Texas, Bill Wright and E. John Gesick's *Texas Kickapoo*, and Jonathan B. Hook's *Alabama-Coushatta Indians*.[9]

In sum, during the past twenty-five years historians have provided a much broader and balanced picture of Native Americans in Texas during the years just prior to the Civil War. For example, the Comanches are understood as much more than a "barrier to civilization," although at times there may be a tendency to gaze at Indians through the same rose-colored glasses used for viewing Anglos for so many years. Not surprisingly, some of the same tendencies may be observed in recent writings on Texans of Mexican descent in 1845–1860. After all, many of the Tejanos who had been forced to adjust to becoming residents of a new republic in 1836 faced an even more wrenching adjustment as they became citizens of the United States after annexation in 1845 while also dealing with a huge influx of Anglos. At least, as Andrés Reséndez points out in *Changing National Identities at the Frontier*, residents of Mexican descent in Texas and New Mexico were already falling into the orbit of the economy of the United States when political control changed, probably easing the transition to some extent. Thus, the story of Tejanos in this period as told in recent accounts is not as negative as that of Indians, but in many ways it is far from positive.[10]

David Montejano's *Anglos and Mexicans in the Making of Texas* is the place to begin an examination of recent historical scholarship on Mexican Americans in antebellum Texas, for it sets the stage and provides an excellent overview of the problems facing those new residents of the United States in 1845. Another important survey is Arnoldo De León's *Mexican Americans in Texas*. Two studies that begin their analysis during the late antebellum period are by Arnoldo De León and Kenneth L. Stewart: *Tejanos and the Numbers Game*, and *Not Room Enough*. Four books that focus on San Antonio and several of its best-known residents well illustrate the complexity of Tejano life during the antebellum years: In *Beyond the Alamo*, Raúl Ramos explains a largely successful adjustment by people of Mexican descent, and Timothy M. Matovina, in *Tejano Religion and Ethnicity*, emphasizes the role of Catholicism in creating an identity for the Tejano community and holding it together; David R. McDonald's *Jose Antonio Navarro* details the life of a leader of the revolution who consistently championed Tejano rights without suffering serious repercussions among Anglos; and, by contrast, Jesús F. de la Teja has edited *A Revolution Remembered: The Memoirs and Selected Correspondence of Juan N. Seguin*, which tells the story of a hero of the Texas Revolution who had to leave his home from 1842 to 1848 and who fought for Mexico in the Mexican-American War before returning to live out his life in Texas. Similarly, Anglo-Texan suspicions forced the DeLeón family of Victoria to leave the state, but they fought back in court and regained their properties; their story is ably told by Ana Carolina Castillo Crimm in *DeLeón: A Tejano Family History*.[11]

Armando C. Alonzo, in *Tejano Legacy*, shows that Tejanos did not necessarily lose everything to Anglo immigrants but rather continued to participate in ranching after 1848 and maintained a sense of identity, too. Andrés Tijerina's *Tejano Empire* also explains how South Texans of Mexican descent held their own against Anglo encroachment. Daniel D. Arreola, in *Tejano South Texas*, delineates the cultural distinctiveness of the region from San Antonio southward. At times marriages united the Anglo and Tejano elites in South Texas, as shown by Jane Clements Monday and Frances B. Vick in *Petra's Legacy: The South Texas Ranching Empire of Petra Vela and Mifflin Kenedy*, the account of a family created by the union of Kenedy, a Pennsylvania-born businessman/rancher, and Vela, the daughter of a former provincial governor.[12]

The movement of Anglos into South Texas after 1845, although relatively peaceful, led at times to serious ethnic conflict. An early example came in 1857 when Anglo teamsters, frustrated at their inability to compete with Mexicans who used oxcarts to transport goods from Indianola on the Gulf to San Antonio, began a campaign of violence against the cart men. This conflict is discussed in Larry Knight's article "The Cart War." A much more notable case of ethnic conflict, the so-called Cortina War of 1859, is described best in Jerry D. Thompson's *Cortina: Defending the Mexican Name in Texas*. This conflict, especially along the border with Mexico, brought companies of Texas Rangers in to join local law enforcement officers. These Ranger units tended to operate largely outside any real control by the State of Texas—formal organization of the Rangers as a professional law enforcement group would come after the Civil War—but even this early they began to build the reputation that would earn them hatred among many Tejanos to this day. Two general histories—Robert M. Utley's *Lone Star Justice* and Charles Robinson's *Men Who Wear the Star*—are attempts at evenhanded treatment of the Rangers. Michael L. Collins in *Texas Devils* and Frederick Wilkins in *Defending the Borders* concentrate on the Rangers of the late antebellum period.[13]

African Americans in late antebellum Texas have received less attention than Indians and Tejanos during the past twenty-five years, but even their story has been told in far greater depth than ever before. Randolph B. Campbell's *Empire for Slavery: The Peculiar Institution in Texas*, the first general history of slavery in Texas, examines all facets of the institution and argues that, regardless of the Lone Star State's position on the frontier, it existed there in fundamentally the same way as in the Old South. In *Los Brazos de Dios*, Sean M. Kelley contends that proximity to Mexico rather than the frontier gave Texas a distinct variant of southern slavery—a borderland plantation society. Although it stops just short chronologically of the late antebellum period, a yet-unpublished dissertation by Andrew Torget, "Between Two Empires: Slavery in the Texas Borderlands," provides in-depth analysis critical to an understanding of the peculiar institution's growth in Texas. James C. Kearney's *Nassau Plantation* offers a view at variance with the usual belief that German immigrants strongly opposed slavery. T. Lindsay Baker and Julie P. Baker's edited *Till Freedom Cried Out* adds narratives from thirty-two Texas freedmen who later relocated to Oklahoma to the large collection of Works Progress Administration narratives from bondsmen in the Lone Star State already available in print. An excellent collection of excerpts from the narratives, originally published in 1974, was made available again in reprint: Ronnie C. Tyler and Lawrence R. Murphy, editors, *The Slave Narratives of Texas.* Elizabeth R. Rabe's article "Slave Children of Texas" reminds readers that children as well as adults paid a terrible price for slavery. Mark Gretchen, in *Slave Transactions of Guadalupe County*, makes a positive contribution by revealing just how much information is available on slavery in county records preserved in local courthouses. The biographical approach to slavery is available in Patricia Smith Prather and Jane Clements Monday's *From Slave to Statesman: the Legacy of Joshua Houston, Servant to Sam Houston.*[14]

Historians during the past quarter-century also have called into question some aspects of the old saying that Texas was heaven for men and dogs and hell for women and oxen. Mark M. Carroll's *Homesteads Ungovernable* and Jean A. Stuntz's *Hers, His, and Theirs* point out that Texas women enjoyed far greater legal rights than did their counterparts in most other parts of the United States. A case study of women in Colorado County by Angela Boswell, *Her Act and Deed*, offers the kind of in-depth examination that shows how much local history can add to our understanding. Adrienne Caughfield's *True Women and Westward Expansion* describes the migration of women from the United States to Texas and interprets their experience as a reflection of both the dominant "cult of true womanhood" and the concept of manifest destiny. In *Hands to the Spindle: Texas Women and Home Textile Production*, Paula Mitchell Marks reminds readers of an important way that women contributed to their families. Biographies such as Light T. Cummins's *Emily Austin of Texas*, Paula Mitchell

Marks's *Turn Your Eyes toward Texas*, and Linda S. Hudson's *Mistress of Manifest Destiny* provide individual perspectives on the lives of notable women.[15]

Although recent studies of the late antebellum years in Texas have concentrated on ethnic groups and women, historians have not completely neglected the state's economy and economic change. Most Texans depended on farming for a living, a subject described and analyzed by C. Allan Jones in *Texas Roots: Agriculture and Rural Life before the Civil War* and by Richard G. Lowe and Randolph B. Campbell in *Planters and Plain Folk*. The development of cattle ranching is discussed from varying perspectives in Don Graham's *Kings of Texas*, Joe S. Graham's *El Rancho in South Texas*, and Terry G. Jordan's *North American Cattle-Ranching Frontiers*. David G. Surdam's article "The Antebellum Texas Cattle Trade across the Gulf of Mexico" points to an extensive export of cattle prior to 1861, contrary to the idea that Texas did not sell beef outside the state in any important way until after the Civil War. Inadequate transportation badly handicapped the economic development of antebellum Texas, and a thorough study of that subject is badly needed. Jacques D. Bagur, in *A History of Navigation on Cypress Bayou and the Lakes*, discusses one use of the state's meagre waterways, but only the railroad held the answer to transportation in a region of great distances and unreliable rivers. Unfortunately, during the antebellum period railroad building in Texas faced not only problems of finance and engineering but issues of public policy as well. Would the state simply give financial assistance to private railroad corporations, or would it construct the roads itself? An article by John Moretta, "The Censoring of Lorenzo Sherwood: The Politics of Railroads, Slavery and Southernism in Antebellum Texas," gives an excellent brief explanation of how during the 1850s private interests used issues related to slavery to destroy Galvestonian Lorenzo Sherwood and his state plan for building railroads.[16]

The economy of antebellum Texas underlay a society that defies simple descriptions. Any "snapshot" view of the state's social structure is likely to convince observers that there were a few households constituting the wealthy elite and a mass of others, including large numbers of poor whites. However, several studies point out convincingly that such snapshots do not take into account the numerous family ties that created economic and social cohesion. This argument is found in Carolyn Earle Billingsley's *Communities of Kinship* and Ricky L. Sherrod's "Plain Folk, Planters, and the Complexities of Southern Society."[17]

As is well known, at the time of annexation in 1845, Texas claimed the Rio Grande as its boundary with Mexico, whereas the latter nation insisted on the Nueces River as the proper dividing line. The boundary dispute was key in bringing on the Mexican-American War a year later, and the Treaty of Guadalupe-Hidalgo, which ended that conflict in 1848, settled the issue in general but not in detail. For recent studies of the war, see Richard Bruce Winders's *Mr. Polk's Army*, which deals with the conflict in general, and his *Crisis in the Southwest*, which focuses on the place of the Lone Star State in the conflict. Christopher Conway's edited *U.S.-Mexican War* provides a collection of documents that offer perspectives on the war from both sides. Michael L. Collins's *Texas Devils*, Charles D. Spurlin's *Texas Volunteers in the Mexican War*, and Frederick Wilkins's *Highly Irregular Irregulars* provide accounts of the often undisciplined Texan soldiers, who, although effective, tended to be the despair of regular army commanders such as Gen. Zachary Taylor. For excellent biographies of two leaders of Texas soldiers in the Mexican-American War, see Thomas W. Cutrer's *Ben McCulloch and the Frontier Military Tradition* and Richard B. McCaslin's *Fighting Stock: John S. "Rip" Ford of Texas*. The controversial treaty that ended the war but left much in dispute is discussed by Richard Griswold del Castillo in *The Treaty of Guadalupe Hidalgo*. Joseph Richard Werne's *Imaginary Line: A History of the United States and Mexico Boundary Survey* and David J. Weber and Jane Lenz Elder's edition of *Fiasco: George Clinton Gardner's Correspondence from the U.S.-Mexican Boundary Survey* describe the great difficulties involved in determining exactly what the treaty would mean to Texans from the Lower Rio Grande to El Paso.[18]

Once Texas joined the Union in 1845 and experienced conflict on the Indian frontier to the west and at the boundary with Mexico to the south, most of the state's people looked to the federal government for military assistance. Joseph G. Dawson, III, with *The Texas Military Experience*, offers several informative chapters on the late antebellum period, and Thomas T. Smith's article "U.S. Army Combat Operations in the Indian Wars of Texas" is an excellent account. In *The U.S. Army and the Texas Frontier Economy*, Smith focuses on the economic impact of the army rather than its military contributions, but in the process he explains the overall importance of the army to early Texas. In similar fashion, Robert Wooster's *Soldiers, Sutlers, and Settlers* deals primarily with social matters but sheds light on the meaning of the military's presence. Four studies that discuss the importance of particular U.S. Army posts to Texas are Thomas T. Smith's *Fort Inge*, Robert Wooster's *Fort Davis*, Ty Cashion's *A Texas Frontier: The Clear Fork Country and Fort Griffin*, and Lawrence John Francell's *Fort Lancaster*. Jerry Thompson edited a valuable collection of documents on the state of forts at the close of the antebellum period in *Texas and New Mexico on the Eve of the Civil War*. Finally, *The Old Army in Texas: A Research Guide to the U.S. Army in Nineteenth-Century Texas*, by Thomas T. Smith, is invaluable for those who wish to pursue research on the military in Texas from 1845 to 1860.[19]

Texas's path from union in 1845 to disunion in 1861 is analyzed in detailed studies that discuss major steps along the way and others that deal with the entire period. Mark J. Stegmaier's *Texas, New Mexico and the Compromise of 1850* explains the crisis of 1850 and the compromise that left many pro-South Texans very unhappy. Joel H. Silbey's *Storm over Texas* argues that annexation constituted a pivotal moment in putting the nation on the road to the Civil War. Daniel Walker Howe's *What Hath God Wrought*, a volume in the Oxford History of the United States, places the story of annexation in its national context. Donald E. Reynolds's *Texas Terror: The Slave Insurrection Panic of 1860 and the Secession of the Lower South* and Michael Phillips's "White Violence, Hegemony, and Slave Rebellion in Dallas, Texas, before the Civil War" tell the story of an event that revealed how fearful Texans were on the eve of disunion. James Marten's *Texas Divided* and Dale Baum's *Shattering of Texas Unionism* deal with the entire period and point to the centrality of slavery as a divisive issue.[20]

Biographies have remained an invaluable approach to the years of building sectional crisis. The two-hundred-year anniversary of Sam Houston's birth in 1993 led to a spate of new studies of the life of that most famous Texan. Although emphasizing his role in the revolution, all also deal with his courageous stand against disunion. These biographies include Marshall DeBruhl's *Sword of San Jacinto* and Randolph B. Campbell's *Sam Houston and the American Southwest*, a volume in the Library of American Biography series. Madge Thornall Roberts, a descendant of Houston, has provided an excellent study of the relationship between Houston and the wife who accomplished the seemingly insurmountable task of reforming the "Big Drunk" in *Star of Destiny*. Roberts also edited four volumes of personal letters, giving readers a fascinating view of the inner Houston. James L. Haley, with *Sam Houston*, has provided the most complete biography in nearly fifty years.[21]

No other Texas leader of the antebellum years approaches the towering stature of Houston, but biographies offer insights into the minds and actions of other important figures. Had not Edward Burleson died in 1851 at age fifty-three, his reputation as a rough and ready fighting man could have made him a force in secessionist Texas. His biography has been written by John H. Jenkins and Kenneth Kesselus. Kenneth Wayne Howell's *Texas Confederate, Reconstruction Governor: James Webb Throckmorton* recounts the life of a leader from North Texas who had the courage to vote no on secession but then supported his state once it became part of the Confederate States of America. John Anthony Moretta's *William Pitt Ballinger* tells the story of a lesser-known secessionist, and David C. Humphrey's *Peg Leg: The Improbable Life of a Texas Hero, Thomas William Ward* describes an old Texan who supported the Union. With *Adventures of a Frontier Naturalist: The Life and Times of Dr. Gideon Lincecum,* editors Jerry Bryan Lincecum and Edward Hake Phillips introduce a largely unknown but highly entertaining (not to say eccentric) secessionist.[22]

In summary, during the past twenty-five years historians of antebellum Texas have brought hitherto underemphasized ethnic groups and women to center stage. There is greater balance in the story, even if in some cases the roles of largely positive and largely negative characters have simply been reversed. Overall, Texas history from 1845 to 1861 is now viewed through a much less triumphal lens, as Anglo men set the stage for secession and a disastrous war.

NOTES

1. David La Vere, *The Texas Indians* (College Station: Texas A&M University Press, 2003); W. W. Newcomb, *The Indians of Texas* (Austin: University of Texas Press, 1961).

2. F. Todd Smith, *From Dominance to Disappearance: The Indians of Texas and the Near Southwest, 1786–1859* (Lincoln: University of Nebraska Press, 2005); Gary C. Anderson, *The Conquest of Texas: Ethnic Cleansing in the Promised Land, 1820–1875* (Norman: University of Oklahoma Press, 2005).

3. Paul H. Carlson, *The Plains Indians* (College Station: Texas A&M University Press, 1998).

4. Pekka Hämäläinen, *The Comanche Empire* (New Haven, Conn.: Yale University Press, 2008).

5. Thomas W. Kavanagh, *Comanche Political History: An Ethnohistorical Perspective, 1706–1875* (Lincoln: University of Nebraska Press, 1996); Gerald Betty, *Comanche Society before the Reservation* (College Station: Texas A&M University Press, 2002); Morris W. Foster, *Being Comanche: A Social History of an American Indian Community* (Tucson: University of Arizona Press, 1991).

6. Paul Carlson and Tom Crum, *Myth, Memory, and Massacre: The Pease River Capture of Cynthia Ann Parker* (Lubbock: Texas Tech University Press, 2010).

7. Brian DeLay, *War of a Thousand Deserts: Indian Raids and the U.S.-Mexican War* (New Haven, Conn.: Yale University Press, 2008).

8. Timothy K. Perttula, *The Caddo Nation: Archaeological and Ethnohistoric Perspectives* (Austin: University of Texas Press, 1992); F. Todd Smith, *The Caddo Indians: Tribes at the Convergence of Empires, 1542–1854* (College Station: Texas A&M University Press, 1995); Timothy K. Perttula and James E. Bruseth, *The Native History of the*

Caddo: Their Place in Southeastern Archeology and Ethnohistory (Austin: University of Texas Press, 1998); F. Todd Smith, *The Caddos, the Wichitas, and the United States, 1846–1901* (College Station: Texas A&M University Press, 1996), and *The Wichita Indians: Traders of Texas and the Southern Plains, 1540–1845* (College Station: Texas A&M University Press, 2000).

9. Thomas A. Britten, *The Lipan Apaches: People of Wind and Lightning* (Albuquerque: University of New Mexico Press, 2009); James L. Haley, *Apaches: A History and Culture Portrait* (Norman: University of Oklahoma Press, 1997); Robert A. Ricklis, *The Karankawa Indians of Texas: An Ecological Study of Cultural Traditions and Change* (Austin: University of Texas Press, 1996); Kelly F. Himmel, *The Conquest of the Karankawas and the Tonkawas, 1821–1859* (College Station: Texas A&M University Press, 1999); Bill Wright, *The Tiguas: Pueblo Indians of Texas* (College Station: Texas A&M University Press, 1993); Bill Wright and E. John Gesick; *The Texas Kickapoo: Keepers of Tradition* (El Paso: Texas Western Press, 1996); Jonathan B. Hook, *The Alabama-Coushatta Indians* (College Station: Texas A&M University Press, 1997).

10. Andrés Reséndez, *Changing National Identities at the Frontier: Texas and New Mexico, 1800–1850* (Cambridge: Cambridge University Press, 2004).

11. David Montejano, *Anglos and Mexicans in the Making of Texas, 1836–1986* (Austin: University of Texas Press, 1987); Arnoldo De León, *Mexican Americans in Texas: A Brief History* (Arlington Heights, Ill.: Harland Davidson, 1993); Arnoldo De León and Kenneth L. Stewart, *Tejanos and the Numbers Game: A Socio-Historical Interpretation from the Federal Censuses, 1850–1900* (Albuquerque: University of New Mexico Press, 1989); Kenneth L. Stewart and Arnoldo De León, *Not Room Enough: Mexicans, Anglos, and Socio-Economic Change in Texas, 1850–1900* (Albuquerque: University of New Mexico Press, 1993); Raúl Ramos, *Beyond the Alamo: Forging Mexican Ethnicity in San Antonio, 1821–1862* (Chapel Hill: University of North Carolina Press, 2008); Timothy M. Matovina, *Tejano Religion and Ethnicity: San Antonio, 1821–1860* (Austin: University of Texas Press, 1995); David R. McDonald, *Jose Antonio Navarro: In Search of the American Dream in Nineteenth-Century Texas* (Denton: Texas State Historical Association, 2011); Jesús F. de la Teja, ed., *A Revolution Remembered: The Memoirs and Selected Correspondence of Juan N. Seguin* (Austin: Texas State Historical Association, 1990); Ana Carolina Castillo Crimm, *DeLeón: A Tejano Family History* (Austin: University of Texas Press, 2004).

12. Armando C. Alonzo, *Tejano Legacy: Rancheros and Settlers in South Texas, 1734–1900* (Albuquerque: University of New Mexico Press, 1998); Andrés Tijerina, *Tejano Empire: Life on the South Texas Ranches* (College Station: Texas A&M University Press, 2008); Daniel D. Arreola, *Tejano South Texas: A Mexican American Cultural Province* (Austin: University of Texas Press, 2002); Jane Clements Monday and Frances B. Vick, *Petra's Legacy: The South Texas Ranching Empire of Petra Vela and Mifflin Kenedy* (College Station: Texas A&M University Press, 2007).

13. Larry Knight, "The Cart War: Defining American in San Antonio in the 1850s," *Southwestern Historical Quarterly* 109 (Jan. 2006): 319–36; Jerry D. Thompson, *Cortina: Defending the Mexican Name in Texas* (College Station: Texas A&M University Press, 2007); Robert M. Utley, *Lone Star Justice: The First Century of the Texas Rangers* (New

York: Berkeley, 2002); Charles Robinson, *The Men Who Wear the Star: The Story of the Texas Rangers* (New York: Random House, 2000); Michael L. Collins, *Texas Devils: Rangers and Regulars on the Lower Rio Grande, 1846–1861* (Norman: University of Oklahoma Press, 2008); Frederick Wilkins, *Defending the Borders: The Texas Rangers, 1848–1861* (Austin: State House Press, 2001).

14. Randolph B. Campbell, *An Empire for Slavery: The Peculiar Institution in Texas, 1821–1865* (Baton Rouge: Louisiana State University Press, 1989); Sean M. Kelley, *Los Brazos de Dios: A Plantation Society in the Texas Borderlands, 1821–1865* (Baton Rouge: Louisiana State University Press, 2010); Andrew Torget, "Between Two Empires: Slavery in the Texas Borderlands, 1820–1845" (Ph.D. diss., University of Virginia, 2009); James C. Kearney, *Nassau Plantation: The Evolution of a Texas German Slave Plantation* (Denton: University of North Texas Press, 2010); T. Lindsay Baker and Julie P. Baker, eds., *Till Freedom Cried Out: Memories of Texas Slave Life* (College Station: Texas A&M University Press, 1997); Ronnie C. Tyler and Lawrence R. Murphy, eds., *The Slave Narratives of Texas* (Austin: Encino Press, 1974, reprint 2006); Elizabeth R. Rabe, "Slave Children of Texas: A Qualitative and Quantitative Analysis," *East Texas Historical Journal* 42 (Spring 2004): 10–24; Mark Gretchen, *Slave Transactions of Guadalupe County, Texas* (Denton: University of North Texas Press, 2009); Patricia Smith Prather and Jane Clements Monday, *From Slave to Statesman: The Legacy of Joshua Houston, Servant to Sam Houston* (Denton: University of North Texas Press, 1993).

15. Mark M. Carroll, *Homesteads Ungovernable: Families, Sex, Race, and the Law in Frontier Texas, 1826–1860* (Austin: University of Texas Press, 2001); Jean A. Stuntz, *Hers, His, and Theirs: Community Property Law in Spain and Early Texas* (Lubbock: Texas Tech University Press, 2005); Angela Boswell, *Her Act and Deed: Women's Lives in a Rural Southern County, 1837–1873* (College Station: Texas A&M University Press, 2001); Adrienne Caughfield, *True Women and Westward Expansion* (College Station: Texas A&M University Press, 2005); Paula Mitchell Marks, *Hands to the Spindle: Texas Women and Home Textile Production, 1822–1880* (College Station: Texas A&M University Press, 1996); Light T. Cummins, *Emily Austin of Texas, 1795–1851* (Fort Worth: Texas Christian University Press, 2009); Paula Mitchell Marks, *Turn Your Eyes toward Texas: Pioneers Sam and Mary Maverick* (College Station: Texas A&M University Press, 1989); Linda S. Hudson, *Mistress of Manifest Destiny: A Biography of Jane McManus Storm Cazneau, 1807–1878* (Austin: Texas State Historical Association, 2001).

16. C. Allan Jones, *Texas Roots: Agriculture and Rural Life before the Civil War* (College Station: Texas A&M University Press, 2005); Richard G. Lowe and Randolph B. Campbell, *Planters and Plain Folk: Agriculture in Antebellum Texas* (Dallas: Southern Methodist University Press, 1987); Don Graham, *Kings of Texas: The 150-Year Saga of an American Ranching Empire* (New York: John Wiley and Sons, 2003); Joe S. Graham, *El Rancho in South Texas: Continuity and Change from 1750* (Denton: University of North Texas Press, 1994); Terry G. Jordan, *North American Cattle-Ranching Frontiers: Origins, Diffusion, and Differentiation* (Albuquerque: University of New Mexico Press, 1993); David G. Surdam, "The Antebellum Texas Cattle Trade across the Gulf of Mexico," *Southwestern Historical Quarterly* 100 (Apr. 1997): 477–92; Jacques D. Bagur, *A History of Navigation on Cypress Bayou and the Lakes* (Denton: University of North Texas Press, 2001); John

Moretta, "The Censoring of Lorenzo Sherwood: The Politics of Railroads, Slavery and Southernism in Antebellum Texas," *East Texas Historical Journal* 35 (Fall 1997): 39–52.

17. Carolyn Earle Billingsley, *Communities of Kinship: Antebellum Families and the Settlement of the Cotton Frontier* (Athens: University of Georgia Press, 2004); Ricky L. Sherrod, "Plain Folk, Planters, and the Complexities of Southern Society: Kinship Ties in Nineteenth-Century Northwest Louisiana and Northeast Texas," *Southwestern Historical Quarterly* 113 (July 2009): 1–31.

18. Richard Bruce Winders, *Mr. Polk's Army: The American Military Experience in the Mexican War* (College Station: Texas A&M University Press, 1997), and *Crisis in the Southwest: The United States, Mexico, and the Struggle over Texas* (Lanham, Md.: Rowman and Littlefield, 2002); Christopher Conway, ed., *The U.S.-Mexican War: A Binational Reader* (Indianapolis, Ind.: Hackett, 2010); Michael L. Collins, *Texas Devils: Ranchers and Regulars on the Lower Rio Grande, 1846–1861* (Norman: University of Oklahoma Press, 2008); Charles D. Spurlin, *Texas Volunteers in the Mexican War* (Austin: Eakin Press, 1998); Frederick Wilkins, *The Highly Irregular Irregulars: Texas Rangers in the Mexican War* (Austin: Eakin Press, 1990); Thomas W. Cutrer, *Ben McCulloch and the Frontier Military Tradition* (Chapel Hill: University of North Carolina Press, 1993); Richard B. McCaslin, *Fighting Stock: John S. "Rip" Ford of Texas* (Fort Worth: Texas Christian University Press, 2011); Richard Griswold del Castillo, *The Treaty of Guadalupe Hidalgo: A Legacy of Conflict* (Norman: University of Oklahoma Press, 1990); Joseph Richard Werne, *The Imaginary Line: A History of the United States and Mexico Boundary Survey, 1848–1857* (Fort Worth: Texas Christian University Press, 2007); David J. Weber and Jane Lenz Elder, eds. *Fiasco: George Clinton Gardner's Correspondence from the U.S.-Mexican Boundary Survey, 1849–1854* (Dallas: Southern Methodist University Press, 2010).

19. Joseph G. Dawson III, *The Texas Military Experience: from the Texas Revolution through World War II* (College Station: Texas A&M University Press, 1995); Thomas T. Smith, "U.S. Army Combat Operations in the Indian Wars of Texas, 1849–1881," *Southwestern Historical Quarterly* 99 (Apr. 1996): 501–31, and *The U.S. Army and the Texas Frontier Economy, 1845–1900* (College Station: Texas A&M University Press, 1999); Robert Wooster, *Soldiers, Sutlers, and Settlers: Garrison Life on the Texas Frontier* (College Station: Texas A&M University Press, 1987); Thomas T. Smith, *Fort Inge: Sharps, Spurs, and Sabers on the Texas Frontier, 1849–1869* (Austin: Eakin Press, 1993); Robert Wooster, *Fort Davis: Outpost on the Texas Frontier* (Austin: Texas State Historical Association, 1994); Ty Cashion, *A Texas Frontier: The Clear Fork Country and Fort Griffin, 1849–1887* (Norman: University of Oklahoma Press, 1996); Lawrence John Francell, *Fort Lancaster* (Austin: Texas State Historical Association, 1999); Jerry Thompson, ed., *Texas and New Mexico on the Eve of the Civil War: The Mansfield and Johnston Inspections, 1859–1861* (Albuquerque: University of New Mexico Press, 2001); Thomas T. Smith, *The Old Army in Texas: A Research Guide to the U.S. Army in Nineteenth-Century Texas* (Austin: Texas State Historical Association, 2000).

20. Mark J. Stegmaier, *Texas, New Mexico and the Compromise of 1850: Boundary Dispute and Sectional Crisis* (Kent, Ohio: Kent State University Press, 1996); Joel H. Silbey, *Storm over Texas: The Annexation Controversy and the Road to Civil War* (New York:

Oxford University Press, 2005); Daniel Walker Howe, *What Hath God Wrought: The Transformation of America, 1815–1848* (New York: Oxford University Press, 2009); Donald E. Reynolds, *Texas Terror: The Slave Insurrection Panic of 1860 and the Secession of the Lower South* (Baton Rouge: Louisiana State University Press, 2007); Michael Phillips, "White Violence, Hegemony, and Slave Rebellion in Dallas, Texas, before the Civil War," *East Texas Historical Journal* 37 (Fall 1999): 25–35; James Marten, *Texas Divided: Loyalty and Dissent in the Lone Star State, 1856–1874* (Lexington: University of Kentucky Press, 1990); Dale Baum, *The Shattering of Texas Unionism: Politics in the Lone Star State during the Civil War Era* (Baton Rouge: Louisiana State University Press, 1998).

21. Marshall DeBruhl, *Sword of San Jacinto: A Life of Sam Houston* (New York: Random House, 1993); Randolph B. Campbell, *Sam Houston and the American Southwest* (Boston: Little Brown, 1993); Madge Thornall Roberts, *Star of Destiny: The Private Life of Sam and Margaret Houston* (Denton: University of North Texas Press, 1993); Madge Thornall Roberts, ed., *The Personal Correspondence of Sam Houston,* 4 vols. (Denton: University of North Texas Press, 1996–2001); James L. Haley, *Sam Houston* (Norman: University of Oklahoma Press, 2002).

22. John H. Jenkins and Kenneth Kesselus, *Edward Burleson: Texas Frontier Leader* (Austin: Texas State Historical Association, 1990); Kenneth Wayne Howell, *Texas Confederate, Reconstruction Governor: James Webb Throckmorton* (College Station: Texas A&M University Press, 2008); John Anthony Moretta, *William Pitt Ballinger: Texas Lawyer, Southern Statesman, 1825–1888* (Austin: Texas State Historical Association, 2000); David C. Humphrey, *Peg Leg: The Improbable Life of a Texas Hero, Thomas William Ward, 1807–1872* (Austin: Texas State Historical Association, 2009); Jerry Bryan Lincecum and Edward Hake Phillips, eds., *Adventures of a Frontier Naturalist: The Life and Times of Dr. Gideon Lincecum* (College Station: Texas A&M University Press, 1994).

CHAPTER 11

Civil War and Reconstruction in Texas, 1861–1874

Carl H. Moneyhon

In 1861, Texans entered an era of potentially revolutionary change as their state seceded from the Union to join the southern Confederacy. Four years of warfare ensued, followed by defeat and then nine years of Reconstruction. The importance of the events connected with this era has attracted a large number of studies by those interested in Texas history. This essay examines the literature addressing Texas history between 1861 and 1874 that has been produced since 1991. It seeks both to provide a comprehensive listing of such works and also to place those works within the context of recent historiographical developments in the general field of American history.

Randolph B. Campbell's essay on the literature of the era of war and Reconstruction, published in 1991 in Walter L. Buenger and Robert A. Calvert's *Texas through Time*, provides a useful benchmark for the beginning of this historiography. The field was in transition at the time, with the advent of what was called the "new social history." The advocates of this type of history sought to produce studies from perspectives other than those of white males. They also brought new methods to their efforts, particularly the use of statistical analysis to examine trends not always apparent in the literary sources. In Reconstruction studies this new approach correlated closely with a revisionist movement that insisted that the era must be examined free of the racist assumptions that underlay traditional interpretations. Campbell summed up the impact of new perspectives in history on the field and also advanced an agenda for further work.[1]

Campbell, agreeing with an earlier assessment by Barry A. Crouch, concluded that significant changes had taken place in the interpretation of the Reconstruction era as a result of the new scholarship. Many of the villains in the traditional story told by Charles W. Ramsdell and William C. Nunn, both scholars in the tradition of William A. Dunning, were cast in a more favorable light. When accepting the aspirations of African American freedmen to security in their lives and property as legitimate claims on society, the work of the Freedmen's Bureau, the U.S. Army, and the state's Republican Party and its leaders came to be seen as positive forces in helping to create a more equitable society. Campbell noted, however, that although inroads had been made into a variety of topics associated with the new social history—urban life, families, women, race, gender, religion, social structure, and even economies—much remained to be done. Scholars seeking topics would find that except in the era of Reconstruction there would be little historiographical debate, because in many cases the literature was "thin" and in others had been "studied so little." As to the future, Campbell's call for future research reflected the importance of the new social history when he asked particularly for scholars to address how the events of this era had changed the very character of life in Texas across time.[2]

Since Campbell's review, both professional and amateur historians have continued to probe this critical era, and the interpretive landscape has continued to shift. The field has come to be dominated even more by the ideas of social history, but in the past twenty years historians have taken even more novel approaches. What has been called the "new cultural history," a response to the perceived inadequacies of social history, has invited scholars to explore the culture or cultures that underlay behavior of individuals within communities. Its advocates have sought in ideas, ritual, popular culture, and memory, among other sources, the key to understanding what has taken place. In addition, a new military history has emerged that challenges the emphasis upon leaders, strategy, and tactics associated with traditional military studies. The historians embracing this approach have taken much from social and cultural histories, asking how communities affected the military. They have also sought to discover the society and culture of military organizations, the impact of society and culture on warfare, and, in the end, the impact of war on society and culture.[3]

Broader historiographical trends have strongly influenced the writing of Texas history. Topically, recent Texas-related scholarship on the Civil War years has addressed a wide variety of problems. Although a considerable amount of research has been carried out on topics related to the war, no comprehensive synthesis yet exists. Until one is written, Ralph A. Wooster's introduction to the era provides a useful basic narrative of events in Texas. In addition, broad overviews of the state at war are available in two new anthologies by Charles D. Grear and Kenneth W. Howell, discussed in more detail below.[4]

Relative to the war, many traditional topics remain in play. The beginning of the war and the state's entry into the Confederacy, of considerable interest in the past, has been a subject of continued interest. Although Walter L. Buenger's 1984 study of secession in Texas offers what is probably the definitive work on the movement's causes, scholars have continued to expand our understanding of what happened and looked particularly at how Texans came to their conclusion regarding the Republican government. Donald Reynolds's study of the slave insurrection panic of 1860 concludes that pro-secession politicians were able to use unexplained fires in northern Texas to play upon the fears of Texans and other southerners, pushing them toward the acceptance of secession. The manipulation of voters by political leaders is also emphasized in James M. Smallwood's general reexamination of the state's march toward secession and by Linda S. Hudson in her study of the role played by the Knights of the Golden Circle in the crisis.[5]

Whether or not Buenger's generalization concerning the broad acceptance of the need for secession is valid has been addressed by the work of Dale Baum. Baum, who offers a prime example of the use of statistics in exploring history, tested this long-advanced theory that the secession vote did not reflect the honest choice of Texas voters by correlating voting and demographic statistics for the secession election. He found that, although suppression of the vote may have taken place in parts of the state, little voter fraud existed overall, that the fraud that occurred did not alter the results, and that the election results truly reflected the desires of the majority of Texas voters.[6]

A related topic that has attracted the attention of historians is the character of obvious anti-Confederate sentiment that emerged during the secession crisis and then persisted throughout the war. Baum, again, brought statistical methods to his study of Texas unionism, asking who the Unionists were and why they failed to mount an effective opposition to the Democratic leadership of the time. Examining Unionist voting patterns across the era, he concluded that the movement contained no cohesive interest group other than those opposed to the Democratic leadership. With no core constituency, elements of the alliance shifted constantly. Baum's conclusions agreed with those of James Marten, who, using traditional narrative sources, identified widely disparate groups moving in and out of the movement, unable to coalesce permanently. Kenneth W. Howell's article on the unionism of James W. Throckmorton points up the eclectic character of those attracted to the movement, showing Throckmorton's opposition to secession to be based primarily on his determination to preserve white supremacy in northern Texas. Once secession had taken place, he quickly abandoned the Unionists, seeking other ways to secure his goal.[7]

Precisely who constituted anti-Confederate dissenters through the war years remains an elusive problem. Richard McCaslin provides some insights into dissent in Collin County, connecting non-southern cultural characteristics of that area with dissent. McCaslin and David Paul Smith also link opposition to Confederate authorities to resistance to conscription after 1862 and subsequently to bands of deserters in the Red River country. Walter D. Kamphoefner sees dissent as widespread in the German communities and concludes that anti-slavery sentiment actually was widespread in the antebellum period. In his study of the German community in Texas, however, Melvin Johnson maintains that the mainstream of that community supported the war effort. For Johnson the only major source of dissent came from what he sees as the liberal element located primarily in the Texas Hill Country.[8]

While historians have made progress in explaining the factors that promoted opposition to the Confederacy, they also have further explored its suppression. Much of the literature has emphasized the heavy-handed and to some degree extralegal means used to suppress those who remained loyal to the Union. David Pickering and Judy Falls provide a graphic portrait of the resistance of Unionists in northeastern Texas, then document the violence used against them by both regular and irregular pro-Confederate forces that worked to crush them. Rick McCaslin also emphasizes the violence of suppression in his study of the "Great Hanging" at Gainesville. McCaslin sees suppression as an inevitable response from within that community, one suffering from the social instability created by war. In such circumstances community leaders, primarily slaveholders in these cases, with no authority to restore order, resorted to vigilante tactics to reestablish security.[9]

Mary Jo O'Rear offers a view of efforts at crushing dissent similar to McCaslin's in her work on the well-known Nueces massacre. A different perspective is offered by Stanley S. McGowen. McGowen asks whether the fight between pro-Union Germans fleeing to Mexico and Confederate forces should be called a battle or a massacre and concludes that it should be considered a legitimate battle because it took place between armed combatants, both prepared for a fight. Thus, although he recognizes that a breakdown of discipline among Confederate troops led to the subsequent murder of many of the Germans who had been taken captive, he downplays the predator-unprotected victim view of the relationship between pro- and anti-Confederate groups.[10] Connected to this event is Frank Wilson Kiel's examination of the memory, often fallacious, that developed surrounding the "Treue der Union" monument commemorating this event constructed at Comfort.[11]

An even more variant conclusion on the story of wartime dissent is advanced by Timothy Crane in his study of violence against Unionists. Crane looks particularly at the scale of violence involved and also at the personal experiences of individual Unionists, both leaders and common men. He concludes that despite some exceptional incidents Confederate authorities did not systematically persecute Unionists and that Confederate civilians generally tolerated their Unionist neighbors.[12]

The matter of identity inherent in the issue of wartime dissent also raises the question of pro-Confederate character in the state. On this matter, scholars have arrived at new conclusions using different approaches. Clayton Jewett, looking primarily at legislative and economic documents and employing statistical analyses of enlistments, concludes that early in the war Texans came to see their interests as different from those of the larger Confederacy. As a result, Texans came to see the war more in terms of protecting local communities than achieving broader national goals. Andrew F. Lang, looking at the secession movement and war years from the perspective of cultural history, concludes that Texans shaped a peculiar version of Confederate nationalism. He finds that as they moved toward secession they looked to the memory of the Texas Revolution more than that of the American Revolution to forge a Confederate identity that allowed them to transcend class divisions. Ironically, this constructed reality also allowed them to ignore completely the fact that slavery was the immediate cause of the war. This, in Lang's view, was the first step toward the creation of a Confederate nationalism tinged with an attachment to a romantic version of the Texas revolution.[13]

The secession movement and wartime dissent have been popular topics among historians interested in the Civil War, but military history has continued to dominate the field.[14] Even this area, however, has been influenced by the new social, cultural, and military histories, with all showing greater concern for the war from the perspective of the common soldier. In campaign histories this interest has been expressed primarily in the integration of letters and diaries produced by these men into the narrative.

Since 1991 historians have been particularly productive in writing campaign histories and have either revised earlier works or written the first history of every major military operation directly related to Texas. The central theme of all of these works has been that, although Texas may not have been the center of warfare, the military action that did take place was important to the overall course of the war nationally. It should be noted that this conclusion is countered to some extent by Joseph G. (Chip) Dawson in his investigation of Confederate strategy. Dawson concludes that probably after the fall of New Orleans and clearly by the late summer of 1863, Texas, for a variety of reasons, was no longer strategically important to the Confederacy, and that the state was in isolation through the last two years of the war.[15]

The first major campaign directly related to Texas was the ill-fated Sibley expedition, which attempted to establish a Confederate bridgehead to the west. The expedition, consisting almost solely of Texas troops, has been of interest to historians for a long time, but Donald Frazier has taken another look, combining an analysis of military leadership and an assessment of strategy and tactics with the experiences of the common soldier. Frazier points to the variety of issues that doomed the campaign, particularly unfavorable weather and the failure of logistical planning. Frazier's overview can be supplemented by more detailed examinations, largely traditional narratives of battles and leaders, of specific battles within that campaign. These include John Taylor's study of the Battle of Val Verde and Taylor and Thomas S. Edrington's history of the Battle of Glorieta Pass.[16]

Overlooked to some degree by earlier scholars, the Union Navy's blockade of the Texas Gulf Coast has received attention in a dissertation by John Fisher. Fisher not only tells the story of the development of the blockade but draws significant conclusions about its impact on Texas. Whereas previous studies suggested that Texans suffered little as a result of the war, Fisher's work contends that the blockade had a considerable impact, not only dislocating the coastal population but producing hardships among all Texans. Challenging long-held views that a majority of Texans came out of the war feeling that they had not been defeated, Fisher asserts that the blockade helped produce demoralization among Texans that ultimately led them to abandon the Confederate cause.[17]

Five subsequent campaigns aimed directly at an occupation of Texas have all received extensive treatment. Stephen A. Dupree reviews the reasons why the national government sought to invade Texas and also the development of its strategy in his study of Gen. Nathaniel Banks. Dupree shows President Lincoln's role in focusing on the state. The president wished to encourage loyalists in the state, put an end to Confederate trade across the border, discourage any French adventures, and seize cotton stored in Texas. Planning the subsequent campaigns fell into the hands of Banks, who Dupree describes as limited by personal failings and conflicts with superior officers, both of which interfered with the implementation of his basic strategy and carrying out successful campaigns.[18]

The first campaign, leading to the Battle of Galveston, is covered in part in Donald Frazier's first volume of a proposed four-volume work on Louisiana and Texas. In it he examines federal strategy leading up to the occupation of Galveston in October 1862, the capture, then subsequent recapture of the city the following January. Frazier concludes that the failure by the federals to hold Galveston was significant to the character of the western war in that it freed up Texas troops for use elsewhere and also prevented an earlier invasion of Texas. The history of Galveston during the war by Edward T. Cotham, Jr., also assesses the importance of that city as a military target, covers early efforts at taking it, then tells the story of its occupation and recovery. More detailed analyses of the Battle of Galveston are provided in essays by Frazier, Cotham, and Donald Willett. Willett and Cotham both emphasize Adm. David Farrgut's unrealistic belief that the city could be held as a component critical to the outcome of the campaign. Cotham agrees with Frazier that the recapture of Galveston changed the immediate course of the war in the Trans-Mississippi region.[19]

The second major campaign, a naval expedition that aimed at a lodgment on the Texas coast, ended in the Battle of Sabine Pass on September 8, 1863. Edward Cotham, in addition to his work on Galveston, provides new insights into this battle, particularly the importance of good engineering in the construction of the fortifications at Sabine Pass in producing victory. He also concludes that the federal defeat resulted from a failure of leaders, in both navy and army, to appreciate the situation they encountered and respond effectively. As with the recapture of Galveston, Sabine Pass, in Cotham's view, altered how troops could be disposed in the Trans-Mississippi, delayed the occupation of Texas, and forced the federals into even more campaigns to achieve that end.[20]

Shortly after the defeat at Sabine Pass, General Banks initiated a third move on Texas in October 1863. This one intended to reach the state by moving along Louisiana's Bayou Teche. This Second Teche campaign, proving as unsuccessful as the federal effort at Sabine Pass, has been examined by Richard G. Lowe, who emphasizes the failure of communication in the Union command, leaving the field commander uncertain of General Banks's particular goals. In addition, an inadequately supported supply line left federals vulnerable to attack and helped bring about their retreat after the Battle of Bayou Bourbeau on November 3.

Lowe's portrayal of the failures of Union command shows a remarkable foreshadowing of similar problems faced in the coming Red River campaign.[21]

At roughly the same time that General Banks initiated the Second Teche campaign, he began a fourth campaign to occupy Texas by sending an expedition to the Rio Grande. This one actually arrived in Texas, and federal troops captured and occupied Brownsville, then moved up the Rio Grande. Stephen A. Townsend and Charles D. Spurlin provide pictures of this occupation, one that kept federal troops remaining on Texas soil until the war's end. Townsend concludes that, although federal forces never moved into the interior as planned, their presence produced significant results by cutting off some trade from Texas into Mexico, bringing the war home to Texans and also blocking any potential alliance between the Confederacy and the French-backed Mexican government. Townsend further contends that the expedition's failure to succeed probably can be blamed on Gen. Henry Halleck's desire to move directly against Houston and Galveston, a plan that led to the withdrawal of large numbers of troops to support campaigns along this line. In his conclusions, Townsend, along with John Fisher, finds that federal military action significantly undermined the Confederate war effort and the morale of both soldiers and civilians.[22]

In the spring of 1864, General Banks began a fifth campaign, this one advancing toward Texas along the Red River. Gary D. Joiner and Michael J. Forsyth have provided important studies of this campaign. As did the other expeditions originating in Louisiana, this one ended in defeat for the federals, the invasion blocked by Confederate victories in the battles of Mansfield and Pleasant Hills. Joiner's work emphasizes the failure of Union command, a pattern similar to that discerned in the Second Teche campaign by Lowe. In addition, Joiner is particularly critical of Gen. E. Kirby Smith for sending troops into Arkansas to attack an already stalled Union advance under Gen. Frederick Steele rather than keeping his force together and attempting to crush Banks after his defeat near Shreveport. Forsyth's study looks more closely at the Confederate inability to deal Banks a decisive defeat and concludes that Banks must be credited with blunting Confederate attacks to achieve a successful withdrawal. He also concludes that Banks's success prevented the Confederate victory from more decisively affecting the war's course.[23]

In addition to action in the defeat of these five invasion efforts, Texas troops were involved in other engagements connected to Union activities in Louisiana. Two of these have been covered by Donald Frazier. Along the Teche in 1862, Frazier shows, Texas cavalry fighting as mounted infantry proved effective on Louisiana's unique terrain, a success that helped develop Confederate tactics used subsequently against the federals. Frazier also chronicles the role of Texas troops in an attempt to relieve the siege at Port Hudson in the summer of 1863. This effort tried to force federals back toward New Orleans with an attack on Gen. Benjamin Butler's supply lines there. Initially successful, the Texans under Gen. Tom Green suffered defeat at Fort Butler outside Donaldsonville.[24]

In addition to the confrontations with Yankees, the war in Texas also involved a defense of the frontier. David Paul Smith provides the first comprehensive overview of the state's efforts to defend the frontier against both Indians and the bands of guerillas and deserters that were pervasive through the Red River country. Another pertinent study for understanding frontier conditions is Jeffery M. Roth's examination of the situation on the northwestern frontier. Both Smith and Roth contend that Texas troops provided a successful defense of the frontier and prevented the receding of the line of settlement. This conclusion has been challenged by Glen Sample Ely, who criticizes the state's Ranger forces as ill disciplined as well as inadequate for the job. He sees the frontier as retreating during the war and holds the failure of the state forces responsible.[25]

How the war ended in Texas has been a question provoking some disagreement. In 1865 the continued occupation of the Rio Grande area led ultimately to the ironic fact that the last battle of the Civil War took place on Texas soil. That encounter, the Battle of Palmetto Ranch of May 12–13, 1865, has been chronicled by Jeffrey W. Hurt. Palmetto Ranch has often been used to show the persistence of a military spirit in Texas, and some work suggests that Texans were willing to fight to the bitter end. John R. Lundberg's study of Granbury's Texas Brigade, for example, insists that, although morale in that unit may have declined after the Battle of Franklin, the men never abandoned their basic attachment to the Confederacy. Other historians, however, have drawn a different picture. Brad Clampitt's study of the breakup of Confederate armies in Texas suggests that at least those Texas soldiers who remained at home readily gave up. Clampitt sees in the collapse of Confederate units without a formal surrender and in the disorder that followed a measure of the disintegration of discipline and morale among troops that had been in process through the spring of 1865. Carl H. Moneyhon, basing his conclusion on Confederate letters, argues that Confederates not only gave up but believed themselves to be defeated and subjugated by the final surrender. These conclusions correspond to those of John Fisher in his study of the blockade and Stephen Townsend in his work on the occupation of the Rio Grande region.[26]

Tied as well to military history have been the recent biographies of military leaders. These reflect the impact of changes in military history with their emphasis upon leaders' characteristics in addition to their skills as tacticians and strategists. Each of these works has concluded that its subject's leadership capacity has been underestimated by previous historians. Typical is Thomas Cutrer's study of Ben McCulloch. Cutrer sees McCulloch, the ill-fated general killed at Pea Ridge in 1862, as superior to many of his contemporaries not only as a strategist and campaign planner but also as a judge of the capabilities of his subordinates. Only the war allowed McCulloch, excluded from professional advancement before the war because of his lack of professional training, to demonstrate his true genius. Jerry Thompson's study of Gen. Henry Hopkins Sibley, though focusing on his entire military career, devotes particular attention to his role in the New Mexico campaign and concludes that factors other than his leadership were critical to that campaign's failure. John C. Waugh's study of Sam Bell Maxey also paints a positive picture of that officer, concluding that Maxey proved remarkably adept at organizing Indian troops and leading them into battle during the Red River campaign and operations associated with it. Perhaps the most remarkable rehabilitation comes in Paul Casdorph's study of John Bankhead Magruder, a subject of considerable criticism before and after his arrival in Texas. Casdorph portrays him as a good military commander for the District of Texas, despite his apparent fondness for drink.[27]

If campaign histories and biographies of leaders have remained largely wedded to the emphasis on battles and leaders characteristic of traditional military history, studies of military organization have been more heavily influenced by the social and cultural components of the new military history. Charles D. Grear best reflects this trend with his works examining why Texans fought. His approach has been to examine traditional literary sources, but looking for the values expressed to determine motivation. Looking at such evidence from men in all types of units and theaters of operation, he concludes that fighting for their communities proved the ultimate motivating force. This drew men from Texas to fight in the older states to the east. It also helps to explain desertion as men left the army to return to Texas when they believed their families needed them to face a military threat.[28]

Unit histories also reflect the shift toward the new military history. Though these histories usually chronicle the marches and battles of divisions, brigades, and regiments, most also look at the characteristics of the men who served, usually employing some form of statistical analysis of their backgrounds. In addition, they generally attempt to explain why these men joined the army and why they fought and continued to fight through the horrors of war. Richard G. Lowe's examination of Gen. John G. Walker's infantry division may be considered a model of the new history. The core of the study is a quantitative analysis of the men in the division. Lowe finds that the men of this unit represented a cross-section of their communities. Rich men fought alongside poor. He discerns little in the way of class conflict. Lowe also addresses the issue of motivation and concludes that the idea of defending their homeland from Yankee invasion led most men in the division into the army and then remained an important motivating force throughout their service.[29]

The importance of community in the military experience evidenced in Lowe's study also is apparent in Charles Brooks's study of Hood's Texas Brigade, a work heavily influenced by new approaches to military history. Brooks observes that to a large extent the civilian community shaped the military experience of these soldiers. Effective leadership ultimately meant conforming to the expectations of leadership brought to the military by these men from their homes. Brooks concludes, then, that good leaders accepted an interactive and relational use of power.[30]

A more traditional study of a larger unit is John R. Lundberg's work on Granbury's Texas Brigade. Lundberg avoids any assessment of the socioeconomic profile of the men of that brigade but does take up the question of the culture within which they operated. He concludes, along with Lowe and Brooks, that they remained closely connected to their home communities and that desertion, when it occurred, usually happened because men returned home to protect their families. On the other hand, Lundberg argues that most morale remained high through numerous defeats at least up to the Battle of Franklin in 1864, a fact that he attributes to good leadership. This same emphasis on the importance of leadership may be found in his study of Texans in the disastrous 1864 Tennessee campaign.[31]

Studies of smaller units, however, produce questions as to exactly what generalizations may be employed to assess the character of the common soldiers. The state's cavalry regiments have attracted particular attention, with new studies of the 1st, 3rd, 10th, 11th, 13th, 28th, Parsons's, and the 1st Texas Legion. Less work has been done on infantry units raised in the state, although several unpublished theses and dissertations have been produced, including studies of the 1st, 7th, 15th, and 19th Texas Infantry regiments. One artillery battery, the 9th Field Artillery, has been studied. Additional attention has been paid to the frontier regiments. Some of these studies are traditional unit history narratives; others include demographic profiles of the men who served and attempt to address their motivation.[32]

What generalizations may be made from these various studies is not completely clear. The character of individual commands has been shown to differ greatly. Some units largely comprised men from a single community, others drew from a wider base. Some of these regiments consisted of large numbers of local elites, as found by Douglas Hale in his study of the 3rd Cavalry. Others simply reflected the social and economic makeup of the community from which they came, the view of George Otott in his study of the 1st Texas Infantry. Randolph B. Campbell's examination of military service by the inhabitants of Harrison County provides further warning about oversimplifying, with his conclusion that young unmarried men rather than a broad cross-section of the men there entered the army.[33]

Scholars also have found widely different motivations among the men. James Newsom's study of the 7th Texas Infantry, for example, concludes that patriotism was the driving force motivating many of the men in that unit. Allen G. Hatley's history of the 11th Texas Cavalry, on the other hand, finds that the men of this unit, many of whom opposed secession, joined the army primarily to protect their families and homes. In his history of the 1st Texas Legion, Hatley determines that its men were more interested in protecting the frontier than serving elsewhere. On the other hand, Richard B. McCaslin's study of the 11th Texas Cavalry, an organization created after the implementation of military conscription, finds little commitment among men basically forced to serve—in short, "conditional Confederates."[34]

In the end, anyone interested in either traditional military history or the questions raised by its newer manifestation will find additional insights in the vast array of letters, diaries, and memoirs that have been published since 1991. New materials are now available on soldiers from the Army of Northern Virginia, the Army of the Tennessee, the Army of Mississippi, and the Trans-Mississippi. These include insights provided by officers of all ranks and also common soldiers, by men who served in a wide variety of circumstances. The writings of men from a variety of different ethnic backgrounds also offer different views of the war. The notebook of Henry O. Gusley even provides the viewpoint of a marine in the Union Navy.[35]

Somewhat connected to military history is the story of the operation of prison camps in Texas during the war. Two studies have been made of Camp Groce near Hempstead, the smallest of the prison camps within the state. Danial Francis Lisarelli provides a narrative account of Camp Groce, based largely on the reminiscences of federal troops incarcerated there. Brad Clampitt offers a more scholarly analysis of this facility and suggest that, although the soldiers there faced many of the same privations as those experienced elsewhere, they did not experience the same horrors of starvation and disease connected with Confederate camps in the East. James Smallwood has written on Camp Ford in Smith County.[36]

Addressing another topic related to the military, Charles D. Grear examines the relationship between white Texans, traditionally averse to any cooperation with Indians, and their Confederate Indian allies. Grear contends that necessity forced cooperation between the two groups, and they fought well together. On the other hand, he also finds that during lulls in action and toward the war's end white prejudice triumphed and relations deteriorated.[37]

As in the older histories, studies of nonmilitary war-related topics have continued to lag behind those of the military. Nonetheless, historians have addressed a wide variety of subjects, including many related to the state's social and cultural history. Politics, a staple of antebellum and post-bellum histories, remains largely unexplored. A provocative exception is Marcus Johnson's thesis on the state supreme court. Johnson contends that the court was politicized during the secession crisis and filled with states-rights advocates, but, ironically, during the war the court's decisions swerved away from a states-rights philosophy. The court's decisions strengthened the authority of the Confederate government relative to that of the state or individuals. Related, in some way, is the development of government-sponsored support for the families of Confederate soldiers, a program documented by Vicki Betts. Another work of interest is an overview by Kenneth E. Hendrickson, Jr., of the service of the three Confederate governors of the state. Hendrickson concludes that each proved remarkably adept at handling the myriad problems they faced. Additional insight into state politics may be gained from the publication of a major primary source, the memoir of Confederate senator Williamson S. Oldham.[38]

Economic history has also been generally overlooked. One exception is David Stieghan's study of Confederate rifle making in the state. In it he raises significant questions about the economy. Documenting the production of more than five thousand rifles for Confederate troops, he asks if this state-sponsored industrialization might have had a long-term impact on the state had the war effort succeeded. Another exception to the general lack of economic study is Carol Taylor's study of the beef cattle industry during the war. An additional study that is particularly provocative is Glen Ely's look at the frontier economy. Ely has discovered that ranchers in western Texas, including Confederate beef contractor John Chisum, began a thriving cattle trade with Union forces in New Mexico as early as 1864.[39]

The war's meaning to local communities socially and economically remains a topic needing more attention, but work has been done in this area. Paul A. Levengood's study of war-time Houston provides insight into that city. He finds that Houston did not experience an economic boom during this period, but neither did its people experience great hardships. Inconveniences existed, but they did not undermine a continuing prosperity. Stephen Chicoine's history of Chappell Hill focuses more on the personal impact of the war on the town's citizens than broader social and economic issues. Bill Stein also focuses more on individuals, including dissidents and slaves, in his study of Colorado County.[40]

Other social and cultural histories also have appeared. Among these is Ronald E. Goodwin and Bruce A. Glasrud's examination of the shifting relationships among whites and blacks as the war progressed and each faced the possibility of an end to slavery. Dale Baum adds to that story with his study of slaves brought into Texas during the war. Angela Boswell's studies of women during the war show their shifting responsibilities and mark a step forward in our understanding of the war's impact on gender. Richard G. Lowe's look at the relationship between Confederate soldiers and their wives and children is a path-breaking work on the character of family life in Texas. In the end, work in this area will also be encouraged by the continued publication of significant primary sources reflecting on life on the home front.[41]

Randolph B. Campbell's work on the long-term impact of the war on Confederate veterans is particularly distinctive as a representative of the interest of social historians. Using a sample of veterans from Harrison County, he finds that they generally returned to a stable life experience, at least in terms of residence, marital status, and occupation. Many of them also became actively involved in local politics. On the other hand, suffering from debilitating wounds and the aftereffects of disease, they died at a rate much higher than men who had not entered the army. Typifying the sort of work involved in the new social history, Campbell's remains alone as a case study.[42]

Unique in their approaches to the history of the war years are two books that focus on using photographs to tell the story. Carl H. Moneyhon and Bobby Roberts use the images of individual soldiers along with their biographical information to weave an overall account of the war. Jerry Thompson and Lawrence Jones's examination of the war on the border adds a distinctive perspective on that area with its narrative accompanied by contemporary photographs that capture the character of the border at that time.[43]

How the war ultimately was reconstructed in memory has been a significant new interest. The recreation of a pro-southern image by former Confederates is shown clearly by Alexander Mendoza in his study of the construction of Confederate statues at the University of Texas at Austin. Kelly McMichael's work on the movement to build Confederate monuments shows the impetus behind these efforts through the nineteenth century. Julie Holcomb addresses the problems of countering this image in the war's sesquicentennial years.[44]

As with studies of the Civil War, the literature on the Reconstruction era also has continued to expand since 1991. It has been dominated by the continued development of the revisionist school and the telling of the Reconstruction story from the perspectives of the nondominant classes. This has involved the continued disassembling of the traditional interpretation of the era provided by Charles W. Ramsdell and William C. Nunn, both associated with what is known as the Dunning school.[45]

Among the components of the traditional narrative was the assertion that occupying military forces preyed upon the civilian population. A major part of that charge centered on assertions that the army used out-of-control African American troops as an occupying force. David Work's study of black troops in Texas finds that there were instances of these soldiers breaking the law and instigating racial incidents. On the other hand, he finds that they were critical in restoring order within the state and helping pressure the French to abandon their adventure in Mexico. These troops also helped protect the freedmen as they adjusted to their new condition. For the most part, Work sees them behaving with restraint and discipline.[46]

The traditional story of the role of the Freedmen's Bureau also has experienced further revision. Barry Crouch has been prominent in this effort, with his various works showing that the Bureau's leadership and agents carried out a sincere effort to improve the lot and protect the freedmen. At the same time, he recognizes the inability of the Bureau to have a larger impact on the state because of its limited resources and the character of the agents. Christopher Bean supports Crouch's basic arguments. His studies of the agency at Marshall and the subassistant Bureau commissioners for the entire state undercut the idea that the Bureau was filled with individuals intent on imposing blacks on the community at the expense of whites. At the same time, he sees the Bureau as run by conscientious men who ultimately helped blacks secure the legal rights to make contracts, to be married, and to secure their suffrage. William Richter's work on individual Bureau agents agrees with this interpretation, although his study of Bureau administration concludes that it was largely out of touch with civilian sensibilities.[47]

The revisionist story of the African American experience continues to undermine the traditional view of black irresponsibility, although more needs to be known about the transition to freedom. Nancy Cohen-Lack's study of the development of the free labor system provides one insight into this change. Cohen-Lack examines the degree to which the emergence of the postwar labor system reflected agency on the part of African American workers and finds that the freedmen emerged from the war with the basic belief that only ownership of land assured full independence in an agricultural society. This belief ultimately thwarted the development of the contract system and helped to produce the system of tenant farming that replaced it.[48]

The success of blacks in achieving land ownership has been addressed by Thad Sitton and James H. Conrad. Using economic statistics, they show that blacks were relatively successful in acquiring land. The number of black landowners increased from 1.8 percent in 1870 to 26 percent in 1890. Their study further explains how blacks were able to accomplish this in the face of white resistance through the era. Dale Baum's study of the freedmen's town in Brazos County, on the other hand, shows the problems blacks encountered in their efforts to obtain and then hold on to land there. Baum finds that, although some blacks managed to acquire land, they constantly faced injustices inflicted on them by enemies and apparent friends. The picture of treachery within the legal system and opposition to black landownership is made even more apparent in his examination of the unsuccessful efforts of Azeline Hearne to hold on to a plantation given to her son by her former master.[49]

An additional study of the transformation to freedom and the development of a new identity among African Americans is Charles A. Israel's inquiry into the development of segregated Protestant churches in Houston. Israel shows that blacks actually moved to create these separate churches in response to the racism they found in white churches. Their separation ultimately was an expression of the desire within the black community to secure equality.[50]

In political history, revisionism has seriously struck at traditional interpretations that suggested that conservative Democratic leadership after the war was the legitimate representative of Texans and that the governments of governors Elisha M. Pease and Edmund J. Davis were illegitimate, imposed from outside, and in the latter case tyrannical and corrupt. Studies of the conservative Democratic leadership clearly show that this group did not represent the state's newly freed black population. The irresponsibility of these leaders and their role in provoking further federal intervention has been examined in several studies of the actions of the Twelfth Legislature and the government of conservative governor James W. Throckmorton. They show how a combination of prewar Democrats and conservative Unionists gained control of the government and to a considerable degree worked to undermine the impact of emancipation. Randolph B. Campbell's examination of the district judges demonstrates the survival of the antebellum political elite after the war and their dominance of the judiciary. Barry Crouch shows that the Black Codes, statutes passed by the Twelfth Legislature, had the clear intent of imposing serious constraints on the freedom of the state's former slaves.[51]

The traditional view that the Republican Party that emerged after congressional intervention in 1867 did not represent legitimate interests within the state has been further undermined by continued examinations of the individuals who joined that party. The traditional picture of a party of ignorant blacks, scalawags, and carpetbagger adventurers from the North has been largely disproved. Barry Crouch provides insight into the African American politicians who became part of the party. Randolph Campbell has shown with his statistical analyses that the majority of white Republican officeholders had been in Texas prior to the war. Most were substantial members of their communities.[52]

Another key to traditional arguments against the legitimacy of the Davis government was that the military policed the election, controlled the counting of the ballots, and awarded Davis a narrow 771 vote victory in the 1869 gubernatorial election. In addition to chapters in his general study of elections through this era, Dale Baum shows, with what must be considered finality, that Gov. Edmund J. Davis was legitimately elected governor. Using statistical methods, Baum shows that given the breakdown in previous elections, even if the counties whose votes were suppressed by fraud and intimidation had been counted, Davis would have won the election. The critical factor in the 1869 election was the failure of white conservatives to turn out at the polls.[53]

Studies are still needed on many of the programs of the Davis administration, particularly the development of public schools and programs of economic development, but the picture has been significantly recast with Barry Crouch and Donaly Brice's examination of its most criticized institution—the state police force. Pointing to the actual citizenship of black Texans and widespread violence aimed at their intimidation, Crouch and Brice radically alter the picture of that much maligned agency with their conclusion that many of the charges leveled against the state police were political in character. Further, they argue that the force was a necessary step toward controlling the violence of the era and that it looked not totally unlike the Texas Rangers that succeeded it. In addition, they show that the force was not used as frequently as has been alleged and that its members were, with some exceptions, model lawmen. In addition, the force's actual racial composition was mostly white, hardly warranting the contemporary charge that it was a black police force.[54]

The actual character of the violence the state police confronted has been one of the more debated issues in Reconstruction studies. The wide variety of perspectives may best be seen in Kenneth Howell's anthology on Civil War violence.[55] Some scholars have seen economic issues behind the violence. Barry Crouch and Donaly Brice's important work on the life of Cullen Baker, one of the more notorious of the region's bad men, concludes that much of Baker's crime resulted from his close relationship with local landowners, who willingly used him to control the labor of their former slaves. Kenneth M. Hamilton also emphasizes economic issues in his study of Harrison County and concludes that the desire of white planters to preserve their wealth was greater than other issues in provoking violence there.[56]

Others have seen politics as the primary issue. Gregg Cantrell is one of the few historians who attempts to apply a statistical analysis to the problem. Seeing a correlation between increases in violence and political events, he concludes that political conflict was a clear cause of violence. James Hathcock's study of Hunt County, a part of the particularly violent north section of the state, also sees violence as political, representing a continuation of the war and resistance to federal authority. Blacks and white Unionists and Republicans, who came to be seen as extensions of that power, became the ultimate focus of this resistance. Likewise, Christopher Bean's study of the murder of George W. Smith, a member of the Constitutional Convention, shows not only that violence was political but that federal authorities simply never were able to mount a response necessary to protect the rights of Unionists and their allies. In examining the Lee-Peacock feud that broke out in the Red River country, James Smallwood, Barry Crouch, and Larry Peacock also see politics as behind events. They conclude that the so-called feud was not a feud at all but a purposeful attack upon agents of the federal government, former slaves, and white Republicans. Robert J. Lee, a leader of one faction, and his associates were intent on continuing the late conflict, in effect launching a second civil war.[57]

Rebecca Kosary offers a slightly different explanation. Finding that violence was often leveled at black women and children as well as men, she observes that such attacks often were sexual in character, and so perhaps not simply racist. Instead she sees them as part of a purposeful campaign to reassert racial control over the black community, subjugating blacks by demonstrating their inability to prevent such attacks.[58]

Chuck Parsons's work on the Sutton-Taylor feud that began in 1868 is the first examination of that confrontation. Simply documenting the events connected with the feud, Parsons effectively portrays what happened but also shows the difficulty of identifying everything, from the basic chronology to who was involved. His work and others ultimately have one thing in common, the agreement that the era was a violent one, justifying, to some extent, the Davis administration's efforts at securing law and order.[59]

In addition to criticism of the state police, another point central to later charges against Governor Davis was that he refused to give up the governorship in 1874 in the midst of what has been called the Coke-Davis imbroglio. As with other aspects of the Davis years, this view has been attacked by scholars. Lance Cooper has reexamined the court case, known as the Semicolon case, and the supreme court's decision. He concludes that the judges' ruling was an analytically sound example of a constitutional interpretation and that Davis was justified, at least in the law, in refusing to accept the legitimacy of the 1873 election. In an examination of Davis's actions in the crisis, Carl Moneyhon contends that the governor could in fact legitimately claim his office beyond January 1874 and concludes that he finally stepped down specifically to avoid a violent confrontation between forces supporting him and his Democratic opponents.[60]

The best recent study addressing the politics of Redemption, touching on it tangentially, is Patrick G. Williams's examination of the Democratic Party in Texas in the years after the Davis administration. Williams emphasizes the importance of migration from older southern states, migration dominated by individuals aligned with the Democratic Party, in bringing a relatively quiet and virtually inevitable end to Reconstruction. Williams, significantly, raises questions about the coalition that overturned Reconstruction, showing the deep divisions within the Democratic Party over policy. Ultimately, only a common goal of overthrowing the Republican government held together a party actually badly divided over railroad policy.[61]

In addition to these studies that focus on Reconstruction at the state level, another significant trend has been to look more closely at events at the local level. Randolph Campbell has been a major proponent of local studies, arguing that until more is known of what took place at the town, city, and county level understanding the larger trends in Reconstruction will be restricted. In his study of local politics in six sample counties, he finds that local conditions, particularly the makeup of populations and economic conditions, affected the political results in each county. Some counties had viable Republican organizations, at least temporarily; others never saw the emergence of local Republican organizations capable of securing power.[62]

Scholars have not rushed to take up Campbell's challenge to look more closely at local affairs during Reconstruction, although some important studies exist. Kenneth Kesselus provides a broader look at the impact of emancipation and Reconstruction on Bastrop County but also shows, as suggested by Campbell, that a large black population made possible a biracial coalition, giving Republicans potential power over a long period of time. Leslie Lovett's consideration of Fort Bend County shows how a large black population influenced that community's politics until the Jaybird-Woodpecker War brought an end to their participation in elections in 1889. Likewise, Bill Stein's study of Colorado County shows the working of a biracial coalition in another county with a sizable black population. Though it is a primary source and not community history per se, Robert J. Robertson's study of the lives of two English immigrants to Beaumont offers one of the few firsthand accounts of life within a Texas community during Reconstruction.[63]

Carl Moneyhon has provided the first effort at creating a synthesis of revisionist research, although it also contains elements of what has been called post-revisionism in its recognition of some problems with the Republican state government. Moneyhon shows that considerable headway has been made in our understanding of the era's politics but also notes that, except for interest in the impact of emancipation on the freedmen, work on social and cultural issues is still warranted.[64]

Some of the most insightful work addressing broader social and cultural questions and dealing with Campbell's view that historians must deal with questions of continuity and discontinuity has been done in works not directly tied to either the war or Reconstruction. Works that cut across the chronological limits set by these two essentially political events include broader studies of traditional topics such as biography and economics but also embrace much of what is considered social and cultural history. Biography, where the chronological boundaries are set by the life of the subject rather than outside events, is one area where it is possible to see change over time. Since 1991 significant additions have been made to the list of biographies of individuals whose lives cut across the middle of the nineteenth century. Insights into the state's conservative Democratic politicians are offered in several works. Kenneth Wayne Howell's biography of Governor Throckmorton, covering the sixty-eight years of his life, concludes that he was a man motivated by personal ambition, ideas of economic advancement, and raw racism who successfully shifted from Unionist to conservative governor to railroad promoter to secure these ends. Louis Gould's biography of Alexander Watkins Terrell, a Civil War regimental commander, Redeemer Democrat, and important state legislator, provides insights into a man whose Civil War experience, most notably the rumors of his cowardice in battle, negatively influenced much of the rest of his political life.[65]

As to the Democratic opponents, much remains to be done. Carl Moneyhon's biography of Governor Davis is the first of this important figure and shows that his views of the rule of law help explain his behavior in the secession crisis, his flight from the state, and his ultimate move into the Republican Party. The lives of other Unionists and Republicans offer potential insight into this period. Andrew J. Hamilton has received attention in an older study but deserves a new look. Others have had older theses or dissertations written about them but need new treatments, including Governor Elisha M. Pease and Unionist and Republican congressman Edward Degener.[66]

In addition there are biographies of individuals who lived through this era but did not hold political or military office. John Moretta's study of Galveston attorney William Pitt Ballinger is an important addition to this genre. Moretta shows Ballinger's conversion from unionism to support of secession, his ideological shift to Confederate nationalism based on his repugnance of what he considered Lincoln's efforts at coercion, his cautious initial acceptance of the results of the war, then ambivalence toward radical Reconstruction. As with other biographers, Moretta demonstrates the complexity of his subject's decision making through this period and the idiosyncratic nature of the historical process. In addition, Philip Caudill's story of William Barry Duncan offers insights into the life of a pioneer cattleman and reluctant Confederate soldier who spent most of his service along the Gulf Coast.[67]

Recent biographies also provide insight into individuals who lived outside the dominant culture and were hardly impacted by the war and its aftermath. Of particular significance is Jerry Thompson's biography of Juan Nepomucino Cortina. Although he spent much of his time in Mexico, Cortina reflects a border world in which war and Reconstruction appear to have had little impact. Similar to the Cortina story is that of the Kiowa chief Santanta by Charles M. Robinson. Santanta would play a significant role in Reconstruction, when Governor Davis used his release in an effort to secure peace on the frontier, but Robinson demonstrates that Santanta's own world consisted of a constant struggle to remain a leader in the face of Kiowa factionalism. In a sense, the story of Santanta points to the existence of parallel courses in the history of the state, with this chief unable to accommodate white demands and remain a leader among his peoples. For whites he became treacherous, whereas within his own culture he simply maneuvered to maintain power. Both biographies provide a warning against simplistic views of what was going on among the people of Texas through this era.[68]

Family history is another genre that crosses traditional chronologies. Published works suggest that some Texans did not suffer through the war and Reconstruction years to the same degree as others in the South. Margaret Swett Henson and Deolece Parmalee's study of the Cartwright family of San Augustine, for example, shows a family that managed to move through the period and secure considerable economic success. Even though the Cartwrights provided men for the Confederate army, the family successfully negotiated the problems of war and Reconstruction to emerge possibly wealthier than they had been in the antebellum years. Harold Hyman's study of the Kempner family of Galveston also shows a successful family, despite the intervention of the war.[69]

Community studies also can cut across time and are particularly useful in addressing the question of social change. Sean M. Kelley's study of life along the Brazos River is one such. Kelley emphasizes contrasting ideals of family that divided ethnic and racial groups in this plantation community before the war, producing an internal frontier. The potential conflicts of this frontier encouraged whites to secede in 1861 in order to protect their idea of the family, an idea that included racial subordination. Reconstruction, in turn, allowed blacks to assert control over their families and also to secure a degree of political power through their alliances with German ethnic groups.[70]

Ty Cashion's examination of the development of communities in the vicinity of Fort Griffin into the 1880s shows that community history can provide insights into economic life. Although his study emphasizes the violence of the area, including Indian- and bandit-related events, it also offers a view of the economic expansion of a settlement despite the war, suggesting, at least in this case, the limited effect of the war on frontier development.[71]

Longitudinal studies of business enterprises also provide insight into the impact of events during these critical years. Kyle Wilkison's study of the effect of railroads on Texas, for example, finds a market revolution beginning during Reconstruction that seriously affected plain folk. Living in relative isolation and sharing basic values, by the end of Reconstruction their world was breaking down. Further increasing land prices, difficulty in buying land, the shift to farm tenancy, and the production of cotton led to a breakdown of traditional values. Michael Moore's thesis on the Henry Jones plantation and ranching operation provides further evidence of the limited effects of the war on the state's economy, showing both the survival of wealth and the complexity of the state's economies during this era. Although the work is not usually associated with the Civil War and Reconstruction, Don Graham's history of the King Ranch and the role of its founder in border politics and troubles is also typical of the sort of work that addresses the broader issues of change over time.[72]

Gender and ethnic studies also have the potential for assessing events over a wider period. Kenneth Stewart and Arnoldo De León's study of the effect of socioeconomic change in the nineteenth century on Mexican Americans is reflective of this possibility. They show that this group failed to share in the increasing prosperity of Anglo-Texans as the development of discrimination against them prevented their movement into the state's more prosperous regions and the commercialization of cattle ranching than the usual Reconstruction-related events. This work also shows the complexity of life in Texas, with its emphasis upon a population whose experiences do not easily fit the generalizations made about Anglos.[73]

Women's history has been the area of social history that has seen the greatest amount of work. Angela Bosell's study of white women in Washington County between 1837 and 1873, based largely on court records, concludes that, although gender roles may have been somewhat different on the frontier, by the war and afterward they were typical of the American South and remained relatively unchanged; activities by some individuals may have strayed from the norm in the frontier period and then during the war, but this did not alter the ideal. Paula Marks's study of household production of textiles also finds that little changed in day-to-day life. Spinning and the weaving of textiles continued to be important, bringing women together within communities and providing a major component of family economics. Francelle Pruitt's study of divorce in Washington and Harrison Counties between 1841 and 1880 shows similar continuity, with Texas women maintaining a relatively high degree of autonomy in the courts and securing equal treatment in the division of property and custody of children. Margaret Breashears's work on the occupational structure and education of women between 1860 and 1920 found little real change as well. Taken as a whole, in addressing the question of continuity versus discontinuity, women's studies suggest that war and Reconstruction produced little but temporary changes in women's roles.[74]

Studies of class also represent a new interest. Linda Newland's study of five families from East Texas who owned one hundred or more slaves is particularly provocative. Determining that four of the five families survived the war and Reconstruction still among the wealthy elite within their communities, Newland contends that the war and Reconstruction had less impact on wealthy Texans than traditional studies and popular mythology claim. Again, from this one study, society appears to have maintained considerable continuity through the war years.[75]

Since 1991 historians have continued to expand our knowledge of Texas through the critical years of war and Reconstruction. Military history has continued to dominate the field, although the shift toward a different sort of military history is apparent. In addition, researchers have made significant movement into other areas of investigation. The study of society and culture called for by Campbell in 1991 has begun to appear, although the literature remains in many respects as thin as he noted. If we are to determine precisely what the war meant for Texans, further investigation is inevitably called for. Existing studies must be tested and further explored before any definitive synthesis of the wartime experience can be realized.

NOTES

1. Randolph B. Campbell, "Statehood, Civil War, and Reconstruction, 1846–76," in *Texas through Time: Evolving Interpretations*, ed. Walter L. Buenger and Robert A. Calvert (College Station: Texas A&M University Press, 1991), 165–96. For insight into the agenda of the "new social history," see Robert Berkhofer, *A Behavioral Approach to Historical Analysis* (New York: Free Press, 1969); and Lee Benson, *Toward the Scientific Study of History* (Philadelphia: Lippincott, 1972).

2. Campbell, "Statehood, Civil War, and Reconstruction," 196; Barry A. Crouch, "'Unmanacling' Texas Reconstruction: A Twenty-Year Perspective," *Southwestern Historical Quarterly* 93 (Jan. 1990): 275–302; Charles William Ramsdell, *Reconstruction in Texas* (New York: Columbia University Press, 1910); William C. Nunn, *Texas under the Carpetbaggers* (Austin: University of Texas Press, 1962).

3. Lynn Hunt, *The New Cultural History* (Berkeley: University of California Press, 1989); Peter Burke, *What Is Cultural History?* (Cambridge: Polity Press, 2004); Mark Moyar, "The Current State of Military History," *Historical Journal* 50 (2007): 225–40; Robert M. Citinio, "Military Histories Old and New: A Reintroduction," *American Historical Review* 112 (Oct. 2007): 1070–90; Maris A. Vinovskis, *Toward a Social History of the Civil War: Exploratory Essays* (Cambridge: Cambridge University Press, 1990).

4. Ralph A. Wooster, *Texas and Texans in the Civil War* (Austin: Eakin, 1995); Charles D. Grear, ed., *The Fate of Texas: The Civil War and the Lone Star State* (Fayetteville: University of Arkansas Press, 2008); Kenneth W. Howell, *The Seventh Star of the Confederacy: Texas during the Civil War* (Denton: University of North Texas Press, 2009). For a basic chronicle of wartime events in Texas, see Archie P. McDonald, "The Civil War and the Lone Star State: A Brief Overview," in Howell, *Seventh Star*, 21–31. Alwyn Barr has provided an overview of nonmilitary publications related to the war era: "The Impact of New Studies about Texas and Texans on Civil War Historiography," in Howell, *Seventh Star*, 2–20; McDonald's essay contains some of the same publications listed by Barr, although it seeks to provide a somewhat different perspective on them.

5. Walter L. Buenger, *Secession and the Union in Texas* (Austin: University of Texas Press, 1984); Donald E. Reynolds, *Texas Terror: The Slave Insurrection Panic of 1860 and the Secession of the Lower South* (Baton Rouge: Louisiana State University Press, 2007); see also Reynolds, "Reluctant Martyr: Anthony Bewley and the Texas Slave Insurrection Panic of 1860," *Southwestern Historical Quarterly* 96 (Jan. 1993): 345–61; James M. Smallwood, "The Impending Crisis: A Texas Perspective on the Causes of the Civil War," in Howell, *Seventh Star*, 32–51; Linda S. Hudson, "The Knights of the Golden Circle in Texas, 1858–1861: An Analysis of the First (Military) Degree Knights," in Howell, *Seventh Star*, 52–69.

6. Dale Baum, "Pinpointing Apparent Fraud in the 1861 Texas Secession Referendum," *Journal of Interdisciplinary History* 22 (Autumn 1991): 201–21.

7. Dale Baum, *The Shattering of Texas Unionism: Politics in the Lone Star State during the Civil War Era* (Baton Rouge: Louisiana State University Press, 1998); James Marten, *Texas Divided: Loyalty and Dissent in the Lone Star State, 1856–1874* (Lexington: University Press of Kentucky, 1990); Kenneth Wayne Howell, "'When the Rabble Hiss, Well May Patriots Tremble': James Webb Throckmorton and the Secession Movement in Texas, 1854–1861," *Southwestern Historical Quarterly* 109 (Apr. 2006): 465–94.

8. Richard McCaslin, "Wheat Growers in the Cotton Confederacy: The Suppression of Dissent in Collin County, Texas, during the Civil War," *Southwestern Historical Quarterly* 96 (Apr. 1993): 526–39; David Paul Smith, "Conscription and Conflict on the Texas Frontier, 1863–1865," *Civil War History* 36 (1990): 250–61; Walter D. Kamphoefner, "New Perspectives on Texas Germans and the Confederacy," in Grear, *Fate of Texas*, 105–121; Melvin Johnson, "A New Perspective for the Antebellum and Civil War Texas German Community" (M.A. thesis, Stephen F. Austin State University, 1993).

9. David Pickering and Judy Falls, *Brush Men and Vigilantes: Civil War Dissent in Texas* (College Station: Texas A&M University Press, 2000); Richard McCaslin, *Tainted Breeze: The Great Hanging at Gainesville, Texas, 1862* (Baton Rouge: Louisiana State University Press, 1992); see also McCaslin, "Wheat Growers in the Cotton Confederacy: The Suppression of Dissent in Collin County Texas, during the Civil War," *Southwestern Historical Quarterly* 96 (Apr. 1993): 526–39, and "The Price of Liberty: The Great Hanging at Gainesville," in Grear, *Fate of Texas*, 53–68.

10. Mary Jo O'Rear, "Reckoning at the River: Unionists and Secessionists on the Nueces, August 10, 1862," in Howell, *Seventh Star*, 85–109; Stanley S. McGowen, "Battle or Massacre? The Incident on the Nueces, August 10, 1862," *Southwestern Historical Quarterly* 104 (July 2000): 65–86.

11. Frank Wilson Kiel, "Treue der Union: Myths, Misrepresentations, and Misinterpretations," *Southwestern Historical Quarterly* 115 (Jan. 2012): 283–92.

12. Timothy Crane, "When Madness Ruled the Hour: Unionists and Confederates in Civil War Texas" (Ph.D. diss., University of Texas, 2003).

13. Clayton E. Jewett, *Texas in the Confederacy: An Experiment in Nation Building* (Columbia: University of Missouri Press, 2002); Andrew F. Lang, "Memory, the Texas Revolution, and Secession: The Birth of Confederate Nationalism in the Lone Star State," *Southwestern Historical Quarterly* 114 (July 2010): 21–35.

14. See Walter F. Bell, "Civil War Texas: A Review of the Historical Literature," *Southwestern Historical Quarterly* 109 (Oct: 2005): 205–34. Although Bell is concerned with broader literature, the primary focus of this essay is on military history; as in the case of the Barr essay, this chapter covers some of the same materials but offers a different perspective.

15. Joseph G. Dawson III, "Texas, Jefferson Davis, and Confederate National Strategy," in Howell, *Fate of Texas*, 1–23.

16. Donald S. Frazier, *Blood and Treasure: Confederate Empire in the Southwest* (College Station: Texas A&M University Press, 1995); John Taylor, *Bloody Valverde: A Civil War Battle on the Rio Grande, February 21, 1862* (Albuquerque: University of New Mexico Press, with the Historical Society of New Mexico, 1995); Thomas S. Edrington and John Taylor, *The Battle of Glorieta Pass: A Gettysburg in the West* (Albuquerque: University of New Mexico Press, 1998).

17. John Fisher, "A Blockaded State: Texas during the Civil War, 1861–1865" (Ph.D. diss., Texas A&M University, 1995).

18. Stephen A. Dupree, *Planting the Union Flag in Texas: The Campaigns of Major General Nathaniel P. Banks in the West* (College Station: Texas A&M University Press, 2008).

19. Donald S. Frazier, *Fire in the Cane Field: The Federal Invasion of Louisiana and Texas, January 1861–January 1863* (Buffalo Gap, Tex.: State House Press, 2009); Edward T. Cotham, Jr., *Battle on the Bay: The Civil War Struggle for Galveston* (Austin: University of Texas Press, 1998), and "'Nothing but Disaster': The Failure of Union Plans to Capture Texas," in Howell, *Seventh Star*, 130–48; Donald Willett, "Without a Fight: The Eighty-Four-Day Union Occupation of Galveston, Texas," in Howell, *Seventh Star*, 110–29; Donald S. Frazier, *Cottonclad! The Battle of Galveston and the Defense of the Texas Coast* (Abilene, Tex.: McWhiney Foundation Press, 1998).

20. Edward T. Cotham, Jr., *Sabine Pass: The Confederacy's Thermopylae* (Austin: University of Texas Press, 2004).

21. Richard G. Lowe, *The Texas Overland Expedition* (Abilene, Tex.: McWhiney Foundation Press, 1998).

22. Stephen A. Townsend, *The Yankee Invasion of Texas* (College Station: Texas A&M University Press, 2006); Charles D. Spurlin, "Hide Your Daughters: The Yankees Have Arrived in the Coastal Bend," in Howell, *Seventh Star*, 149–66.

23. Gary D. Joiner, *One Damn Blunder from Beginning to End: The Red River Campaign of 1864* (New York: Rowland and Littlefield, 2002), *Through the Howling Wilderness: The 1864 Red River Campaign and Union Failure in the West* (Knoxville: University of Tennessee Press, 2006), and "Defending the Lone Star: The Texas Cavalry in the Red River Campaign," in Howell, *Seventh Star*, 189–207; Michael J. Forsyth,

The Red River Campaign of 1864 and the Loss by the Confederacy of the Civil War (Jefferson, N.C.: McFarland, 2010).

24. Donald S. Frazier, "Texans on the Teche: The Texas Brigade at the Battles of Bisland and Irish Bend, April 12–14, 1863," *Louisiana History* 32 (Autumn 1993): 417–35, and "'The Battles of Texas Will be Fought in Louisiana': The Assault on Fort Butler, June 28, 1863," *Southwestern Historical Quarterly* 104 (Jan. 2001): 333–64.

25. David Paul Smith, *Frontier Defense in the Civil War: Texas' Rangers and Rebels* (College Station: Texas A&M University Press, 1992); see also Smith, "The Elm Creek Raid, 1864: State and Confederate Defense and Response," *Military History of the Southwest* 19 (1989): 121–36, "Conscription and Conflict on the Texas Frontier, 1863–1865," *Civil War History* 36 (1990): 250-61, and his more recent "The Limits of Dissent and Loyalty in Texas," in *Guerillas, Unionists, and Violence on the Confederate Home Front*, ed. Daniel Sutherland (Fayetteville: University of Arkansas Press, 1999), 133–50. Jeffery M. Roth, "Civil War Frontier Defense Challenges in Northwest Texas," *Military History of the West* 30 (2000): 21–44; Glen Sample Ely, "Gone from Texas and Trading with the Enemy: New Perspectives on Civil War West Texas," *Southwestern Historical Quarterly* 110 (Apr. 2007): 439–64.

26. Jeffrey W. Hurt, *The Final Fury: Last Battle of the Civil War: Palmetto Ranch* (Austin: University of Texas Press, 2002); John R. Lundberg, *Granbury's Texas Brigade: Diehard Western Confederates* (Baton Rouge: Louisiana State University Press, 2012); Bradley R. Clampitt, "The Break-Up of the Confederate Trans-Mississippi Army, 1865" (Thesis, University of North Texas Press, 2001), "The Breakup: The Collapse of the Confederate Trans-Mississippi Army in Texas, 1865," *Southwestern Historical Quarterly* 108 (Apr. 2005): 499–534, and *The Confederate Heartland* (Baton Rouge: Louisiana State University Press, 2011). Carl H. Moneyhon, "'I Seemed to Have No Thought of the Past, Present, or Future': Texans React to Confederate Defeat," in Howell, *Fate of Texas*, 137–53.

27. Thomas W. Cutrer, *Ben McCulloch and the Frontier Military Tradition* (Chapel Hill: University of North Carolina Press, 1993); Jerry Thompson, *Confederate General of the West: Henry Hopkins Sibley* (College Station: Texas A&M University Press, 1996); John C. Waugh, *Sam Bell Maxey and the Confederate Indians* (Abilene, Tex.: McWhiney Foundation Press, 1998); Paul D. Casdorph, *Prince John Magruder: His Life and Campaigns* (New York: Wiley, 1996).

28. Charles Grear, *Why Texans Fought in the Civil War* (College Station: Texas A&M University Press, 2010), "'If We Should Succeed in Driving the Enemy Back Out of My Native State': Why Texans Fought East of the Mississippi River during the Civil War," in Howell, *Fate of Texas*, 37–52, and "Texans to the Home Front: Why Lone Star Soldiers Returned to Texas during the War," *East Texas Historical Journal* 45 (Fall 2007): 14–25.

29. Richard G. Lowe, *Walker's Texas Division, C.S.A.: Greyhounds of the Trans-Mississippi* (Baton Rouge: Louisiana State University Press, 2004).

30. Charles E. Brooks, "The Social and Cultural Dynamics of Soldiering in Hood's Texas Brigade," *Journal of Southern History* 67 (Aug. 2001): 535–72.

31. John R. Lundberg, *Granbury's Texas Brigade: Diehard Western Confederates* (Baton Rouge: Louisiana State University Press, 2012), and *The Finishing Stroke: Texans in the 1864 Tennessee Campaign* (Abilene, Tex.: McWhiney Foundation Press, 2003).

32. Stanley S. McGowen, *Horse Sweat and Powder Smoke: The First Texas Cavalry in the Civil War* (College Station: Texas A&M University Press, 1999); Douglas Hale, *The Third Texas Cavalry in the Civil War* (Norman: University of Oklahoma Press, 1993); Martha Crabb, *All Afire to Fight: The Untold Tale of the Civil War's Ninth Texas Cavalry* (New York: Fort Post Road Press, 2000); Church Carlock and V. M. Owens, *History of the Tenth Texas Cavalry Dismounted Regiment* (North Richland Hills, Tex.: Smithfield Press, 2001); Allen G. Hatley, *Reluctant Rebels: The Eleventh Texas Cavalry Regiment* (Hillsboro, Tex.: Hill College Press, 2006); Thomas Reid, *Spartan Band: Burnett's 13th Texas Cavalry in the Civil War* (Denton: University of North Texas Press, 2005); Anne J. Bailey, *Between the Enemy and Texas: Parson's Texas Cavalry in the Civil War* (Fort Worth: Texas Christian University Press, 1989); M. Jane Johansson, *Peculiar Honor: A History of the 28th Texas Cavalry, 1862–1865* (Fayetteville: University of Arkansas Press, 1998); Jeffrey D. Murrah, *None but Texians: A History of Tery's Texas Rangers* (Austin: Eakin Press, 2001); Allen G. Hatley, *The First Texas Legion* (Eagle Lake, Tex.: Centex Press, 2004); James L. Newsom, "Intrepid Gray Warriors: The 7th Texas Infantry, 1861–1865" (Ph.D. diss., Texas Christian University, 1995); George Edward Otott, Jr., "Antebellum Social Characteristics of the Officers and Men in the First Texas Infantry, Confederate States Army" (M.A. thesis, California State University, Fullerton, 2003); Blake R. Hamaker, "Making a Good Soldier: A Historical and Quantitative Study of the 15th Texas Infantry, Confederate States of America" (M.A. thesis, University of North Texas, 1998); John D. Perkins, *Daniel's Battery: The Ninth Texas Field Battery* (Hillsboro, Tex.: Hill College Press, 1961). For a study of the frontier regiments, see John W. Gorman, "Frontier Defense: Enlistment Patterns for the Texas Frontier Regiments in the Civil War," in Howell, *Seventh Star*, 70–84; see also Anne J. Bailey, *Texans in the Confederate Cavalry* (Abilene, Tex.: McWhiney Foundation Press, 1998).

33. Hale, *Third Texas Cavalry*; Otott, "Antebellum Social Characteristics"; Randolph B. Campbell, "Fighting for the Confederacy: The White Male Population of Harrison County in the Civil War," *Southwestern Historical Quarterly* 104 (July 2000): 23–39.

34. Newsom, "Intrepid Gray Warriors"; Hatley, *Reluctant Rebels*, and *First Texas Legion*; Richard B. McCaslin, "Conditional Confederates: The Eleventh Texas Cavalry West of the Mississippi River," *Military History of the Southwest* 21 (Spring 1991): 87–99.

35. Jerry D. Thompson, *Westward the Texans: The Civil War Journal of Private William Randolph Howell* (El Paso: Texas Western Press, 1990); Douglas John Carter, *As It Was: Reminiscences of a Soldier of the Third Texas Cavalry and the Nineteenth Louisiana Infantry* (Austin: State House Press, 1990); Edward B. Williams, *Rebel Brothers: The Civil War Letters of the Truehearts* (College Station: Texas A&M University Press, 1995); Richard G. Lowe, ed., *A Texas Cavalry Officer's Civil War: The Diary and Letters of James C. Bates* (Baton Rouge: Louisiana State University Press, 1999); George Skoch and Mark W. Perkins, eds., *Lone Star Confederate: A Gallant and Good Soldier of the 5th Texas Infantry* (College Station: Texas A&M University Press, 2003); Rex H. Stever and Barbara M. Stever, *Oi Callie: The Civil War Letters of Brandt Badger* (Dallas: Taylor, 2004); Thomas W. Cutrer, ed., *Our Trust Is in the God of Battles: The Civil War Letters of Robert Franklin Bunting, Chaplain, Terry's Texas Rangers, C.S.A.* (Knoxville: University of Tennessee

Press, 2006); Donald S. Frazier and Andrew Hillhouse, *Love and War: The Civil War Letters and Medicinal Book of Augusts V. Ball* (Buffalo Gap, Tex.: State House Press, 2010); Jerry Thompson, ed., *Tejanos in Gray: Civil War Letters of Captains Joseph Rafael de la Garza and Manuel Yturri* (College Station: Texas A&M University Press, 2011); Edmund Louis Burnett, ed., *Civil War Letters of Louis Lehman: With Alexander Terrell's and James B. Likens' Texas Cavalry Regiments, 1863–1864* (Hillsboro, Tex.: Hill College Press, 2011); Charles D. Spurlin, ed., *The Civil War Diary of Charles A. Leuschner* (Austin: Eakin Press, 1992); Walter Kamphoefner and Wolfgang Helbich, *Germans in the Civil War: The Letters They Wrote Home* (Chapel Hill: University of North Carolina Press, 2006); Edward T. Cotham, Jr., *The Southern Journey of a Civil War Marine: The Illustrated Note-book of Henry O. Gusley* (Austin: University of Texas Press, 2006); Thomas T. Smith, Jerry D. Thompson, Robert Wooster, and Ben E. Pingenot, "San Antonio and the Secessionists, 1861–1862: From the Reminiscences of Maj. Gen. Zenas R. Bliss," *Southwestern Historical Quarterly* 110 (July 2006): 69–108.

36. Brad Clampitt, "Camp Groce, Texas: A Confederate Prison," *Southwestern Historical Quarterly* 104 (Jan. 2001): 365–84; Danial Francis Lisarelli, *The Untold Story of Camp Groce CSA* (Boca Raton, Fla.: Universal, 1999); James M. Smallwood, "Prison City, Camp Ford: Largest Confederate Prisoner-of-War Camp in the Trans-Mississippi," in Howell, *Seventh Star*, 208–25.

37. Charles D. Grear, "Red and White Fighting the Blue: Relations between Texans and Confederate Indians," in Howell, *Seventh Star*, 167–88.

38. Marcus E. Johnson, "Responding to the Exigencies of War: The Supreme Court of Texas during the Civil War" (M.A. thesis, Baylor University, 2001); Vicki Betts, "'A Sacred Charge upon Our Hands': Assisting the Families of Confederate Soldiers in Texas, 1861–1865," in Howell, *Seventh Star*, 246–67; Kenneth E. Hendrickson, Jr., "The Confederate Governors of Texas," in Howell, *Seventh Star*, 228–45; Clayton E. Jewett, *Rise and Fall of the Confederacy: The Memoir of Senator Williamson S. Oldham, CSA* (Columbia: University of Missouri Press, 2006).

39. David S. Stieghan, "The Confederate Rifle Makers of Texas" (M.A. thesis, Stephen F. Austin State University, 1996); Carol Taylor, "Feed the Troops or Fight the Drought: The Dilemma Texas Beef Contractors Faced in 1861–1865," in Howell, *Seventh Star*, 287–300; Ely, "Gone from Texas."

40. Paul A. Levengood, "In the Absence of Scarcity: the Civil War Prosperity of Houston, Texas," *Southwestern Historical Quarterly* 101 (Apr. 1998): 401–26; Stephen Chicoine, *The Confederates of Chappell Hill, Texas: Prosperity, Civil War, and Decline* (Jefferson, N.C.: McFarland, 2005); Bill Stein, "Distress, Discontent, and Dissent: Colorado County, Texas, during the Civil War," in Howell, *Seventh Star*, 301–16.

41. Ronald E. Goodwin and Bruce A. Glasrud, "On the Edge of First Freedoms: Black Texans and the Civil War," in Howell, *Seventh Star*, 268–86; Dale Baum, "Slaves Taken to Texas for Safekeeping during the Civil War," in Grear, *Fate of Texas*, 83–104; Angela Boswell, "The Civil War and the Lives of Texas Women," in Grear, *Fate of Texas*, 69–82; Richard G. Lowe, "Warriors, Husbands, and Fathers: Confederate Soldiers and Their Families," in Grear, *Fate of Texas*, 25–36. For primary sources related to life on the home front, see Erika L. Murr, ed., *A Rebel Wife in Texas: The Diary and Letters of Elizabeth*

Scott Neblett, 1852–1864 (Baton Rouge: Louisiana State University Press, 2001); M. Jane Johansson, *Widows by the Thousand: The Civil War Letters of Theophilus and Harriet Perry, 1862–1864* (Fayetteville University of Arkansas Press, 2000); Bruce S. Cheesman, ed., *Maria von Blücher's Corpus Christi: Letters from the South Texas Frontier, 1849–1879* (College Station: Texas A&M University Press, 2002); Paula Mitchell Marks, *When Will the Weary War Be Over? The Civil War Letters of the Maverick Family of San Antonio* (Dallas: Book Club of Texas, 2008); Michael R. Haslip, ed., *Sketches of Kate James: Dallas County Pioneer* (Garland, Tex.: Garland Landmark Society, 2009); and Ginny McNeill Raska and Mary Lynne Gasaway Hill, eds., *The Uncompromising Diary of Sallie McNeill, 1858–1867* (College Station: Texas A&M University Press, 2009).

42. Randolph B. Campbell, "After the Surrender: The Postwar Experiences of Confederate Veterans in Harrison County, Texas," in Grear, *Fate of Texas*, 121–36.

43. Carl H. Moneyhon and Bobby Roberts, *Portraits of Conflict: A Photographic History of Texas in the Civil War* (Fayetteville: University of Arkansas Press, 1998); Jerry Thompson and Lawrence T. Jones III, *Civil War and Revolution on the Rio Grande Frontier: A Narrative and Photographic History* (Austin: Texas State Historical Association, 2004).

44. Alexander Mendoza, "Cause Lost but Not Forgotten: George Washington Littlefield, Jefferson Davis, and Confederate Memories at the University of Texas at Austin," in Grear, *Fate of Texas*, 155–80; Kelly McMichael, *Sacred Memories: The Civil War Monument Movement in Texas* (Denton: Texas State Historical Association, 2009); Julie Holcomb, "'Tell It Like It Was': Texas, the Civil War, and Public History," in Grear, *Fate of Texas*, 181–96.

45. Charles W. Ramsdell, *Reconstruction in Texas* (New York: Columbia University Press, 1910); William C. Nunn, *Texas under the Carpetbaggers* (Austin: University of Texas Press, 1962).

46. David Work, "United States Colored Troops in Texas during Reconstruction, 1865–1867," *Southwestern Historical Quarterly* 109 (Jan. 2006): 337–57.

47. Barry Crouch, *Freedmen's Bureau and Black Texans* (Austin: University of Texas Press, 1992), and *The Dance of Freedom: Texas African Americans during Reconstruction*, ed. Larry Madaras (Austin: University of Texas Press, 2007); Christopher Bean, "'A Most Singular and Interesting Attempt': The Freedmen's Bureau at Marshall, Texas," *Southwestern Historical Quarterly* 110 (Apr. 2007): 465–85, and "A Stranger amongst Strangers: An Analysis of the Freedmen's Bureau Subassistant Commissioners in Texas, 1865–1868" (Ph.D. diss., University of North Texas, 2008); William C. Richter, "'The Raider Rules the Day': Colonel DeWitt C. Brown and the Freedmen's Bureau in Paris, Texas, 1867–1868," *Southwestern Historical Quarterly* 93 (Jan. 1990): 303–32, and *Overreached on All Sides: The Freedmen's Bureau Administrators in Texas, 1865–1868* (College Station: Texas A&M University Press, 1991).

48. Nancy Cohen-Lack, "A Struggle for Sovereignty: National Consolidation, Emancipation, and Free Labor in Texas, 1865," *Journal of Southern History* 58 (Feb. 1992): 57–98.

49. Thad Sitton and James H. Conrad, *Freedom Colonies: Independent Black Texans in the Time of Jim Crow* (Austin: University of Texas Press, 2005); Dale Baum, "Burdens of Landholding in a Freed Slave Settlement: The Case of Brazos County's 'Hall's Town,'"

Southwestern Historical Quarterly 113 (Oct. 2009): 185–204, and *Counterfeit Justice: The Judicial Odyssey of Texas Freedwoman Azeline Hearne* (Baton Rouge: Louisiana State University Press, 2009).

50. Charles A. Israel, "From Biracial to Segregated Churches: Black and White Protestants in Houston, Texas, 1840–1870," *Southwestern Historical Quarterly* 101 (Apr. 1998): 429–58.

51. Randolph B. Campbell, "The District Judges of Texas in 1866–1867: An Episode in the Failure of Presidential Reconstruction," *Southwestern Historical Quarterly* 93 (Jan. 1990): 357–77; Barry A. Crouch, "All the Vile Passions: The Texas Black Codes of 1866," *Southwestern Historical Quarterly* 97 (July 1993): 13–34.

52. Barry A. Crouch, "Hesitant Recognition: Texas Black Politicians, 1865–1900," *East Texas Historical Journal* 31 (Spring 1993): 41–58; Randolph B. Campbell, "Scalawag District Judges: The E. J. Davis Appointees," *Houston Review* 14, no. 2 (1992): 75–88, and "George W. Whitemore: East Texas Unionist," *East Texas Historical Journal* 28 (1990): 17–28.

53. Dale Baum, "Chicanery and Intimidation in the 1869 Gubernatorial Race," *Southwestern Historical Quarterly* 97 (July 1993): 37–54.

54. Barry A. Crouch and Donaly E. Brice, *The Governor's Hounds: The Texas State Police, 1870–1873* (Austin: University of Texas Press, 2011).

55. Kenneth W. Howell, ed., *Still the Arena of Civil War: Violence and Turmoil in Reconstruction Texas, 1865–1874* (Denton: University of North Texas Press, 2012).

56. Barry A. Crouch and Donaly E. Brice, *Cullen Montgomery Baker, Reconstruction Desperado* (Baton Rouge: Louisiana State University Press, 1997); Kenneth M. Hamilton, "White Wealth and Black Repression in Harrison County, Texas: 1865–1868," *Journal of Negro History* 84 (Autumn 1999): 340–59.

57. Gregg Cantrell, "Racial Violence and Reconstruction Politics in Texas, 1867–1868," *Southwestern Historical Quarterly* 93 (Jan. 1990): 333–55; James Hathcock, "The Role of Violence in Hunt County, Texas, during Reconstruction" (M.A. thesis, University of North Texas, 2004); Christopher B. Bean, "Death of a Carpetbagger: The George Washington Smith Murder and Stockade Trial in Jefferson, Texas, 1868–1869," *Southwestern Historical Quarterly* 112 (Jan. 2009): 263–92; James M. Smallwood, Barry A. Crouch, and Larry Peacock, *Murder and Mayhem: The War of Reconstruction in Texas* (College Station: Texas A&M University Press, 2003).

58. Rebecca Kosary, "To Degrade and Control: White Violence and the Maintenance of Racial and Gender Boundaries in Reconstruction Texas, 1865–1868" (Ph.D. diss.: Texas A&M University, 2006).

59. Chuck Parsons, *The Sutton-Taylor Feud: The Deadliest Blood Feud in Texas* (Denton: University of North Texas Press, 2009).

60. Lance Cooper, "'A Slobbering Lame Thing'? The Semicolon Case Reconsidered," *Southwestern Historical Quarterly* 101 (Jan. 1998): 321–39; Carl H. Moneyhon, "Edmund J. Davis in the Coke-Davis Election Dispute of 1874: A Reassessment of Character," *Southwestern Historical Quarterly* 100 (Oct. 1996): 131–51.

61. Patrick G. Williams, *Beyond Redemption: Texas Democrats after Reconstruction* (College Station: Texas A&M University Press, 2007).

62. Randolph B. Campbell, *Grass-Roots Reconstruction in Texas, 1865–1880* (Baton Rouge: Louisiana State University Press, 1997).

63. Kenneth Kesselus, *History of Bastrop County, Texas, during Reconstruction* (Bastrop, Tex.: Wash Jones Press, 2011); Leslie Lovett, "The Jaybird-Woodpecker War: Reconstruction and Redemption in Fort Bend County, Texas, 1869–1889" (M.A. thesis, Rice University, 1994); Bill Stein, "Consider the Lily: The Ungilded History of Colorado County, Texas," *Nesbitt Memorial Library Journal: A Journal of Colorado County History* 9 (Jan. 1999): pt. 7, 3–39; vol. 10 (Jan. 2000): pt. 8, 3–62; Robert J. Robertson, *Her Majesty's Texans: Two English Immigrants in Reconstruction Texas* (College Station: Texas A&M University Press, 1998).

64. Carl H. Moneyhon, *Texas after the Civil War: The Struggle of Reconstruction in Texas* (College Station: Texas A&M University Press, 2004).

65. Kenneth Wayne Howell, *Texas Confederate, Reconstruction Governor: James Webb Throckmorton* (College Station: Texas A&M University Press, 2008); Lewis L. Gould, *Alexander Watkins Terrell: Civil War Soldier, Texas Lawmaker, American Diplomat* (Austin: University of Texas Press, 2004); A. Christian Klemme, "The Rise, Fall, and Redemption of Oran M. Roberts" (M.A. thesis, University of North Texas, 2004); Dede Casad, "The Lives and Legacies of Two Texas Governors, Richard Coke and Lawrence Sullivan Ross. Two Governors: A Comparative Study" (Ph.D. diss., University of Texas at Dallas, 2001).

66. Carl H. Moneyhon, *Edmund J. Davis: Texas Unionist, Civil War General, Republican Governor* (Fort Worth: Texas Christian University Press, 2010).

67. John Anthony Moretta, *William Pitt Ballinger: Texas Lawyer, Southern Statesman, 1825–1888* (Austin: Texas Historical Association, 2000); Philip Caudill, *Moss Bluff Rebel: A Texas Pioneer in the Civil War* (College Station: Texas A&M University Press, 2009).

68. Jerry Thompson, *Cortina: Defending the Mexican Name in Texas* (College Station: Texas A&M University Press, 2007); Charles M. Robinson III, *Satanta: The Life and Death of a War Chief* (Austin: State House Press, 1997).

69. Margaret Swett Henson and Deolece Parmalee, *The Cartwrights of San Augustine: Three Generations of Agricultural Entrepreneurs in Nineteenth-Century Texas* (Austin: Texas State Historical Association, 1993); Harold M. Hyman, *Oleander Odyssey: The Kempners of Galveston, Texas, 1854–1980s* (College Station: Texas A&M University Press, 1990).

70. Sean M. Kelley, "Plantation Frontiers: Race, Ethnicity, and Family along the Brazos River of Texas, 1821–1886" (Ph.D. diss., University of Texas at Austin, 2000).

71. Ty Cashion, *A Texas Frontier: The Clear Fork Country and Fort Griffin, 1849–1887* (Norman: University of Oklahoma Press, 1966).

72. Kyle Grant Wilkison, "The End of Independence: Social and Political Consequences of Economic Change in Texas, 1870–1914" (Ph.D. diss., Vanderbilt University, 1995); Michael Moore, "Settler, Slaves, Sharecroppers and Stockhands: A Texas Plantation-Ranch, 1824–1896" (M.A. thesis, University of Houston, 2001); Don Graham, *Kings of Texas: The 150-Year Saga of an American Ranching Empire* (New York: John Wiley and Sons, 2003).

73. Kenneth L. Stewart and Arnoldo De León, *Not Room Enough: Mexicans, Anglos, and Socioeconomic Change in Texas, 1850–1900* (Albuquerque: University of New Mexico Press, 1993).

74. Angela Boswell, *Her Acts and Deeds: Women's Lives in a Rural Southern County, 1837–1873* (College Station: Texas A&M University Press, 2001); Paula Mitchell Marks, *Hands to the Spindle: Texas Women and Home Textile Production, 1822–1880* (College Station: Texas A&M University Press, 1996); Francelle Pruitt, "'But a Mournful Remedy': Divorce in Two Texas Counties, 1841–1880" (M.A. thesis, University of North Texas, 1999); Margaret Breashears, "An Analysis of Status: Women in Texas, 1860–1920" (M.A. thesis, University of North Texas, 1999).

75. Linda S. Newland, "The Persistence of Antebellum Planter Families in Postbellum East Texas" (M.A. thesis, University of North Texas, 1998).

CHAPTER 12

Reformers, Populists, and Progressives, 1875–1915

Jessica Brannon-Wranosky

The close of Reconstruction, ironically, was more of a beginning for Texas reform activism than an end. At a time when Bourbon Democrats had positioned themselves to retake total control of state, and for that matter regional, politics, cracks in their pedestals of power began to emerge in the form of dissenters—people refusing to return to Old South–style society and politics. The Lone Star State's residential composition had changed demographically and politically since the eve of the Civil War. In many ways, the increased diversity created the opportunity for a variety of groups to question the power structure long dominated by planter-class white men. Questioning did not equate to removing, though, and no one factor or theme dominated Texas more during the years between Reconstruction and the Roaring Twenties (1875–1920) than the tug of war between generations of conservatives and reformers.

In the past twenty years, academics have produced a vast array of published material discussing the different facets of reformer's lives and activities in Texas in the late nineteenth and early twentieth centuries. In addition to the increased amount of work covering this period are the historical acknowledgments and discoveries of the new layers of heterogeneity that existed in Texas during these decades. Several previous, now definitive, works on Texas activism in the decades after Reconstruction continue to be influential in the development of the field. Any historiographical overview that did not take a moment to acknowledge some of these important studies and their authors would be incomplete.

Some of these earlier studies absolutely necessary for individuals looking to increase their knowledge of late nineteenth- and early twentieth-century reform in Texas are Alwyn Barr's *Reconstruction to Reform*, Merline Pitre's *Through Many Dangers Toils and Snares*, Robert McMath's *Populist Vanguard*, and Lewis Gould's *Progressives and Prohibitionists*. Additionally, though not specifically about Texas, Robert Wiebe's *Search for Order, 1877–1920* continues to have an immense influence on the discussion of Gilded Age–Progressive Era activism in theoretical structure, but in very broad national strokes. Recent scholarship has built upon these and other influential works by examining how enormously diverse communities of reformers actually were and how varied were the avenues for change. As is usually the case, to understand the current historiographical trends one has to be familiar with their rhetorical foundation.[1]

Depending on the subject matter and the community discussed, historians have started to indicate that there were three chronological periods separating different types of reform during these decades. The first, the age of grassroots reform, lasted through the late 1880s before many of the statewide reform associations were organized. The second, the People's Party decade and the rise of the reform faction of the Texas Democratic Party, lasted somewhere between the early 1890s into the first decade after the turn of the twentieth century. Finally, the era of the progressive Democratic Party faction began by the end of the first decade of the twentieth century and ran at least until 1920.

The first period's grassroots and early reformers are more easily defined by those they were reacting to than by a single thread or developmental model, because they acted in limited and somewhat isolated and individualistic or localized ways. These individuals (and local groups) were often trying to get the Redeemer Democrats to institute change or remove them altogether from power. Thus, the chronological period belonging to the grassroots reformer era in Texas coincides with what historian Patrick Williams describes as the Redeemer "generation of Democrats that had come of age by 1861, engineered Reconstruction's collapse during the 1870s, and continued to dominate Texas politics until the election of James S. Hogg as governor in 1890."[2]

In *Beyond Redemption*, Patrick Williams discusses these "Redeemer" or "Bourbon" Democrats who reclaimed control over state affairs at the end of Reconstruction. These planter-class conservatives claimed that their regained rule would differ enormously from that of Reconstruction Texas and that along with low taxes and debt reduction this group promised to usher in a better and more efficient state. Yet within a few years these Democrats began to realize that to make their claims materialize was not going to be as easy as they thought.

The state fell further into debt despite cuts in government-sponsored programs, including law enforcement and education. The centralized political control exercised by state Democratic Party leaders was not unusual for former Confederate states, argues Williams. Yet, the enormous growth in the state's population from new settlers meant that a growing number of Texans were not on board or at least not automatically deferent to the state's political power structure. Instead, a disconnect between the state's leaders and much of the general population existed, and many in the state became increasingly disenchanted with the Redeemer/Bourbon/conservative Democrats and looked for other solutions and reform. By the 1880s, Texas reformers began to act—especially at the grassroots level. Though Williams does not prescribe to examining the Texas Democratic Party by looking at internal factions, the Redeemer party leaders were this generation's placeholders for future generations of conservative Democrats.

Walter Buenger, in *The Path to a Modern South*, examines one of the areas of the state in which there was a concentration of reform activists in the late nineteenth century, northeastern Texas. This book is a wealth of local history information. Yet readers should not misinterpret this study as one with a short reach or limited application. Instead, Buenger inspects the development of the New South through a local lens and argues that the larger southern linear deviation from residual antebellum leftovers can be ascertained by focusing on this specific area of Texas. In other words, if you look at northeastern Texas during this period, it becomes clear the steps the South took to become the New South. As part of his argument, Buenger follows several grassroots reform groups, which he describes as "factions," that fought against conservative Democratic control in Texas during these decades. By 1887, he writes, "Northeast Texas fell into roughly five groups . . . conservatives, social reformers, economic reformers, insurgents, and black Republicans."[3]

Within Buenger's different factions were groups looking to solidify their connections and project different agendas toward reform. In *No Saloon in the Valley*, James D. Ivy examines the development of one of the earliest statewide social reform movements—temperance/prohibition. Beginning with a visit and 1882 tour of the state by Frances Willard, national president of the Women's Christian Temperance Union, Ivy explains how Texas grassroots organizing of local WCTU chapters grew to form networks of reformers fighting against alcohol abuse and conservative political supporters of keeping Texas "wet." The author argues that soon after the WCTU began to establish in the state, unlike at the national level, Texas men started to take the lead in the fight for increased prohibition regulations. Women continued to hold the central offices for the Texas WCTU and affiliated local chapters, but men directed the politicization of the larger cause and connected organizations including a single-issue reform political party, the Prohibition Party. Ivy's argument, though, should not lead readers to believe that Texas women were apolitical during these years.[4]

On the contrary, as Jessica Brannon-Wranosky explains in the first portion of her dissertation, "Southern Promise and Necessity," and in a forthcoming contribution to the University of Georgia's series Southern Women, after a period of individual advocacy for woman suffrage during Reconstruction, woman suffragists in the Lone Star State started traveling and organizing grassroots women's rights activities across Texas. In some cases, reformers worked exclusively under the auspices of woman suffrage work, whereas other activists often advocated women's voting rights as part of their efforts on behalf of temperance, labor, or other political and social issues. These grassroots activities created alliances with the national women's rights associations, the American Woman Suffrage Association and the National Woman Suffrage Association, and were enormously important in educating local audiences on information about the need for women's voting rights. Brannon-Wranosky illustrates that by doing so reformers gathered support, made contact with other activists, and slowly chipped away at social and cultural resistance. Thus, their efforts provided a foundation for the next stage of suffrage organizing—the creation of a state and local woman suffrage reform associations during the 1890s.[5]

As Elizabeth Hayes Turner finds in her study, *Women, Culture, and Community in Galveston Texas, 1880–1920*, reaction to Democratic Party rule or patriarchal dominance was not always the stimulus for the beginning of grassroots organizing and reform. Her study highlights that women's urban church auxiliaries created outreach networks and began to provide neighborhood and city-level aid to residents as cities grew and their populations diversified. As these women's aid groups further solidified their associational organization into a systematic method of social service, around the turn of the twentieth century, their orderly progressivism provided the foundation for emergency services and urban rebuilding after the 1900 hurricane that almost wiped out Galveston. Turner's study encompasses the leaps between reform generations into that of the progressives. Founders of the nineteenth-century aid associations passed the reigns to younger civic activists who either added new purpose to existing clubs or founded their own. Thus, Turner argues, the associational evolution further blossomed as Galveston's women leaders participated in the formation of larger more powerful groups, including the Texas Federation of Women's Clubs, the state woman suffrage associations, and their Galveston affiliates.[6]

Elizabeth Enstam, in *Women and the Creation of Urban Life*, finds that Dallas's ladies aid and benevolent society reform efforts, like those in Galveston, most often grew from members' connections or experiences within women's church auxiliaries. Yet, as both Turner's and Enstam's books also firmly establish, just because some of the early women's citywide networks formed on platforms of more social reform did not disqualify these groups or their future members from participating in a variety of political reform movements, including women's rights activities. By nature, this type of reform was a direct rejection of conservative male dominance at the local, state, and national levels.[7]

Additionally, the conservatism against which some Texan reformers fought was not always limited to a faction of the Texas Democratic Party. During the years after Reconstruction, levels of racial and ethnic discrimination and violence increased across the South and the nation—including Texas. In *Catarino Garza's Revolution on the Texas-Mexico Border*, Elliott Young provides a detailed analysis of one grassroots reformer's quest to combat nativist and ethnic discrimination north of the United States–Mexico border and corrupt procorporate policies of Mexico's president Porfirio Díaz. The Díaz regime, often referred to as the Porfiriato, lasted from 1876 until 1911, when he was forcibly removed by Mexican revolutionaries. The revolution lasted from 1910 to 1920, but Garza started speaking out against and fighting the Porfiriato decades before. During his revolutionary attempt, though unsuccessful, Garza made similar charges as those voiced by later revolutionaries, including that Díaz's attempt to modernize Mexico came at the price of selling the country piecemeal and allowing foreign corporate interests to enslave the Mexican people. Furthermore, while the nation's resources and citizen labor were being handed to foreign investors, the only individuals benefiting from the relationships were the corporate heads and political elites of the Porfiriato. Young suggests that these earlier attempts to oust Díaz were essential in building grassroots support for the later successful revolution. Interestingly, the same conservative agrarian Democratic Party leaders whom other Texan reform groups rallied against also proved to be the allies north of the border to whom Díaz fled in exile. The purpose of Young's study is, in fact, to illustrate the transnational nature of some reform messages.[8]

Thad Sitton and James Conrad's *Freedom Colonies* explores the creation of black towns as a grassroots social and cultural reform movement from the late nineteenth through the mid-twentieth century. The book details many of the towns' locations and the elements that made up the daily lives of their residents. To create a separate existence in order to escape many of the limitations and dangers of Jim Crow America, many African Americans created opportunities for political and civic leadership control over community schools and churches and increased safety in both public and private life. Sitton and Conrad provide chapters on education, land acquisition and ownership, and the establishment of community churches in Texas black towns.[9]

Freedom Colonies is not an exhaustive study, though, as the authors readily point out, and there is room for much more study on the subject in both Texas and other areas of the United States. The autonomy and safety gained by self-segregated communities during the Jim Crow era appear to have provided, at least for a time, increased opportunities for success. Yet there were also sacrifices. This type of community removal was similar to what would be called in the twenty-first century "going off the grid." This equated to a community level of self-reliance that often also resulted to limited resources. Jim Crow–based separation, in either forced or voluntary forms, also came with a price. As Debra A. Reid examines in *Reaping a Greater Harvest*, white Texans used, for example, their segregated access to research funding and institutions of higher education to establish improved agricultural practices. Not having access to these scientific advancements and knowledge, black farming communities were thus placed at a growing disadvantage. This was not a reality only for black towns but for all African Americans and other minorities.[10]

A series of groups representing some of these political power minorities attempted a national political coup against the dominant Democratic and Republican parties during the 1890s, resulting in the brief existence of one of the most successful third parties in U.S. history—the People's/Populist Party. Rarely do political histories discuss these years and not give some mention of the effect populists had on the environment run by campaigning, elections, and legislative actions. During a time of heighted urbanization and industrialization complicated by a nationwide economic depression peaking in 1893, labor organizations and mutual aid farmer's associations began aligning into the national People's Party. Many Texans were intimately involved in every stage of this political building, and in 1891 Texas experienced the creation of its state-level People's Party, which lasted into 1897. A series of classic studies released prior to the 1990s looked to explain the Populists, their limited success, and subsequent demise. Yet in recent years historians have begun to provide a further diversified look at the multifaceted populist movement.

In his *Populist Vision*, Charles Postel examines the movement from a national scale and in the first part of the book traces its activism back to the reform era that followed Reconstruction. His attention to the grassroots populist political activism through agrarian union/cooperative associations during the 1870s and 1880s places this book as one that examines activism during both the grassroots and the 1890s reform periods. Postel argues that Populist/People's Party founders by the 1890s envisioned a confederation of industrial organizations with the purpose of systematically aligning the Farmers' Alliance and Industrial Union, the National Farmers' Alliance, the Colored Farmers' Alliance, the Farmers' Mutual Benefit Association, the Knights of Labor, the Women's Alliance, the Citizen's Alliance, and other reform groups. This confederation, which became the national political party shortly after its first meetings, built on a foundation established by its affiliate organizations through local grassroots activities and association building during the previous decades. An article by Worth Robert Miller and Stacy G. Ulbig, "Building a Populist Coalition in Texas, 1892–1896," also looks at coalition building, but at a much closer scale, focusing on events specifically in Texas and during the height of populist activity. Together, these two works provide an excellent view of organizational process and political networking.[11]

Kenneth and John B. Rayner and the Limits of Southern Dissent and *Feeding the Wolf: John B. Rayner and the Politics of Race*, both by Gregg Cantrell, dive into the discussion of populists and race. John B. Rayner was Texas's central African American Populist leader. His father, Kenneth, had been an important white political figure and active supporter of the Whig Party and then Republican during the post–Civil War era. In both books, Cantrell discusses the importance of race-based rhetoric and political connections in the activities of third-party politics in Texas. Twenty-first-century researchers and history enthusiasts seeking recent works on Texas populism should start with these two names—Cantrell and Postel. Cantrell also has a book forthcoming from Yale University Press on the People's Party in Texas, which promises to be an excellent coverage of the third-party movement. Together, Cantrell's books and *Populist Vision* cover the ins and out of the decade's third-party politics but also bring new and much needed discussion to the table by delving into the gendered, racial, and labor dynamics that shaped and were defined by populist activism.[12]

Added to this group of important works on Texas populism are Worth Robert Miller's "Building a Progressive Coalition in Texas" and Kyle G. Wilkison's

Yeomen, Sharecroppers, and Socialists. Collectively these two pieces look at the political and social directions taken by some populists after the fall of the movement. The void left at the end of previous works suggested by omission that People's Party supporters simply faded into their rural surroundings and lost interest in politics all together after the 1896 series of election losses. Not so, argue Miller and Wilkison. Instead, Miller points out that reform faction Democratic Party leaders approached some of the former Populist leaders to try to mend cracks in their foundation and solidify reform Democratic control permanently. In the process, after the turn of the century some of these former Populists became involved in supporting the creation of a series of election laws, known as the Terrell Laws, which attempted to remove the questionable means conservative Democrats had used to control elections. In doing so they began the systematic disfranchisement of black voters. Wilkison's book, on the other hand, follows the twentieth-century northeastern Texans at the local level who exemplified the archetype "common man" and made up the majority of populist supporters during the late nineteenth century. He finds that after the fall of the People's Party the lives of small farmers began to change, in part because of the economy, urbanization, and political trends out of their control. Many of these individuals had to find new livelihoods or move to new locations to survive.[13]

One of the areas of populist Texas history that still needs increased attention is women and gender research. A chapter in Cantrell's forthcoming book and one in Postel's book on gender and women in the Populist movement are good moves in that direction. Additionally, *Women in the Texas Populist Movement* is a collection of women's letters to the Texas Populist news organ, the *Southern Mercury*. Edited by Marion K. Barthelme, this is an enormously useful source on the topic. A biographical article on Populist leader Ellen Lawson Dabbs by Ruth Karbach also brings light to the subject. And Brannon-Wranosky's 1890s chapter in "Southern Promise and Necessity" illustrates that woman suffrage organizing included women from all three political parties in Texas during this decade—the Democratic, the Republican, and the People's. This portion of the study finds that the political schism between parties was one reason the first woman suffrage association in Texas, the Texas Equal Rights Association, eventually crumbled. Many of the suffragists during this decade were Populists, and thus this is a source of information on women in the movement. Overall, even though a few have started chipping away at this area of discussion, there is still a need for a full study on Texas Populist women.[14]

In the past two decades, historians have also focused on a broader sense of reform at the end of the nineteenth century in addition to the populist revolt. Leading much of this direction have been scholars who discuss different aspects of the clubwoman movement in Texas, which began to organize during the 1890s out of existing local ties from church and temperance associations. Turner and Enstam look closely at the interconnected dynamics of certain urban environments as springboards for local, state, and national women's activism in their examinations of Galveston and Dallas. Judith N. McArthur's book and Megan Seaholm's dissertation take a broader approach by dissecting women's civic activity starting in the 1890s and running through 1920. McArthur's *Creating the New Woman* follows Texas women from their 1890s work with the WCTU and local church societies through their involvement with the Texas Federation of Women's Clubs to their involvement with suffrage and their success with winning Texas primary suffrage in 1918. Turner's, McArthur's, and Enstam's books add an important historiographical element to the discussion of Progressive Era Texas and southern women's history.[15]

Jeffrey Zemler's "The Texas State Building and the Women's World's Fair Exhibit Association of Texas" takes the timeline established by Turner, McArthur, and others back even further to the dawn of the decade. His study uncovers civic booster activities tying women from across the state together during the campaign to ensure Texas representation at the 1893 World's Fair. This study provides a look at many of the women who became the founding leaders of the Texas Federation of Women's Literary Clubs in 1897, which changed its name to the Texas Federation of Women's Clubs in 1899, but in connection with civic activism years before the creation of the Texas Federation or its entry into progressive reform.[16]

The 1890s were also the decade during which the study of Texas history emerged as a version of educational reform. As Richard McCaslin discusses in *At the Heart of Texas*, the birth of the Texas State Historical Association started with the dual purpose of preserving the state's heritage and encouraging an academic study of history as part of the progressive professionalism movement. During the same period, as McArthur explains, the Texas Federation of Women's Clubs and affiliated organizations began establishing public libraries across the state. This initiative also led to the establishment of the Texas State Library and Archives, as David B. Gracy explores in *The State Library and Archives of Texas*. As part of this historical preservation trend during the 1890s, heritage associations in Texas began to link local and state auxiliaries to national associations. Those in Texas included the United Daughters of the Confederacy, which Kelly McMichael Stott discusses in her dissertation, and the Daughters of the Republic of Texas, which Mark Fish highlights in his biographical dissertation on Mary Jones. These heritage and historically minded organizations—just as much about posterity as the past—increasingly aimed toward progressive measures after the turn of the twentieth century.[17]

Historians who delineate between the reform and populist generation and that of the progressives in Texas history define the beginning of the state's "Progressive Era" sometime between 1907 and 1911. Some historians define its beginnings at the time when the old reformers and next generation of progressives in the Texas Democratic Party garnered enough support to gain control of the gubernatorial primary and get Thomas Campbell nominated and subsequently elected. Others often refer to the 1911 meeting of the University of Texas Alumni (eventually to be called Texas Exes). At this alum meeting, organizers and speakers addressed political and social issues of the period and began carving out progressive political space, using the university as both a locale and rallying point to begin a full-scale assault on the state's conservative political machine. Janet Schmelzer's new biography on Thomas Campbell, *Our Fighting Governor*, fills an important void and adds to this discussion. Beyond this historiographical debate, though, it has become accepted that the gray space between 1907 and 1911 was the corridor for the next generation to enter into debates and fights with conservatives.[18]

This new generation saw both the creation of new reform networks and the transition of existing ones. Included in these was the renewed and largest woman suffrage push in state history and the continued rise of clubwomen's activities in multiple forms and through various venues. Judith N. McArthur and Harold L. Smith's *Minnie Fisher Cunningham* provides an analysis of Progressive Era activism and woman suffrage reform through a biographical lens. This essential book for those looking at twentieth-century reform networks focuses on one of the century's most politically active Texans. By following the life of "Minnie Fish," a nickname given to her by Franklin Delano Roosevelt, the authors highlight several Progressive Era movements including the last stages of votes-for-women activity in the Lone Star State. Additionally, this biography uncovers an enormous amount regarding what happened to progressives after 1920 and the effect progressive thought had on politics during the 1920s, New Deal reforms, 1950s politics, and beyond.[19]

Some progressive reforms or endeavors begun during this decade, between 1910 and 1920, continued into the following decades, thus broadening the effect Texas reformers had on the state's history. For example, Bernadette Pruitt's article in the *Journal of Urban History* and her book *The Other Great Migration* show that African Americans often moved from the rural South to urban areas in the region seeking new environments for opportunity. This action was a source of reform because it created potential by changing the migrant's lives and the cities in which they settled. Pruitt's work also adds enormously to the growing historiography on the "Great Migration" by showing that African American migration during these years was not aimed exclusively at Northeast and Midwest cities.[20]

In his dissertation "Portrait of a Southern Progressive," Mark Stanley follows Texas Speaker of the House, governor, and reformer Pat Neff in a political biography that places Neff at the center of several reform and progressive circles and movements in Texas and the larger South. Like McArthur and Smith, Pruitt, and others, Stanley shows that not all reformers' activities were confined to one generation of change. Instead, Neff got his political start as a Texas House of Representatives member, and then Speaker, during the early progressive period. Then, after a break from state politics, he reentered activism in the name of prohibition on the eve of ratification of the Eighteenth Amendment by Texas progressives. He was elected governor in 1920 and 1922 and later became president of Baylor University. Many of the state's progressive environmental reforms instituted during the 1920s and continuing into the 1930s have a Neff connection.[21]

Many of the reform and progressive legacies created in Texas during these years were established as part of financial trusts. Reform Democrat James "Jim" Hogg had been at the center of the reform community in the 1890s. After his gubernatorial terms he entered private practice and an oil speculation partnership in Houston (which became Texaco after his death), and it paid off enormously. The wealth and industrial holdings he and his children propagated were part of a larger industrial growth that changed the face of the nation and much of the world during these decades. After his death in 1906, son William "Will" Hogg assumed the leadership of the Hogg empire and direction. This included being the lead political voice of the family. William was the next generation, a progressive. The family money was used for three purposes—funding family indulgences and creating and preserving both a civic and a political family legacy. To the civic legacy Will's only sister, Ima Hogg, and one of his younger brothers, Mike, participated adamantly. Kate Sayen Kirkland delves into the formation and reach of the Hogg family's civic legacy in *The Hogg Family and Houston*. By placing the family in the realm of the financial social investors of the period, she highlights how reform-minded families backed with industrially produced wealth changed the face of the Lone Star State and the nation.[22]

That these multigenerational reform endeavors and progressive measures continued after the traditionally defined Progressive Era has often led historians to rethink the limitations of the predetermined "progressive" box. Historian Robert S. Maxwell, for example, argues that the Progressive Era in Texas actually lasted through the 1920s. There is more room in this discussion for future works to take a stand or at least offer an opinion. Additionally, another often used descriptor for southern progressivism and Texas progressivism comes from southern historian C. Vann Woodward—the idea of progressivism "for whites only." Scholars need to be careful not to let the discriminatory practices of many white progressives limit the depth of the era's research to investigation of Anglos as sources of progressive reform. Recent works have begun to highlight how ethnically and racially diverse progressive reformers in the South actually were.[23]

Tejano progressive José Tomás Canales, ironically, got his start as part of the conservative Democratic Party machine, as Richard Henry Ribb outlines in his dissertation on Canales's early reform activities. The further Canales moved into state politics, though, the further he aligned with issues championed by the reform and progressive factions of the party. As Ribb argues, by the end of the 1910s this state representative was using the power of his office to press a full investigation and subsequent reorganization of the Texas Rangers in connection with repeated violent actions against Tejanos in South Texas.[24]

The First Waco Horror, by Patricia Bernstein, also discusses the work of progressives in Texas against mob violence after the lynching of Jesse Washington in Waco, Texas, in 1916. The seventeen-year-old's violent death made national news and caught the attention of W. E. B. DuBois and other National Association for the Advancement of Colored People leaders. DuBois asked woman suffragist Elisabeth Freeman, who was already in Texas on a suffrage speaking and organizing tour, to investigate the incident. *The First Waco Horror* gives a detailed account of the lynching, Freeman's investigation, and the aftermath. Bernstein argues that the NAACP's involvement and activist efforts in the lynching helped to shape its methods and national notoriety.[25]

In conclusion, although there has been a large rise in the histories covering areas of post-Reconstruction reform and conservative activity in Texas over the past twenty years, there are countless holes still left to fill. For example, the president who took the helm of the Colored Division of the national Woman's Christian Temperance Union in 1898, Eliza E. Peterson, lived in Texarkana. She traveled the United States for well over a decade gaining support and members in the African American community. Peterson was in the process of visiting

Harriet Tubman and was among a limited few at the abolitionist icon's bedside when Tubman died. Despite how famous and well-connected Peterson seems to have been, we know almost nothing about her or African American activism in the temperance movement. Moreover, work still needs to be done on the Texas Association of Colored Women's Clubs during this era to tie black women's activism in Texas into a larger national dialogue. During the late nineteenth and early twentieth century, Tejanas across the state organized local *sociedades mutualistas* (mutual aid societies) in a number of cities. The investigation and study of these groups would provide new layers to a number of fields. In a similar vein, black churches were centers of political and social activism, as were social and fraternal organizations; historians need to seek sources of information in connection with these associations, which would have enormous potential to broaden our understanding of this era.[26]

Additionally, as several historians have pointed out, there was an all-out war between reform and progressive wings of the Democratic Party and the conservative faction, which often controlled the politics of the state. Reformers and progressives rallied behind some individuals in hopes of deseating some of the conservative stronghold office holders. Although recent biographical studies on "Colonel" Edward House and Alexander Watkins Terrell have added enormously to our understanding of two of the Democratic Party's powerhouses during this period, a central example of a study needing to be done is a biography of James Hogg. There is a lengthy biography of Hogg in existence, but it is over half a century old. There is no need to rework a study simply because of age, but in the time since its publication the profession has changed immensely in outlook and access to source location and retrieval methods. There is a need for a new, inclusive, and critical look at James Hogg.[27]

Moreover, Samuel Palmer Brookes, president of Baylor University, was a much more central political figure than many historians have realized. His papers at the Texas Collection and University Archives at Baylor University hold correspondence and other documents that reveal secret dealings with progressive Democrats vying for control of Texas politics and strategies through which they hoped to remove conservative leaders including U.S. senator Charles A. Culberson. There is definitely a story there.

In general, as historian Lewis Gould and many others have discussed, Texas universities were a haven for reform and progressive thought and organizing. Historians should look more closely at institutions of higher learning for evidence of reform and progressive activity, but also as entities in themselves. These were often controlled environments away from the conservative-led

Democratic Party surroundings and were places where liberal activism could take root and flourish. There are also gaping holes on the other side of the political fence; there is still a need for good biographies on conservative Democrat leaders Joseph Weldon Bailey and James Ferguson. Overall, there remains a lot to be done and discovered about Texas between Reconstruction and the Roaring Twenties.[28]

NOTES

1. Alwyn Barr, *Reconstruction to Reform: Texas Politics, 1876–1906* (Austin: University of Texas Press, 1971); Merline Pitre, *Through Many Dangers Toils and Snares: The Black Leadership of Texas, 1868–1900* (Austin: Eakin Press, 1985); Robert C. McMath, Jr., *Populist Vanguard: A History of the Southern Farmers' Alliance* (Chapel Hill: University of North Carolina Press, 1975); Lewis L. Gould, *Progressives and Prohibitionists: Texas Democrats in the Wilson Era* (Austin: University of Texas Press, 1973); Robert H. Wiebe, *Search for Order, 1877–1920* (New York: Hill and Wang, 1967). This list is not meant to be all inclusive but simply to suggest a few of the key classic works discussing late nineteenth- and early twentieth-century Texas reformers.

2. Patrick G. Williams, *Beyond Redemption: Texas Democrats after Reconstruction* (College Station: Texas A&M University Press, 2007), 179.

3. Walter L. Buenger, *The Path to a Modern South: Northeast Texas between Reconstruction and the Great Depression* (Austin: University of Texas Press, 2001), 5.

4. James D. Ivy, *No Saloon in the Valley: The Southern Strategy of Texas Prohibitionists in the 1880s* (Waco, Tex.: Baylor University Press, 2003).

5. Jessica S. Brannon-Wranosky, "Southern Promise and Necessity: Texas, Regional Identity, and the National Woman Suffrage Movements, 1868–1920" (Ph.D. diss., University of North Texas, 2010), and "Mariana Thompson Folsom: Nineteenth-Century Woman's Rights Activist," in *Texas Women: Their Histories, Their Lives*, ed. Elizabeth Hayes Turner, Stephanie Cole, and Rebecca Sharpless (Athens: University of Georgia Press, forthcoming, 2014–2015).

6. Elizabeth Hayes Turner, *Women, Culture and Community: Religion and Reform in Galveston, Texas, 1880–1920* (New York: Oxford University Press, 1997).

7. Elizabeth York Enstam, *Women and the Creation of Urban Life: Dallas Texas, 1843–1920* (College Station, Texas: Texas A&M University Press, 1998).

8. Elliott Young, *Catarino Garza's Revolution on the Texas-Mexico Border* (Durham, N.C.: Duke University Press, 2004).

9. Thad Sitton and James H. Conrad, *Freedom Colonies: Independent Black Texans in the Time of Jim Crow* (Austin: University of Texas Press, 2005).

10. Rhonda Ragsdale, "A Place To Call Home: A Study of the Self-Segregated Community of Tatums, Oklahoma, 1894–1970" (Master's thesis, University of North Texas, 2005); Debra Ann Reid, *Reaping a Greater Harvest: African Americans, the Extension Service, and Rural Reform in Jim Crow Texas* (College Station: Texas A&M University Press, 2007).

11. Postel, *Populist Vision*; Worth Robert Miller and Stacy G. Ulbig, "Building a Populist Coalition in Texas, 1892–1896," *Journal of Southern History* 74 (May 2008): 255–96.

12. Gregg Cantrell, *Kenneth and John B. Rayner and the Limits of Southern Dissent* (Urbana: University of Illinois Press, 1993), and *Feeding the Wolf: John B. Rayner and the Politics of Race, 1850–1918* (Wheeling, Ill.: Harlan Davidson, 2001).

13. Worth Robert Miller, "Building a Progressive Coalition in Texas: The Populist-Reform Democrat Rapprochement, 1900–1907," *Journal of Southern History* 52 (May 1986): 163–82; Kyle G. Wilkison, *Yeomen, Sharecroppers, and Socialists: Plain Folk Protest in Texas, 1870–1914* (College Station, Texas A&M University Press, 2008).

14. Marion K. Barthelme, ed., *Women in the Texas Populist Movement: Letters to the Southern Mercury* (College Station: Texas A&M University Press, 1997); Ruth Hosey Karbach, "Ellen Lawson Dabbs: Waving the Equal Rights Banner," in Turner et al., *Texas Women;* Jessica S. Brannon-Wranosky, "Southern Promise and Necessity: Texas, Regional Identity, and the National Woman Suffrage Movement, 1868–1920" (Ph.D. diss., University of North Texas, 2010).

15. Turner, *Women, Culture, and Community*; Enstam, *Women and the Creation of Urban Life*; Megan Seaholm, "Earnest Women: The White Woman's Club Movement in Progressive Era Texas, 1880–1920" (Ph.D. diss., Rice University, 1988); Judith N. McArthur, *Creating the New Woman: The Rise of Southern Women's Progressive Culture in Texas, 1893–1918* (Urbana: University of Illinois Press, 1998).

16. Jeffrey Zemler, "The Texas State Building and the Women's World's Fair Exhibit Association of Texas," *Southwestern Historical Quarterly* 115 (July 2011): 19–43.

17. Richard B. McCaslin, *At the Heart of Texas: One Hundred Years of the Texas State Historical Association, 1897–1997* (Austin: Texas State Historical Association, 2007); McArthur, *Creating the New Woman*; David B. Gracy II, *The State Library and Archives of Texas: A History, 1835–1962* (Austin: University of Texas Press, 2010); Kelly McMichael Stott, "From Lost Cause to Female Empowerment: The Texas Division of the United Daughters of the Confederacy, 1896–1966" (Ph.D. diss., University of North Texas, 2001); Mark Fish, "Mary Jones: Last First Lady of the Republic of Texas" (Ph.D. diss., University of North Texas, 2011).

18. For examples of historians discussing or providing structure for this delineation, see Barr, *Reconstruction to Reform*; Miller, "Building a Progressive Coalition"; Brannon-Wranosky, "Southern Promise and Necessity"; Gould, *Progressives and Prohibitionists*; and Gould, *Alexander Watkins Terrell.* Janet Schmelzer, *Our Fighting Governor: The Life of Thomas M. Campbell and the Politics of Progressive Reform in Texas* (College Station: Texas A&M University Press, 2014).

19. Judith N. McArthur and Harold L. Smith, *Minnie Fisher Cunningham: A Suffragist's Life in Politics* (Oxford: Oxford University Press, 2003).

20. Bernadette Pruitt, "For the Advancement of the Race: African-American Migration to Houston, 1914–1940," *Journal of Urban History* 31 (May 2005): 435–78, and *The Other Great Migration: The Movement of Rural African Americans to Houston, 1900–1941* (Texas A&M University Press, 2013).

21. Mark S. Stanley, "Portrait of a Southern Progressive: The Political Life and Times of Gov. Pat M. Neff of Texas, 1871–1952" (Ph.D. diss., University of North Texas, 2011).

22. Kate Sayen Kirkland, *The Hogg Family and Houston: Philanthropy and the Civic Ideal* (Austin: University of Texas Press, 2009).

23. Robert S. Maxwell, "Texas in the Progressive Era, 1900–1930," in *Texas: A Sesquicentennial Celebration*, ed. Donald W. Whisenhunt (Austin: Eakin, 1984), 173–200; C. Vann Woodward, *Origins of the New South, 1877–1913* (1951; reprint, Baton Rouge: Louisiana State University Press, 1971), 369.

24. Richard Henry Ribb, "José Tomás Canales and the Texas Rangers: Myth, Identity, and Power in South Texas, 1900–1920" (Ph.D. diss., University of Texas at Austin, 2001). See also David Montejano, *Anglos and Mexicans in the Making of Texas, 1836–1986* (Austin: University of Texas Press, 1987); and Evan Anders, *Boss Rule in South Texas: The Progressive Era* (Austin: University of Texas Press, 1982).

25. Patricia Bernstein, *The First Waco Horror: The Lynching of Jesse Washington and the Rise of the NAACP* (College Station: Texas A&M University Press, 2005).

26. McArthur, *Creating the New Woman*, 17; Milton C. Sernett, *Harriet Tubman: Myth, Memory, and History* (Durham: Duke University Press, 2007), 175–76.

27. Godfrey Hodgson, *Woodrow Wilson's Right Hand: The Life of Colonel Edward M. House* (New Haven, Conn.: Yale University Press, 2006); Lewis L. Gould, *Alexander Watkins Terrell: Civil War Soldier, Texas Lawmaker, Diplomat* (Austin: University of Texas Press, 2004); Robert C. Cotner, *James Stephen Hogg: A Biography* (Austin: University of Texas Press, 1959).

28. Lewis L. Gould, "The University Becomes Politicized: The War with Jim Ferguson, 1915–1918," *Southwestern Historical Quarterly* 86 (Oct. 1982): 256–76.

CHAPTER 13

World War I through World War II

Patrick Cox

Texas changed remarkably in the first four decades of the twentieth century. At the beginning of the century, the state still resembled and reflected its ties to those of the defeated Confederacy. Texas in the early 1900s remained largely rural, heavily dependent on agriculture, mainly poor with little in social services or public education, and staunchly segregated. By the end of World War II, Texas was poised on the doorstep of modernization. Although it was still strongly attached to southern culture and lagging behind in public services, notable changes had taken place. Larger cities, improved infrastructure, a strong petrochemical industry and financial sector, and a growing population changed the face of the state. Though still a segregated society at the end of World War II, the foundations of the modern civil rights movement in Texas were in place. Along with these changes, new Texas leadership provided a notable impact on national policy that would forever change the role of the federal government and its relationship with states and local communities.

For an understanding of Texas and its links to southern culture and progressivism, many important works provide comprehensive overviews and analyses of this distinct region of the United States. These include the classic work by C. Vann Woodward, *Origins of the New South, 1877–1939*. Other outstanding contributions are George Brown Tindall's *Emergence of the New South, 1913–1945* and V. O. Key's *Southern Politics in State and Nation*.[1] Key provided an exceptional, groundbreaking study on Texas and the rest of the southern states. Each of these studies has withstood the test of time and provided insightful interpretations that are important to an understanding of the unique role played by southern progressives in the early twentieth century.

The Progressive Era of the early twentieth century resulted in profound changes in Texas as well as the entire nation. Social and economic reforms helped set the stage for the modernization of Texas and its emergence from the southern sphere of influence. Many of the changes sought during the Populist movement of the 1890s began to take place even as the group as an organized force disappeared into the history books. Farmers and rural residents gained from railroad regulation, an expanding economy, and higher commodity prices. Urban residents benefited from a growing population, better communications, transportation, and public services. Women and religious groups took center stage in putting forward an agenda of prohibition and reform. However, the state's minority populations suffered significant setbacks as a result of progressive victories. The state's progressive leadership systematically excluded African Americans and Mexican Americans from political participation and from nearly all benefits derived from social and economic changes. Segregation in Texas became an entrenched, defined pattern of life throughout the state, and it largely remained in this stage until cracks began to appear in the New Deal and World War II era.

In the past thirty years, more historians who study Texas and the Southwest have launched research into the Progressive Era and early twentieth century. Lewis L. Gould's *Progressives and Prohibitionists* and Norman Brown's *Hood, Bonnet and Little Brown Jug* both provide a comprehensive look at the social, economic, and political changes that occurred during these times. No study of the Progressive Era in Texas can ignore these excellent, well-documented perspectives. Another study on the politics of the era is reflected in a series of essays contained in *Profiles in Power: Twentieth-Century Texans in Washington, D.C.*, edited by Kenneth E. Hendrickson, Jr., Michael L. Collins, and Patrick Cox.[2]

Racial segregation and conflict intensified in the early twentieth century. Texas ranked third among all states for lynching African Americans during this period. Race riots erupted in the larger cities of Dallas and Houston and smaller cities in East Texas. Some progressives and religious organizations began to criticize the lynchings and other lawlessness openly. The *Dallas Morning News*, *Houston Chronicle*, and *San Antonio Express* began news coverage and editorials in protest of the violence. Some of this reaction stemmed from concern in the growing urban business community and among religious leaders. Concern rose over fear of harming the image of the communities to northern investors and business interests. The Association of Southern Women for the Prevention of Lynching, led by Jessie Daniel Ames of Georgetown, Texas, began during this era.

Several works highlighting activists, progressive, and related organizations on gender, race, and class issues are noteworthy. James R. Green authored *Grass Roots Socialism*. *The Texas Left*, edited by David O'Donald Cullen and Kyle G. Wilkison, contains essays detailing the challenges provided by Texas socialists, labor activists, women's movements, and minority organizations during the Progressive Era. Judith N. McArthur's *Creating the New Woman* offers a comprehensive look at women's organizations and suffrage in this era. Another groundbreaking work is Charles C. Alexander's *Ku Klux Klan in the Southwest*. This study contains the dark side of the progressive movement as evoked by the rise of the hooded order and an era of fear in the 1920s. For an introspective look at one urban Texas community, *White Metropolis* by Michael Phillips contains an extensive look at the complex racial and class relationships in Dallas especially during the twentieth century.[3]

The war and patriotic fervor that erupted in the nation were a godsend to advocates of the prohibition of alcohol and women's suffrage. Prohibition supporters argued that alcohol was a waste of vital resources, a threat to American soldiers, and a tool of the German kaiser. On April 14, 1917, the day the country declared war on Germany, U.S. senator Morris Sheppard of Texas introduced the prohibition amendment to Congress. Congress passed the amendment in December 1917, and it was sent to the states for ratification. Sheppard became nationally known as the "Father of National Prohibition."

Suffrage advocates turned their rhetorical guns on the newspapers and business leaders of the community to press their cause. As part of their campaign, women suffrage leaders enthusiastically volunteered for projects linked to the war effort. They worked on food conservation drives, sales of war bonds, and efforts to raise medical supplies and clothing. Women's rights activists noted that the "alien enemy has paid his poll tax" while "our sons and brothers and husbands" were in the service and effectively disfranchised. Judith N. McArthur and Harold L Smith's *Minnie Fisher Cunningham* is a study of the suffrage movement and the life of one of the premier activists in twentieth-century Texas. In addition, McArthur's *Creating the New Woman* provides a more comprehensive look at women's progressive roles. An excellent regional study illustrating the new role of professional women in the movement is Jacqueline Masur McElhaney's *Pauline Periwinkle and Progressive Reform in Dallas*. The career of a leader of Texas women's clubs of the era is examined by Kelley M. King in

Call Her a Citizen: Progressive Era Activist and Educator Anne Pennybacker. The career of another female leader in Texas education of those decades is the subject of Debbie Mauldin Cottrell's *Pioneer Woman Educator: The Progressive Spirit of Anne Webb Blanton.*[4]

A more focused regional perspective of this era with its political, social, and economic upheaval is offered in *Boss Rule in South Texas* by Evan Anders. The author provides a colorful and insightful look at the region and the unique development of the rural area bosses who controlled the minority Anglo population and the majority Mexican American residents. *Sawdust Empire,* by Robert S. Maxwell and Robert D. Baker, is an economic and social history of the Texas lumber industry. Their work is also a groundbreaking volume on environmental history, with East Texas as the stage. Walter L. Buenger authored *The Path to a Modern South,* which provides a comprehensive examination of life, society, and change during the Progressive Era. Reviewing the social and economic change of the early 1920s from the vantage point of the state's major metropolitan dailies, *The First Texas News Barons* by Patrick Cox covers the major issues of prohibition, suffrage, racial strife, and the Ku Klux Klan.[5]

Isolationist sentiment remained strong in Texas but changed significantly with the buildup and onset of World War I. Germany's submarine warfare created concern, but Texans were more concerned with German attempts to encourage Mexico to renew hostilities against the United States. Germany was especially interested in keeping America out of the European war and became involved in the internal affairs of Mexico during its revolution. Violence along the Rio Grande and the political unrest during the prolonged revolution became major contributing factors to U.S. entry into the war. Although no monograph exists that focuses entirely on all aspects of Texas and World War I, some studies note the importance and impact of the Great War on the state and its citizens. A good introduction is provided in Ralph Wooster's *Texas and Texans in the Great War.*[6]

For tensions along the border in the World War I era, see Benjamin H. Johnson's *Revolution in Texas.*[7] The unrest along the Rio Grande during the Mexican Revolution of 1910–1920 increased federal involvement along the border. The prolonged military activity prepared the U.S. Army for war. Texans gained valuable experience working with large troop units with modern weapons. Many Texans volunteered for military service and entered the draft. Over 989,000 men registered and nearly 200,000 enlisted and saw service during the war. Several hundred Texas women served as nurses. One nurse and 5,170 men died in the service. Of these deaths, a third occurred in the United States as a result of the influenza epidemic of 1918. Four Texans received the Medal of Honor for service in the war.

Perhaps the single most important Texan during World War I was Col. Edward M. House. The consummate insider of his era, House served as the chief diplomat and political advisor to President Woodrow Wilson. In an administration with an impressive number of Texans in the Cabinet, House stood the tallest until his dispute with the president during the peace negotiations in Paris in 1919. *Woodrow Wilson's Right Hand* by Godfrey Hodgson is the best biography of the man and his roles as presidential counselor and confidant. House served as the first of many influential Texas political leaders who would rise to power during the twentieth century.[8]

The outbreak of World War I in Europe initially created economic havoc in Texas and the rest of the South. Cotton, the primary cash crop, dropped in price as the conflict disrupted international trade. However, by 1915, demand for cotton, oil, and other agricultural and manufactured products by the Allied forces had reversed the trend. When the United States entered the war in 1917, Texas farmers and businesses benefited from the national mobilization effort. Cotton prices rose from a low of seven cents per pound to thirty-five cents per pound in 1919. The Houston Ship Channel was enlarged, and the Bayou City emerged as the largest inland seaport in the nation as a result of wartime traffic. Bank deposits rose and employment increased across the state. The Texas oil industry, with its history of instability in the early 1900s with the Spindletop discovery, had experienced a decline similar to cotton when the war began in Europe. As a result of the demands created by the war, the oil industry ascended to become the major industrial activity in the state. Along with this expansion, the industry increased its political influence in both Austin and Washington, D.C.

Several works provide valuable insight on the development of the oil industry and other businesses. *Giant under the Hill*, by Jo Ann Stiles, Judith Walker Linsley, and Ellen Walker Rienstra, is the most recent and insightful publication on the first oil boom in the state. Diana Davids Olien and Roger M. Olien authored *Oil in Texas*, which covers the boom years of the early twentieth century and the industry's tremendous impact on the state and its culture. *Bless the Pure and Humble*, by Nicholas George Malavis, covers the expansion of the industry with both historical and legal perspectives. David Prindle's *Petroleum Politics and the Texas Railroad Commission* and Carl C. Rister's classic study *Oil! Titan of the Southwest* provide important and very readable insights into this important industry. *But Also Good Business*, by Walter L. Buenger and Joseph A. Pratt, illustrates the influence of banking and finance and their involvement in the petroleum, timber, and cotton industries. Another noteworthy and well-written business and community history is *Texas Merchant: Marvin Leonard and Fort Worth*, by Victoria Buenger and Walter L. Buenger.[9]

The Mexican Revolution of 1910–1920 made a dramatic impression on Texas residents and altered life and business during this era. The internal conflict south of the Rio Grande often overshadowed events in Europe leading up to and including World War I. Most Texans viewed the fighting in Europe as monumental yet distant; the unrest along the Mexican border led Texans of all persuasions to call for Washington's intervention and federal troops. Sensational coverage by Texas newspapers—featuring the Plan of San Diego, Pancho Villa's raid on Columbus, New Mexico, and a steady stream of stories about attacks on Americans and their property—resulted in an increased sense of insecurity and belligerence, within the state and in the rest of the Southwest. The revelation of alleged German offers of assistance to Mexico in early 1917 seemingly affirmed calls for preparedness and intervention. The exposure of German foreign secretary Arthur Zimmermann's offer to return to Mexico lands lost to the United States in the Treaty of Guadalupe eliminated all support for Germany. Sympathy for the German American community disappeared, and the remaining pacifist sentiments lost their influence as Texans enthusiastically mobilized for war.[10]

This prewar scenario in Texas differed significantly from that in the rest of the nation primarily because of the exposure to the Mexican Revolution. Problems associated with the revolution had little effect on most Americans until the appearance of the Zimmermann note in March 1917. From a regional perspective, however, Mexico played a substantive role in affairs and attitudes in Texas well before the revelation of Zimmermann's decoded message.[11]

David Montejano's classic *Anglos and Mexicans in the Making of Texas* covers many the conflicts between Mexican Americans and Texans during this period. The Rio Grande Valley and Trans-Pecos areas of the state became a virtual war zone from 1915 to 1918. Another well-documented view of the conflict is in Don M. Coerver and Linda B. Hall's *Texas and the Mexican Revolution*. Patrick Cox covers the period with a focus on media coverage and political reaction in his previously cited *The First Texas News Barons*. Arnoldo De León's *Mexican Americans in Texas* also provides insight into the impact on Mexican Americans during this turbulent period. The Rio Grande Valley of far South Texas was aflame during this same period. Many Texas newspapers carried accounts of "Mexican bandits" and their raids on ranches and small communities north of the river. Train derailments, burned bridges, and other property damage were attributed to these mounted raiders. In reactions to these attacks, many Tejano families lost their farms, homes, and their lives during this unsettled period. *War Scare on the Rio Grande* provides a fascinating, graphic look at both sides of the Rio Grande brought on by the Mexican Revolution.[12]

With the market crash on Wall Street in October 1929, the vast majority of people in America and throughout Texas could not comprehend the economic and social storm to come. The popular Herbert Hoover, in his first year of office after his resounding victory in 1928, also refused to recognize the problem. Like most Americans, he believed that the economy was sound and that the market would correct itself. Most Texas officials and business and civic leaders supported President Hoover's views. However, hard times quickly followed as the national economy sank faster than the *Titanic* and the nation's once optimistic outlook dropped along with wages and jobs. Nearly two years after the Wall Street crash, every economic sector was showing a decline. New construction disappeared completely in every Texas city and community. Commodity prices dropped to nineteenth-century levels. The oil industry continued to pump money and jobs into the state's economy but could not absorb all of the unemployed workers. The discovery of oil in the great East Texas field in 1931 that drew people from Texas and surrounding states failed to offset growing unemployment. An estimated ten thousand laborers who traveled to the East Texas boom area could not find jobs. In Houston, where oil was stored, refined, and shipped, nearly one in four remained out of work. Hobo camps popped up along the San Antonio River and other Texas communities; on this topic, see *The South and the New Deal*, by Roger Biles.[13]

By 1931 the darkening economic clouds had become even more menacing. Banks around the state began to close for lack of funds and from unsound investments. Foreclosures of businesses and farms began to rise. Also, in urban areas layoffs began to increase as businesses reduced their payrolls and scaled back production and services. The Texas National Bank in Fort Worth closed its doors in January 1930 when it could not provide money to all of its depositors. In September 1931, San Antonio's City Central Bank and Trust Company failed. People remained nervous about their money in local banks. Many hid money in mattresses and buried cash in jars behind their homes.[14]

Several relevant works cover the Great Depression in Texas and its impact. George Norris Green's *The Establishment in Texas Politics* examines the state's Democratic leadership from Austin to Washington with a focus on the economic, racial, and social collisions that made Texas politics a contact sport. Chandler Davidson's *Race and Class in Texas Politics* is another critical study of the influence the Texas wealthy and powerful exerted over state and national politics. Keith J. Volanto's *Texas, Cotton, and the New Deal* is an in-depth study of the difficulties facing farm families in rural Texas who relied on the traditional southern crop. Likewise, Neil Foley's *White Scourge: Mexicans, Blacks, and Poor Whites in Texas Cotton Culture* provides a critical examination of the racial and economic difficulties of this era; see also Foley's *Quest for Equality*. Julia Kirk Blackwelder authored *Women of the Depression*, a solid work on the ethnic and gender issues during the 1930s in the Alamo City.[15]

Next to President Roosevelt, Vice President John Nance Garner of Uvalde became the single most influential person in the early New Deal years. Garner's political knowledge combined with the respect he held among his colleagues in Congress was invaluable. Per the customs of the era, Garner's whiskey drinking and poker playing with his congressional colleagues helped lubricate the legislative process for the New Deal. Garner stayed with FDR through the landslide victory of 1936, but the team divided over Garner's criticism of expanding the New Deal, FDR's ill-fated court-packing plan, and the president's opposition to many of Garner's friends in the 1938 elections. Garner opposed FDR's effort to seek a third term and unsuccessfully sought the Democratic presidential nomination in 1940. He left Washington in 1941 with a vow never to return to the nation's capital—a place where he had served for nearly forty years. Although no modern biography of Garner has been published, a critique of his contributions and other Texans can be found in Hendrickson and colleagues' previously cited *Profiles in Power*.

A significant number of other Texas political leaders rose to prominence during the 1930s as well. The best biography on Sam Rayburn is by D. B. Hardeman and Donald C. Brown, two studies by Anthony Champagne are useful as well. Rayburn's stature and contributions to the nation were astounding, and his record as the longest-serving Speaker of the House remains unsurpassed. Rayburn also was the coauthor of the Rural Electrification Authority, which literally brought most of the American countryside out of the dark ages in the late 1930s and 1940s. A biography on financial leader Jesse Jones by Steven Fenberg, *Unprecedented Power*, is the story of the Texas banker who administered the Reconstruction Finance Corporation through the Great Depression and converted the agency into a wartime defense program for World War II.[16]

Another notable Texan made his mark when he first appeared as a young maverick congressman in 1937. Lyndon Johnson won a surprising special election and immediately ingratiated himself with Sam Rayburn and FDR.

Johnson campaigned on his unyielding support for the New Deal programs in Texas and for bringing electricity to Central Texas and the rest of rural America. Johnson's early life and career are the subject of myriad books and studies. Probably the best and most insightful are Robert Dallek's *Lone Star Rising* and Robert Caro's *Years of Lyndon Johnson*. Also worthwhile is Doris Kearns Goodwin's *Lyndon Johnson and the American Dream*.[17]

The 1936 Texas Centennial became a landmark event throughout the state and lifted both Texan spirits and the local economy. Reviewing the accomplishments of the centennial year, the editors of the *Texas Almanac* believed the events signaled a "return of prosperity" and "served the purpose of bringing full realization that the old Texas had passed—that the centennial event meant more than the passing of a mere historic milestone." Agriculture and the oil and gas industry still held great wealth for the state's citizens and businesses. After 1936, expanded opportunities in manufacturing would begin to rival the traditional source of wealth in Texas. Texas had finally passed "into cultural and economic adulthood." Though financial progress remained difficult in the Great Depression, the Texas centennial celebration created new opportunities and a changing image of the state and its residents.[18] The best study of the Texas Centennial is provided by Kenneth B. Ragsdale in *The Year America Discovered Texas*. Ragsdale provides the most comprehensive study of centennial events and activities throughout the state. In addition, the previously cited *First Texas News Barons* by Patrick Cox covers the event through the perspective of the news media, with a discussion of how the Texas western image and ethos evolved during this era.[19]

Unlike the divisions and reservations by isolationists and in the ethnic German communities in World War I, Texans were nearly unanimous in supporting the war effort after the Japanese surprise attack on Pearl Harbor. The best two volumes to cover the domestic and war fronts from the regional perspective are Ralph Wooster's *Texas and Texans in World War II* and *1941: Texas Goes to War*, edited by James Ward Lee and colleagues.[20]

There are several other works of import on World War II Texas: Robert Thonhoff, *Camp Kenedy, Texas*; Robert L. Wagner, *The Texas Army: A History of the 36th Division in the Italian Campaign*; Michael R. Waters, *Lone Star Stalag: German Prisoners of War at Camp Hearne*; Lee Carraway Smith, *A River Swift and Deadly: The 36th "Texas" Infantry Division at the Rapido River*; David Westheimer, *Sitting It Out: A World War II POW Memoir*; and Melanie Wiggins, *Torpedoes in the Gulf: Galveston and the U-Boats;* see also Joyce Gibson Roach's collection *Collective Heart: Texans in World War II*. Likely the most prolific historian covering World War II Texas is former Neiman Marcus executive Thomas E. Alexander. Among his well-crafted works are *The Wings of Change*, *The Stars Were Big and Bright*, and *The One and Only Rattlesnake Bomber Base*.[21]

As part of the massive war effort, women became an essential part of the workforce. Women worked in almost every conceivable job as men left to join the armed services, including factory positions, raising farm produce and cattle, and testing and flying airplanes, as well as military service. The most noted Texas woman involved in World War II, Oveta Culp Hobby, is the subject of two recent studies. One, Debra L. Winegarten's *Oveta Culp Hobby*, is a biography with attention paid to the war period; the other, Vanessa A. Crockford's M.A. thesis from the Army War College, examines Hobby's impact as the wartime leader of the Women's Army Auxiliary Corps. Other new works detailing the role of Texas women at war include Cindy Weigand's overview of the subject, *Texas Women in World War II*, and two books detailing the role of Texas's women pilots—Harry Franklin Snapp's *Pioneer Women in West Texas Skies* and Alyce Stevens Rohrer's *Girls of Avenger*. Overall, the general topic of women in the war effort needs additional attention from historians.[22]

The state's minority populations also provided strong support for the war and helped further the civil rights movement in Texas. One of the best accounts of this phenomenon is from Maggie Rivas-Rodriguez, editor of *Mexican Americans and World War II*. An important analysis that considers Mexican Texans on the home front is Emilio Zamora's *Claiming Rights and Righting Wrongs*.[23]

Many biographies, unit histories, and wartime experiences of Texans have been published, and the list continues to grow thanks to the interest Americans retain in World War II. Don Graham's *No Name on the Bullet: A Biography of Audie Murphy* is an excellent study of the small-town Texan who became a national hero and star. Tom Hatfield's *Rudder* is a comprehensive study of the life and times of the war hero who later became Texas land commissioner and president of Texas A&M University.[24]

In summary, many changes took place in Texas between 1900 and 1945 that influenced the growth, outlook, economy, society, and culture of the state. These were watershed decades in the formation of what would emerge after World War II and is now recognized as modern Texas. Although much more research and analysis are needed on the people, places, issues, and events of this era, publications of the past thirty years have provided a much more thorough understanding of this unique place we call Texas.

NOTES

1. C. Vann Woodward, *Origins of the New South, 1877–1913* (Baton Rouge: Louisiana State University Press, 1951); George Brown Tindall, *The Emergence of the New South, 1913–1945* (Baton Rouge, Louisiana State University Press, 1967); V. O. Key, Jr., *Southern Politics in State and Nation* (New York: Alfred A. Knopf, 1949).

2. Lewis L. Gould, *Progressives and Prohibitionists: Texas Democrats in the Wilson Era* (Austin: University of Texas Press, 1973, rev. 1994); Norman Brown, *Hood, Bonnet and Little Brown Jug: Texas Politics 1921–1928* (Austin: University of Texas Press, 1984); Kenneth E. Hendrickson, Jr., Michael L. Collins, and Patrick Cox, eds., *Profiles in Power: Twentieth-Century Texans in Washington, D.C.* (Austin: University of Texas Press, 2004).

3. James R. Green, *Grass Roots Socialism: Radical Movements in the Southwest, 1895–1943* (Baton Rouge: Louisiana State University Press, 1978); David O'Donald Cullen and Kyle G. Wilkison, eds., *The Texas Left* (College Station: Texas A&M University Press, 2010); Judith N. McArthur, *Creating the New Woman: The Rise of Southern Women's Progressive Culture in Texas, 1893–1918* (Urbana: University of Illinois Press, 1998); Charles C. Alexander, *The Ku Klux Klan in the Southwest* (Lexington: University of Kentucky Press, 1965); Michael Phillips, *White Metropolis: Race, Ethnicity, and Religion in Dallas, 1841–2001* (Austin: University of Texas Press, 2006).

4. Judith N. McArthur and Harold L Smith, *Minnie Fisher Cunningham: A Suffragist's Life in Politics* (New York: Oxford University Press, 2005); Jacqueline Masur McElhaney, *Pauline Periwinkle and Progressive Reform in Dallas* (College Station: Texas A&M University Press, 1998); Kelley M. King, *Call Her a Citizen: Progressive Era Activist and Educator Anne Pennybacker* (College Station: Texas A&M University Press, 2010); Debbie Mauldin Cottrell, *Pioneer Woman Educator: The Progressive Spirit of Anne Webb Blanton* (College Station: Texas A&M University Press, 1993).

5. Evan Anders, *Boss Rule in South Texas* (Austin: University of Texas Press, 1982); Robert S. Maxwell and Robert D. Baker, *Sawdust Empire: The Texas Lumber Industry, 1830–1940* (College Station: Texas A&M University Press, 1983); Walter L. Buenger, *The Path to a Modern South: Northeast Texas between Reconstruction and the Great Depression* (Austin: University of Texas Press, 2001); Patrick Cox, *The First Texas News Barons* (Austin: University of Texas Press, 2005).

6. Ralph Wooster, *Texas and Texans in the Great War* (Abilene, Tex.: State House Press, 2010).

7. Benjamin H. Johnson, *Revolution in Texas: How a Forgotten Rebellion and Its Bloody Suppression Turned Mexicans into Americans* (New Haven, Conn.: Yale University Press, 2005).

8. Godfrey Hodgson, *Woodrow Wilson's Right Hand: The Life of Colonel Edward M. House* (New Haven, Conn.: Yale University Press, 2006).

9. Jo Ann Stiles, Judith Walker Linsley, and Ellen Walker Rienstra, *Giant under the Hill: A History of the Spindletop Oil Discovery at Beaumont, Texas* (College Station: Texas A&M University Press, 2002); Diana Davids Olien and Roger M. Olien, *Oil in*

Texas: The Gusher Age, 1895–1945 (Austin: University of Texas Press, 2002); Nicholas George Malavis, *Bless the Pure and Humble: Texas Lawyers and Oil Regulation, 1919–1936* (College Station: Texas A&M University Press, 1996); David Prindle, *Petroleum Politics and the Texas Railroad Commission* (Austin: University of Texas Press, 1984); Carl C. Rister, *Oil! Titan of the Southwest* (Norman: University of Oklahoma Press, 1957); Walter L. Buenger and Joseph A. Pratt, *But Also Good Business: Texas Commerce Banks and the Financing of Houston and Texas, 1886–1986* (College Station: Texas A&M University Press, 1986); Victoria Buenger and Walter L. Buenger, *Texas Merchant: Marvin Leonard and Fort Worth* (College Station: Texas A&M University Press, 2008).

10. The best study of foreign involvement in Mexico during the revolution remains Friedrich Katz, *The Secret War in Mexico: Europe, the United States and the Mexican Revolution* (Chicago: University of Chicago Press, 1984).

11. Many books with a national perspective comment on Texas, along with examinations of the national debate, ethnic divisions, isolationist sentiments, and pivotal events that influenced political affairs and the nation's entry into World War I. A select group of national and regional histories includes Arthur S. Link, *Woodrow Wilson and the Progressive Era, 1910–1917* (New York: Harper and Brothers, 1954), and *Wilson: The Struggle for Neutrality, 1914–1915* (Princeton, N.J.: Princeton University Press, 1960). Link is Wilson's best-known biographer and editor of his personal papers. Other historians with similar views on neutrality and intervention are Robert H. Ferrell, *Woodrow Wilson and World War I, 1917–1921* (New York: Harper and Row, 1985); and Ross Gregory, *The Origins of American Intervention in the First World War* (New York: W. W. Norton, 1971). Recognized historians who base their conclusions on southern opinions include Dewey W. Grantham, *The South in Modern America* (New York: Harper Collins, 1994); Glenn Justice, *Revolution on the Rio Grande* (El Paso: Texas Western Press, 1992); David Montejano, *Anglos and Mexicans in the Making of Texas, 1836–1986* (Austin: University of Texas Press, 1987); and James Sandos, *Rebellion in the Borderlands: Anarchism and the Plan of San Diego, 1904–1923* (Norman: University of Oklahoma Press, 1992).

12. Montejano, *Anglos and Mexicans*; Don M. Coerver and Linda B. Hall, *Texas and the Mexican Revolution: A Study in State and National Border Policy, 1910–1920* (San Antonio, Tex.: Trinity University Press, 1984); Arnoldo De León, *Mexican Americans in Texas: A Brief History* (Arlington Heights, Ill.: Harlan Davidson, 1993); Frank N. Samponaro, Paul J. Vanderwood, and Robert R. Runyon, *War Scare on the Rio Grande: Robert Runyon's Photographs of the Border Conflict, 1913–1916* (Austin: Texas State Historical Association, 1990).

13. Roger Biles, *The South and the New Deal* (Lexington: University Press of Kentucky, 1994).

14. The impact of these events can be seen in a series of essays written by the students of Robert C. Cotner in *Texas Cities and the Great Depression* (Austin: Texas Memorial Museum, 1974).

15. George Norris Green, *The Establishment in Texas Politics: The Primitive Years 1938–1957* (Westport, Conn.: Greenwood Press, 1979); Chandler Davidson, *Race and Class in Texas Politics* (Princeton, N.J.: Princeton University Press, 1990); Keith J. Volanto,

Texas, Cotton, and the New Deal (College Station: Texas A&M University Press, 2005); Neil Foley, *The White Scourge: Mexicans, Blacks, and Poor Whites in Texas Cotton Culture* (Berkeley: University of California Press, 1997), and *Quest for Equality: The False Promise of Black-Brown Solidarity* (Cambridge, Mass.: Harvard University Press, 2010); Julia Kirk Blackwelder, *Women of the Depression: Caste and Culture in San Antonio, 1929–1939* (College Station: Texas A&M University Press, 1984).

16. D. B. Hardeman and Donald C. Brown, *Rayburn: A Biography* (Austin: Texas Monthly Press, 1987); Anthony Champagne, *Congressman Sam Rayburn* (New Brunswick, N.J.; Rutgers University Press, 1984), and *Sam Rayburn: A Bio-Bibliography* (Westport, Conn.: Greenwood Press, 1982); Steven Fenberg, *Unprecedented Power: Jesse Jones, Capitalism, and the Common Good* (College Station: Texas A&M University Press, 2011).

17. Robert Dallek, *Lone Star Rising: Lyndon Johnson and His Times, 1908–1960* (New York: Oxford University Press, 1991); Robert Caro, *The Years of Lyndon Johnson: The Path to Power* (New York: Vintage, 1982); Doris Kearns Goodwin, *Lyndon Johnson and the American Dream* (New York: St. Martin's Press, 1991).

18. *Texas Almanac Supplement*, 1937 (Dallas: A. H. Belo, 1936), 4.

19. Kenneth B. Ragsdale, *The Year America Discovered Texas, Centennial '36* (College Station: Texas A&M University Press, 1987).

20. Ralph Wooster, *Texas and Texans in World War II* (Austin: Eakin Press, 2005); James Ward Lee et al., eds., *1941: Texas Goes to War* (Denton: University of North Texas Press, 1991).

21. Robert Thonhoff, *Camp Kenedy, Texas* (Waco, Tex.: Eakin Press, 2003); Robert L. Wagner, *The Texas Army: A History of the 36th Division in the Italian Campaign* (Austin: State House Press, 1972); Michael R. Waters, *Lone Star Stalag: German Prisoners of War at Camp Hearne* (College Station: Texas A&M University Press, 2006); Lee Carraway Smith, *A River Swift and Deadly: The 36th "Texas" Infantry Division at the Rapido River* (Austin: Eakin Press, 1989); David Westheimer, *Sitting It Out: A World War II POW Memoir* (Houston: Rice University Press, 1992); Melanie Wiggins, *Torpedoes in the Gulf: Galveston and the U-Boats, 1942–1943* (College Station: Texas A&M University Press, 1995); Joyce Gibson Roach, *Collective Heart: Texans in World War II* (Austin: Eakin Press, 1996); Thomas E. Alexander, *The Wings of Change: The Army Air Force Experience in Texas during World War II* (Abilene, Tex.: McWhiney Foundation Press, 2003), *The Stars Were Big and Bright: The United States Army Air Forces and Texas during World War* II (Austin: State House Press, 2008), and *The One and Only Rattlesnake Bomber Base: Pyote Army Airfield in World War II* (Abilene, Tex.: State House Press, 2005). See also Louis Fairchild, *They Called It the War Effort: Oral Histories from World War II, Orange, Texas* (Austin: Eakin Press, 1993).

22. Debra L. Winegarten, *Oveta Culp Hobby: Colonel, Cabinet Member, Philanthropist* (Austin: University of Texas Press, 2014); Vanessa A. Crockford, "Oveta Culp Hobby and Her 'Lieutenants': Transformational Leadership in Action in the Women's Army Auxiliary Corps of World War II" (M.A. thesis, U.S. Army Command and General Staff College, Fort Leavenworth, Kans., 2003); Cindy Weigand, *Texas Women in World War II* (Lanham, Md.: Republic of Texas Press, 2003); Harry Franklin Snapp, *Pioneer Women*

in West Texas Skies: Women Airforce Service Pilots of World War II (Abilene, Tex.: Rupert N. Richardson Press, Hardin Simmons University, 1994); Alyce Stevens Rohrer, *Girls of Avenger* (Bloomington, Ind.: Xlibris, 2002).

23. Maggie Rivas-Rodriguez, ed., *Mexican Americans and World War II* (Austin: University of Texas Press, 2005); Emilio Zamora, *Claiming Rights and Righting Wrongs: Mexican Workers and Job Politics in World War II* (College Station: Texas A&M University Press, 2009).

24. Don Graham, *No Name on the Bullet: A Biography of Audie Murphy* (New York: Viking, 1989); Tom Hatfield, *Rudder: From Leader to Legend* (College Station: Texas A&M University Press, 2011).

CHAPTER 14

Modernizing Texas, 1945–1980

Sean P. Cunningham

Benefiting from the interpretational distance that comes with the passage of time, the historiography of modernizing Texas, defined here as the period between 1945 and 1980, has matured in several important ways since the early 1990s. This developing scholarship has resulted in an increasingly diversified portrait of Texas history since the end of World War II. Recent historians have been effective in not only unpacking the multifaceted narratives of modernizing Texas but also explaining the state's experience within broader regional and national contexts. As a result, literature on the recent Texas past has and continues to break new ground as bridges are built to connect themes in political, social, economic, and cultural history.

To study Texas history between 1945 and 1980 is to discuss the state's response to globalization, the Cold War, the quest for civil rights, industrial and postindustrial economics, oil, urbanization and suburbanization, shifting demographics, and a social milieu that struggled with an increasingly pluralistic, postmodern, and relativistic American culture. Texas history since 1945 further demands attention to the state's regional identity. Scholars have long debated whether Texas is historically more southern or western, but since 1945 those categories have been blurred by the emergence of a new regional category—Sunbelt. These factors collectively considered, the dominant storyline of Texas history between 1945 and 1980—and the one that most visibly connects the other strands—remains the birth of two-party politics and the rise of modern conservatism. In the decades after World War II, the once invisible and powerless

Texas Republican Party transformed itself into the undisputed home for state conservatives. Along the way, the Texas GOP also became the state's dominant political party—so dominant, in fact, that some contemporary observers have wondered whether Texas is effectively, once again, a one-party state.

Historians have been interested in several questions related to this development. One of the most deceptively simple is the temporal genesis of this transformation. When did realignment in Texas begin, and why? Several scholars have addressed these questions, but three recent studies stand out. In 2005, Ricky F. Dobbs published *Yellow Dogs and Republicans: Allan Shivers and Texas Two-Party Politics*. Dobbs contends that the birth of partisan realignment can be traced to the hyper-anticommunist political culture of the early 1950s and the response of establishment Democrats (like Allan Shivers) to the presidential campaigns of Dwight Eisenhower. Essentially a biography of Shivers, Dobbs's study nevertheless speaks to the broader question of the modern Texas GOP's origins. Kenneth Bridges contributed to this discussion with *Twilight of the Texas Democrats: The 1978 Governor's Race*. Though not incompatible with Dobbs's argument, Bridges sees Bill Clements's surprising defeat of John Hill in the state's 1978 gubernatorial contest as a crucial turning point for the state Republican Party's legitimacy as an institution focused on winning elections and transforming Texas's long-held aversion to the GOP. And Sean P. Cunningham's *Cowboy Conservatism* broadens and connects these analyses by assessing the various changes to Texas's political culture between the 1950s and 1980s. Here we see that Republican growth was affected by several socioeconomic and cultural forces that conflated during the 1960s and 1970s to enable an emerging and popular image of liberalism as weak, amoral, and failed. Put differently, as the Sunbelt ethos of limited government, social tradition, and anticommunism grew increasingly synonymous with Texas Republican visions of conservatism and antiliberalism, the state GOP exacerbated ideological divisions within the Democratic Party to create, in many Texans' minds, a political bifurcation that almost demanded the realignment of state conservatives to the Republican fold. Taken together, these three monographs suggest multicausal and nonlinear answers to questions concerning the temporal origins and development of conservative Texas Republicanism.[1]

Historians and political scientists have long been interested in other aspects of modern Texas political history, as well. Though not exclusively focused on the Texas experience, several monographs incorporate Texas into analyses of the South's modernization in the decades after World War II. Specifically related to the question of political realignment, Earl and Merle Black's *Rise of Southern*

Republicans and Byron E. Shafer and Richard Johnston's *End of Southern Exceptionalism* are particularly impressive in that both see the locus of southern electoral change in congressional, state, and local races rather than in presidential campaigns. Both reflect methods more common to the social sciences, but in doing so they complicate historians' understanding of what motivated political change in the postwar South and how Texas did or did not fit into those regional patterns of realignment.[2]

Historians have been more aggressive in placing Texas within a southern context than within a national one, with a handful of notable exceptions. Among these is Douglas Rossinow's *Politics of Authenticity*. Rossinow examines student culture at the University of Texas at Austin from the early Cold War through the 1960s as a window into the popular quest for "authenticity" that marked much of youthful liberalism during the golden age of counterculture. An attempt to speak to the shifting nature of national liberalism, Rossinow's study of Austin is, simultaneously, an important examination of postwar Texas youth culture.[3]

Most efforts to connect Texas to modern national politics have been made through presidential biographies. Most of those have focused on Lyndon Johnson. The most effective and well contextualized of these is Robert Dallek's two-volume biography, *Lone Star Rising* and *Flawed Giant*. Dallek's work is methodologically sound, interpretively balanced, and insightful on both Johnson's personal character and the circumstantial complexities that shaped his career.[4]

A handful of studies on George H. W. Bush are also worth noting. John Robert Greene's *Presidency of George Bush* and Ryan J. Barilleaux and Mark J. Rozell's *Power and Prudence* mark the earliest and best critical assessments of the Bush presidency, though neither deals in any effective way with Bush's longer political career in Texas. Herbert S. Parmet's *George Bush* offers a much more substantive examination of Bush's longer political career and argues that the Connecticut-raised Bush was ultimately victimized by the disconnect that emerged during the 1960s between his moderate Republican convictions and his ambition, set in an emerging context of Sunbelt conservatism. Though at times his work is analytically limited, Parmet offers a glimpse into the dynamics of Texas political culture and the discomfort that moderate Republicans experienced as they were torn between their party's established leadership and an emerging conservative backlash at the grass roots.[5]

As of 2013, no effective scholarly work exists on the early career of George W. Bush, though several studies have connected him with Texas oil interests and power—usually corrupted power. Kevin Phillips—former Republican strategist and architect of Richard Nixon's infamous "southern strategy"—has authored several books along these lines, including *American Dynasty* and *American Theocracy*. In *American Theocracy*, Phillips uses the term "Texification" to describe the shift in American political culture he connects to George W. Bush and, particularly, corporate elements that contributed financially to Bush's political career.[6] Though less focused on the Bushes, similar and effective studies have been done on the relationship among oil, politics, and Texas power, including Bryan Burrough's *The Big Rich*, which is particularly useful for scholars interested in the lives of the so-called Big Four of Texas oil—Roy Cullen, H. L. Hunt, Clint Murchison, and Sid Richardson.[7]

Effective biographies also exist for several other key figures shaping post-1945 Texas politics. One of the best is Patrick Cox's *Ralph W. Yarborough*, which can be read as a complement to the scholarship that deals with the shifting nature of Texas political culture, contextualized by the rise of modern conservatism. Other political studies have effectively collected shorter biographies into one volume using an overarching theme. Among these is *The House Will Come to Order*, in which Patrick Cox and Michael Phillips examine the evolving nature and influence of the Texas Speaker of the House.[8]

It is not surprising that historians interested in modernizing Texas have prioritized the dynamics of a shifting political culture. However, just as much (and perhaps more) progress has been made in the scholarship dealing with race, ethnicity, and civil rights, though that literature has also been influenced by issues related to political activism and civic inclusion. These trends are as true of post-1945 Texas historiography as they are of twentieth-century American historiography more broadly, though studies rooted in Texas offer a comparatively greater focus on the experience of Mexican Americans.[9]

A good place to begin any study of Mexican Americans and Texas politics since 1945 is Rodolfo Rosales's *Illusion of Inclusion*. Rosales's book effectively uses the city of San Antonio not only as a mirror on the racial dynamics of state politics but also as a lens for understanding Sunbelt economic developments at the local level. His study is also noteworthy for the ways in which it applies municipal policy implementation to civic engagement, commercial boosterism, and competing notions of ethnic identity. Rosales's study of San Antonio might be effectively paired with Marc Simon Rodriguez's *Tejano Diaspora*, which breaks new ground by connecting Mexican American social and political culture as it developed in South Texas with an emerging ethnic consciousness and political activism in the American Midwest. By explaining the South Texas roots of Mexican American activism in other regions of the country,

Rodriguez makes a significant contribution to scholars hoping to connect the racial and ethnic complexities of modernizing Texas to changes nationwide.[10]

No historian interested in Mexican American political activism in Texas can ignore organizations like the League of United Latin American Citizens (LULAC) or La Raza Unida Party. Fortunately, the influence of both organizations has been well chronicled.[11] Among the most prolific scholars concerned with these organizations, and with Mexican American political activism broadly, is Ignacio M. García. At least two of García's books on this topic are worth mentioning: *United We Win: The Rise and Fall of La Raza Unida Party* remains relevant as an accessible and passionate introduction to one of the most influential Mexican American political organizations of the early 1970s. *Viva Kennedy* explores the emergence of Mexican American political identity in Texas related to John F. Kennedy's 1960 presidential campaign, as well as the rising expectations for political inclusion that accompanied JFK's ascension to the White House.[12]

One of the best recent studies on the relationship between ethnic identity and the origins of Mexican American political activism is Patrick Carroll's impressive microhistory *Felix Longoria's Wake*, which centers on the funeral arrangements for U.S. Army private Felix Z. Longoria, a native of South Texas killed in action in the Philippines during World War II. When Longoria's widow made plans to bury her deceased husband in his home town of Three Rivers, the local cemetery's director resisted on the grounds that area whites would object to a Mexican American being buried in a space customarily reserved for whites. Through Carroll's engrossing narrative, readers are forced to deal with blurred notions of whiteness in tandem with Cold War sensibilities informing the meaning of patriotism, anticommunism, and American identity. It is an effective study that further introduces one of the key figures of early Mexican American political activism—Hector P. García and his American G.I. Forum—in addition to offering a unique perspective on Lyndon Johnson's early political ambitions.[13]

Several historians have also focused on South Texas in an effort to explain the origins and growth of Mexican American political activism and cultural identity in the decades after World War II. Scholars should find this literature rich but might also do well to expand it by applying similar thematic approaches to other Texas regions.[14]

There have been a handful of helpful, recent monographs on Mexican American labor and work culture. Effectively diversifying the historiography rooted in South Texas, these titles include Scott Cook's *Mexican Brick Culture in the Building of Texas*, Zargosa Vargas's *Labor Rights Are Civil Rights*, Monica Perales's *Smeltertown*, and, most recently, Deborah Cohen's *Braceros*. Each makes an important contribution to the field of ethnohistory and labor in Texas, and Cohen's book is particularly engaging as a form of transnational/border history.[15]

Scholars also continue to pursue "whiteness studies," which have been particularly en vogue since the early 1990s. Arnoldo De León's *Ethnicity in the Sunbelt* takes a generational view of Mexican American identity as related to political engagement in Houston. This book is especially helpful for scholars trying to understand the complicated and mixed strategies employed by Mexican Americans seeking admission into the state's white-dominated societies. Less a whiteness study than a history of political activism, David Montejano's *Quixote's Soldiers* works well with De León's study of ethnicity in Houston. *Quixote's Soldiers* is also valuable for its skilled incorporation of class and gender as tools for analysis.[16]

Nationally, most historians interested in the civil rights movement continue to focus on the African American experience. In *Fighting Their Own Battles*, Brian D. Behnken takes this historiography in a relatively new and important direction. Behnken contrasts the organizational strategies developed by African Americans and Mexican Americans in Texas between 1940 and 1975, illustrating not only that these strategies were quite different but that widespread intolerances held by leaders in both camps prevented a coherent, united political front.[17] The post-1945 historiography on African Americans in Texas is also well developed, though comparatively less attention has been paid to it in recent years. Nevertheless, scholars interested in understanding the ways in which African Americans have adjusted to and battled against social, cultural, and political norms in the Lone Star State should have no difficulty finding both useful introductions and studies more acutely focused on aspects of segregation, discrimination, and the pursuit of civic and political equality.[18]

The politics of school desegregation has commanded a great deal of attention among Texas historians. One of the best and most recent contributions to this literature is Amilcar Shabazz's *Advancing Democracy*. Shabazz's study effectively challenges long-held perceptions that Texas managed to desegregate its public schools and universities in relative peace. Tracing Heman Sweatt's short career at the University of Texas Law School, Shabazz illuminates aspects of the civil rights era in Texas that have been overshadowed by more dramatic happenings in other states and at later times. Gary Lavergne's study *Before Brown*, which explores the earlier half of the Sweatt narrative, provides a nice complement to Shabazz's study, as does Dwonna Goldstone's *Integrating the 40 Acres.*[19]

These studies of the University of Texas at Austin notwithstanding, considerably more attention has been paid to the desegregation of public primary and secondary schools in Texas than to desegregation at colleges and universities. Historians should have little trouble accessing scholarship on the ramifications of this struggle, much of which has utilized local case studies.[20] Other scholars have found that educational reform more broadly also provides a gateway for exploring aspects of the civil rights era in Texas. By exploring understudied aspects of race and education, many scholars have subsequently advanced a trend that encourages the conflation of social, cultural, and political methods to the benefit of a historiography concerned with the evolving and diverse character of modernizing Texas.[21]

In 2004, Ruth P. Morgan contributed to the historiography of race and civil rights in Texas with *Governance by Decree*, which explores both the political impact of the Voting Rights Act of 1965 in Dallas and the impact of that law on the shifting structure of Dallas's local government. Morgan reveals a mixed legacy. With minority enfranchisement came opportunities for both legitimate representation and corruption, as minority leaders sometimes misused their newly elected offices. Morgan's study adds dimension to the post-1945 historiography dealing with race in Texas, which continues to develop. Along these lines, *White Metropolis* by Michael Phillips and *The Dallas Myth* by Harvey J. Graff also deserve mention.[22]

Regional development and identity are also crucial components of the developing historiography of modernizing Texas. Scholars interested in placing Texas within the larger story of an emerging and increasingly urban postwar Sunbelt would be wise to consult both Gerald N. Nash's *Federal Landscape* and Bruce Schulman's *From Cotton Belt to Sunbelt.* Both illuminate the relationship among federal defense industries, economic regulation, and growth. Though neither focuses exclusively on Texas, historians seeking to understand Texas's regional identity (or exceptionalism) will benefit from reading Nash and Schulman.[23] More recent is the extremely effective study edited by Michelle Nickerson and Darren Dochuk, *Sunbelt Rising.* Again, though not a study singularly focused on Texas, *Sunbelt Rising* draws on the historiography of contested regional identity, the South, and the impetus for economic, urban, and political development both conservative and liberal in nature.[24]

Prisons have become a stereotypically highlighted aspect of Sunbelt regional character; though a few historians have approached the history of law enforcement and prisons in post-1945 Texas, none as of 2011 have offered a comprehensive overview of the relationship between prisons, law enforcement, and that character.[25]

Obviously, economics is one of the key aspects to understanding Texas in the decades after World War II. Most economic histories of modernizing Texas have emphasized development in urban centers like Dallas, Fort Worth, Houston, San Antonio, and Austin. These studies are closely related in method and focus to studies concerned with suburbanization and demographic change. Most have further recognized that finance, construction, defense, energy, agriculture, and technology have been the most influential sources of economic growth. Texas is well entrenched in the broader narrative that sees World War II and the early Cold War as a context for the growing relationship of federal investment, defense industries, and economic growth. As the United States fought and won a global war, then prepared for the possibility of another, Texas grew more urban and industrial—thanks in part to the efforts of men like Jesse H. Jones, whose work through the Reconstruction Finance Corporation helped make federal contracts a source of great wealth and opportunity for many Texans. In the years following World War II, thousands of Texans moved from farms to factories and from the working class to the middle class, particularly in the state's biggest cities, where the impact of federal capital was felt most substantially. Historians have certainly recognized the power of these economic forces, but the literature needs and continues to expand.[26]

Lately, attention has been given to economic development and suburbanization in the Dallas-Fort Worth metroplex, and a few recent studies have focused on development in Austin, one of the state's fastest growing cities and perhaps the most representative of the impact of new technology on reshaping the national and global image of the Texas economy.[27]

Scholars have largely avoided synthesizing the economic history of modern Texas, choosing instead to connect with urban studies and to explain developments in a single location rather than the state as a whole. Though these urban studies have revealed much about the forces behind modern Texas's explosive economic growth, fewer scholars have taken the time to assess urbanization's impact on a rural Texas in sharp declension in recent years. The importance of a globalized market for Texas agriculture has been addressed by such scholars as Clayton Brown, but more needs to be done on the social, cultural, and political ramifications of urban and suburban economic development in smaller communities.[28]

More historians are also investigating the relationship between economic development and environmental conservation. South and East Texas have received the bulk of that attention, though some recent studies are expanding not only the field's geographic reach but its interconnectivity with social and cultural history as well. Still, the environmental history of modern Texas remains an emerging field in need of continued growth and exploration.[29]

Scholars in recent years have also grown increasingly interested in cultural memory as an aspect of Texas exceptionalism and regional identity. One of the best studies along these lines is Leigh Clemons's *Branding Texas*. Clemons succinctly comments on the construction of a distinctly Texan ethos, reflected in and reinforced through various forms of public entertainment. Her deconstruction of gender norms in Texas is particularly sharp. Scholars should also be interested in *Lone Star Pasts*, edited by Gregg Cantrell and Elizabeth Hayes Turner. This collection of essays is particularly helpful as an example to graduate students seeking methodological grounding for their own studies into the construction of modern social memory and popular Texas history.[30]

Cultural histories of modernizing Texas have addressed an array of other topics as well. A handful of studies look at developments in broadcasting and journalism, including several overviews of news coverage related to the assassination of John F. Kennedy, though this critical episode in both Texas and American history still deserves a comprehensive, scholarly analysis—preferably one focused on the tragedy's social, cultural, and political impact rather than various whodunit conspiracies. The best and most accessible option for someone looking to find a book on the immediate aftershocks from Kennedy's murder in Dallas should consult Steven Gillon's *The Kennedy Assassination—24 Hours After*.[31]

It should further surprise no one that Texas's sports-centric culture has captured the attention of numerous authors; a few are particularly worth mentioning as effective examples of how to use popular entertainment as a window into social, cultural, and political history. One of these is John Eisenberg's autobiographical *Cotton Bowl Days*, in which the author comments on, among other things, the emergence of a political far right in Dallas during the late 1950s, as well as the Kennedy assassination's impact on social and political consciousness.[32] However, the most influential and culturally significant study to use sports as a window on modern Texas is, without question, H. G. Bissinger's monumentally successful *Friday Night Lights*. Published in multiple editions, this book inspired a television show and Hollywood movie of the same name. The book is ostensibly a history of the 1988 Odessa Permian High School football team, but it is far more than that. Using football as a lens, Bissinger magnifies aspects of race, gender, class, and politics in West Texas, highlights cultural divisions premised on each of these categories, and exposes gross deficiencies in the Texas educational system of the late 1980s. When first released, *Friday Night Lights* made a popular splash that should in no way disqualify it as a valuable resource for scholars interested in the history of Texas, and especially West Texas. Though not a classically academic book, and certainly not above scholarly criticism, *Friday Night Lights* remains, at the very least, a model and potential staging point for deeper examinations into the interplay of race, gender, class, and social identity in modern Texas.[33]

Steven L. Davis has been more effective than most in writing about Texas literary history. His studies have shed light on oft-ignored aspects of Texas cultural history. These include *J. Frank Dobie* and *Texas Literary Outlaws*. Still, there is room for additional work on the literary and intellectual history of modernizing Texas.[34] There is also room for more scholarship on Texas music, though a small handful of books have at least opened a door for historians interested in Texas's placement within the broader narrative of contemporary popular music.[35]

Clearly, the historiography that addresses modernizing Texas has matured in several ways since the early 1990s. Significant advancements have been made in the scholarly understanding of Texas's recent political, social, economic, and cultural history. This historiography is now qualitatively stronger, but it is substantially larger as well—so large that, in a forum such as this, it is impossible to address every relevant book, journal article, book chapter, or dissertation added to library shelves each year. Such growth is to be expected and welcomed. As new generations of historians approach the story of modernizing Texas, that past becomes less and less recent. Contexts change. New interpretations emerge. Revision of the established narratives is inevitable. These are all healthy and necessary reflections on a field that continues to provide fertile soil for the cultivation of historical understanding. It will be interesting to see how historians have changed that understanding of modernizing Texas when the scholarship is reassessed in another twenty or so years.

NOTES

1. Ricky F. Dobbs, *Yellow Dogs and Republicans: Allan Shivers and Texas Two-Party Politics* (College Station: Texas A&M University Press, 2005); Kenneth Bridges, *Twilight*

of the Texas Democrats: The 1978 Governor's Race (College Station: Texas A&M University Press, 2008); Sean P. Cunningham, *Cowboy Conservatism: Texas and the Rise of the Modern Right* (Lexington: University Press of Kentucky, 2010). For more on Texas conservatism, see, for example, Jonathan Schoenwald, "The Case of General Edwin A. Walker," in *A Time for Choosing: The Rise of Modern American Conservatism* (New York: Oxford University Press, 2001), chap. 4. Conservative religious influences rooted in Texas can also be found in Daniel K. Williams, *God's Own Party: The Making of the Christian Right* (New York: Oxford University Press, 2010); and Darren Dochuk, *From Bible Belt to Sunbelt: Plain-Folk Religion, Grassroots Politics, and the Rise of Evangelical Conservatism* (New York: W. W. Norton, 2011). Five older texts are also worth considering: George N. Green, *The Establishment in Texas Politics: The Primitive Years, 1938–1957* (Norman: University of Oklahoma Press, 1979); Roger M. Olien, *From Token to Triumph: The Texas Republicans since 1920* (Dallas: Southern Methodist University Press, 1982); Don Carleton. *Red Scare! Right Wing Hysteria, Fifties Fanaticism and Their Legacies in Texas* (Austin: Texas Monthly Press, 1985); John R. Knaggs, *Two-Party Texas: The John Tower Era, 1961–1984* (Austin: Eakin Press, 1986); and Chandler Davidson, *Race and Class in Texas Politics* (Princeton, N.J.: Princeton University Press, 1990).

2. Earl Black and Merle Black, *The Rise of Southern Republicans* (Cambridge, Mass.: Harvard University Press, 2002); Byron E. Shafer and Richard Johnston, *The End of Southern Exceptionalism: Class, Race, and Partisan Change in the Postwar South* (Cambridge, Mass.: Harvard University Press, 2006). See also Michael Lind, *Made in Texas: George W. Bush and the Southern Takeover of American Politics* (New York: Basic Books, 2003); Steven Lawson, *In Pursuit of Power: Southern Blacks and Electoral Politics, 1965–1982* (New York: Columbia University Press, 1987); Numan V. Bartley, *The New South, 1945–1980: The Story of the South's Modernization* (Baton Rouge: Louisiana State University Press, 1995); and Jack Bass and Walter DeVries, *The Transformation of Southern Politics: Social Change and Political Consequence since 1945* (Athens: University of Georgia Press, 1995).

3. Douglas Rossinow, *The Politics of Authenticity: Liberalism, Christianity, and the New Left in America* (New York: Columbia University Press, 1998). For more on Texas liberalism, see David Cullen and Kyle G. Wilkison, eds., *The Texas Left: The Radical Roots of Lone Star Liberalism* (College Station: Texas A&M University Press, 2010); and William S. Clayson, *Freedom Is Not Enough: The War on Poverty and the Civil Rights Movement in Texas* (Austin: University of Texas Press, 2010).

4. Robert Dallek, *Lone Star Rising: Lyndon Johnson and His Times, 1908–1960* (New York: Oxford University Press, 1991), and *Flawed Giant: Lyndon Johnson and His Times, 1961–1973* (New York: Oxford University Press, 1999). See also by Robert A. Caro, *The Years of Lyndon Johnson: The Path to Power* (New York: Knopf, 1982), *Means of Ascent: The Years of Lyndon Johnson* (New York: Alfred A. Knopf, 1990), *Master of the Senate: The Years of Lyndon Johnson* (New York: Knopf, 2002), and *The Passage of Power: The Years of Lyndon Johnson* (New York: Knopf, 2012); and Irving Bernstein, *Guns or Butter: The Presidency of Lyndon Johnson* (New York: Oxford University Press, 1996). For tighter examinations of the Johnson presidency, see Julie Leininger Pycior, *LBJ and Mexican Americans: The Paradox of Power* (Austin: University of Texas Press, 1997); Thomas Clarkin, *Federal Indian Policy in the Kennedy and Johnson Administrations,*

1961–1969 (Albuquerque: University of New Mexico Press, 2001); Hal K. Rothman, *LBJ's Texas White House: "Our Heart's Home"* (College Station: Texas A&M University Press, 2001); and Sean J. Savage, *JFK, LBJ, and the Democratic Party* (Albany: State University of New York Press, 2004).

5. John Robert Greene, *The Presidency of George Bush* (Lawrence: University Press of Kansas, 2000); Ryan J. Barilleaux and Mark J. Rozell, *Power and Prudence: The Presidency of George H. W. Bush* (College Station: Texas A&M University Press, 2004); Herbert S. Parmet, *George Bush: The Life of a Lone Star Yankee* (New York: Scribner, 1997).

6. Kevin Phillips, *American Dynasty: Aristocracy, Fortune, and the Politics of Deceit in the House of Bush* (New York: Viking, 2004), and *American Theocracy: The Peril and Politics of Radical Religion, Oil, and Borrowed Money in the 21st Century* (New York: Viking, 2006). See also Robert Bryce, *Cronies: Oil, the Bushes, and the Rise of Texas, America's Superstate* (New York: PublicAffairs, 2004).

7. Bryan Burrough, *The Big Rich: The Rise and Fall of the Greatest Texas Oil Fortunes* (New York: Penguin Press, 2009). For more on Texas oil, see Jane Wolfe, *The Murchisons* (New York: St. Martin's Press, 1989); and Roger M. Olien, *Wildcatters: Texas Independent Oilmen* (College Station: Texas A&M University Press, 2007). For more on political corruption, see Mickey Herskowitz, *Sharpstown Revisited: Frank Sharp and a Tale of Dirty Politics in Texas* (Austin: Eakin Press, 1994).

8. Patrick Cox, *Ralph W. Yarborough: The People's Senator* (Austin: University of Texas Press, 2001); Patrick L. Cox and Michael Phillips, *The House Will Come to Order: How the Texas Speaker Became a Power in State and National Politics* (Austin: University of Texas Press, 2010). See also Kenneth Hendrickson, Jr., and Michael L. Collins, *Profiles in Power: Twentieth Century Texans in Washington* (Austin: University of Texas Press, 2004); and Brian McCall, *The Power of the Texas Governor: Connally to Bush* (Austin: University of Texas Press, 2009). For more on modernizing Texas using civil rights and second-wave feminism as lenses for analyses, see Judith N. McArthur and Harold L. Smith, *Texas through Women's Eyes: The Twentieth Century Experience* (Austin: University of Texas Press, 2010); other examples include Mike Cochran, *Claytie: The Roller-Coaster Life of a Texas Wildcatter* (College Station: Texas A&M University Press, 2007); James Reston, Jr., *The Lone Star: The Life of John Connally* (New York: Harper and Row, 1990); Carolyn Barta, *Bill Clements: Texian to His Toenails* (Austin: Eakin Press, 1996); Dan Murph, *Texas Giant: The Life of Price Daniel* (Austin: Eakin Press, 2002); and Mary Beth Rogers, *Barbara Jordan, American Hero* (New York: Bantam Books, 1998). A few good studies of political women have been published, including Nancy Young and Lewis L. Gould, *Texas, Her Texas: The Life and Times of Frances Goff* (Austin: Texas State Historical Association, 1997); and Nancy Baker Jones and Ruthe Winegarten, *Capitol Women: Texas Female Legislators, 1923–1999* (Austin: University of Texas Press, 2000). Other political biographies worth noting are Gary A. Keith, *Eckhardt: There Once Was a Congressman from Texas* (Austin: University of Texas Press, 2007); Laura F. Cavazos, *A Kineno Remembers: From the King Ranch to the White House* (College Station: Texas A&M University Press, 2008); Dave McNeely and Jim Henderson, *Bob Bullock: God Bless Texas* (Austin: University of Texas Press, 2008); and Nancy

Beck Young, *Wright Patman: Populism, Liberalism, and the American Dream* (Dallas: Southern Methodist University Press, 2000).

9. The standard introduction to this topic remains David Montejano, *Anglos and Mexicans in the Making of Texas, 1836–1986* (Austin: University of Texas Press, 1987), though only Part 4 deals specifically with the post-1945 period. Still, students of modernizing Texas should be familiar with this study. Phyllis McKenzie, *The Mexican Texans* (College Station: Texas A&M University Press, 2004), is worth noting as a more concise introduction, with chapters 3 and 4 being most relevant to modern Texas history. For another concise introduction, see Arnoldo De León, *Mexican Americans in Texas: A Brief History*, 3rd ed. (Wheeling, Ill.: Harlan Davidson, 2009).

10. Rodolfo Rosales, *The Illusion of Inclusion: The Untold Political Story of San Antonio* (Austin: University of Texas Press, 2000); Marc Simon Rodriguez, *The Tejano Diaspora: Mexican Americanism and Politics in Texas and Wisconsin* (Chapel Hill: University of North Carolina Press, 2011). See also Robert D. Auerbach, *Deception and Abuse at the Fed: Henry B. Gonzalez Battles Alan Greenspan's Bank* (Austin: University of Texas Press, 2008).

11. For examples, see Benjamin Marquez, *LULAC: The Evolution of a Mexican American Political Organization* (Austin: University of Texas Press, 1993); Craig A. Kaplowitz, *LULAC, Mexican Americans, and National Policy* (College Station: Texas A&M University Press, 2005); and Armando Navarro, *La Raza Unida Party: A Chicano Challenge to the U.S. Two Party Dictatorship* (Philadelphia: Temple University Press, 2000).

12. Ignacio M. García, *United We Win: The Rise and Fall of La Raza Unida Party* (Tucson: University of Arizona Press, 1989), and *Viva Kennedy: Mexican Americans in Search of Camelot* (College Station: Texas A&M University Press, 2000); two additional studies by García worth reading are *Hector P. García: In Relentless Pursuit of Justice* (Houston: Arte Publico Press, 2002), and *White, but Not Equal: Mexican Americans, Jury Discrimination, and the Supreme Court* (Tucson: University of Arizona Press, 2008). For additional legal studies focused on Mexican Americans, see Louise Ann Fisch, *All Rise: Reynaldo G. Garza, the First Mexican American Federal Judge* (College Station: Texas A&M University Press, 1996); and Carlos R. Soltero, *Latinos and American Law: Landmark Supreme Court Cases* (Austin: University of Texas Press, 2006).

13. Patrick Carroll, *Felix Longoria's Wake: Bereavement, Racism, and the Rise of Mexican American Activism* (Austin: University of Texas Press, 2003).

14. For scholarship focused on Mexican American identity and political activism in South Texas, see, for example, Amando Navarro, *The Cristal Experiment: A Chicano Struggle for Community Control* (Madison: University of Wisconsin Press, 1998); Gilberto J. Quezada, *Border Boss: Manuel B. Bravo and Zapata County* (College Station: Texas A&M University Press, 1999); Chad Richardson, *Batos, Bolilos, Pochos, and Pelados: Class and Culture on the South Texas Border* (Austin: University of Texas Press, 1999); Daniel D. Arreola, *Tejano South Texas: A Mexican American Cultural Province* (Austin: University of Texas Press, 2002); and Anthony Quiroz, *Claiming Citizenship: Mexican Americans in Victoria, Texas* (College Station: Texas A&M University Press, 2005).

15. Scott Cook, *Mexican Brick Culture in the Building of Texas, 1800s–1980s* (College Station: Texas A&M University Press, 1998); Zargosa Vargas, *Labor Rights Are Civil Rights:*

Mexican American Workers in Twentieth-Century America (Princeton, N.J.: Princeton University Press, 2005); Monica Perales, *Smeltertown: Making and Remembering a Southwest Border Community* (Chapel Hill: University of North Carolina Press, 2010); Deborah Cohen, *Braceros: Migrant Citizens and Transnational Subjects in the Postwar United States and Mexico* (Chapel Hill: University of North Carolina Press, 2011).

16. The seminal example of "whiteness studies" remains David Roediger, *The Wages of Whiteness: Race and the Making of the American Working Class*, rev. ed. (New York: Verso Books, 1999). Arnoldo De León, *Ethnicity in the Sunbelt: Mexican Americans in Houston* (College Station: Texas A&M University Press, 2001); David Montejano, *Quixote's Soldiers: A Local History of the Chicano Movement, 1966–1981* (Austin: University of Texas Press, 2010). See also Carlos Kevin Blanton, "George I. Sanchez, Ideology, and Whiteness in the Making of the Mexican American Civil Rights Movement, 1930–1960," *Journal of Southern History* 72 (Aug. 2006): 569–604. For similar studies that rely more heavily on religion as a framework for analysis, see Roberto R. Trevino, *The Church in the Barrio: Mexican American Ethno-Catholicism in Houston* (Chapel Hill: University of North Carolina Press, 2006); and Paul Barton, *Hispanic Methodists, Presbyterians, and Baptists in Texas* (Austin: University of Texas Press, 2006). At least three studies have examined Mexican American women's experience since 1945: Vicki Ruiz, *From out of the Shadows: Mexican Women in Twentieth-Century America* (New York: Oxford University Press, 1998); Jose Angel Gutierrez, Michelle Melendez, and Sonia Adriana Noyola, eds., *Chicanas in Charge: Texas Women in the Public Arena* (Lanham, Md.: AltaMira Press, 2006); and Cynthia Orozco, *No Mexicans, Women, or Dogs Allowed: The Rise of the Mexican American Civil Rights Movement* (Austin: University of Texas Press, 2009).

17. Brian D. Behnken, *Fighting Their Own Battles: Mexican Americans, African Americans, and the Struggle for Civil Rights in Texas* (Chapel Hill: University of North Carolina Press, 2011); for a similar study, see Neil Foley, *Quest for Equality: The Failed Promise of Black-Brown Solidarity* (Cambridge, Mass.: Harvard University Press, 2010).

18. For instance, see Alwyn Barr, *Black Texans: A History of African Americans in Texas, 1525–1995* (Norman: University of Oklahoma Press, 1996); Alwyn Barr and Robert A. Calvert, eds., *Black Leaders: Texans for Their Times* (Austin: Texas State Historical Association, 1990); and Bruce A. Glasrud and James M. Smallwood, eds., *The African American Experience in Texas: An Anthology* (Lubbock: Texas Tech University Press, 2007). For similar studies focused exclusively on Houston, see Howard Beeth and Cary D. Wintz, eds., *Black Dixie: Afro-Texan History and Culture in Houston* (College Station: Texas A&M University Press, 2000); and Robert D. Bullard, *Invisible Houston: The Black Experience in Boom and Bust* (College Station: Texas A&M University Press, 1987). For information on African American women in post-1945 Texas, see, for instance, Bruce A. Glasrud and Merline Pitre, eds., *Black Women in Texas History* (College Station: Texas A&M University Press, 2008); and Merline Pitre, *In Struggle against Jim Crow: Lulu B. White and the NAACP, 1900–1957* (College Station: Texas A&M University Press, 1999).

Several good studies have used sports as a lens for understanding the black Texas experience, including Frank Fitzpatrick, *And the Walls Came Tumbling Down: Kentucky, Texas Western, and the Game That Changed American Sports* (New York: Simon and Schuster, 1999); Robert J. Robertson, *Fair Ways: How Six Black Golfers Won Civil Rights in Beaumont, Texas* (College Station: Texas A&M University Press, 2005); and Charles H. Martin, *Benching Jim Crow: The Rise and Fall of the Color Line in Southern College Sports, 1890–1980* (Urbana: University of Illinois Press, 2010). See also Michael R. Botson, Jr., *Labor, Civil Rights, and the Hughes Tool Company* (College Station: Texas A&M University Press, 2005).

19. Amilcar Shabazz, *Advancing Democracy: African Americans and the Struggle for Access and Equity in Higher Education in Texas* (Chapel Hill: University of North Carolina Press, 2004); Gary M. Lavergne, *Before Brown: Heman Marion Sweatt, Thurgood Marshall, and the Long Road to Justice* (Austin: University of Texas Press, 2010); Dwonna Goldstone, *Integrating the 40 Acres: The 50-Year Struggle for Racial Equality at the University of Texas* (Athens: University of Georgia Press, 2006).

20. For studies on Houston, see Thomas R. Cole, *No Color Is My Kind: The Life of Eldrewey Stearns and the Integration of Houston* (Austin: University of Texas Press, 1997); William Henry Kellar, *Make Haste Slowly: Moderates, Conservatives, and School Desegregation in Houston* (College Station: Texas A&M University Press, 1999); and Guadalupe San Miguel, Jr., *Brown, Not White: School Integration and the Chicano Movement in Houston* (College Station: Texas A&M University Press, 2001). For studies on Dallas, see Glenn Linden, *Desegregating Schools in Dallas: Four Decades in the Federal Courts* (Dallas: Three Forks Press, 1995); and Robyn Duff Ladino, *Desegregating Texas Schools: Eisenhower, Shivers, and the Crisis at Mansfield High* (Austin: University of Texas Press, 1996).

21. Paul A. Sracic, *San Antonio v. Rodriguez and the Pursuit of Equal Education: The Debate over Discrimination and School Funding* (Lawrence: University Press of Kansas, 2007); Guadalupe San Miguel, Jr., *"Let All of Them Take Heed": Mexican Americans and the Campaign for Educational Equality in Texas, 1910–1981* (Austin: University of Texas Press, 1987); Carlos Kevin Blanton, *The Strange Career of Bilingual Education in Texas, 1836–1981* (College Station: Texas A&M University Press, 2004); Gene B. Preuss, *To Get a Better School System: One Hundred Years of Education Reform in Texas* (College Station: Texas A&M University Press, 2009); Larry Cuban, *As Good as It Gets: What School Reform Brought to Austin* (Cambridge, Mass.: Harvard University Press, 2010).

22. Ruth P. Morgan, *Governance by Decree: The Impact of the Voting Rights in Dallas* (Lawrence: University Press of Kansas, 2004); Michael Phillips, *White Metropolis: Race, Ethnicity, and Religion in Dallas, 1847–2001* (Austin: University of Texas Press, 2006); Harvey J. Graff, *The Dallas Myth: The Making and Unmaking of an American City* (Minneapolis: University of Minnesota Press, 2008). On race and political access, see Debra A. Reid, ed., *Seeking Inalienable Rights: Texans and Their Quests for Justice* (College Station: Texas A&M University Press, 2009).

23. Gerald N. Nash, *The Federal Landscape: An Economic History of the Twentieth-Century West* (Tucson: University of Arizona Press, 1999); Bruce J. Schulman, *From Cotton Belt to Sunbelt: Federal Policy, Economic Development, and the Transformation of the South, 1938–1980* (New York: Oxford University Press, 1991).

24. Michelle Nickerson and Darren Dochuk, *Sunbelt Rising: The Politics of Space, Place, and Region* (Philadelphia: University of Pennsylvania Press, 2011); see specifically Volker Janssen, "Sunbelt Lock-Up: Where the Suburbs Met the Super-Max," 217–39.

25. For examples of work done on law enforcement in Texas, see Gary M. Lavergne, *A Sniper in the Tower: The Charles Whitman Murders* (Denton: University of North Texas Press, 1997); Steven Hamon Wilson, *The Rise of Judicial Management in the U.S. District Court, Southern District of Texas, 1955–2000* (Athens: University of Georgia Press, 2002); Dwight D. Watson, *Race and the Houston Police Department, 1930–1990: A Change Did Come* (College Station: Texas A&M University Press, 2005); Robert M. Utley, *Lone Star Lawmen: The Second Century of the Texas Rangers* (New York: Oxford University Press, 2007); and Howard Campbell, *Drug War Zone: Frontline Dispatches from the Streets of El Paso and Juarez* (Austin: University of Texas Press, 2009). On prisons in modern Texas, see Chad R. Trulson and James W. Marquart, *First Available Cell: Desegregation of the Texas Prison System* (Austin: University of Texas Press, 2009); Ben M. Crouch and James W. Marquart, *An Appeal to Justice: Litigated Reform of Texas Prisons* (Austin: University of Texas Press, 1989); James W. Marquart, Sheldon Ekland-Olson, and Jonathan E. Sorensen, *The Rope, the Chair, and the Needle: Capital Punishment in Texas, 1923–1990* (Austin: University of Texas Press, 1993); William T. Harper, *Eleven Days in Hell: The 1974 Carrasco Prison Siege in Huntsville, Texas* (Denton: University of North Texas Press, 2004); and David M. Horton and George R. Nielson, *Walking George: The Life of George John Beto and the Rise of the Modern Texas Prison System* (Denton: University of North Texas Press, 2005).

26. Among the many good books on Texas economic development since 1945 are Joseph A. Pratt and Christopher J. Castaneda, *Builders: Herman and George R. Brown* (College Station: Texas A&M University Press, 1999); and Howard J. Erlichman, *Camino del Norte: How a Series of Watering Holes, Fords, and Dirt Trails Evolved into Interstate 35 in Texas* (College Station: Texas A&M University Press, 2006). On Houston's economy, see Walter Buenger and Joe Pratt, *But Also Good Business: Texas Commerce Banks and the Financing of Houston and Texas* (College Station: Texas A&M University Press, 1986); George T. Morgan, Jr., and John O. King, *The Woodlands: New Community Development, 1964–1983* (College Station: Texas A&M University Press, 1987); and Joe R. Feagin, *Free Enterprise City: Houston in Political-Economic Perspective* (New Brunswick, NJ: Rutgers University Press, 1988).

27. On Dallas-Fort Worth, see Robert B. Fairbanks, *For the City as a Whole: Planning, Politics, and the Public Interest in Dallas, Texas, 1900–1965* (Columbus: Ohio State University Press, 1998); William H. Wilson, *Hamilton Park: A Planned Black Community in Dallas* (Baltimore: Johns Hopkins University Press, 1998); J'Nell L. Pate, *Livestock Legacy: The Fort Worth Stockyards, 1887–1987* (College Station: Texas A&M University Press, 2000); and Victoria Buenger and Walter Buenger, *Texas Merchant: Marvin Leonard and Fort Worth* (College Station: Texas A&M University Press, 2001). On Austin, see Kenneth B. Ragsdale, *Austin, Cleared for Takeoff: Aviators, Businessmen, and the Growth of an American City* (Austin: University of Texas Press, 2004); Linda Scarbrough, *Road, River, and Ol' Boy Politics: A Texas County's Path from Farm to Supersuburb* (Austin: Texas State Historical Association, 2005); and William Scott Swearingen, Jr., *Environmental City: People, Place, Politics, and the Meaning of Modern Austin* (Austin: University of Texas Press, 2010).

28. A good source for understanding changes in Texas agribusiness is Clayton D. Brown, *King Cotton in Modern America: A Cultural, Political, and Economic History*

since 1945 (Jackson: University Press of Mississippi, 2011). See also John Opie, *Ogallala: Water for a Dry Land* (Lincoln: University of Nebraska Press, 1993); T. Lindsay Baker, *More Ghost Towns of Texas* (Norman: University of Oklahoma Press, 2003); and Phillip G. Pope, "Missing Places: Small Town Decline in the Texas Panhandle since 1945" (Ph.D. diss., Texas Tech University, 2012).

29. For examples, see Dick Bartlett, *Saving the Best of Texas: A Partnership Approach to Conservation* (Austin: University of Texas Press, 1995); James J. Cozine, Jr., *Saving the Big Thicket: From Exploration to Preservation, 1685–2003* (Denton: University of North Texas Press, 2004); Martin V. Melosi and Joseph A. Pratt, *Energy Metropolis: An Environmental History of Houston and the Gulf Coast* (Pittsburgh, Pa.: University of Pittsburgh Press, 2007); and Kenna Lang Archer, "Damning the River of the Arms of God: The People of the Brazos and Their Unwieldy River" (Ph.D. diss., Texas Tech University, 2012). Several historians have used Lady Bird Johnson as a means for exploring Texas environmental history, including Lewis L. Gould, *Lady Bird Johnson: Our Environmental First Lady* (Lawrence: University Press of Kansas, 1999); and Jan Jarboe Russell, *Lady Bird: A Biography of Mrs. Johnson* (New York: Scribner, 1999).

30. Leigh Clemons, *Branding Texas: Performing Culture in the Lone Star State* (Austin: University of Texas Press, 2008); Gregg Cantrell and Elizabeth Hayes Turner, eds., *Lone Star Pasts: Memory and History in Texas* (College Station: Texas A&M University Press, 2006). Memory studies focused on the Alamo have been the most popular way for historians to tackle contemporary cultural identity formation in Texas. Arguably the best of these is James E. Crisp, *Sleuthing the Alamo: Davy Crockett's Last Stand and Other Mysteries of the Texas Revolution* (New York: Oxford University Press, 2005); related studies include Holly Beachley Brear, *Inherit the Alamo: Myth and Ritual at an American Shrine* (Austin: University of Texas Press, 1995); Dan Kilgore and James E. Crisp, *How Did Davy Die? And Why Do We Care So Much?* (College Station: Texas A&M University Press, 2010); and Randy Roberts and James S. Olson, *A Line in the Sand: The Alamo in Blood and Memory* (New York: Free Press, 2001).

31. On the media, see Richard Schroeder, *Texas Signs On: The Early Days of Radio and Television* (College Station: Texas A&M University Press, 1998); Aida Barrera, *Looking for Carrascolendas: From a Child's World to Award-Winning Television* (Austin: University of Texas Press, 2001); and Patrick Cox, *The First Texas News Barons* (Austin: University of Texas Press, 2005). On the JFK assassination and journalism, see Bob Huffaker, Bill Mercer, George Phenix, and Wes Wise, *When the News Went Live: Dallas 1963* (Lanham, Md.: Taylor Trade Publishing, 2004); and Robert B. Semple, ed., *Four Days in November: The Original Coverage of the John F. Kennedy Assassination* (New York: St. Martin's Press, 2003). Steven M. Gillon, *The Kennedy Assassination—24 Hours After: Lyndon B. Johnson's Pivotal First Day as President* (New York: Basic Books, 2009).

32. John Eisenberg, *Cotton Bowl Days: Growing Up with Dallas and the Cowboys in the 1960s* (New York: Simon and Schuster, 1997); see also Terry Frei, *Horns, Hogs, and Nixon Coming: Texas vs. Arkansas in Dixie's Last Stand* (New York: Simon and Schuster, 2002); and David G. McComb, *Spare Time in Texas: Recreation and History in the Lone Star State* (Austin: University of Texas Press, 2008).

33. H. G. Bissinger, *Friday Night Lights: A Town, a Team, and a Dream* (Cambridge, Mass.: Da Capo Press, 1990, 2000); see also Carlton Stowers, *Where Dreams Die Hard:*

A Small American Town and its Six-Man Football Team (Cambridge, Mass.: Da Capo Press, 2005).

34. Steven L. Davis, *J. Frank Dobie: A Liberated Mind* (Austin: University of Texas Press, 2009), and *Texas Literary Outlaws: Six Writers in the Sixties and Beyond* (Fort Worth: Texas Christian University Press, 2004). Others examples are Keith L. Bryant, *Culture in the American Southwest: The Earth, the Sky, the People* (College Station: Texas A&M University Press, 2001); Megan Barnard, ed., *Collecting the Imagination: The First Fifty Years of the Ransom Center* (Austin: University of Texas Press, 2007); Alan Gribben, *Harry Hunt Ransom: Intellect in Motion* (Austin: University of Texas Press, 2008); and James S. Olson, *Making Cancer History: Disease and Discovery at the University of Texas M. D. Anderson Cancer Center* (Baltimore: Johns Hopkins University Press, 2009).

35. Barry Shank, *Dissonant Identities: The Rock'n'Roll Scene in Austin, Texas* (Hanover, N.H.: Wesleyan University Press, 1994); Andy Bradley and Roger Wood, *House of Hits: The Story of Houston's Gold Star/SugarHill Recording Studios* (Austin: University of Texas Press, 2010). For more on Mexican American/Tejano music, see Yolanda Broyles-Gonzalez, *Lydia Mendoza's Life in Music: La Historia de Lydia Mendoza* (New York: Oxford University Press, 2001); and Guadalupe San Miguel, Jr., *Tejano Proud: Tex-Mex Music in the Twentieth Century* (College Station: Texas A&M University Press, 2002).

CHAPTER 15

Recent Texas, 1981 to the Present

Bruce A. Glasrud, Light Townsend Cummins, and Cary D. Wintz

In December 2000, Texas lieutenant governor James Richard "Rick" Perry assumed the office of governor as George W. Bush prepared to become the forty-third president of the United States. By December 2013, although two-term President Bush had been out of office for five years, Governor Perry remained in office, and he should serve until January 2015. This would give Perry fourteen years in the governor's mansion, making him the longest-sitting governor in Texas history and one of the longer in the United States. The political endurance of Perry following the popular George W. Bush cemented the state of Texas as a solidly "red" state in the twenty-first-century vernacular. Such a lengthy career as governor ought to lend to some remarkable studies. It also leads to questions: Will he run again for the presidency, in spite of his poor showing in the 2012 primaries? Who will succeed him as governor—a Democrat, or will Republicans continue to own the office? The above comments and questions lead to two issues connected to historians: first, they are not any better political prognosticators than anyone else, and second, historians seldom write about "recent" topics. For historians of the recent past, it is sometimes difficult to achieve the necessary distance in order to arrive at an objective interpretation of people and events.

The above scenario regarding Governor Perry provides evidence to those points. Despite his lengthy tenure in office, little of a scholarly nature has been written about Governor Perry. He was featured in Gail Collins's op-ed book *How the Lone Star State Hijacked the American Agenda*, but, as telling as the portrait is, the nation likely has more to fear from itself than from the Lone Star State. Perry, remember, achieved few positive results in his presidential campaign. No book and few interpretive articles have covered his successive administrations or examined the extent to which his years in office have solidified control by a governor designed by the Texas Constitution to be a weak executive. Primary sources abound and will leave students with solid topics for research in the future, should any wish to examine Perry's legacy. Governor Perry has written two books, and these also can assist the historian. *On My Honor: Why the American Values of the Boy Scouts Are Worth Fighting For* was published in 2008. A conservative Republican, in this book Perry emphasizes the positive impact of the organization on the youth of America. His second book, *Fed Up! Our Fight to Save America from Washington*, was published in 2010; it contains Perry's arguments for a limited central government.[1]

The dearth of historical examination also afflicts other Texas politicians of recent vintage. We know of no works that cover the lives, or careers, of former governor Mark White or of senators Phil Gramm, John Cornyn, or Lloyd Bentsen. Both Gramm and Cornyn do have biographies published about them from Books on Demand, authored by Jesse Russell and Ronald Cohn, articles originally printed in and by Wikipedia. Senator Gramm also published *The Role of Government in a Free Society*, a book that provides extensive insight into his views on government and the economy. When Senator Bentsen became U.S. secretary of the treasury, a small thirty-two page book by John Hamilton provided some information about the newly appointed secretary.[2] On the other hand, not only has Republican senator Kay Bailey Hutchison authored two interesting studies of women leaders and politicians, *American Heroines* and *Leading Ladies*, she has been the recipient of studies, including the critical early biography by Arthur Frederick Ide, *From Stardom to Scandal*. She obviously had not fallen too far since her years in the U.S. Senate came after the Ide book. More recently Hutchison also was the recipient of one of the Russell/Cohn books-on-demand.[3]

Charismatic leaders William P. "Bill" Clements and Ann Richards have been discussed by students and scholars. On Clements, see the well-written study by Carolyn Barta.[4] On Governor Richards, the not always favorable book by Mike Shropshire and Frank Schaefer, *The Thorny Rose of Texas*, is a fun read. One can garner much personal information from Ann Richards and Peter Knobler's *Straight from the Heart*. The best work on Ann Richards is Jan Reid's *Let the People In*. Reid pays attention to Richard's style and character.[5] Governor Richards's former husband, David Richards, in *Once upon a Time in Texas*, with humor and compassion describes his and others' lives on the liberal and Democratic side of Texas politics.[6] Without support from her gubernatorial opponent, West Texas iconoclast Clayton Williams, Richards might have lost the election of 1990. An insightful study is Sue Tolleson-Rinehart and Jeanie R. Stanley's *Claytie and the Lady*. For more on Williams, consult Mike Cochran's *Claytie*.[7]

It would be remiss if we did not mention the two Texans who also served as U.S. presidents during these years—George H. W. Bush and George W. Bush. An excellent place to begin with the forty-first president is *George Bush: The Life of a Lone Star Yankee*, by Herbert S. Parmet. The senior Bush, although not born a Texan, moved to Texas and later became Ronald Reagan's vice president during his presidency. Bush followed Reagan as president and served from 1989 through 1992. A study of the man who became the forty-third president is Clarke Rountree's *George W. Bush: A Biography*. Bush junior served as president for two terms, from 2001 through 2008. Kevin Phillips has written a critical assessment of the overall influence of the Bush family: *American Dynasty*.[8]

Beginning with the election of 1978, Texas underwent considerable change. Not the least feature was the election of Republican William P. "Bill" Clements as governor. For the impact of this election, see Kenneth Bridges's *Twilight of the Texas Democrats*. Clements was the first Republican elected governor of Texas since Reconstruction. Although Democrats Mark White (1983–1987) and Ann Richards (1991–1995) would hold office as governors after 1980, Republicans gained control of state political life. That change has been evident in most of the major issues of the past thirty years, among them population growth, immigration, redistricting (including voter gerrymandering), drug wars, the economy, defective infrastructure, urbanization, public education, and personal issues including abortion, sexual preference, and religion. These and other topics have been covered by historians as well as by writers and scholars from other disciplines. A short overview of this recent period can be found in Rupert N. Richardson, Adrian Anderson, Cary D. Wintz, and Ernest Wallace's "Republican Texas, 1985–2008" in *Texas: The Lone Star State*. Its historiography is covered in Nancy Beck Young's "Beyond Parochialism" in *Beyond Texas through Time*.[9]

The period began with the tumultuous 1980s. That decade is well described and analyzed in M. Ray Perryman's *Survive and Conquer*. It is too bad that Perryman or someone else did not continue into the nineties and the twenty-first century.[10] Scholars do, however, continue to research, analyze, and explain the political aspects of those years. Brian McCall, for example, in *The Power of the Texas Governor*, provides an analysis of the influence and, to a lesser extent, ability of Texas governors of those years. McCall's book is helpful in gaining a sense of what these governors accomplished. Other Texas political leaders arose in the Texas House of Representatives. It was a place for skilled performers, as Patrick Cox and Michael Phillips relate so well in *The House Will Come to Order*.[11] As noted by Dave McNeely and Jim Henderson, in *Bob Bullock: God Bless Texas*, lieutenant governors in Texas wield considerable power and influence. Bullock is a classic example of what could be and was accomplished by someone in this position.[12]

Liberals proudly called Texas home at the beginning of the 1980s, yet in a few years their influence virtually disappeared. They celebrated the leading role of liberal leaders such as Ralph Yarborough and Henry B. Gonzalez. Gonzalez challenged Alan Greenspan, as discussed in Robert D. Auerbach, *Deception and Abuse at the Fed*. One liberal Democratic congressman, Bob Eckhardt, is portrayed by Gary A. Keith in *Eckhardt: There Once Was a Congressman from Texas*. A colorful, hardworking politico, Eckhardt aided and encouraged many junior congressmen from across the nation, including Tennessee leader and later vice president Al Gore. However, not all liberals were politicians, as Don E. Carleton reports in *A Breed So Rare: The Life of J. R. Partin, Liberal Texas Oil Man*.[13]

As the political careers of Ann Richards, Kay Bailey Hutchison, and earlier Barbara Jordan illustrate, women entered politics in increasing numbers beginning in the 1970s and have continued to do so. Nancy Baker Jones and the late Ruthe Winegarten capture the spirit and abilities of those women who served in the Texas legislature in *Capitol Women*. During these years the ethnic and cultural background of female public officials changed, and more Latinas held office. Information on this group can be located in *Políticas: Latina Public Officials in Texas*, by Sonya García and colleagues. The influence of a San Antonio legislator can be noticed in Sharon A. Navarro's *Latina Legislator: Letitia Van de Putte and the Road to Leadership*.[14]

As García's collection emphasizes, one of the important demographic changes in Texas during the past thirty years has been the significant increase in the percentage of and population of peoples of Mexican and other Latin American nations' descent. One example, as Louise Ann Fisch notes in *All Rise: Reynaldo G. Garza*, was the appointment of a Mexican American to the federal bench. Mexican Americans, or Tejanos, organized and created the Raza Unida Party, a story described by Ignacio M. García in his study *United We Win*. The Mexican American influence has spread, shows Matt Rodriquez in *The Tejano Diaspora*.[15]

As mentioned earlier, one of the issues of import during the past thirty years, especially with the wrangling between Democratic and Republican parties over the 1965 Voting Rights Act regulation of preclearance, was that of redistricting, an issue that eventually brought about the downfall of a powerful Texas politician, Thomas Dale "Tom" DeLay, the House majority leader. That is Steve Bickerstaff's emphasis in *Line in the Sand*. To attempt balance on the issue, DeLay published, with Stephen Mansfield, a memoir titled *No Retreat, No Surrender*. Such redistricting conflicts escalated, and as reported by Steven Wilson led to an increased federal judicial system watching the process. Wilson's book, *The Rise of Judicial Management in the U.S. District Court, Southern District of Texas*, skillfully explores the growth of the southern district court for Texas.[16]

The majority of both scholarly and nonscholarly publications connected with recent Texas, the years beyond 1980, have referenced or dealt directly with Texas politics. Such books sell and are perhaps easier to focus on than broader-ranging studies of an increasingly urbanized and diverse state. However, there also has been, if not a proliferation, at least a modicum of studies that concern nonpolitical issues and concerns in the Lone Star State. The most significant and perplexing book is that produced by Steve Murdock and colleagues, *The New Texas Challenge: Population Change and the Future of Texas*, which calls on Texans to pay attention to the demographic changes taking place in the Lone Star State, changes that affect such vitally important issues as public education, housing, urban and suburban growth, and, quite naturally, politics. Murdock's book will continue to retain our attention, even as the numbers change.[17]

As Murdock reports, immigration from Mexico, both legal and illegal, challenges the state and the nation. For more on that topic, see the succinct study by Charles Bowden and Julian Cardona, *Exodus/Exodo*, which analyzes the many ramifications of the migration from Mexico to the Lone Star State. Bowden earlier noted the severe problems associated with the drug trafficking and trade in his sensational *Down by the River*.[18] The relationship of drugs, money, murder, and family continues to haunt cities in Texas, particularly border cities such as El Paso, Laredo, Houston, and San Antonio.

Cities like those mentioned above have grown substantially in both population and expanse during the past thirty years. Survival of the cities and their inhabitants depends on energy in many differing respects. An examination of energy in Houston and the Texas Gulf Coast can point to the needs of the city, as well as to the environmental protections a city and region need in order to establish responsible urban growth, according to Martin V. Melosi and Joseph A. Pratt in their enlightening collection *Energy Metropolis: An Environmental History of Houston and the Gulf Coast*. Urban growth has not been the only feature of development in recent Texas, as Linda Scarbrough notes in her first-rate study of Williamson County, *Road, River, and Ol' Boy Politics*.[19]

Rivaling Steve Murdoch's collection on population and demographic statistics as a vital work to use in writing and thinking about twenty-first-century Texas, to our way of thinking, is a work by economists Louis J. Rodriguez and Yoshi Fukasawa. Their edited and collected study, *The Texas Economy: 21st Century Economic Challenges*, is a must for any historian examining and writing about the recent past in the Lone Star State. Joseph A. Pratt and Christopher J. Castaneda deal with one important aspect of economic development in their study *Builders: Herman and George R. Brown*.[20]

All has not been work with no play in recent Texas. Texans, as well as individuals from around the nation, travel to San Antonio to visit the Alamo, perhaps the most important historical symbol of the Lone Star State's mythical and mystical past. This spirit and focus were the concept for a well-constructed book by Holly Beachley Brear titled *Inherit the Alamo*. Texans also love football, whether on the professional, collegiate, or high school level. Compared to other states, it is high school football that is most often remarked upon. Just recently, for example, citizens in a community near Dallas built a $60 million stadium for their high school football team. Sam Houston State University professor Ty Cashion, in a well written and researched work, considers the impact of football on Texas and Texas communities in *Pigskin Pulpit*. Texans also like and revel in music. One of the greatest of Texas musicians is the old pro, and everlasting singer and writer, Willie Nelson. Joe Nick Patoski captures the life and influence of Nelson in *Willie Nelson: An Epic Life*.[21]

Whether discussing politics, economics, demographics, or immigration, Texas history over the past thirty years has been interesting, exciting, and fraught with varied interpretations and arguments. The final answers likely wait for future historians to explore and explain. In so doing, they will borrow from some of the works mentioned in this essay.

NOTES

1. On George W. Bush, see his *Decision Points* (New York: Crown, 2010), and *Speaking of Freedom: The Collected Speeches* (New York: Scribners, 2009). Gail Collins, *How the Lone Star State Hijacked the American Agenda* (New York: W. W. Norton, 2012); Rick Perry, *On My Honor: Why the American Values of the Boy Scouts Are Worth Fighting*

For (New York: Stroud and Hall, 2008), and *Fed Up! Our Fight to Save America from Washington* (New York: Little, Brown, 2010).

2. Jesse Russell and Ronald Cohn, *John Cornyn* (Miami: Books on Demand, 2012), and *Phil Gramm* (Miami: Books on Demand, 2012); Phil Gramm, *The Role of Government in a Free Society: A Collection of Speeches and Articles* (Irving, Tex.: Fisher Institute, 1982); John C. Hamilton, *Secretary of the Treasury Lloyd Bentsen* (Minneapolis: ABDO and Daughters, 1993).

3. Kay Bailey Hutchison, *American Heroines* (New York: Harpers, 2006), and *Leading Ladies* (New York: Harpers, 2008); Arthur Frederick Ide, *From Stardom to Scandal: The Rise and Fall of Kay Bailey Hutchison* (London: Monument Press, 1993); Jesse Russell and Ronald Cohn, *Kay Bailey Hutchison* (Miami: Books on Demand, 2012).

4. Carolyn Barta, *Bill Clements: Texian to His Toenails* (Austin: Eakin Press, 1996).

5. Mike Shropshire and Frank Schaefer, *The Thorny Rose of Texas: An Intimate Portrait of Governor Ann Richards* (New York: Carol, 1994); Ann Richards and Peter Knobler, *Straight from the Heart: My Life in Politics and Other Places* (New York: Simon and Schuster, 1989); Jan Reid, *Let the People In: The Life and Times of Ann Richards* (Austin: University of Texas Press, 2012).

6. David Richards, *Once upon a Time in Texas: A Liberal in the Lone Star State* (Austin: University of Texas Press, 2002).

7. Sue Tolleson-Rinehart and Jeanie R. Stanley, *Claytie and the Lady: Ann Richards, Gender, and Politics in Texas* (Austin: University of Texas Press, 1994); Mike Cochran, *Claytie: The Roller-Coaster Life of a Texas Wildcatter* (College Station: Texas A&M University Press, 2007).

8. Herbert S. Parmet, *George Bush: The Life of a Lone Star Yankee* (New York: Transaction, 1977); Clarke Rountree, *George W. Bush: A Biography* (New York: Greenwood Press, 2010); Kevin Phillips, *American Dynasty: Aristocracy, Fortune, and the Politics of Deceit in the House of Bush* (New York: Viking, 2004).

9. Kenneth Bridges, *Twilight of the Texas Democrats: The 1978 Governor's Race* (College Station: Texas A&M University Press, 2010); Rupert N. Richardson, Adrian Anderson, Cary D. Wintz, and Ernest Wallace, "Republican Texas, 1985–2008," in *Texas: The Lone Star State*, 10th ed. (Boston: Prentice-Hall, 2010), 385–408; Nancy Beck Young, "Beyond Parochialism: Modernization and Texas Historiography," in *Beyond Texas through Time: Breaking Away from Past Interpretations*, ed. Walter L. Buenger and Arnoldo De León (College Station: Texas A&M University Press, 2011), 221–69.

10. M. Ray Perryman, *Survive and Conquer: Texas in the '80s—Money—Power—Tragedy . . . Hope!* (Dallas: Taylor, 1991).

11. Brian McCall, *The Power of the Texas Governor: From Connally to Bush* (Austin: University of Texas Press, 2009); Patrick Cox and Michael Phillips, *The House Will Come to Order: How the Texas Speaker Became a Power in State and National Politics* (Austin: University of Texas Press, 2010).

12. Dave McNeely and Jim Henderson, *Bob Bullock: God Bless Texas* (Austin: University of Texas Press, 2008).

13. Robert D. Auerbach, *Deception and Abuse at the Fed: Henry B. Gonzalez Battles Alan Greenspan's Bank* (Austin: University of Texas Press, 2008); Gary A. Keith, *Eckhardt:*

There Once Was a Congressman from Texas (Austin: University of Texas Press, 2007); Don E. Carlton, *A Breed So Rare: The Life of J. R. Partin, Liberal Texas Oil Man, 1896–1992* (Austin: Texas State Historical Association, 1998).

14. Nancy Baker Jones and Ruthe Winegarten, *Capitol Women: Texas Female Legislators, 1923–1999* (Austin: University Press, 2000); Sonya García et al., *Políticas: Latina Public Officials in Texas* (Austin: University of Texas Press, 2008); Sharon A. Navarro, *Latina Legislator: Letitia Van de Putte and the Road to Leadership* (College Station: Texas A&M University Press, 2008). On Barbara Jordan, see Mary Beth Rogers, *Barbara Jordan: American Hero* (New York: Bantam Books, 1998).

15. Louise Ann Fisch, *All Rise: Reynaldo G. Garza, the First Mexican American Federal Judge* (College Station: Texas A&M University Press, 1996); Ignacio M. García, *United We Win: The Rise and Fall of the Raza Unida Party* (Tucson: University of Arizona Press, 1989); Matt Rodriquez, *The Tejano Diaspora: Mexican Americanism and Ethnic Politics in Texas and Wisconsin* (Chapel Hill: University of North Carolina Press, 2011).

16. Steve Bickerstaff, *Line in the Sand: Congressional Redistricting in Texas and the Downfall of Tom DeLay* (Austin: University of Texas Press, 2010); Tom Delay and Stephen Mansfield, *No Retreat, No Surrender: One American's Fight* (New York: Sentinel HC, 2007); Steven Hamon Wilson, *The Rise of Judicial Management in the U.S. District Court, Southern District of Texas, 1955–2000* (Athens: University of Georgia Press, 2002).

17. Steve H. Murdock et al., *The New Texas Challenge: Population Change and the Future of Texas* (College Station: Texas A&M University Press, 2003).

18. Charles Bowden and Julian Cardona, *Exodus/Exodo* (Austin: University of Texas Press, 2008); Charles Bowden, *Down by the River: Drugs, Money, Murder, and Family* (New York: Simon and Schuster, 2003).

19. Martin V. Melosi and Joseph A. Pratt, eds., *Energy Metropolis: An Environmental History of Houston and the Gulf Coast* (Pittsburgh, Pa.: University of Pittsburgh Press, 2007); Linda Scarbrough, *Road, River, and Ol' Boy Politics: A Texas County's Path from Farm to Supersuburb* (Austin: Texas State Historical Association, 2005).

20. Louis J. Rodriguez and Yoshi Fukasawa, eds., *The Texas Economy: 21st Century Economic Challenges* (Wichita Falls, Tex: Midwestern State University Press, 1996); Joseph A. Pratt and Christopher J. Castaneda, *Builders: Herman and George R. Brown* (College Station: Texas A&M University Press, 1999).

21. Holly Beachley Brear, *Inherit the Alamo: Myth and Ritual at an American Shrine* (Austin: University of Texas Press, 1995); Ty Cashion, *Pigskin Pulpit: A Social History of Texas High School Football* (Austin: Texas State Historical Association, 1998); Joe Nick Patoski, *Willie Nelson: An Epic Life* (New York: Little, Brown, 2008).

Contributors

Matthew M. Babcock is Assistant Professor of History at the University of North Texas at Dallas and has also taught at Austin College. He earned his Ph.D. in history at Southern Methodist University, with a dissertation concentrated on "Turning Apaches into Spaniards." Babcock's teaching and research interests focus on North American frontiers and borderlands, particularly the colonial Southwest.

Alwyn Barr is Professor Emeritus of History at Texas Tech University and a former chair of the history department. Among his authored books are *Black Texans: A History of African Americans in Texas, 1528–1995* and *African Texans.* He also has edited, with Robert A. Calvert, *Black Leaders: Texans for Their Times*, and has written the Introduction to *Black Cowboys of Texas*, edited by Sara R. Massey, as well as several journal articles on African American history. He is a former president of the Texas State Historical Association and a board member of Humanities Texas.

Jessica Brannon-Wranosky is Assistant Professor of History at Texas A&M University–Commerce. She received her Ph.D. in history from the University of North Texas. Her research interests are U.S. women's history, southern history, enfranchisement and suffrage history, and digital humanities. Her current book project examines the roles generations of Texas suffragists played during decades of campaigning in the South from Reconstruction through the ratification of the Nineteenth Amendment, and she is the author of anthology and academic journal articles and the digital media author for *Give Me Liberty: An American History* by Eric Foner. Brannon-Wranosky is an active member and office holder in several professional associations including the Texas

State Historical Association board of directors, the Southern Association for Women Historians, and the Southern Historical Association.

Randolph B. "Mike" Campbell is Regents' Professor of History at the University of North Texas. He also serves as editor of the Texas State Historical Association publication *Southwestern Historical Quarterly.* Campbell is a specialist in antebellum and reconstruction history. Among his prize-winning books are *An Empire for Slavery: The Peculiar Institution in Texas, Grass-Roots Reconstruction in Texas,* and *Gone to Texas: A History of the Lone Star State.*

Patrick Cox is President of Patrick Cox Consultants. He received his Ph.D. in history from the University of Texas at Austin. Cox and Kenneth E. Hendrickson, Jr., are the editors of *Writing the History of Texas.* Cox is coauthor of *The House Will Come to Order: The Texas House Speakers* and authored *The First Texas News Barons* and the award-winning *Ralph W. Yarborough: The People's Senator.* He is former associate director of the Dolph Briscoe Center for American History at the University of Texas of Austin and is a fellow of the Texas State Historical Association.

Light Townsend Cummins is the Guy M. Bryan, Jr., Professor of History at Austin College. He is a member of the Texas Institute of Letters and the Philosophical Society of Texas and a lifetime fellow of the Texas State Historical Association. He was named a Minnie Stevens Piper Professor in 2006. Cummins is the author or editor of eleven academic books and several dozen scholarly articles dealing with Texas history along with two best-selling college textbooks, popular-oriented essays, and numerous book reviews. He recently completed a book length biography of Dallas sculptor Allie V. Tennant. Cummins served as the official state historian of Texas from 2009 to 2012.

Victoria H. Cummins is Professor of History at Austin College in Sherman, Texas, teaching a variety of courses on Latin American and U.S. history. She holds a Ph.D. from Tulane University. Her current research deals with Texas regional art and artists in the interwar period, a project that grew out of an interest in the influence of the Mexican muralists in the United States. In addition to scholarly publications on these topics, she has a chapter-long biographical study of art historian Frances B. Fisk forthcoming in a volume of the University of Georgia Press series Southern Women. Her current book project, tentatively titled "Muses to Modern Culture: Women and the Advancement of the Visual Arts in Texas, 1900–1940," is being coauthored with Light Cummins.

Sean P. Cunningham is Associate Professor of History at Texas Tech University. He received his Ph.D. from the University of Florida. With particular research and teaching interests in post-1945 American political culture, Cunningham published his first book, *Cowboy Conservatism: Texas and the Rise of the Modern Right*, in 2010. He published his second book, *American Politics in the Postwar Sunbelt: Conservative Growth in a Battleground Region*, in 2014.

Arnoldo De León, the C. J. "Red" Davidson Professor of History at Angelo State University, is an acknowledged leader in the history of peoples of Mexican descent in Texas and U.S. history. De León is the author of numerous works including *Racial Frontiers: Africans, Chinese, and Mexicans in Western America*, *North to Aztlán: A History of Mexican Americans in the United States*, and *The Tejano Community, 1836–1900*.

Bruce A. Glasrud is Professor Emeritus of History, California State University, East Bay, and Retired Dean, School of Arts and Sciences, Sul Ross State University. He specializes in the history of African Americans in Texas and the American West and coedited *Tracking the Texas Rangers*, *Texas Labor History*, *Making East Texas*, *East Texas*, *West Texas History*, and *Bibliophiling Tejano History*.

James C. Kearney received his Ph.D. from the University of Texas at Austin. His first book, *Nassau Plantation: The Evolution of a Texas German Slave Plantation*, appeared in 2009. His second book, *Friedrichsburg: A Novel*, won the Summerfield G. Roberts award for the best Texas History book of 2012. An annotated translation of Detlev Dunt's *Reise nach Texas* (1834) will appear in 2015. He is currently collaborating with a German colleague, Ulf Debelius, on a comprehensive history of the *Adelsverein*. Kearney teaches a course on European immigration in Texas at the University of Texas at Austin.

Richard B. McCaslin is Professor of History and chair of the department at the University of North Texas. His particular fields of interest are Texas history and nineteenth-century U.S. military history. Among his many publications are *At the Heart of Texas: One Hundred Years of the Texas State Historical Association*, *Fighting Stock: John S. "Rip" Ford of Texas*, and *Tainted Breeze: The Great Hanging at Gainesville, Texas, 1862*.

Carl H. Moneyhon is Professor of History at the University of Arkansas, Little Rock. A specialist in the American Civil War and Reconstruction, he has written extensively on the Texas experience during these years. Among his works are *Texas after the Civil War: The Struggle of Reconstruction* and *Edmund J. Davis of Texas: Civil War General, Republican Leader, Reconstruction Governor*.

Rebecca Sharpless is Associate Professor of History at Texas Christian University. From 1991 to 2006 she directed the Baylor University Institute for Oral History. In addition to oral history, Sharpless focuses on the history of women in the southern United States. Among her publications are *Fertile Ground, Narrow Choices: Women on Texas*

Cotton Farms, 1906–1940 and *Cooking in Other Women's Kitchens: Domestic Workers in the South, 1865–1960*. She is coediting a volume of essays on Texas women for the University of Georgia Press series Southern Women.

F. Todd Smith is Professor of History at the University of North Texas. He received his Ph.D. from Tulane University. He is interested particularly in the Southern Plains Indians and in the U.S. borderlands. Smith's publications include *From Dominance to Disappearance: The Indians of Texas and the Near Southwest, 1786–1859*, *The Caddo Indians*, and *The Wichita Indians*.

Cary D. Wintz is Distinguished Professor of History at Texas Southern University, where he has taught since 1971. Wintz is the author/editor of nearly twenty books, including *Black Culture and the Harlem Renaissance*, *Harlem Speaks*, and *the Encyclopedia of the Harlem Renaissance*. He is also coauthor on the last three editions of *Texas: The Lone Star State*, coeditor of *Major Problems in Texas History*, and author of other works on African Americans in Texas.

Richard B. Wright is Associate Professor of Art at Texas A&M International University. He holds degrees in art history from Wesleyan University and the University of Virginia. His primary research interests are the architectural history of Texas and the south-central United States from about 1900 to 1975, along with the urban history of Texas and the Southwest.

Index of Authors

Index of Titles

CPSIA information can be obtained
at www.ICGtesting.com
Printed in the USA
BVOW09s0459310517
485563BV00001B/32/P

9 780806 146195